Approaches to Co

Also by Brian L. Lancaster

Mind, Brain and Human Potential: The Quest for an Understanding of Self
Elements of Judaism

Approaches to Consciousness

The Marriage of Science
and Mysticism

Brian L. Lancaster

palgrave
macmillan

First published 2004 by
PALGRAVE MACMILLAN
Houndmills, Basingstoke, Hampshire RG21 6XS and
175 Fifth Avenue, New York, N.Y. 10010
Companies and representatives throughout the world

PALGRAVE MACMILLAN is the global academic imprint of the Palgrave Macmillan division of St. Martin's Press, LLC and of Palgrave Macmillan Ltd. Macmillan® is a registered trademark in the United States, United Kingdom and other countries. Palgrave is a registered trademark in the European Union and other countries.

ISBN 978-0-333-91275-1 (hardback)

ISBN 978-0-333-91276-8   ISBN 978-1-137-09057-7 (eBook)
DOI 10.1007/978-1-137-09057-7

A catalogue record for this book is available from the British Library.

A catalog record for this book is available from the Library of Congress.

10   9   8   7   6   5   4   3   2   1
13   12   11   10   09   08   07   06   05   04

Contents

Figures

Tables and Boxes

Tables

Boxes

Preface

It is a mistake to think of science and mysticism as non-overlapping realms of human endeavour. Science and mysticism share a common interest, namely that of advancing our grasp of reality. Despite the fact that the 'reality' to which mysticism points may not immediately correspond to that studied by science, the approaches to knowledge articulated in these two paths significantly intersect. Whilst mysticism contends with a reality that is, in part, unseen and non-physical, it would be incorrect to dismiss it as having no concern with the observable world of the senses and the overt phenomena of mind. For example, Jewish and Islamic mystics view an understanding of the seen world as a key to knowledge of the 'higher' worlds, for it is believed that all is built on a principle of correspondence. Indeed, the roots of modern science are to be found in the influence these traditions had on renaissance Christian mystics in their quests to know the forces that shape the known world.

A complementary picture to that of mysticism's interest in *this* world is given by the thrust of modern science to extend its territory beyond the concrete reality to which its techniques are primarily directed. The unseen reality of consciousness has become a challenge to science, just as the physical nature of brain activity has become a topic of interest for the mystical challenge to know the limits of human potential.

A true marriage – one made in heaven, as it might be said – harnesses two forces that can share a common ground, yet strives to create something distinctive through the creative tension between those forces. A marriage is not made of sameness, and the divergence between science and religion does not disqualify them as bedfellows. A third cannot be born unless commonality and difference are measured in the crucible.

Two specific issues lie at the heart of the potential dialogue between science and mysticism. The first concerns the nature of the forces that shape the physical world. Recent years have seen much speculation over the relationships between mysticism and quantum mechanics and astrophysics. While quantum mechanics represents the most accurate map we have of the forces that shape physical reality, its terms of reference lead far beyond the cosy scientific territory of direct observables. Mystical texts similarly abound in speculation about the nature of concealed forces that may be known only through their expression in the physical world. The distinctiveness of the mystical approach arises in this context with the enriching spice of *purpose*. *Why* is the world as it is? And *of what value* is the challenge to grasp the patterning in the forces that seem to bring order out of chaos?

Consciousness constitutes the second issue that brings science and mysticism into dialogue. A stirring of scientific interest in consciousness over the second half of the twentieth century seems to have been galvanized into a concerted thrust as we enter the twenty-first. Consciousness is sometimes seen as the major challenge that remains standing in the path of the juggernaut of science. It is often portrayed as a proverbial nut that will surely be cracked, given time, just as all the phenomena that seemed mysterious in previous ages have come to be explained scientifically.

Yet it cannot be doubted that consciousness is different. Consciousness is the inner citadel; the essence of what it is to be human. We know it from the inside; or rather, *it is the quality of knowing itself*. Here lies the common ground with mysticism, for none have charted the territory of the phenomena of mind more richly than those who walked the path of mysticism. The mystical knowing of God has been identified with knowing the roots of thought and consciousness. And in relation to non-theistic forms of mysticism, enlightenment is equated with the glowing transparency of a mind that is fully known to itself. In both cases, insight into consciousness has been integral to the path of perfection.

The challenge to understand consciousness demands a harmony of inquiry between science and mysticism. Subtle features of the mind, noticed only by mystics schooled intensively in introspective methods, may provide the key for interpreting data thrown up by the relevant sciences. Such mystical insights might enable a richer comprehension of cognitive neuroscientific data concerning perception and memory, for example. And, in complementary fashion, these scientific data can enrich the spiritual quest to explore consciousness inwardly.

The approach I adopt through these pages is rooted in this complementarity between scientific and mystical ways of addressing consciousness. The grail of understanding consciousness demands *a marriage of science and mysticism*. It requires that the data available through the externalized means of science be integrated with the insights culled from the more internally-directed inquiry of mysticism.

Just as mysticism brings the qualities of meaning and purpose to our knowledge of the physical world, so it enriches the science of consciousness through its emphasis on the goal of *transformation*.

Mystics who develop subtle comprehension of the minutiae of consciousness do so in service of the quest for transformation. The spiritual traditions are founded on the notion that self-knowledge contributes to the soteriological path to a transformed world. Despite the fact that the religious tone of such ideas sets them fundamentally apart from the worldview of science, they nevertheless have a bearing on the need discernible in contemporary culture for elements of moral purpose to be introduced into the otherwise arid realm of science. The move towards a science of consciousness may be a sign of a nascent cultural transformation whereby the values traditionally aligned with religion are integrated more broadly into a post-secular society.

Consciousness is not simply the most recent in a line of phenomena to confront the scientist. More fundamentally, it has been the need for cultural regeneration that has seeded the desire to probe the mystery of consciousness. A culture that has no place for mystery is one that is effectively closed to its own creative roots. I believe that the marriage of science and mysticism in the pursuit of consciousness is reawakening the search for meaning, which is the vital heart of a healthy culture.

There are many individuals who have contributed to my path of inquiry into the ways of consciousness, and I wish to record my thanks to them. They know who they are, and I have no desire to list their names (nor would they want it!). Should they discern something of their influence in these pages, then that is acknowledgement enough. Beyond that, I take responsibility for what is presented in my own name. Some have taught me through teaching, and some have taught me through listening. And some taught me simply through silence....

For over more than a decade, I have been privileged to teach many inspiring students on the MSc programme in Consciousness and Transpersonal Psychology at Liverpool John Moores University. They travelled heroically to be there, when all I had to do was turn up. My thanks go to them, for they stimulated my work beyond measure.

Thanks are due to my wife, Irene. Without complaint, she endured the months during which the charms of the word-processor rivalled her for my attentions. More than this, she worked tirelessly on the drafts. A discerning eye for content and grammar, what more could she give? And, finally, thanks to my daughters, Kalela and Esther. How I valued their input! The title 'Beyond Within' was Kalela's inspired contribution, and Esther watched over the artwork. More than this, it is undoubtedly the unofficial duty of children to keep you sane ... I think they succeeded ...

Brian L. Lancaster

Part I
Towards a Unitary Discipline of Consciousness Studies

Chapter 1
The Big Picture

On asking the right questions

The emanation of the Holy Ancient One proceeds as the emanation which is the essence of all further emanations. It is the
supernal, concealed wisdom which includes all that follows.... It
is the inner consciousness[1] of the Holy Ancient One – a
consciousness that spreads through all dimensions.
(*Zohar* 3:289a, *Idra Zuta*)[2]

[O]ne who is *compresent* with the Divine Presence is a Watcher,
an Awakened One ... his degree of awakening is proportionate
to his reciprocal compresence with God.
(Abd Al-Karim Jili, cited in Corbin, 1976/1990, p. 152)

The pure Brahman becomes the witnessing consciousness.
(Radhakrishnan, 1953, p. 903)

For the author of the *Zohar*, consciousness is a quality of the
divine. In the act of creation such consciousness gives rise to all
that is, both physical and mental. Our consciousness becomes
an echo of the primordial divine consciousness. In the Sufi
tradition, represented here by the fourteenth-century Jili,
mystics endeavour to align themselves with God, since only
then do they awaken to full consciousness. Again, at the heart
of such teaching is the view that there is only one consciousness
– that of the divine, the essence of any power to observe.
Finally, Radhakrishnan reminds us that the oldest of the world's
established religions, Hinduism, continues to teach this simple
message: that the seemingly human power to observe, or

3

witness, is nothing other than the pure divine source – *Brahman* – shining through us.

Despite the myriad shades found in particular teachings, a degree of consensus seems to be evident amongst all the spiritual traditions: whatever consciousness is, it is not *merely* human and biological. This idea constitutes the primary point of contrast with the scientific quest to understand consciousness, epitomized in Searle's assertion that:

> Consciousness ... is a biological feature of human and certain animal brains. It is caused by neurobiological processes and is as much a part of the natural biological order as any other biological features such as photosynthesis, digestion, or mitosis.
>
> (Searle, 1992, p. 90)

For Searle, as for the majority of contemporary philosophers and neuroscientists, consciousness is unequivocally a biological phenomenon.

Further diversity is introduced when we consider the views of some of the pioneers of quantum physics, for whom consciousness is not so much a biological phenomenon as a concomitant of the physical properties of our universe. Nobel prize winners Wigner (1972) and Bohm (1980), for example, insist that consciousness is intrinsic to the framework of quantum mechanics.

With views as diverse as these, how is it possible for us to advance towards a unitary discipline of consciousness studies? To those who hold consciousness to be a product of the brain alone, the notion that it is actually a *spiritual* property having a non-physical reality is simply unfounded from the evidence they deem acceptable. More than this, the spiritual perspective introduces a worldview fundamentally at odds with that of contemporary science. In the other direction, those professing belief in a spiritual view of consciousness will remain unshaken by claims that they are clinging to unsubstantiated ideas. It is incontrovertibly the case that the evidence available regarding the brain and consciousness does not necessarily contradict the view that consciousness derives from some form of *higher* realm. The fact is that, while the brain is clearly the organ of consciousness in the sense that it is responsible for the forms in our minds at any given time, there is as yet no definitive evidence that the brain itself *creates* consciousness.

Given the seeming chasm between these viewpoints, why should we endeavour to argue for a unitary discipline of consciousness studies? Those with such disparate worldviews may, at best, politely respect one another's views, but would have no basis for meaningful dialogue. Since this book explicitly seeks to integrate transpersonal, psychological and biological approaches to consciousness, it will be clear that I myself believe that there is a basis for dialogue. In part, such dialogue is necessary simply because many are seeking it. The challenge presented by the study of consciousness is central to our shared sense of *soul*, and relates to the urgency of forging a spiritual path while honouring the observations available through the tools of science. More than this, I intend to show that a sharing of insights across the various areas of study can encourage those involved to ask the right kinds of questions of the data to which they have immediate access. A discipline of consciousness studies should be *integrative*, encouraging a sharpening of interpretation within its subsidiary areas of study. Such an integrative approach is, in fact, not new. The great spiritual traditions, *the sacred sciences of the soul*, as Nasr (1993) calls them, have always sought to grapple with 'data' available from diverse sources about the nature of the mind. Indeed, these traditions were critically involved in the foundations of modern science (Griffin, 2000; Wallace, 2000; Wightman, 1972; Yates, 1964), and may be expected to continue to develop through the fruits of the scientific approach.

What, then, are the right questions to be asking about consciousness? Framing the right questions is always the key to a productive inquiry. Over recent years there have been many books on consciousness, each attempting to answer what the author had construed as *the* central questions about consciousness: What is its nature? How does it arise? What is its relation to unconsciousness? As Baars (1988, 1997) notes, this latter type of question is particularly important since it is only by pointing up features of comparison that we can generally clarify what something *is* – effectively, we know an entity by knowing what it is not. Clearly, if we had no conception of darkness, then the notion of light would be meaningless. Therefore, it is the method of *contrastive analysis* that Baars advocates in the pursuit of consciousness.

Baars employs his contrastive method to specify those features that differentiate between conscious and unconscious aspects of cognitive processes such as perception and memory. In brief, Baars notes that unconscious processes are generally more efficient and faster than conscious ones. Unconscious processes operate in parallel, resulting in a level of multitasking absent from consciousness. I shall be exploring Baars' theory further in Chapter 5 when addressing the cognitive approach to consciousness. However, I mention Baars' method here, at the outset, since it may be taken as a paradigm for the broad range of disciplines which will concern us. The contrastive method applies on a considerably larger scale than that envisaged by Baars himself, for, in order to make any kind of meaningful claim, all approaches to consciousness demand a basis of comparison. I will therefore use an extended principle of contrastive analysis to distil central questions for each of the approaches to be considered.

At the outset we confront a problem. In employing our extended contrastive analysis paradigm, with what is consciousness to be contrasted? Clearly, the answer should logically be that the comparison is with that which is *not* consciousness – just as the comparison of light is with that which is not light, namely darkness. The problem is, however, that it is not so simple for us to name unequivocally that which is not consciousness. Indeed, the range of approaches to consciousness depends pivotally on our view of what exactly is *not* consciousness.

In the first sense, that which is not consciousness may be thought of as the material world of objects, both physical and biological. With this statement we are entering the discourse of philosophy. What is the relation of consciousness to these objects? In the starkest sense, either they are fundamentally distinct, as proposed by *dualists*; or they are in some sense part of the same realm of reality, as suggested by *monists*. In either case, the question we must confront concerns the *relationship* between consciousness and the material/biological realm.

Panpsychists would tend to deny the original premise in the previous paragraph, since they hold that mind is a property of the whole physical world, and is not limited only to brains, for example.[3] If mind is a property of the natural world, then its most elusive feature, consciousness, is to be explained in terms of properties of the natural world as a whole, and not simply as a product of the brain. Most people's general intuition is opposed to panpsychism; consciousness is one thing, rocks and seas are another. In making such an assertion, however, we emphasize *personal* consciousness. Perhaps the seed of consciousness is to be found in the natural world, but the consciousness that we experience is tied specifically to the individual brain. This, in turn, raises the question of what it is about my own consciousness that seems to cut me off from the consciousness suggested in panpsychism as a property of the whole. This question begins to differentiate between traditional philosophy and the approach of mysticism and spirituality. Mystics have asserted the oneness between their own consciousness and that of the cosmos as a whole, usually in the theistic sense of a divine unity.

Spiritual traditions are generally concerned in one way or another precisely with this question about why we are not more aware of the continuity between ourselves and the greater whole. They present the practitioner with techniques and ways of living directed towards overcoming this sense of separateness.

A further possible comparison with consciousness enters at this point. Most people, with the exception of panpsychists, would view the physical world as constituting the appropriate contrast to consciousness. However, there is also a contrast 'upwards', as it were.[4] In many spiritual traditions, normal, or mundane, consciousness is viewed as being distinct from 'higher' consciousness. For example, *Vedic* teachings (the earliest stratum of Hinduism) underpin Sri Aurobindo's notion of a divine, or 'supramental' consciousness that contrasts with the 'lower' realm of mundane human consciousness (Cornelissen, 2001). Questions triggered by this comparison would tend to focus on the nature of such higher consciousness. What do those who claim to have had such experiences report, and how might such a view be incorporated into psychological and scientific perspectives on consciousness? An important question to consider in this context concerns any additional capacities claimed as being available to one who accesses, or reaches, higher levels of consciousness. Religious traditions condemn the kind of narcissism that simply wishes to revel in the *experience* of supposed higher states. Such experience is viewed as leading to some more tangible gain in terms of a divinely-sanctioned role in relation to others and the world as a whole. Experiences of self-transformation, and the acquisition of wisdom, are stages towards achieving that role. Inevitably, additional questions arise here – what exactly is meant by self-transformation, and what distinguishes wisdom from the ordinary accumulation of skills and information?

Retreating from the rarefied realms of mysticism, an additional contrastive feature is given shape by Freud's topographical model of the mind. From the point of view of psychoanalysis, that which is not conscious is *unconscious*. Freud's distinctive input here lay in his analysis of the specific dynamics that distinguish the unconscious from the conscious system of the mind. In terms of our extended paradigm of contrastive analysis, it is the mode of *thought* that differentiates the two systems. Thinking that proceeds unconsciously (Freud's *primary process*) contrasts with conscious thought (the *secondary process*) in being irrational, symbolic and devoid of a normal time sense.

Central to both psychoanalytic and cognitive approaches to consciousness, and its contrast with the unconscious, is the nature of self. In simple terms, *I* (self) am the centre of my conscious world. And yet, paradoxically, I may feel most alive, most highly conscious perhaps, when I do not really have any reflective sense of self. How can we resolve this paradox? What role does self play in consciousness?

The disciplines of cognitive psychology and neuroscience – the areas Baars primarily had in mind in establishing his method of contrastive analysis – have seen the greatest level of research interest into consciousness over recent years. The critical question addressed by these disciplines concerns the features that differentiate unconscious from conscious processes. This question tends to focus on time-dependent sequences of operations. To take a perceptual example, various stages of brain processing must ensue before I become conscious of the external entity that is producing flickering energy patterns on my retina, or in my cochlea. Key operations are *preconscious* in the sense that they precede my becoming conscious of some entity or other. The question of interest, then, concerns the critical transition from preconscious to conscious. What is it that renders the former conscious?

In addition to such momentary transitions, our interest encompasses the larger scale *transformations* between different *states of consciousness*. This will be considered more fully in the next section. However, my survey of the key questions involved in approaching consciousness would not be complete without recognizing the need to ask about factors involved when there is a major transition from one conscious state to a different one. The concept of the 'preconscious' may be highly relevant here. For example, depth psychology suggests that preconscious processing can trigger insights leading to breakthroughs in therapy.[5] Similarly, the creative leaps associated with moments of genius seem to entail suspension of normal conscious processing in favour of more preconscious activity. The problem is that it is unclear whether the term 'preconscious' means the same thing to cognitive scientists as it does to depth psychologists.

Problems of terminology haunt the study of consciousness. In the first place, the term 'consciousness' itself carries diverse meanings, thus muddying the clarity of analysis. Second, we have this problem of the 'preconscious'. In the terminology of cognitive neuroscience, processes are deemed preconscious during a brief time period prior to their reaching consciousness. In contrast to the cognitive view, the more therapeutic and spiritual branches of psychology conceive of the preconscious as a region of the mind that is largely distinct from the conscious mind. Brevity need not be a defining feature of preconscious processing. An idea may be processed 'preconsciously' even for a prolonged period. The idea is being formulated, as it were, at the margins of the mind.

For therapeutic and spiritual psychology, then, processes that are preconscious are viewed as taking place beyond the focal conscious region of the mind. They involve images, memories and thoughts which do not achieve full consciousness but are nevertheless not totally outside consciousness. James (1890/1950) seems to have had such processes in mind when writing of the 'fringe of relations' that surrounds a state of consciousness. The fringe concerns features of consciously perceived words or images that do not themselves enter directly into consciousness. These fringe features nevertheless contribute significantly to our comprehension of the words or images themselves (Mangam, 1993; Weinberger, 2000). In his later work analysing religious experience, James (1902/1960) refers to the 'transmarginal or subliminal region' (p. 462), akin to his earlier notion of the 'fringe', as being central to the kinds of transformations seen in conversion or mystical states. Mavromatis (1987) relates fringe consciousness to that state between waking and sleep known as *hypnagogia*, during which imagery is pronounced. More recently, Revonsuo *et al.* (2000) introduce the term 'peripheral consciousness' to refer to subjective experience on the borderline between the fully conscious and the nonconscious.

There is no shortage of labels for this 'twilight' conscious state. Neither is there a shortage of claims made for the role it may play in major transformations, whether they are therapeutic, spiritual or creative. But specifying what exactly characterizes the state is not so straightforward. Why is psychological and spiritual transformation dependent on the 'dreamy subliminal', to use another of James' terms?

The major premise of this book is that an integrative approach to consciousness is critical for answering these kinds of questions. In the case of the preconscious, for example, different specialist areas can contribute to a broad understanding that will be richer than a view deriving from any one area in isolation. As I shall elaborate, the insights from cognitive neuroscience into the nature of preconscious processing can, for example, advance our understanding of transformative mystical techniques. Contemporary mysticism is enriched when the use of millennia-old transformational techniques is grounded in sound data gleaned through scientific study. But as this book will illustrate, there is also an important influence in the other direction. Interpretation of scientific data can be enhanced when viewed through a lens provided by introspective traditions.

In summary, beyond the specific questions that we seek to answer, there is one question that characterizes the value of approaching consciousness studies as a unitary discipline. What do the insights from different areas of inquiry lend to each other in advancing our quest to understand consciousness and to enrich our lives?

The significance of transpersonal psychology

> Let empiricism once become associated with religion, as hitherto, through some strange misunderstanding, it has been associated with irreligion, and I believe that a new era of religion as well as of philosophy will be ready to begin.
>
> (James, 1909/1977, p. 142)

There are two faces to transpersonal psychology. One is succinctly characterized by Parsons' phrase, 'Psychology *as* religion' (Parsons, 1999, p. 12). This face speaks to those who seek the kind of transformational paths that have traditionally been the domain of the religions, and more especially of religious mysticism. Transpersonal psychology draws on the practices developed within spiritual traditions, and attempts to classify both the practices and their effects on the individual. It further classifies the levels of being, or of consciousness, which are encountered as the individual progresses on a path of transformation. Its strength lies in the richness of the interconnections it has established between diverse systems of thought which have historically addressed the human predicament and our spiritual potential. Its appeal lies in its attempts to transcend the cultural boundaries between all the various spiritual maps on which it is able to draw. It presents a 'way for today' – an integrated paradigm of transcendence for a world desperate to honour pluralism.

This first face is characteristically oriented towards change. Its practitioners engage with psycho-spiritual techniques in order to achieve some degree of transformation. Delineation of the levels of consciousness that might be encountered is largely presented for reasons of guidance. Just as the great spiritual traditions of the past presented stories and images depicting the ways to freedom and enlightenment, so the speculative systems of transpersonal psychology may be viewed as maps of the 'terrain' likely to be encountered on the journey to higher realization.

The other face of transpersonal psychology is oriented towards scientific psychology. It shares with the latter the goal of explaining processes and states of the mind. This second face seeks to understand features of the everyday mental landscape, including perception, emotion, memory, thinking and the construction of identity. It is not restricted to those states and processes which are related directly to 'transpersonal experiences', and, accordingly, shares common ground with cognitive neuroscience and other branches of psychology.[6]

Many works within transpersonal psychology ignore, or make only fleeting reference to, this second face. Transformative experience and higher states of knowing are the primary issues of interest. Conversely, studies into consciousness from cognitive and neuroscientific perspectives rarely have any place for an input from a transpersonal vision. Never the twain shall meet! I believe this to be an unfortunate state of affairs, which is to the detriment of progress in the understanding of consciousness. As the following pages will illustrate, the common ground between a transpersonal approach and the approaches associated with more mainstream areas of psychology is important since it enables generative dialogue between the overtly spiritual, and the mundane, study of consciousness. It provides the critical bridge between approaches which otherwise can appear irreconcilable due to differences in their goals and the scale of their ambition.

The distinctive element that sets this second face of transpersonal psychology apart from the other branches of psychology is its implicit relation to the transformational imperative of the first face. A transpersonal approach to the study of perception, for example, is distinct from that of cognitive neuroscience in its goal of understanding the elements of transformation. What is it about the processes of perception that limits individuals in their vision of the world? How might these processes be transformed, leading to an enhanced level of functioning? In short, the second face of transpersonal psychology is that branch of psychology that studies processes of the mind within the overall context of the transformational imperative.

Seen in this light, transpersonal psychology is heir to the sacred sciences of the soul (Nasr, 1993). Islamic, or Vedic, science, for example, studied the nature of mind in all its forms because *self-knowledge is intrinsically transformational*. Knowledge of the mundane is the opening to any interest in higher realms of consciousness. And this is so for two related reasons. First, if transformation is the goal, you can only start from where you stand. Buddhist wisdom literature, for example, analyses the mind in intricate detail specifically in order that those who study it might recognize features which lock them into limiting states. Recognition is the first step towards intervention and self-mastery.

Second, in the classical statement of esoteric systems of thought, the 'microcosm' reflects the 'macrocosm'. Or, as Corbin (1958/1969) expresses it in his study of Sufism, 'to everything that is apparent, literal, external, exoteric ... there corresponds something hidden, spiritual, internal, esoteric' (p. 78). As he remarks, this concept is the 'central postulate of esotericism and esoteric hermeneutics'. In the words of the *Zohar*:

> The Holy One, blessed be He ... made this world corresponding to the world above, and everything which is above has its counterpart here below, and everything here below has its counterpart in the sea; and yet all constitutes a unity.
>
> (*Zohar* 2:20a)

The individual – as microcosm – 'is made on the model of the world above' (*Zohar* 1:186b). The correspondence extends further: even

God and man are isomorphic (Shokek, 2001), in that they 'share the same structure and are logically equivalent' (p. 6). According to this system of thought, the dynamics of the soul are mirrored in the structure and functions of the bodily organs: 'Man's soul can be known only through the organs of the body, which are the levels that perform the work of the soul. Consequently, it is both known and unknown' (*Zohar* 1:103b).

In these terms, one studies the 'organs' in order to know the 'soul'. Stripped of specific theistic content, we could read these passages as suggesting, in our present context, that the mundane realm of human mental processes operates by means of the same principles as those which operate at higher levels. Knowledge of neural and mundane psychological processes may be seen as transformational because, through this micro-macrocosmic parallelism, it gives insight into the realm of the soul. Brain function, for example, might be reflective of the dynamics of the psyche, or even of intra-divine processes. Similarly, study of the principles by which the mundane ego operates may give insight into the nature of a supposed higher self. If the 'lower' recapitulates the 'higher', then study of the 'lower' reveals the ways of the 'higher'.

Immediately, we confront terms which strain at the leash of a scientific worldview – what is the ontological status of a supposed 'higher self'; why posit differing levels, and levels of what, exactly? Is not the brain the *cause* of any dynamics of the psyche? These questions will be addressed in subsequent sections of this chapter. For now I wish to emphasize the potential for dialogue between disciplines focusing on the study of the mind from different perspectives. The central consideration is whether study of the key organizing principles at work in the mundane function of the brain can seed our understanding of deeper, transformational functions, and vice versa.

I can only give hints of an answer here, for the principles need to be studied in detail, as they will be in subsequent chapters. In brief, and by way of example, the approach of neurophysiology suggests two major operational features that are critical for the study of consciousness: *binding* and *re-entrance*. Consideration of both features will reveal correspondences with principles described in mystical systems of thought as pertaining to the relationship between human and divine levels of being. As will be analysed in more detail in Chapter 4, binding refers to the mechanisms employed by the brain for integrating neural responses. These mechanisms establish coherence amongst the oscillating patterns of neural responses. For example, they ensure that the brain's responses to individual elements in a visual scene are organized globally in order to enable recognition. In short, binding is critical to the brain's ability to signal the presence of meaningful objects. Re-entrance refers to neural pathways originating in 'higher' brain areas, which course back to influence processing in 'lower' areas. Re-entrance plays a critical role in binding, since it enables higher-level analysis of perceptual properties to bring about appropriate ordering of lower-level systems. Without re-entrance, coherence in neural firing patterns could not develop.

Familiarity with both the physiological processes and the numerous mystical writings that bear on analogous themes suggests that binding and re-entrance may correspond to the mystical ideas of *unification* and the *reflexivity* of consciousness, respectively. Unifications are meditative practices directed towards integration of the mind and its relation to the divine. The goal of all mysticism entails recognition and realization of the unity said to lie behind all manifestation. Practices such as meditation attempt to achieve resonant, harmonious integration across a hierarchy of bodily, psychological and transcendent levels. While neurophysiological research points to the functional value of coherence in neural systems, insight gleaned through meditative unification can suggest the mystical value of coherence throughout physical, psychological and spiritual realms.

In Jewish mysticism, practices of unification take on eschatological significance, for ultimately 'there shall be perfection above and below, and all worlds shall be united in one bond' (Scholem, 1941/1961, p. 233). The Godhead is viewed as the object of these practices for it is, as it were, in need of the re-integration that can be achieved through human agency.[7]

> The drawing out of divine influence is connected with the mystery of unification, which, according to the Kabbalah, is the most important activity that men can engender within the Godhead.
> (Tishby 1949/1989, p. 948)

Tishby cites a source that well conveys the cosmic significance of unification:

> The righteous and the pious and the men who perform great deeds pray on their own and they unify the great name [of God]

and tend the fire of the altar that is in their hearts. Then, out of pure thought, all the *sefirot* [divine emanations] are unified and are linked one to another until they extend to the source of the flame whose height is infinite.

(p. 949)

What the neurones are doing at one level – binding parts into a meaningful whole – the soul, according to this scheme, achieves on the higher plane of emanation.

The neurophysiological concept of re-entrance relates to the more cosmic notion of *reflexivity*. Reflexivity is a keynote theme of much mystical literature, and suggests that the goal of spiritual practice is to effect a clear reflection back to the source of consciousness. Lao Tzu asks in the *Tao Te Ching*, 'Can you polish your mysterious mirror and leave no blemish?' (Lao Tzu, 1963, p. 66). The Islamic philosopher and mystic, Ibn Arabi, similarly uses the metaphor of the polished mirror to convey the idea of the meeting between the image of God and the mystic in the moment of mystical union. He writes:

And when the real ... had brought into being
the world entire
as a shaped form
without spirit
the world was like an unpolished mirror
... [W]hat was required
was the polishing of the mirror
that is the world
And Adam was that very polishing
of that mirror....
(Cited in Sells, 1994, pp. 72–3)

As Sells explains, the 'polishing of the mirror' is achieved by reaching completeness, at which time the ego is transcended and there is nothing to obscure the purity of divine reflection. Adam represents the paradigm of this state of purity.

As we will discuss in Chapter 4, consciousness seems to be dependent on re-entrant neural systems. In cerebral terms, neural activity from 'lower' to 'higher' regions functions to trigger the re-entrant pathways, which engender an alignment between the 'higher' and 'lower' regions, eventuating in consciousness.

Mystical perspectives on reflexivity suggest an analogous sequence. The human ('lower') effects a link to the divine ('higher'), bringing about an alignment between the two, as symbolized in the idea of consciousness as mirror for divine reflection.

While such parallels may seem tenuous at this juncture, my claim is simply that they merit further study. Such study represents the subtext of this book. My interest lies in the various approaches that have been adopted for the study of consciousness, and the extent to which they interrelate with each other and may be advancing towards a richer picture of the nature of consciousness. It is worth emphasizing at the outset that the vision of trans-personal psychology which ensues from this examination can be regarded as integrally enmeshed with all systems of psychology. According to this vision, transpersonal psychology is not to be seen as an additional layer of some kind of investigative cake, a layer that can readily be ignored when asking questions about the mech-anisms of consciousness. On the contrary, it has a major contribu-tion to make at all levels. Perhaps, to extend the metaphor, it might be thought of as the raising agent for the whole cake.

In this connection, Ferrer (2000, 2002) has made the critical point that transpersonal theory, if it is to be genuinely contiguous with the great spiritual traditions, should be concerned with ways of *knowing*, not *experiencing*. He rightly observes that 'the aim of most contemplative traditions is not "to have experiences," but rather to realize and participate in special states of discernment' (2000, p. 232). Were the subject matter of transpersonal psychol-ogy restricted to human experience, with the discipline directing itself only to the phenomenological description and classification of states of being, then it would have no role in relation to the more physically-oriented and functional approaches to conscious-ness. However, to the extent that its focus is *knowledge*, pertaining to the *how* as well as the *why* of systems in action, both human and non-human, it can be seen to have a bearing on all approaches to consciousness.

The point is well exemplified by a further set of correspon-dences, this time between some recent theorizing in neuroscience and the Buddhist understanding of mental processes. Zeki (2003) reports that his studies of the neurophysiology of vision lead him to view the visual system as comprising a series of functional nodes, each of which has a distinctive conscious correlate. He argues that the commonly-held view of consciousness as single and unified is mistaken. Instead, visual consciousness is comprised, as he puts it, of 'many microconsciousnesses'. Zeki and Bartels (1999) have commented that many find these conclusions difficult to accept on account of the widespread belief in the unity of consciousness. However, to anyone with more than a fleeting knowledge of Buddhism, this conclusion accords strikingly with Buddhist thought. A transpersonal perspective, drawing on such spiritual tradition, may have a role to play in promoting the kind of view that Zeki has articulated.

A sophisticated analysis of perception is presented in the Abhidhamma of the Theravada school of Buddhism, a section of the *Pali* canon dealing with science and metaphysics. This tradition holds that the seemingly unbroken processes of perception and thought mask their true character, which entails a series of discrete 'moments'. In each moment, a distinctive consciousness arises, is briefly sustained, and decays (Lancaster, 1997a, 1997b). The eleventh-century *Summary of Abhidhamma* ('Abhidhammattha-Sangaha') states that when an object stimulates the visual system:

> [First] consciousness of the kind that apprehends sensations ... rises and ceases. Immediately after this there rise and cease in order – visual consciousness, seeing just that visible object; recipient consciousness receiving it; investigating consciousness investigating it; determining consciousness determining it.
>
> (Aung, 1910/1972, p. 126)

I shall leave for the present a more detailed consideration of the precise function of each of these moments, or stages, in the perceptual process. Suffice it to state that these 'consciousnesses' are all understood as arising prior to the final registering of a meaningful perceptual image, and would not be detectable to an untrained mind (untrained, that is, in the discipline of introspection through meditation). Indeed, according to Collins (1982), the Buddhist commentators calculated a figure of 1/74,642 seconds per moment of consciousness! Whatever credence we give to such a figure,[8] it is clear that the moments could realistically be equated with the kinds of preliminary analysis that Zeki ascribes to the functional nodes in the visual system. The point for our purposes is that the Buddhist position asserts categorically that individual consciousnesses are associated with these moments, and therefore Zeki's term 'microconsciousnesses' accords fully with the Buddhist analysis. Rhys Davids' term for the Buddhist concept here, 'flashes of consciousness' (1914, p. 179), possibly captures the parallel more effectively.

It should thus be evident that a two-way dialogue between neuroscience and Buddhist introspective psychology may prove fruitful in specifying the relationship between perceptual processes and consciousness. Neuroscientists sceptical of Zeki's departure from an engrained way of thinking about consciousness (as being one and undivided) could gain from the realization that a sophisticated introspective analysis arrived at such a view hundreds of years ago. And in the other direction, modern Buddhists interested in the specification of 'moments' in thought and perceptual processes could learn enormously from the rich understanding of visual processing that neuroscience has developed. In general, as Hunt (1984, 1985) has argued, the study of states of mind associated with mysticism may be invaluable as a source of understanding which the more 'objective' methods of cognitive neuroscience cannot provide.

More fundamentally, the common ground here illustrates the ramifications of a transformational perspective to the seemingly most scientific of levels of explanatory analysis. As Goleman (1991) reminds us, Buddhism views the systematic study of the mind and its workings as being at the heart of spiritual life. A level of awareness capable of detecting relatively early stages in perceptual processing is essential if one is to transcend the possibly negative, and therefore prejudicial, labelling of sensory images. Without such awareness, one is effectively victim to seemingly automatic, perceptual processes. Writing of one of the early stages in the perceptual process, a modern commentator on the Abhidhamma system conveys the point:

> [T]here appears to be a choice or free will. If the object is determined wrongly on the false data as being permanent, of the nature of a self, with attachment or ill-will, then the ... [later] thoughts will be immoral. If the object is determined correctly as being impermanent, without self, with notions of renunciation, love and kindness, then the thoughts that follow will be moral.
>
> (Jayasuriya, 1963, p. 43)

A transpersonal perspective brings a sense of meaning and purpose into the otherwise cold world of cognitive neuroscience's picture of the mind. Varela, Thompson and Rosch (1991) go so far as to assert that the dialogue between Buddhism and cognitive science can play a key part in the challenge 'to build and dwell in a planetary world' (p. 254). Transpersonal psychology, which is the branch of psychology most equipped to bring forward such discussions of Buddhist and other spiritual insights, should be seen as an essential component of the quest to understand consciousness at all levels. Not only does it contribute to a systematic formulation of the issues involved in transformations of consciousness (first face, discussed above), it also provides models and explanatory frameworks which may have significant bearing on the interpretation of data available from neuroscience, cognitive science and depth psychology. For these reasons, transpersonal psychology gains a scholarly entrance into the 'no man's land' (Rosch, 2000) between science and the world's meditative and contemplative traditions. As Rosch notes, both these great areas of human endeavour have developed rigorous investigative techniques and rules for constructing theories about ourselves and our world. The challenge is that of yoking the two in our quest for consciousness.

Levels of explanation

The three realms of inquiry mentioned above – neuroscience, cognitive science and depth psychology – together with that associated with spirituality and mysticism, constitute the four approaches to consciousness on which I shall be focusing. I do not claim that these approaches are exclusive, and indeed we shall encounter others (such as those deriving from modern physics and evolutionary biology). Nevertheless, these four generally cover the range of methods and explanatory frameworks that bear significantly on the challenge with which consciousness presents us.

In using the phrase 'Approaches to Consciousness' in the title of this book, I am making reference to a number of meanings. The term 'approach' has the general sense of moving towards something, and in our present context, conveys the idea that we have been moving towards consciousness as a major topic of study over the past 30 years or so. A second connotation of the phrase 'approaches to consciousness' is also significant. The phrase conveys the sense of moving inwardly to explore one's own consciousness. It is noteworthy that both these connotations have been evident in the resurgence of interest in consciousness studies over recent times. The academic interest in consciousness has not developed independently of the more general shift in society towards inward exploration. Cultural change plays a huge role in setting the parameters through which academic inquiry operates. It not only has a bearing on relative intangibles, such as the general worldview, but also impacts on issues such as financial and institutional backing for the research projects that shape the progress of science.

Both these senses of the book's title are significant. However, I am primarily using the term 'approach' to emphasize two critical issues in the study of consciousness. First, there is the issue of methodology, which determines both the kinds of research questions that can be asked and the form of conclusions likely to be drawn from them. Second, a given 'approach' entails the use of specific terms relating to the kinds of structures and processes which are employed in attempting to explain phenomena. Table 1.1 specifies how these two issues differ across the four areas of inquiry specified above. As will be seen from the table, not only do the key methods differ across the areas but also the apposite terms for explanation differ, giving rise to what is best described as *explanatory pluralism* (Looren de Jong, 2001). Disagreements between researchers interested in the nature of consciousness arise largely through differences in their respective views of what constitutes appropriate explanatory terms. Table 1.1 makes an invaluable starting point for our inquiry since it maps the terrain, clearing the way for meaningful dialogue.

The areas of inquiry can be seen to correspond to a hierarchy of *levels*. The levels are essentially defined by the scale of organization implied in the terms adopted for explanation. The upper three levels employ non-physical explanatory concepts, and, as indicated in the table, correspond to differing types of experiences. For the moment I will leave open the question of the 'reality' of the explanatory concepts. We should simply acknowledge the diversity in our approach to explanation. An explanation for some phenomenon in terms of neural communication is clearly at a different level from an explanation couched in terms of contact with a Jungian archetype, or in terms of some kind of transcendent presence. That a person may have an experience of 'God' is beyond dispute. What must remain open is whether the appropriate route to explanation involves supernatural realms (Level 1) or some form of unusual neural activity (Level 4).

Related to the drive towards explanation is the need to understand *causation*.

Our primary interest lies with these two terms. What *causes* consciousness and how might we *explain* consciousness? Logically the terms are reciprocal: if I could demonstrate that region X in the brain is the cause of consciousness, then I would have effectively succeeded in explaining consciousness. In reality, we have no definitive evidence of the causation of consciousness, which leads some to suggest that consciousness is a primary quality of the universe; it is not *caused*, it simply *is* (Lancaster, 1991). Just as we are unable to explain what *caused* matter to exist, or life to originate, so the causation of consciousness must remain mysterious. However, as in these other cases, the ultimate mystery need not obscure our interest in studying properties of the phenomenon. We may, accordingly, seek explanations and causes for features of conscious experience.

Take the example of mystical experience. A whole area of inquiry – *neurotheology* (d'Aquili and Newberg, 1999; Newberg, d'Aquili and Rause, 2001) – has recently sprung up, which seeks to specify the brain activity accompanying religious and mystical states. Newberg defines neurotheology as that field of study which brings the sciences of neurophysiology and neuropsychology to bear on matters of religious experience and theology. Neuroscience can certainly demonstrate that the activity of certain brain systems is altered whilst an individual is meditating, for example. The question is what implications do such observations carry? Are the altered conditions the *cause* of the meditative experience, or merely a *correlate* of that experience? And reciprocally, do such observations provide us with the *explanation* of such experience?

This is where the levels of Table 1.1 come in. The following outline briefly sketches examples of the kinds of explanations for spiritual states that we find at each of the levels.

Spiritual/mystical

Throughout the world's religious traditions, discussions of the highest mystical states have invariably drawn on an understanding of God and other transcendent concepts, such as levels of the soul.[9] As far as explanation is concerned, the distinctive features of mystical experience are *explained* to the satisfaction of those sharing the Level 4 outlook by suggesting that they arise through union

TABLE 1.1 Four levels of inquiry into consciousness

Approach	Methods	Explanatory structures/ processes	Experiential equivalents
Level 4: Spiritual/ mystical	Access to revelation Contemplative and ritual practices • Meditation • Prophecy • Analysis of sacred language	Transcendent systems/ quantal systems • Higher self/soul etc. • Ground of being • Pure consciousness • Emanated principles • Godhead	Experience of • 'emptiness' • God/'All-Self'/ observing self • pure consciousness • the numinous
Level 3: Depth-psychological	Hermeneutics • Analysis of syndromes associated with psychic damage • Etymology and other analyses of linguistic meaning • Analysis of myth	Systems of the psyche • Self/ego • Conscious vs unconscious processes • Dynamic structure of the unconscious: complexes, archetypes, symbols • Affective states • Meaning-making processes	Experience of • the numinous • moments of significance • 'deep' selfhood/ archetypal self • 'therapeutic' meaning – the meaning behind overt images and words, etc.

TABLE 1.1 continued

Approach	Methods	Explanatory structures/ processes	Experiential equivalents
Level 2: Cognitive and neuro- psychological	Scientific positivism • Psychophysics: experimental study of experience • Analysis of syndromes associated with brain damage • Computer modelling	Cognitive systems/ informational systems • Self re *explicit* processing • Conscious vs nonconscious processes • Representations (schemata) • Affective states • Functional devices • IT metaphors	Experience of • 'I' • everyday meaning in memories, perceptions, emotions and thoughts • selfhood
Level 1: Neuro- physiological	Scientific positivism • Brain imaging • Electrophysiological recording • Neurochemistry • High-energy physics	Neural systems/quantal systems • Brain centre(s) for consciousness • Patterns of neural communication • Re-entrant systems (efferent/afferent) • Timing of neural responses • Sub-neuronal activity	

with God, or with the 'Absolute'. More than this, the mystical state is placed in the context of a shared and meaningful system of thought, allowing communication between fellows. Subtle distinctions between states may be recognized in the shared Level 4 outlook, a feature which forms the basis of most esoteric and mystical teaching systems. All this is lost when explanations are given solely in terms of the other, lower levels.

Consider the following example. Adapting Aristotelian and Neoplatonic terminology, Rabbi Isaac of Acre (late thirteenth to mid-fourteenth century) writes of the ascent to unity with the divine:

> If the soul of the isolated person [i.e., in isolated devotion] deserves to apprehend and cleave to the Passive Intellect, it is called Passive Intellect ... and likewise when it ascends further and cleaves to the Acquired Intellect, it becomes the Acquired Intellect; and if it merited to cleave to the Active Intellect, then it itself [becomes] Active Intellect; and if you shall deserve and cleave to the Divine Intellect, happy are you because you have returned to your source and root.
>
> (Cited in Idel, 1988a, p.133)

Each of these different terms for the intellect, that is, 'Passive', 'Acquired', 'Active', conveyed a distinctive meaning to the mediaeval mind, giving rise to a shared appreciation of Rabbi Isaac's schematization of the stages entailed in reaching the unitive state. Later, in Chapter 7, I will consider how we might understand the *Active Intellect* in psychological terms that are meaningful today. But, for the present, I wish to emphasize that the state was *explained* not only by reference to the encounter that seems to define it, but also in terms of what was involved in reaching it. The terms had *currency* and *explanatory value* for those sharing the perspective.

Depth-psychological

Whether conceived in negative or positive terms, the approach of depth psychology understands spiritual states as involving complexes of the unconscious. For Freud, the 'oceanic feeling', as he termed the oneness associated with mysticism, resulted from a regression to an infantile, narcissistic state prior to the ego's detaching itself from the world around it (Freud, 1930/1961; see also Parsons, 1999). Moreover, Freud famously saw the *Oedipus complex* as the explanation for other, more formed, spiritual states. Although his attitude to religious and mystical states was distinct from that of Freud, Jung's explanations are similarly couched in terms of psychodynamic complexes. He posited a *transcendent function* to the psyche, which underpins the quest for higher integration. Critical to this quest is the encounter with archetypal complexes, which gives rise to the kinds of numinous feelings (Otto, 1917/1923) experienced in spiritual states. For Jung, then, as for Freud, when seeking a meaningful *explanation* of such states, we should look into the organization of the psyche.

Cognitive

A central theme in cognitive discussions of consciousness is representation, by which is meant the ability of a system to constitute itself (or a subset of itself) to correspond in some way to something other than itself. Following Hebb's classic formulation of *cell assemblies* (Hebb, 1949), we may conceive of neuronal systems as dynamically forming into integrated groupings, each of which represents some entity in the world we experience. It has been proposed that one such representation, that of *self*, plays a critical role in determining what we are conscious of (Kihlstrom, 1993; Lancaster, 1991, 1993b; Metzinger, 2000, 2003).[10] I shall discuss these ideas more fully later in Chapter 5, but for now we need to recognize how such thinking can offer explanations of mystical states (Blackmore, 1986; Brown, 1977; Claxton, 1996; Lancaster, 1997a, 1997b, 2000c). In brief, a mystical state is thought to arise following attenuation of the self-representation together with a concomitant shift towards normally preconscious processes. Again, details of the argument will be explored later, but this outline should illustrate the way in which an *explanation* of a mystical state can be couched in terms that are meaningful at the cognitive level.

Neurophysiological

Whilst the above cognitive approach to explanation makes reference to neuronal systems, its key terms of reference involve terms such as 'representation' and 'self', the meaning of which is not advanced by further neuroscientific specification. Level 1, by contrast, is characterized by the attempt to arrive at such specification. D'Aquili and Newberg (1993) elaborate the presumed neural basis of different kinds of spiritual states. For example, passive meditation is thought to trigger intense stimulation of structures in the hypothalamus and medial forebrain bundle, which is a large fibre tract projecting from the midbrain to many regions of the forebrain. At the same time there is a total deafferentation (that is, loss of functional input) to the left and right posterior-superior parietal lobes. The authors 'believe that this results in the subject's attainment of a state of rapturous transcendence and absolute wholeness which carries such overwhelming power and strength with it that the subject has the sense of experiencing absolute reality' (p. 189). Their conviction is that, 'the principle of selective stimulation and deafferentation of various brain structures accompanied by various patterns and degrees of intensity of limbic stimulation may hold the key to explaining most, if not all, religious experiences' (p. 196). The emphasis here is clearly on neural, not cognitive (and certainly not psychodynamic) systems.

These four approaches illustrate the difference between the idea of explanation and that of reductive causation. We can explain spiritual or mystical experience at any of the levels (that is, in terms of union with the Active Intellect; activation of one or more archetype; reorganization of cognitive representations; or neural systems functioning in distinctive ways), yet the predominant scientific view would hold that only the last has the ring of authenticity about it. And that is because it indicates the material cause of the experience. The focus of debate on consciousness is essentially concerned with the legitimacy of positing forms of causation other than this reductive one (Wallace, 2000).

It should be understood that, crucially, there are two senses in which we can explain a given phenomenon. First, we can explain it in terms of constructs that convey an adequate picture for us to gain a meaningful view of the phenomenon. Second, we can explain it in terms of the real events causing it. The critical issue revolves around the meaning of the tiny word 'real'. If, for example, I were asked to explain some event occurring in a computer game, it would probably be of little help to start discoursing on the electronic phenomena in some tiny lump of silicon. Nor, I suspect, would an elaboration of the subtleties of *machine code* (or whatever the intricacies of the software are) be what my questioner was looking for. Perhaps something along the lines of, 'the curtain concealed an enemy alien who fired a laser gun while you were examining the mysterious scroll,' might hit the mark! As will be evident, the 'curtain', 'scroll' and so on, are not real, but constitute the appropriate explanatory terms in this case.

This example serves to illustrate the way in which a level of explanation may be appropriate even though not couched in terms of the generative cause. There is, of course, an important distinction between the computer game example and the case of consciousness. In the former we know that the images on the screen are truly caused by electronic events, because we built it that way. The final and complete explanation of the game is indeed at an electronic level. We have an *a priori* reason for understanding causation. In the case of consciousness, on the other hand, we have no such *a priori* basis for ascribing causation. In this case, therefore, to infer that the final and complete cause of consciousness lies at the level of bioelectrical events in the brain (paralleling the computer) is not legitimate in the way that it is in the case of the computer game.

Ontology and epistemology

The most challenging consideration in this discussion of causation and explanation concerns the reality of the levels indicated in Table 1.1. It is perfectly evident that the objects and beings in the computer game are not real in a fundamental sense. They clearly have value in a semantic sense, and they can *seem* all too real when the player is engaged in the game. But they have no ontological status. Is this also true of the levels in Table 1.1? Our understanding of causation in relation to consciousness will be critically influenced by our answer to this question.

Ontology refers to the status of entities in terms of their essential existence, or being. In general, if I state that some object – the table in front of me, for example – is *real*, I mean that it exists as an object in the physical world independently of me. This is an ontological statement. If I were to state that consciousness, or the realm of mind, is real in the sense that it exists separately from the physical realm – separate from the physical matter of the brain, for example – then I am an ontological dualist. This position is famously associated with the philosophy of Descartes, who conceived of mind and matter as essentially different 'stuffs'.

In relation to Table 1.1 we may keep an open mind about ontology. For example, whether or not the Godhead at Level 1 really exists, the need for explanations of phenomena in spiritual or mystical terms may still hold, in much the same way as we need explanations of the computer game in terms of 'curtains' or 'mysterious scrolls'. To understand this, we need to introduce a second technical term, *epistemology*. Epistemology refers to the ways in which we generate knowledge and understanding. An epistemological dualist, then, holds that the mind, or consciousness, can be known in two distinctly separate ways. It can be known from within, that is, as *experience*, or it can be known from the outside by studying its correlates in the appropriate physical realm – generally, the brain, but also including wider spheres such as the environment (Abram, 1996). Whilst epistemological dualists might argue that these two routes to knowing the nature of consciousness possess quite distinct properties and dynamics, they do not claim that they depict two separate realities (Bogen, 1998). The critical claim is simply that experiential knowledge will not be understood from without, and that, in any approach to consciousness, such knowledge is an indispensable adjunct to data generated by physical science (Varela and Shear, 1999; Velmans, 2000).

Table 1.1 implies an extension of this principle to other levels. We might contend, for example, that there are distinctive properties associated with experience gained at the spiritual/mystical level, which cannot be known from any of the other levels. Or, we might take the Freudian line that religious experience is best explained in terms of an unconscious complex. This is not to imply that the complex exists (ontologically) apart from Level 1; it is simply to assert that any meaningful insight into the issue under examination depends on explication of the complex in its own terms.[11] As Freud wrote, 'The theoretical structure of psychoanalysis that we have created is in truth a superstructure, which will one day have to be set upon its organic foundation. But we are still ignorant of this' (1916–17/1963, p. 389).

When it comes to *causation*, the two kinds of explanation will give radically different pictures. If we adopt a belief that there are *ontological differences* between the levels indicated in Table 1.1, then it follows that particular kinds of experience could be caused by entities existing at one or more levels. A mystical experience may be caused by contact with some form of higher being, such as an angel or God, for example. If, by contrast, a merely *epistemo-logical* view of the differences between levels were assumed, then most would argue for physical causation. On this view, while recognizing that it may be valuable to discuss mystical experience in terms of angels or God, most would assign its cause to activity of the brain alone.

It is possible that entities at all levels are ontologically real. Not only are neurones real, but so also are the cognitive self and other representations, as also are archetypes and/or other unconscious complexes and the ground of being itself. Unlike dualism, which restricts its reference to the two realms of mind and body, we have here a view which might be named *ontological pluralism*, suggesting that reality consists of a hierarchy of ontologically distinct levels.

Given that dualism is criticized on the grounds that it posits the existence of an indemonstrable realm (that of 'thinking stuff'), it may be difficult to justify this extreme of ontological pluralism. Nevertheless, the question at issue concerns the grounds on which we decide that any entity constitutes an ontological reality. A view widely held today asserts that only the entities studied by physics are the basic elements of the real, a viewpoint known as *material-ism*. Closely related to this view is that of *physicalism*, which asserts that the mind is determined solely by causes which are physical in nature. These two perspectives differ subtly in that a materialist denies the existence of any reality other than the physical, whereas a physicalist asserts only that we need consider no reality other than the physical in attempting to understand all features of the mind. A physicalist can remain agnostic about the possible reality of non-material entities such as a soul. It seems to me that some hair-splitting is going on here, since it is hard to imagine what a 'soul' would be were it bereft of connection to the mind.

The question is, what grounds are there for adhering to the ontology of materialism or physicalism? The post-enlightenment worldview, associated with the successes of science, holds that physical things are real, whilst the status of cognitive, archetypal or mystical entities is, at best, open to doubt. Neurones, and other structures of the brain, are seen as real because they are constituted by the entities studied by physics. 'Selves' and other psychody-namic complexes are not so constituted, and therefore have been seen as having epistemological status only. Yet, as Radder (2001) points out, we are on shaky ground if we suggest that physics itself embraces a single unified ontology. Not only has the ontology embraced by physics changed over time, but also different physicists currently hold a range of conflicting ontologies. Writing of quantum mechanics, the root of almost all contemporary physics, Radder notes that 'The ontology of this theory – what it tells us about the basic structure of the world – has been and still is the subject of a variety of different, and often conflicting, interpretations' (p. 778). For example, some contemporary ontologies in physics support the notion of action at a distance, whilst others do not, and some advocate a role for the consciousness of the observer in determining the values of physical properties to be measured, whilst, again, some do not. Radder is led to conclude that:

> There is no reason at all why psychologists should endorse physicalism. If they do, they subscribe either to an ontology that has no positively specifiable content or to a doctrine that changes with every fundamental change in physics. Moreover, if physicalists rely on current, quantum-mechanical physics, they may well end up adhering to an ontology that is not physicalist in the common sense of exclusively referring to material objects that move, and act causally, in space and time.
>
> (Radder, 2001, p. 781)

There are, of course, a variety of ontologies that could be squared with Table 1.1. The ontological pluralist view mentioned above could assert four separate levels of reality, or it could accommodate the notion that any three are genuinely distinct. In line with threefold pluralism, for example, we might suggest that *neural* (as a subset of the physical), *psychological* (that is, combining Levels 2 and 3) and *transcendent* constitute the three ontologically distinct realms of our cosmos. According to this approach, the reason for separating Levels 2 and 3 would not be ontological but epistemological – some psychological structures are best understood in cognitive terms and others are better explicated in psychodynamic terms. Traditional dualism would see a division between Level 1 and all the higher levels. An alternative position, one in accordance with a number of mystical traditions, would assert that none of the levels are real as such, but that together they constitute veils of illusion progressively surrounding the only reality, that of spirit, which courses through all of them.

The alternatives are many, and the evidence by means of which we might choose between them seems inadequate. My interest for the present simply lies in examining the implications of the foregoing for our understanding of *causation*. The viewpoint of *materialism* allows for *upward causation* only. Any experience for which the terms employed in Levels 2, 3 or 4 may be epistemologically useful, is understood as having been caused by the only real events, namely those of Level 1. Alternatively, a viewpoint ascribing some form of existence to the other levels (ontological dualism or pluralism) could raise the additional possibility of *downward causation*. The brain events that accompany an experience would then be construed as having been caused by the experience. Downward causation can carry the added implication that a system specified at lower levels may have been structured in order to fulfil a function in relation to a reality of a higher kind.[12]

Upward causation gives rise to *reductive explanations*; downward causation implies *teleological explanations* (Figure 1.1).[13] The former are the stock-in-trade of traditional science. The latter rarely enter into mainstream scientific discourse. Teleological explanations sit at the fringe of 'new-paradigm science' with a view such as Goswami's that the physical brain evolved to meet the needs of spirit or consciousness to become known to itself (Goswami, 1993). Teleology is the term applying to the view that developments arise due to the purpose or design that is served by them. Teleology is exemplified by the creationist argument that the complexity in biological function is suggestive of intelligent design.

Emergentism, as advocated, for example, by Sperry (1969, 1995), suggests a species of downward causation devoid of any teleological implications. The term 'emergence' is used to suggest that properties evident at one level cannot be conceptually reduced to the structures apparent at the lower level. The paradigmatic example is that of *water*. A description of water may include terms such as colourless, wet, flowing and so on, which cannot be witnessed at the more reductive level of hydrogen and oxygen atoms. Sperry's theory may be classed as being physicalist without being materialist. He understands consciousness in physicalist terms, inasmuch as it can only come into being on account of the physical brain processes which cause it to arise. However, the theory is not materialist since consciousness is understood as bearing properties that cannot be reduced to the electro-chemical processes of the brain. Consciousness is a dynamic emergent property of brain activity. The aspect of downward causation is seen in Sperry's argument that this emergent property has the power to direct brain activity – a process which has been labelled 'retroaction' (Bogen, 1998). In the terms of Table 1.1 such retroaction exemplifies a higher level causing a specific pattern of organization to arise at a lower level. Sperry, then, recognizes two levels, each with its own dynamics and each having causative effects on the other.

The appeal to the paradigm of water here can be slightly misleading, however. Our scientific understanding of the properties of hydrogen and oxygen atoms *does* provide a basis for explaining the macro properties of water. For example, liquidity arises by dint of the effect energy levels have on the properties of the bonds between the atoms. In contradistinction, there is *no* basis in current neuroscience for explaining how the macro properties, namely those of consciousness, arise from the known properties of neurones. Either we must take it as an act of faith that science will give us the basis for such emergence, or we must accept a materialist stance and reject emergence. The alternative to these viewpoints is the proposition that consciousness is not dependent solely on the physical activity of the brain. It may be ontologically separate (*dualism* or *ontological pluralism*); it may be the only ontological reality (*idealism*); or it may be a property of matter in general (*holophysicalism*).[14]

A further problem with emergentism concerns the ontological status of the emergent property. The appeal to physicalism serves to avoid awkward metaphysical claims of some kind of separate reality. But it is not clear how any emergent dynamic pattern could act in the proposed way to interact with the physical system. Again, appeals to liquidity in relation to water or any analogous example do not help since there is no downward causation involved.

In brief, emergent phenomena are clearly a feature of physical and biological systems. However, it is not exactly clear *how* the postulated downwards causation from emergent properties occurs. In biology, for example, Goodwin (1994) proposes that the healing ability of organisms to reconstitute themselves following damage is 'an emergent property of life that is not explained by the properties of the molecules out of which organisms are made' (p. 163). Again, we have not unequivocally established how the emergent property of the organism as a whole effects such healing.

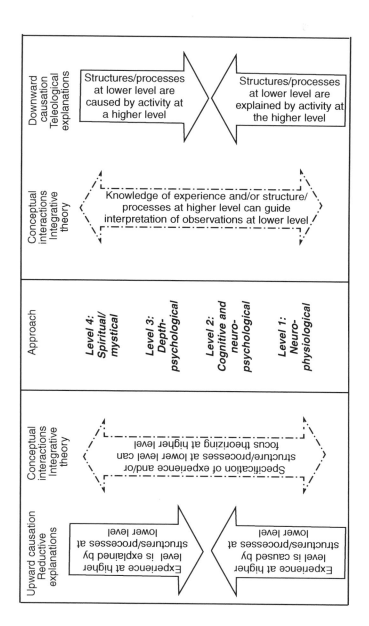

FIGURE 1.1 Approaches to consciousness and/or conscious states which involve bridging across different levels of explanation

While many suggest that emergent fields of some kind are involved, there is little by way of established fact. It is unclear, to take just one key aspect, whether such organizing fields are physical, as Goodwin proposes, or non-physical (Sheldrake, 1981).

Libet (1994) has proposed a field theory of the consciousness–brain relationship, in which consciousness is seen as constituting a field that effects changes within the structural activity of the physical brain. The exact nature of the field is left somewhat vague, on the grounds that contemporary biology and physics provide inadequate data. In Libet's view, we await the appropriate breakthrough. Another proponent of a brain field theory of consciousness, McFadden (2002), argues that we already possess adequate data. According to him, there is substantial supporting data for his proposal that electromagnetic brain fields constitute the physical substrate of consciousness. Despite the attraction of these field theories in terms of their opposition to strong reductionism, there is as yet no consensus over the means whereby downward causation from a brain field may operate. Probably the most promising approach is that offered by quantum physics. Non-local quantum effects may give rise to discrete brain states. I will examine quantum theories of consciousness and the brain in more detail in Chapter 4.

Downward causation is the 'holy grail' for those who seek integration between scientific and religious approaches. The religious categories of 'above' and 'below' would be related by a scientifically-ordained principle. Griffin (2000) notes that, 'As downward causation becomes re-established as a general fact, pervasive of nature at all levels, the notion of downward causation from God, or the universe as an inclusive individual to its parts, will no longer seem so aberrant' (p. 105). As already indicated, however, such optimism rather oversteps the current scientific position. In the study of consciousness, there are a number of mysteries awaiting solution (or maybe there is just one mystery which takes a number of guises). The basis of presumed downward causation is one such mystery.

Figure 1.1 summarizes these discussions about possible relationships among the levels pertaining to consciousness. To the extent that these levels may imply ontological differences, our concern will lie with *causation* and *explanation* (outer columns). If we assume no ontological differences, then it is *integrative theory* that will interest us (inner columns). My term 'integrative theory' is meant to convey the principle that a full treatment of consciousness requires comparative analysis of data from the different levels in Table 1.1. For example, observations at a higher level may prove valuable in interpretation of data at a lower level, and vice versa – data from a lower level may constrain our view of the meaning of experiences at the higher level. The third logical possibility is the more esoteric notion of correspondence introduced above. According to this view (which may be understood as a species of Leibniz's *psychophysical parallelism*), each level articulates fundamental principles in its own distinctive fashion, as with the examples of binding and re-entrance discussed earlier.[15]

Table 1.1 and Figure 1.1 give us a framework for recognizing the issues involved when studies bridge the levels. Many of the promising developments in consciousness studies entail hybrid relationships in this way. For example, *neuro-psychoanalysis* (Solms, 2000; Solms and Turnbull, 2002) employs methods from both neuroscience and psychoanalysis. Moreover, it recognizes that explanatory structures from both neurological (Level 1) and psychoanalytic (Level 3) approaches may be required to fully understand psychiatric states. To take another example, *neurotheology* has both reductive and emergent aspects, which can easily be plotted against the levels of the tables. Neurotheology has demonstrated that a spiritual experience is correlated with activity in specific brain regions, thereby suggesting a role for those regions in the generation of the state (reductive). At the same time, its proponents hint towards a more ontological view of a higher reality: 'Absolute Unitary Being is a plausible, even probable possibility' (Newberg, d'Aquili and Rause, 2001, p. 171).

Levels, quadrants, and everything...

The study of consciousness touches on much that is central to our beliefs and values. As Tart remarks, 'Consciousness is not just of academic and scientific interest: consciousness is our very mode of being and the source of the values by which we live our life' (2000, p. 255). Indeed, it seems to me that the explosion of interest in consciousness research over the past decade or so is not simply about a specific topic that is yet to be understood. It is, more significantly, the latest chapter in the quest to understand ourselves, which has dignified humankind throughout many different ages.

This gives rise to what is, at one and the same time, the fascination and the Achilles' heel of consciousness studies. Perhaps the scope of the project is simply too large, and progress may be expected to arise only when we restrict ourselves to a circumscribed topic. The contrary argument is advanced by those, like me, who stress the need for integration across traditionally separate disciplines. Nevertheless, to title a book *A Brief History of Everything* (Wilber, 1996; see also Wilber, 2000a) takes some confidence! At the root of Wilber's all-encompassing approach is his rejection of the view that the basis, or generative cause, of consciousness is to be found in physical or biological systems alone, as is claimed by those advocating a more restrictive approach:

> [C]onsciousness is not located merely in the physical brain, nor in the physical organism, nor in the ecological system, nor in the cultural context, nor does it emerge from any of those domains. Rather, it is anchored in, and distributed across, all of those domains with all of their available levels.
>
> (Wilber, 1997, p. 83)

Wilber emphasizes what he calls the *spectrum of consciousness*. For him, consciousness pervades all levels in a hierarchy extending from physical matter to the Godhead:

> In simplified form, this spectrum appears to range from subconscious to self-conscious to superconscious; from prepersonal to personal to transpersonal; from instinctual to mental to spiritual; from preformal to formal to postformal; from instinct to ego to God.
>
> (Wilber, 1997, p. 81)

Wilber's ideas derive primarily from developmental theories, including those focused in psychological, astrophysical and evolutionary observations. His own theory builds connections between these developmental approaches and the more inclusive notion of the *Great Chain of Being*. The Great Chain of Being is a concept associated in the West with Aristotle and Plotinus in particular, but it is also found throughout later Neoplatonic formulations and in the teachings of various Eastern authors. Plotinus' concept stressed the continuity across diverse forms in a hierarchical series from the most basic form of existence to the perfect form of God. In Wilber's hands, the hierarchy becomes distributed over four quadrants by introducing the dimensions of interior–exterior and individual–collective.

Wilber's hierarchical formulation has been criticized on the grounds that, without adequate justification, it privileges certain spiritual states over others (Ferrer, 2002; Helminiak, 1998; Krippner, 2000; Lancaster, 2001; Parsons, 1999); that its supposed all-inclusiveness is achieved only at the cost of distorting some of the religious traditions on which it draws (Schlamm, 2001); and that it perpetuates what is, in the eyes of his critics, an outmoded masculine orientation to development and spirituality (Heron, 1998; Wright, 1998). While not wishing to downplay the impact of these criticisms, for the present I wish to emphasize the significance of Wilber's portrayal of the 'big picture' and its importance for consciousness studies.

Wilber's concept of the spectrum of consciousness is predicated on his insistence that a number of fundamental principles recur at all levels of the cosmos, including the levels of matter, life and mind. This perspective derives from the concept of the Great Chain of Being, and strongly underpins his 'integral theory of consciousness' (Wilber, 1997, 2000b). Wilber is uncharacteristically reticent, however, when it comes to probing into the neurophysiological and neurocognitive approaches to consciousness (Wilber, 1999, p. 617). He seems to be satisfied that these young disciplines still await major progress. Consequently, he ignores the possible expression of the recurring principles in these areas, and hardly discusses interactions between these sciences and other areas, or levels, of inquiry. My own view is that the kind of integrative approach that Wilber advocates has much to gain from research evidence already available from cognitive neuroscience. This should become clear in future chapters. Wilber heroically sets a framework and an agenda, but, in relation to neuroscience, he hardly penetrates into the terrain of integration.

The framework laid out in Table 1.1 and Figure 1.1 is less ambitious than Wilber's, in that it omits reference to social and cultural domains. It focuses on the levels of explanation which are most frequently encountered in consciousness studies. More to the point, it is not intended as a map of developmental stages.[16] Its primary terms of reference are methodology and explanation. Through the latter in particular, it serves to emphasize the integrative approaches that are increasingly important if we are to progress in consciousness studies.

In addition to its presentations of a pluralism of explanatory structures, Table 1.1 portrays a pluralism of methods. In particular, when seeking integration between the data of science and those drawn from religious mysticism, it may be misleading to attempt to fit both within a common methodological framework. Ferrer (2002) has criticized Wilber specifically for his attempt to assimilate the methods of religion to those of science. Wilber (1998/2001) proposes a *marriage* between the scientific and spiritual spheres by arguing that all authentic knowing derives from a common form of method, which is that generally viewed as 'scientific'. For Wilber, the approach of spirituality relies on the same three foundational aspects as does 'hard' science. These three are *injunction* (training in the appropriate discipline), *data* (the results obtained by following the discipline), and *falsifiability* (subjecting the theories that are derived from the data to further test). He asserts that:

> [R]eligion's great, enduring, and unique strength is that, at its core, *it is a science of spiritual experience* (using 'science' in the broad sense as direct experience, in any domain, that submits to the three strands of injunction, data, and falsifiability).
>
> (Wilber, 1998/2001, p. 169, italics original)

As Ferrer points out, the problem here is that much that is deemed authentic within the religious traditions does not submit to the falsifiability claim as readily as Wilber implies. Demarcating those elements that cannot be squared with the ways of science as not belonging to the 'spiritual core' of religions is an artificial imposition on the traditions themselves. Moreover, it is states of knowing rather than experiencing that have invariably been extolled in religious mysticism. For these reasons, the marriage we seek between science and religious mysticism may not be well served by Wilber's championing of the scientific method. Ferrer is adamant: '*Wilber's marriage not only perpetuates the dissociations of the modern era, but also renders the legitimation of spiritual knowledge hopeless*' (2002, p. 55, italics original).

In Part II, I will comment more specifically on these, and other, issues of methodology in the context of the diverse approaches to consciousness as they are encountered. For the present, it is sufficient to note that a 'marriage' that, at the outset, places severe limitations on what one of the partners can bring to the relationship is untenable.

In summary, the 'big picture' sees the challenge to understand consciousness as being central to our aspirations at both individual and societal levels. The major terrain for approaching consciousness is mapped by the four levels of Table 1.1: the neural, cognitive, depth-psychological and mystical levels. Each level not only contributes to our conceptualization of consciousness, but also needs to be informed by the others. This dynamic of interrelationship across the levels becomes focused in the role of causation. As discussed above, both downward and upward directions of causation may need to be considered. In particular, over the following chapters I will adduce reasons for viewing consciousness as comprising elements which involve both causative directions. Each level may contribute distinctive aspects to the structural and self-related features of consciousness. However, the essence of consciousness, its distinctive ineffable quality, transcends these aspects of structure and self, and resists the claims of scientific analysis. This essential, phenomenal core of consciousness is incapable of further analysis, and might be thought of as a window into the *otherness* at the heart of things.

Chapter 2
A Common Purpose?

It is time for the much-heralded return of consciousness as a subject matter of psychology to enter a new phase. This new phase would serve to take us well beyond explaining and justifying the return of consciousness, and beyond those empirical investigations that we hope are contributing to our understanding of the nature and character of consciousness. Let us not continue to make the wasteful mistake that psychologists have repeatedly made during this century. Let us not spend our career, or a good part of it, following the data from one study to the next to the next, wherever the data may lead us and without effectual concern regarding the larger picture. Instead of assuming that scientific progress will take care of itself if we just follow certain basic rules of 'good science', let us join together, consciously and deliberately to develop the theory of consciousness by whatever means necessary.

(Natsoulas, 1995, p. 303)

The need for consciousness studies

What is a *discipline*? The word implies limitations, and accordingly, when used in the sense of a branch of instruction, it should alert us to the importance of boundaries in our approach to knowledge. Paramount in this context are the boundaries of subject matter and methodology. Consciousness studies may therefore be considered to be a unitary discipline if two key conditions are met. First, consciousness must be able to be defined coherently and in a form which demarcates it from the subject-matter of other disciplines. Second, there must be a shared concept of method amongst those engaged in consciousness studies. While it is not essential that all subscribe to a monolithic doctrine of method, there must be agreed boundaries regarding the format of demonstrations which can be accepted as advancing understanding of the subject matter.

It does not take an overdose of cynicism to note that neither of these conditions has been adequately met in the case of the study of consciousness. As will be discussed later in this chapter, defining consciousness is notoriously problematic, and there is considerable debate over the range of legitimate methods of study. But the problem is perhaps more fundamental than this, since statements about consciousness are quintessentially statements of *belief*. Some authors believe that consciousness is generated only by the brain (neurophysicalism); others that it is a property of the physical world 'at large' (holophysicalism); and others that it is an echo of the divine (supernaturalism). When it comes to defining consciousness, these kinds of beliefs are always in evidence, whether they are made explicit or not (Baruss, 2001). Simply put, there is inadequate evidence to allow us unequivocally to establish one of these perspectives over the others. Authors who hold the view that the brain is the seat of consciousness are fitting the data from cognitive neuroscience into their general belief system. Within the framework of a *physicalist* worldview, the brain is presented as the obvious candidate for the 'organ of consciousness'. However, the identical data will be incorporated into a different worldview by an author whose approach emphasizes a transcendent source of consciousness. From this supernaturalist perspective, the brain may be presented as the agent generating particular conscious contents, but is not itself the source of consciousness. Given that the data themselves cannot privilege one view over the other, distinguishing between theories of these kinds becomes a matter of favouring one belief system over another.

The question essentially concerns the *origin* of consciousness, and its relation with other entities. Is consciousness uniquely a product of a highly-evolved brain? Might a machine be conscious? Is consciousness a feature of the natural world as a whole? Or, does it derive from some supernatural source? As far as the study of consciousness is concerned, beliefs are both *necessary* and *dangerous*. They are necessary on account of the present inadequacy of the data themselves, which do not directly address the truly fundamental questions about the nature of consciousness.

They are dangerous, for the obvious reason that they tend to cloud our understanding of what is, and what is not, evidence for a particular point of view.

When assessing whether an area of study constitutes a discipline, a third consideration is the approach to *explanation*. All strands of inquiry seek to classify aspects of the subject matter in order to advance towards their explanation. As we discussed in the previous chapter, when it comes to consciousness, the processes and/or structures advanced for explanatory purposes vary considerably in scale, and dialogue becomes decidedly strained amongst those professing diverse views about which scale is appropriate.

All this suggests that we might be fighting a losing battle in arguing for a unitary discipline of consciousness studies. There is, however, a fourth consideration that becomes critical here, namely the *aspirations of society*. An area of inquiry may be considered a distinct discipline *if society considers it as such*. Over the past 20 years or so, it has become evident from a variety of sources – popular and academic books on consciousness, media interest in consciousness, online and paper journals focusing specifically on consciousness – that the discipline is a *de facto* reality. We might quibble over the extent to which consciousness studies represents a genuinely unitary discipline rather than an exercise in interdisciplinary co-operation. But this need not distract from the major point. The resurgence of interest in consciousness has been driven as much by society as a whole as it has by scientists, psychologists, or philosophers. There has been a *need* for consciousness studies.

The interdisciplinary imperative

We stand at the threshold of a new era in modern science ... with the coming of the neuroscience revolution. Before, pure science was able to brush the philosophical questions aside and, indeed, banished all but the most positivist rhetoric from the discussion of what constituted scientific reality. Now, the neuroscience revolution, with its interdisciplinary communication between the basic sciences, its cross-fertilization of methods, and its focus for the first time on the biology of consciousness, appears to have important humanistic implications far beyond the dictates of the reductionistic approach that spawned it.

(Taylor, 1999a, p. 468)

Taylor makes the above statement in the context of comparing two giants in the history of psychology, William James and Sigmund Freud. His interest lies especially in their respective approaches to a scientific psychology. Both James and Freud avowed the value of empiricism in their work, yet both – in different ways – had to come to terms with what they saw as inadequacies in the epistemologies with which they had begun to investigate the nature of mind. James rejected the prevailing empiricism, which, as he wrote at the beginning of his *Principles of Psychology*, had constructed a *'psychology without a soul'* (James, 1890/1950, p. 1, italics original). He favoured instead his approach of *radical empiricism*. This rejected the supremacy of positivism, with its reductionistic orientation, stressing instead the critical importance of observing experience directly. James emphasized that philosophical debate about the mind is meaningful only when we include *all* features of experience, in particular those relations between the individual data of experience which themselves point to the complexity of mind. Undue simplification loses the very heart of the topic.

Early in his career, Freud came to the realization that the neurological systems of explanation in which he had been trained were inadequate for an effective analysis of the mind. In particular, the complex issues surrounding the aetiology of the neurotic symptoms presented by his patients could not be unravelled in neurological terms. The impasse he encountered was filled by his development of psychoanalysis, which as he later wrote, 'must keep itself free from any hypothesis that is alien to it, whether of an anatomical, chemical, or physiological kind, and must operate entirely with purely psychological auxiliary ideas...' (1915–16/ 1963, p. 21). This approach meant that hermeneutics, symbolism and meaning rather than neurones and their energies became the essential terms of reference.

My interest here lies in the 'new era' to which Taylor refers. He notes the importance of an interdisciplinary thrust towards the big questions of our day, especially those directed towards understanding the 'biology of consciousness'. His critical assertion is that the neuroscience revolution lies at the heart of this new era. However, further reflection will confirm that neuroscience does not happen in a vacuum, and that the directions it takes are significantly a product of the aspirations of the society of which it is part.

Consider the underpinnings of the 'neuroscience revolution' itself. What factors have precipitated this revolution? New technologies that allow sophisticated imaging of the anatomy and function of brain systems have certainly produced a quantum shift in the richness of neuroscientific information available. However, the term 'revolution' connotes something more than merely an increase in data. More fundamentally, there have been major changes in the kinds of questions that neuroscientists are confident about asking. There has been a tangible shift to research questions focusing directly on experience.

The technological developments have underwritten this shift. For example, a PET scan can be employed to indicate exactly which areas of the brain become active during specified experiences, such as those associated with meditation, dreaming, or remembering. Prior to the technological breakthroughs, any attempt to map regions of the brain in relation to experience was either somewhat crude (as in EEG studies, for example), or invariably *indirect*. Direct exploration of the human brain had to await a post-mortem examination – hardly the best time for investigating experience! At best, post-mortem examination could give evidence of some presumed relation between physical pathology and past, generally aberrant, experience, as in neurological cases. Alternatively, research focused on animals' brains – again, with the consequence that experiential data would be lacking. The 'neuroscience revolution' lies fundamentally, so it seems to me, in the *positioning of experience at the centre of our agenda.*

This focus on experience within neuroscience is very much a reflection of changes at a more cultural level. Since the mid-twentieth century we have witnessed a movement towards the privileging of experience over other, more utilitarian, values in western society as a whole. Seen in this context we may appreciate that a complex two-way interaction operates between cultural developments and developments in neuroscience (as indeed has always been the case with our attempts to understand the mind).

Tarnas has argued that paradigm shifts in science have an *archetypal* basis. In his view, a given paradigm becomes ascendant due to processes unfolding within the collective mind:

A paradigm appears to account for more data, and for more important data, it seems more relevant, more cogent, more attractive, fundamentally because it has become archetypally appropriate to that culture or individual at that moment in its evolution.

(Tarnas, 1991/1996, p. 448)

The shift within psychological science and neuroscience towards studying consciousness may be best understood in terms of this kind of an archetypal influence. Tarnas' transpersonal orientation is evident in his conception that the shift has been towards a participatory consciousness reconnected to the universal. While the technological developments mentioned above have been enormously important, the rise of consciousness studies in our day cannot be understood without reference to deep processes operating at a collective level. Indeed, from the archetypal point of view, the technological developments themselves are part of the unfolding paradigm. They have been catalyzed by the paradigm shift, as well as contributing to its consolidation.

All this suggests that the interdisciplinary nature of consciousness studies is broader than Taylor implies, for it is not merely with the 'basic sciences' that neuroscience has links. While it may be argued that developments in neuroscience have humanistic implications, as Taylor observes, it is equally important to recognize the opposite influence: that issues at a humanistic, and more generally at a cultural, level have a role in shaping the course of neuroscience.[1] Consequently, it is not simply a question of the neuroscientist liaising with the molecular biologist, the quantum physicist, or the computer scientist. Considerably broader dialogue, extending beyond traditional confines of science, may be appropriate. Flanagan moves in this direction in his understanding of the interdisciplinary approach to consciousness. He argues that progress depends on adopting a 'natural method' in which a wide diversity of sources of data is coordinated:[2]

Start by treating different types of analysis with equal respect. Give *phenomenology* its due. Listen carefully to what individuals have to say about how things seem. Also, let the psychologists and cognitive scientists have their say. Listen carefully to their descriptions about how mental life works, and what jobs if any consciousness has in its overall economy. Third, listen carefully to what the neuroscientists say about how conscious mental events of different sorts are realized, and examine the fit between their stories and the phenomenological and psychological stories. But phenomenology, psychology, and neuroscience are not enough. Evolutionary biology and cultural and psychological anthropology will also be crucial players.

(Flanagan, 1995, p. 1104)

Over recent years several hybrid terms have been coined, which clearly reflect the thrust towards the kind of multidisciplinary approach envisioned here. Varela (1996) uses the term 'neurophenomenology' to convey the importance of subjecting experience to complex, phenomenological analysis before attempting to relate it to states and processes of the brain. 'First-person methods' are used in order to enable participants to detect the subtle features of experience normally taken for granted, for example in relation to awareness of time (Varela, 1999). Only when precise features of consciousness have been adequately delineated introspectively, may one begin to interpret 'third-person' cognitive-neuroscientific data.

As already noted in Chapter 1, Solms uses the term 'neuro-psychoanalysis' to convey the complementarity between psycho-analysis and neuroscience. We often hear that neuroscience is increasingly successful in describing the neural correlates of mental states. However, the precise make-up of states is not always as transparent as might appear. In addition, specifying brain regions responsible for the states can be overly simplistic. Solms (2000) gives the example of patients with damage in the perisylvian region of their right hemispheres. A superficial examination of these patients' problems indicates disturbance to various psychological abilities – spatial perception, emotional expression, and attention. However, rather than infer that the right hemisphere is responsible for these specific functions, Solms argues that a more fundamental problem underlies these specific psychological symptoms. The patients are suffering a regression, best understood in psycho-analytical terms, on account of the loss of their normal relation-ship to external objects. A realistic understanding of the function of the damaged brain region requires a psychoanalytic model, which is why the hybrid approach is favoured. Bringing classical psychoanalytical terms to bear on the problem, Solms concludes that the region damaged in these patients is normally responsible for transforming primitive, narcissistic ways of relating to objects into the mature and realistic orientation of a healthy person.

What unites the approaches of Solms and Varela is the recogni-tion that superficial analysis of experience will result in misleading maps of the brain sites and processes which may be involved. We require more incisive means for understanding the deeper structure of experience, a structure which may not be readily available to immediate introspection. It is for this reason that approaches such as phenomenology (Varela) and psychoanalysis (Solms) are critical for consciousness studies as a whole.

Newberg and d'Aquili's *neurotheology* offers a third example of such contemporary hybrids. As discussed in Chapter 1, the link here is between religious or spiritual experience and study of brain function. Again, it would be naïve to expect a direct correspondence between experience and the functioning of specific brain regions. Clearly, just because someone claims to have seen an angel, it does not follow that we should expect a region of their brain, which may have been active at the time of the experience, to be specialized for recognizing angels. Persinger (1987) argues that the central feature of many spiritual experiences is some kind of *sensed presence*. He understands experiences such as that of seeing an 'angel' as comprising two distinct elements. First, there is a propensity to sense a 'presence' of some kind. Second, the presence may be subjectively clothed according to shared expectations within the individual's culture, or even sub-group. For example, a sensed presence for someone engaged with Christianity may take on the kind of angelic form typically portrayed in Christian iconography.

Persinger has demonstrated that activity in a specific brain region (the hippocampus together with its associations with the right temporal lobe) can trigger experiences of this kind. Whether the presence is experienced as an angel, a disembodied soul, or an alien, may be more to do with the contributions of other brain regions. Again, any suggestion of a presumed cerebral basis of spiritual experience critically depends on our analysis of what constitutes the primary features of the experience.

This issue is considerably more complex than may appear, since the immediate form of our experiences may mask their inner structure. The core experience may not be immediately transparent. In this context, we may note the debate as to whether or not cultural expectancies determine the form of mystical experiences. According to the *essentialist* school of thought (Forman, 1990, 1998) a core mystical experience – that of pure consciousness devoid of mental content – transcends the particularities of cultural and cognitive factors. Opposed to this view is the *contextualist* viewpoint of Katz and others who argue that *all* experience is culturally mediated (see contributors to Katz, 1978a, 1992a):

[T]he experiences themselves are inescapably shaped by prior linguistic influences such that the lived experience conforms to a preexistent pattern that has been learnt, then intended, and then actualized in the experiential reality of the mystic.

(Katz, 1992b, p. 5)

I shall examine this debate in more detail in Chapter 3. For the present, it is sufficient to note that such contradictory views held by scholars of mystical writings complicate the challenge for neurotheology. If we accept Forman's approach, the mystic's experience reveals the fundamental quality of consciousness – *pure consciousness*, an observational ability lacking any informational content. From Katz's corner, the experience reveals only a distinctive form of conscious content. Any 'void' is merely a conditioned void, and therefore gives no indication of a real, underlying empty conscious function. It would be like a computer screen displaying a uniform whiteness which had been generated by complex workings of a programme in the machine. Given these two diverse views, what should the neurotheologist be searching for – a brain correlate of a mediated nothingness or of a pure nothingness?

In these days of relatively effective brain imaging, understanding the structure of subjective experience is more of a challenge than that of deciphering the specifics of brain activity. In principle, it is essentially straightforward to observe regions of the brain 'lighting up'; the difficulty comes in knowing how the various parts of the brain may be related to the given experience. This is where the kinds of complex analyses of experience as conducted by the various hybrids we have discussed are essential. In this challenge, we have the strongest argument for recognizing a unitary discipline of consciousness studies. Under circumstances in which the interdisciplinary input becomes critical for significant progress in any one of the individual disciplines, we have breached the boundary between what might have been thought of as a vague grouping of diverse individuals with a shared interest and a unitary discipline in the area of that interest.

A neuroscientist may possess in abundance the various skills required for generating appropriate third-person data, and yet may lack a crucial element of introspective insight necessary to grasp exactly where those data contribute to a model of conscious processes (Baruŝs, 2001; Lancaster, 1997a). Wallace (1999) notes that 'Buddhists regard the undisciplined mind as an unreliable instrument for examining mental objects, processes, and the nature of consciousness' (p. 176). Such a mind only becomes 'disciplined' in this context through prolonged engagement with a practice such as meditation and clear *training* in introspection. To the extent that *all* sciences of consciousness depend to some extent on introspection to guide interpretation of data, Wallace's statement suggests the critical need for those with 'disciplined' minds to work with those whose own discipline embraces the traditional scientific method and a grasp of the relevant complex instrumentation. The ideal, of course, is for the two characteristics – a grasp of the fundamentals of science and the insight associated with meditative training – to be present within the one individual. But it does not stop there: we would additionally require our expert in consciousness studies to have a sound grasp of the basis of philosophical inquiry, familiarity with phenomenological methods and an understanding of the ramifications of quantum physics – at least! Clearly, we need a forum within which such areas of expertise may be shared; we need a unitary discipline of consciousness studies.

On methodology

The foregoing raises the additional question of methodology. An expert in an area of inquiry is not simply one who has read the relevant books and papers. Fundamentally, it is the ability to *engage* with the methodology that brings a full appreciation of the issues. It is clearly unrealistic to base any appraisal of consciousness studies as a distinctive discipline on its adoption of a distinctive methodology. There is no single method that covers all approaches to consciousness. Even Flanagan's *naturalistic method*, encountered above, which has the strength of its accommodation of diverse inputs, would exclude those who see some non-physical dimension in consciousness.

Essentially, we need to recognize that the term 'method' is used in three distinctive ways. First, and most typically, it is used to refer to the investigative technique adopted. The scientific method classically incorporates a number of critical features, including the controlled manipulation of variables, a third-person perspective, and the repeatability of observations. First-person methods, by comparison, focus on the very subjectivity that science classically eschewed. As Varela and Shear (1999) note, it is not simply a question of 'just taking a look' at our own experience. Rather, methods have been developed which systematically attempt to examine 'what it is that we can and cannot have access to, and how this distinction is not rigid but variable' (p. 2).

The second sense of 'method' in the context of consciousness studies involves the integration of concepts from diverse approaches. It is this sense that Flanagan has in mind with his 'naturalistic method'. Models of the nature of consciousness and conscious information processing may be derived from insightful consideration of all legitimate methodologies (in the above first sense). The contemporary philosophical approach to consciousness may be equated effectively with this second sense. Major works on consciousness by authors such as Block, Flanagan and Guzeldere (1997), Chalmers (1996), Dennett (1991) and Velmans (2000) exemplify this second meaning of 'method'. The strength of these authors' works does not derive from any empirical research into the subject that they may have conducted themselves. Rather, these authors have arrived at significant models of consciousness on the basis of their analysis of the data from the research of others.

The third sense in which the term 'method' is used concerns the transformation of consciousness. There are numerous methods, largely culled from practices associated with spiritual traditions, for training an individual towards experiences of states of consciousness that differ from the normal state. Some argue that such experiences are an essential prerequisite for any research into consciousness. This statement is immediately contentious – many adopting a scientific approach to consciousness would view this quest for personal trans- formation as irrelevant to the search for useful data. Nevertheless, as we saw above, an undisciplined mind – one, that is, which has not experienced transformative states – makes a poor observer of consciousness. It has repeatedly been argued by those interested in consciousness studies and who have also worked within spiritual traditions, that training in one or more spiritual discipline is essential for an appreciation of the subtleties of consciousness. Failure to engage in a practice such as meditation or esoteric ritual of some form would be akin to a cookery 'expert' never having tasted a cooked dish. Braud and Anderson (1998) insist that research should be considered a transformative process itself. And Harman (1993) asserts that 'The scientist who would explore the topic of conscious- ness ... must be *willing to risk being transformed* in the process of exploration (p. 139, italics original).

Now, while it would be impossible to define consciousness stud- ies by reference to an agreed methodology ('method' sense 1), we may legitimately define it in terms of integration across the three meanings of 'method' elaborated above. Consciousness studies might be defined as the discipline that respects the three senses of 'method' elaborated above. On this basis, for example, neuroscientists who deny the value of first-person transformative experience effectively place themselves outside the orb of consciousness studies. Of course, this does not mean that their research has no value. Indeed, much brain research that investigates correlates of consciousness may fall into this category, and I shall be making extensive use of it in later chapters. It is simply to assert that their restrictive stance places them outside the integrative framework of consciousness studies. Similarly, supernaturalists who reject the value of a scientific methodology must be viewed as being outside the discipline of consciousness studies.

The emphasis on integration is critical. It is not simply that some may choose to take an integrative view, as might be the case were an interest in transformational states an optional extra. Rather, the absence of an integrative perspective will inevitably render critical aspects of consciousness obscure.

Basic questions about how we become conscious of sensory images, thoughts, or memories, are most incisively answered when we can draw both on the insights from spiritual traditions and on relevant research data from scientific psychology. Indeed, in this vein, Wallace (2000) explicitly calls for a concerted, collaborative project into consciousness on the part of professional cognitive scientists and 'professional contemplatives' (p. 178). Such collaboration may be essential for dealing with the so-called *hard problem* of consciousness (Chalmers, 1995, 1996) – that of explaining why and how physical matter should have any relation to a property which seems so totally different from it, namely consciousness. Wilber (1999) is correct in asserting that the hard problem is answered in the wisdom traditions of the world's religions. As he remarks, the answer is however obscured to those who have not experienced the 'higher unitive states' to which the practices developed in those traditions are directed. In such a state, one may grasp directly the integrative source of what we ordinarily experience as mind and matter – these two are no longer separate and the problem of their interrelation simply evaporates. Yet, such an answer can have no currency to one married only to the vicissitudes of science or rational philosophy.

The challenge of consciousness studies is not simply that of gathering more data on the subject. Rather, it is the challenge to

move beyond our compartmentalized scheme of things in order
that society might re-balance its sense of values. Again, I think it
appropriate to turn the classical question around. We should be
asking, not whether consciousness studies is a legitimate discipline,
but what is it about ourselves and our society that makes this discipline legitimate for us today. I have already indicated the beginnings of an answer, and it will be consolidated throughout the
following chapters. Essentially, we are experiencing an archetypal
shift in perspective, a reorganizing of the *zeitgeist*, which necessitates a revaluing of the spiritual. Not only is the spiritual becoming an increasingly important source of meaning for many who are
no longer nourished through traditional religions, it is also entering the discourse of knowledge, with a significant upsurge of interest in the dialogue between science and spirituality/religion. It
might be more accurate to state that spiritual ideas are *re-entering*
the discourse of knowledge, for the shift to which I refer takes us
back to the heyday of the sacred sciences of the soul, as they were
last in evidence during the Renaissance.

A Neo-Renaissance

Indeed, to grasp fully the significance of consciousness studies
today, we need to return to the roots of modern science in the
period of the Renaissance. According to Heller (1967/1978), the
Renaissance 'was a revolution in the conception of man ... [in
which] humanity awakened for the first time, as *humanity*, to self-
consciousness' (p. 452). There are significant parallels between this
awakening to self-consciousness in the Renaissance and what we
might describe as an awakening to consciousness itself in our day.
The Renaissance was spawned when a spirit of exploration lodged
in the psyche of the day. Just as fifteenth- and sixteenth-century
explorers encouraged a broader urge to go beyond the confines of
the known world, so in our day the journey beyond our planet has
seeded an exploratory impetus in the collective psyche. A second
parallel with our day concerns the encounter with other traditions.
In the early Renaissance, departures in thought were triggered
largely through contact firstly with Greek ideas, translated and
reformulated by Islamic scholars, and secondly with kabbalistic
approaches to scripture, brought into European thought largely via
Jewish converts to Christianity. In our day, a different encounter –

that with Eastern traditions – has similarly had enormous impact, significantly influencing our approach to spirituality and the nature of mind. A third, provocative parallel is that between the invention of printing and the IT revolution. Just as printing led to a quantum leap in the scale on which ideas could be transmitted, so has the microchip engineered a globalization of knowledge unique in history.

The parallels between the intellectual shift that occurred during the Renaissance and that influencing us today intriguingly extend to the role of method. Like science itself, approaches to method arise in cultural and social context. Vermersch (1999) has observed that the disappearance of introspectionism coincided with troubled times in Europe. Its heyday as far as modern psychology is concerned developed over some 30 years prior to the First World War, and its return to some degree of acceptance begins in the 1960s, when a generation that grew up in peacetime began to flex its muscles. Again, the comparison with the early Renaissance is striking. As Wightman (1972) observes, the flowering of the Italian Renaissance occurs in a roughly 40-year period at the beginning of the fifteenth century when 'the [Italian] peninsula came as near as it ever had done to the reign of peace' (p. 113). Settled times may seed a turning inwards towards the meaning and potential of experience.

More than this, we may discern some poignant lessons for the rise of consciousness studies by considering the way in which the roots of modern science grew from the Renaissance interest in magic. Wightman notes that:

> In conditions of unsurpassed mastery of mathematical, logical, and aesthetic form in classical Greece 'modern science' did *not* emerge; in the High Middle Ages – perhaps more justifiably called an 'Age of Reason' than is the eighteenth century – a new and somewhat different impulse emerged but petered out; only at the culmination of the 'Renaissance' was 'science' in very much the modern acceptance of the term brought to birth.... [O]ne factor is present [during the Renaissance] ... and not only present but pervasively and increasingly so, that in the other two progressive ages remained very much in the background.... [It is the] obsession with the possibility of allying the human mind with 'supernatural' powers to bring about miraculous changes.
>
> (Wightman, 1972, p. 143)

This 'obsession' engendered a distinctive *experimental* attitude, which, coupled with the general Renaissance tendency towards the exploration of nature, became a harbinger of the scientific method (Yates, 1964). Neoplatonic concepts – especially the idea of emanation and that of correspondence between macrocosmic and microcosmic realms – were critical for key Renaissance thinkers, including Marsilio Ficino, his pupil, Pico della Mirandola, Cornelius Agrippa of Nettesheim, and Johannes Kepler. Heller captures the common theme of the Renaissance as follows:

> If the whole of reality – the universe – is infinite and universal, then man (the microcosm) must also be infinite and universal, and so – inseparably – he must be capable of knowing the infinite and universal. And since experience shows that the body is neither infinite nor universal, there must be in man 'something' of the infinite and universal. The reflection cannot differ from that which the mirror reflects.
>
> (Heller, 1967/1978, p. 417)

The major figures of the early Renaissance gained access to a number of kabbalistic texts (Dan, 1997) which impressed on them the potential continuity between the supposed ancient Hermetic doctrines of the *Corpus Hermeticum* and those to be gleaned within the Bible.[3] Yates argues that the attitude towards uncovering hidden regularities beneath the surface of things, which Pico gleaned from his kabbalistic studies, together with the eagerness to engage in active, magical experimentation, were seminal for the rise of modern science:

> The profound significance of Pico della Mirandola in the history of humanity can hardly be overestimated. He it was who first boldly formulated a new position for European man, man as magus using both Magic and Cabala to act upon the world, to control his destiny by science.
>
> (Yates, 1964, p. 116)

The point for our purposes is that the Renaissance *magus* epitomizes an integration of the three meanings of method enunciated above. His magical experiments were a means for discovering some of the secrets of nature (sense 1); his thought pivoted around themes culled from diverse sources, striving for a grand synthesis (sense 2); and his quest was to reach a knowledge of the divine through participation in the Neoplatonic mysteries (sense 3). Most importantly, as Griffin (2000) has argued, for the Renaissance magus, the natural world he studied was animate, imbued with a world soul.

The seventeenth-century demise of this *Neoplatonic-magical-spiritualist* tradition (as Griffin calls it) in favour of the mechanistic one, which came to dominate science, represents one of the great ironies of history. Social and theological factors, rather than rational or empirical ones, underlay the rise of the mechanistic outlook that is often viewed as synonymous with good science. The irony is discerned in the role played by the Church. In order to reinforce its view of a transcendent God, beyond the confines of the natural world, it supported a view of matter as inert. It condoned, or even shaped, the views of those such as Robert Boyle and Isaac Newton, who argued that matter has no intrinsic dynamic, and that any movement of matter comes about only by dint of the influence of the Creator existing outside the natural world. This position paved the way towards the development of mechanistic science. It radically opposed the Renaissance magical view, which had celebrated and explored divine immanence. Whereas the Renaissance magician engaged with the natural world specifically in order to encounter the divine forces active within it, the seventeenth-century scientist studied the natural world in order to understand its dependence on a distant God. Ironically, then, the mechanistic science that began as a force for strengthening belief in a transcendent God, ends in the nineteenth and twentieth centuries by removing any kind of divine involvement in the natural world.

This necessarily brief treatment of complex historical developments (for details, see Griffin, 2000 and references cited there) is presented to illustrate the dichotomy which seems to be opening up in consciousness studies. Two major camps may be discerned, which bear striking resemblance to the two groups illustrated here. What we may call the *neo-Renaissance* camp sees consciousness as a fundamental property of the world, which cannot be reduced to brain activity alone. For some in this camp, consciousness is a naturalistic property. For others, whilst consciousness fills the world, its essence is ontologically transcendent, a view fully paralleling the renaissance conception that God is immanent in nature and transcendent in His essence. This camp is characterized by its emphasis on integrative and participatory research (Braud and

Anderson, 1998; Harman and Clark, 1994; Josephson and Rubik, 1992; Skolimowski, 1994), which includes the three meanings of 'method' enunciated earlier.

The other camp, that of the *neo-reductionists*, holds fast to the direction which science took in the seventeenth century. For those in this camp, consciousness is not an intrinsic property of all matter, but is generated – in some as yet undiscovered way – specifically by a class of computational activities. Some (for example, Searle, 1992, 1998) argue that such activities have to be biological to qualify. Others (for example, Dennett, 1997; Minsky, 1987) argue that consciousness arises whenever some threshold level of computational complexity is achieved, whatever medium might be involved (hence, a super-complex computer would be conscious). What unites this neo-reductionist camp is its faith in the exclusive value in classical third-person methodology – 'method' in its first sense above.

Crick's 'astonishing hypothesis' is typical of the neo-reductionists. The hypothesis asserts that:

'You,' your joys and your sorrows, your memories and your ambitions, your sense of personal identity and free will, are in fact no more than the behavior of a vast assembly of nerve cells and their associated molecules.

(Crick, 1994, p. 3)

Yet there is nothing astonishing here at all! It merely rehashes faith in the 'nothing but-ism' articulated by many before and since. Both the mind and its equally awkward partner, consciousness, are nothing but the brain, which, in turn, is nothing but vast assemblies of nerve cells and molecules. More recently, Taylor (1999; John Taylor, not Eugene Taylor cited earlier) argues that those who do not place their faith in neuroscience and the theory of computational neuroscience are 'heading down the track in the wrong direction, away from the winning post' in the 'race to understand consciousness' (p. 9). This bizarre statement wins my award (to continue in his vein) in the 'heavyweight anti-interdisciplinary approaches to consciousness' category!

In summary, we should note that the neo-Renaissance approach conveys much more than merely an extra dimension of investigative technique. It constitutes a distinctive worldview that not only includes a holistic emphasis, but also effectively articulates a creed for living. A 1992 symposium on consciousness and extended science, whose conclusions are reprinted in Box 2.1, introduces terms like *conscience, humility* and *enhancing the meaning of life.* The conclusions read like a manifesto, resounding with great ideals and a cause to unify its advocates. There is, of course, the danger here that moves towards a more liberated view of ways to investigate consciousness eventuate in its own *behemoth.* A set of principles will become enshrined that not only defines ways of study but also prescribes, in the name of a liberal or 'new age' ethos, the kinds of conclusions which can be tolerated. Thankfully, we have not yet reached such an undesirable state of affairs, but the possibility must surely give grist to the neo-reductionists' mill.

BOX 2.1 Principles of an 'extended science' relevant to consciousness studies

The conclusions from the January 1992 Athens Symposium on Science and Consciousness present a thorough overview of the major principles of an 'extended' science, as the authors term it. They include the following 11 points:

1. The study of consciousness should be concerned not just with definitions of consciousness but with descriptions of its mode of operation. The phenomena of consciousness should be studied in the aspect of subjectively lived experience rather than exclusively in terms of objective data (as is most often the case with cognitive psychology). As a result, an extension is needed in the concept of what constitutes science, defined as knowledge or the quest for knowledge.

2. The 'extended science' is envisioned as in principle a continuum of activity ranging from science as it is currently practised to the humanities and the arts, and possibly including insights that may be gained from spiritual or religious practices. It will explicitly include consciousness in its many dimensions, including creativity; the use of symbol, myth and metaphor; the role of the feminine; the historical perspective; and cross-cultural aspects.

3. There are many artificial dualities to be overcome by the

---

extended science. These dualities or splits owe their origins both to contemporary science and to the dominant paradigm, and include those between ourselves and nature, mind and body, mind and matter, the feminine and the masculine, the observer and the observed, science and values, inductive versus deductive logic, and philosophy and science. In particular, science cannot be divorced from philosophy, because one always brings some philosophy to bear in one's thinking.

4. We need to move from the fragmentation that reductionism produces to principles of complementarity and integration, from 'either/or' to 'both/and' thinking. The conventional notion of causality as local and physical needs to be broadened to take account of networks of causation, non-local interconnectedness, and correlations. The world has suffered from the conventional fragmentary approach, its integrity violated by considering only the parts and thus losing sight of the whole. Again, it must be recognised that no single language or approach can grasp the richness or elusiveness of nature; thus the new science should be open to new and multiple approaches.

5. While science has conventionally been regarded as an objective endeavour leading to the truth about the nature of reality, we need to shift our thinking towards regarding its insights as being context dependent, and to recognising that all approaches to reality are value-influenced. We need actively to address the limitations of scientific approaches, verification, and theories, and to find a place in our worldview for personal knowledge gained through introspection. The importance of intuition as a contributing factor in the process by which knowledge advances needs to be fully acknowledged. Language itself can provide an effective means of exploring quasi-objectively what has previously been characterised as being purely subjective.

6. The extended science will develop in its scope beyond the conventional framework to the qualitative attributes of being and feeling, and will stress the importance of quality as well as quantity. The range of scientific

information will expand to include the anecdotal and the more tenuous aspects of nature. Ways of codification and utilisation of such 'soft' information need to be developed. There is the recognition and the acceptance that insights of the extended science occupy a domain that falls in between ignorance and precise knowledge.

7. A radically different attitude needs to be cultivated in the new science. The old humility (humus = the earth; hence humility = close to the earth), awe, wonder, and delight in the cosmos, which is the beginning of all science, must be restored. These are critical to regaining a reverence for nature. We feel that the attitude that predominates in science at present is arrogance, which has fostered dogmatism and scientism. In doing science, we should let the phenomena speak for themselves, rather than forcibly impose our hypotheses on the phenomena. The importance of the scientist's attitude towards his or her work, preconceptions, and deeper motivations must be stressed. Effects, however subtle, of the experimenter on the experiment are to be anticipated and must be examined; thus self-examination on the part of the experimenter must be included as part of the scientific process so as to make the processes of description more complete.

8. There is a novel role for the scientific collective in the new science. A newly emergent group creativity, perhaps involving a 'group mind' that exhibits camaraderie and cooperativeness in regard to solving problems in addition to the creativity of the individual should be nurtured, recognising that the power of the harmonious group is complementary to traditional Western individualism.

9. Any studies on consciousness must acknowledge the inherent wholeness and unity of the body/mind, and equally avoid losing sight of the total person. The holistic point of view, contrasting with the admittedly highly successful alternative of assuming a Cartesian split and operating under largely reductionistic principles, seems essential in order to study consciousness in its full subtlety, and to explore its deep interrelationship with the realm of the physical.

10. The foundations of contemporary science, and its limitations, should be taught to and understood by all scientific practitioners. While the uniqueness of both individuals and groups presents difficulties for formalising a science of consciousness, consciousness studies are to be regarded nonetheless as having equal status to the physical sciences.

11. The new science, as science with both consciousness and conscience, will concern itself with the consequences of science to the individual, society, and the whole world: it is a science for the integrity of both people and planet that should be translatable into action. The potential value to life of the discipline as a whole should not be compromised by the pursuit of more limited goals. At a personal level, the new science should help people be able to comprehend themselves and their place in nature, facilitate the development of empathic processes which aid mutual understanding, and enhance the meaning of life for individuals and for society.

Reprinted with permission from Josephson, B. & Rubik, B. (1992) The challenge of consciousness research. *Frontier Perspectives*, 3 (1), 15–19.
See also: http://www.tcm.phy.cam.ac.uk/~bdj10/mm/articles/athens.txt

Belief and the explanatory gap

Given the shift in neuroscience towards research into the concomitants of experience, it became inevitable that we should be faced with the challenge of consciousness, since the mystery of experience is *one and the same* as the mystery of consciousness. Before considering in more detail the various ways in which the term 'consciousness' is understood, let us note at the outset the *inward* aspect that characterizes all experience, the essential *subjective quality*. Nagel (1974) famously construed this as the '*what it is like to be ...*' dimension. To take his example, how can we ever know what it is like to be a bat? We could probe the bat's brain and

Knowing experience [handwritten note in top margin]

observe its behaviour in the most intricate detail, yet we could never *know its experience*. There is a critical aspect to consciousness which is seemingly forever closed to outside investigation (see also McGinn, 1991).[4]

For all the intensive study of neural activity relating to conscious states, there is no evidence to explain the nature of the relationship. Whatever the experience may be *about*, it remains fundamentally mysterious as to *why* activity in brain systems should *be experienced*. As has repeatedly been pointed out by those who are willing to face the conundrum of mind, no amount of detail as revealed by current scientific inquiry into the processes operating in such systems – whether they be living brains or artificial computing devices – penetrates directly into the ultimate *why* of experience. Clearly, we may gather information indicating why our experience takes one form or another, but such insight does not answer the question of why *qualia* – the term intended to cover the 'raw feels' of experience – arise in the first place. Here lies the explanatory gap, as it has been termed (Levine, 1983), and the reason why belief plays a critical role in consciousness studies.[5]

In a recent treatment of the subject, Levine conveys the central point as follows:

> As I now look at my red diskette case, I'm having a visual experience that is reddish in character. Light of a particular composition is bouncing off the diskette case and stimulating my retina in a particular way. That retinal stimulation now causes further impulses down the optic nerve, eventually causing various neural events in the visual cortex. Where in all of this can we see the events that explain my having a reddish experience? There seems to be no discernible connection between the physical description and the mental one, and thus no explanation of the latter in terms of the former.
>
> (Levine, 2001, pp. 76–7)

This conundrum is not new, of course. The common general sense we have that consciousness and mind are of a totally different order to that of physical matter has dominated thinking since earliest times. In the seventeenth century, Descartes wrote that these two realms can only interact because it has been so ordained by God. Such appeal to a divine solution did not preclude Descartes from speculating about the brain location of the interaction. Famously, Descartes thought that the pineal gland was the locus for interactions between the brain and the mind. However, not only were there no convincing grounds in the seventeenth century for proposing the pineal gland for this role, but there continues to be no adequate evidence for 'plugging the gap' in our day, as Levine's arguments attest.

Using Descartes' critical thesis that, unlike matter, mind has no spatial properties, the great neurophysiologist of the early twentieth century, Sherrington, captured the essence of the problem: 'how shall a spatial wheel cog into unextended mechanism or the non-spatial drive a spatial wheel?' (Sherrington, 1940, cited in Vesey, 1964, p. 326). There are various philosophical positions that have been adopted in relation to the explanatory gap, the detail of which need not concern us here (for reviews, see Carrier and Mittelstrass, 1991; Globus, Maxwell and Savodnik, 1976; Hardcastle, 1995; Velmans 2000). Suffice it to say that a range of mutually exclusive possibilities has been proposed, each of which is seen by its author(s) as compatible with *all* available evidence. It is not the *data* that differ across the views, but the belief system of the author, as I discussed earlier.

Materialism and *physicalism* have already been discussed in Chapter 1. Both these beliefs eventuate in the view that there is essentially no gap. Churchland (1989), for example, argues that consciousness, understood in folk psychological terms as a non-physical entity, will disappear from our theorizing when we have gained sufficient scientific understanding. The fate of 'consciousness' would become comparable to terms such as 'phlogiston', once thought to be critical for combustion, or '*élan vital*', postulated as the ingredient critical for transforming organic into living matter. Both these terms have disappeared from our treatment of the respective phenomena, because adequate physical and biological explanations became available and replaced them. The terms are thus now superfluous. Materialism and physicalism would not normally be described as *beliefs*. They point to what we *know* (that is, the reality of the material physical world), and extrapolate to what we do not yet know (the physical basis of consciousness), without positing anything unfounded. Nevertheless, this very extrapolation is an act of faith, and should be understood as such when comparing different views on the explanatory gap.

Naturalism holds that that there is no reality other than that of the natural world. Naturalism is, accordingly, akin to physicalism. However, the term is often used in a non-reductive sense which differs significantly from brain-focused physicalism. I use the term 'holophysicalism' to distinguish this non-reductive approach from that of 'neurophysicalism'. Griffin's (2000) naturalism, for example, sees experience as a universal dimension of the natural world. For him, as for Whitehead and Hartshorne before him, there is no explanatory gap since all matter intrinsically carries this experiential dimension.[6] It is claimed that pan-experientialism receives support from ideas in quantum mechanics and astrophysics to the effect that consciousness is implicated in the physical world. Despite much speculation, however, no definitive basis for consciousness in either of these disciplines is yet forthcoming. Again, we must recognize that all such theories take a leap of faith at some point. McGinn, for example, proposes that:

> The origin of consciousness *somehow* draws on those properties of the universe that antedate and explain the occurrence of the big bang. If we need a pre-spatial level of reality to account for the big bang, then it may be this very level that is exploited in the generation of consciousness.
>
> (McGinn, 1995, p. 24, italics added)

When we consider the level of uncertainty involved in that 'somehow' and in our understanding of the phenomena 'antedating the big bang', the extent of the leap of faith becomes evident.

A similar leap of faith is required for neurophysicalist approaches. In a recent paper, Crick and Koch present a framework for explaining consciousness in terms of brain systems. At the outset they warn that:

> The most difficult aspect of consciousness is the so-called 'hard problem' of qualia, the redness of red, the painfulness of pain, and so on. No one has produced any plausible explanation as to how the experience of the redness of red could arise from the actions of the brain. It appears fruitless to approach this problem head-on. Instead, we are attempting to find the neural correlate(s) of consciousness (NCC), *in the hope* that when we can explain the NCC in causal terms, this will make the problem of qualia clearer.
>
> (Crick and Koch, 2003, p. 119, italics added)

The *hope* expressed here is the article of faith of neurophysicalism. The hoped-for breakthrough may indeed arrive; but, in its absence, all claims to have found the scientific explanation of consciousness remain just that – claims.

Opposed to naturalistic theories are those that include reference to some form of non-material dimension that transcends the domain of the natural world – *supernaturalism*. Supernaturalism would include those versions of *dualism* and *monism* that posit a non-physical realm of mind. Eccles (for example, 1989) adopts a dualistic position which holds that the non-material 'self-conscious mind' interacts with sites in the brain. Although Eccles sees the details of this interaction as involving quantum phenomena, which many take as a springboard to naturalistic accounts, his understanding of the mind explicitly sets it apart from the natural world: 'Since materialist solutions fail to account for our experienced uniqueness, I am constrained to attribute the uniqueness of Self or Soul to a super-natural spiritual creation' (p. 237).

Wilber and others who elaborate on the Neoplatonic *Great Chain of Being* might be classed as *supernaturalistic monists*, on the grounds that they consider everything to be a manifestation of spirit (or consciousness), which itself transcends the natural world. As Huston Smith reminds us, the initial link in the chain is radically transcendent:

> [T]his ontological ultimate is radically transcendent, which does not keep it from being fully immanent too for those who have eyes to see it. Denotatively, it is Anaximander's 'boundless' or 'infinite,' Plato's 'Idea of the Good,' Plotinus's 'One,' and Spinoza's 'Deus sive natura.' It is the initial link in the Great Chain of Being that proceeds from it.
>
> (Smith, 1981, p. 36)

On what grounds might we advance one or another of these philosophical positions over the others? Scientific data alone are certainly inadequate to the task. It is unduly simplistic to think that anyone veering towards holophysicalism or supernaturalism does so because their credulity outweighs their critical faculties. Proponents of these views would have it the other way round. For example, belief in the *closure principle*, which is one of the central tenets of reductionistic science, can lead to a rejection of legitimate evidence. The closure principle holds that the physical universe is causally closed, meaning that no non-physical phenomena can causally influence physical matter. Griffin gives an illustration of the problem in defence of his naturalist position. The illustration concerns the evidence for parapsychology, which Griffin finds to be difficult to dismiss. His major contention is that it is the worldview of reductionistic science that blocks a fair-minded appraisal of the evidence. The very possibility of some kind of bi-directional causality between mind and matter is rejected in *a priori* fashion, on account of the presumed infallibility of the closure principle.

Similarly, the supernaturalist Wade (1996) cites considerable evidence in support of her view that 'A physically transcendent source [of consciousness] ... predates physical life at the moment of conception and survives it after death' (p. 249). The supernaturalist position is supported by evidence of seemingly veridical memories of previous lives (Haraldsson, 2001; Stevenson, 1997), memories of conception and birth experiences (Chamberlain, 1990; Grof, 1985), and near-death experiences (van Lommel, 2002). All these lines of evidence are contentious, and it is probably fair to say that they rarely achieve more than a reinforcing of the pre-existing beliefs of those who read them – whether those beliefs are for or against the supernaturalistic viewpoint.

The grounds for adopting one '-ism' over another inevitably entail somewhat broader considerations. The available data may certainly play a role. For example, some have been persuaded against materialism by the data arising from well-controlled studies in parapsychology. However, the orientation that an individual adopts to consciousness is fundamentally an expression of their attitude to more global issues including the meaning and purpose of life itself. As Baruss (2001) rightly points out, whilst a researcher's ontological beliefs can largely be bracketed when it comes to any other branch of science, they are central when it comes to consciousness.

Defining consciousness

What is consciousness? There is no need to define so familiar a thing, something which is continually present in every one's experience. I will not give a definition, for that would be less clear than the thing itself.

(Henri Bergson, cited in Pickering and Skinner, 1990, p.27)

There are indeed problems in defining consciousness, for all definitions invariably invoke substance, process or function to explicate the term under consideration. In the case of consciousness, such attributes are either irrelevant, or incapable of being specified unambiguously. Whatever its relation to substance may be, consciousness is not itself a substance. Is it a process? Some, such as Thatcher and John would have it so:

> Consciousness is a process in which information about multiple individual modalities of sensation and perception is combined into a unified multidimensional representation of the state of the system and its environment, and integrated with information about memories and the needs of the organism, generating emotional reactions and programs of behaviour to adjust the organism to its environment.
>
> (Thatcher and John, 1977, p. 294)

For Jaynes, 'consciousness is an operation rather than a thing, a repository, or a function' (1976/1990, p. 65). However, for others, the emphasis on process shades readily into function. Indeed the whole approach known as *functionalism*, which is strongly identified with cognitive psychology, melds process and function. Consciousness thus becomes identified with the processes of attention, or of working memory, or with the processes which broadcast information throughout the brain (Baars, 1988, 1996). Yet none of this can convey that essential phenomenological component – the inner quality of experience. As Velmans neatly quips, 'We are not just human *doings*, we are also human *beings*' (2000, p. 97).

A further problem arises with the circularity in many proposed definitions. Statements defining consciousness in terms of awareness hardly help, since the term 'awareness' is no less mysterious than 'consciousness'. The elusive element in the latter is equally elusive in the former. What is needed is some way of penetrating into the phenomenological quality itself.

As Chalmers (1996) points out, definitions commonly refer to qualities that are more fundamental than the item being defined. The definition attempts to convey the item's composition, or elements of its function. Yet consciousness cannot be approached in this way since its hallmark is its indivisibility, its unity. We can introduce parallel words to try to convey its essence, but we cannot specify its components. Thus, as we noted earlier, consciousness equates to the *having of experience*, and therefore there is *something it is like* to be a conscious organism (Nagel, 1974). We can also elaborate the idea of consciousness by using more tangible metaphors. A favourite is that of light (Lancaster 1991; Neumann, 1949/1974). Light is intangible; it cannot itself be seen, but enables everything else to be seen. Moreover, light eludes unambiguous specification – sometimes it is particulate and other times it is wave-like. Some regard consciousness as a kind of searchlight, illuminating otherwise unconscious contents of the mind. A somewhat different metaphorical conception is Revonsuo's (1995, 1999) suggestion based on the idea of virtual reality. For him, consciousness is the brain-created experience that '*I*' am directly present in a world outside the brain. Revonsuo argues that all the machinery for the experience lies within the brain, just as the machinery for a virtual reality experience lies within the electronics of the machine. The virtual reality metaphor seems apt. Yet, the problem with such accounts is that the essential question of how machinery generates experience (be it in the nature of a searchlight or of virtual reality) is not addressed. As I concluded in an earlier work, 'Beyond the use of metaphor all we can really say is, *consciousness is*' (Lancaster, 1991, p. 1).

While the quest for an all-satisfying definition may be fruitless, it is essential that we clarify the specific features which the approaches under consideration in this book try to describe, model, and perhaps explain. Many authors make the important point that the term 'consciousness' can convey a variety of differing meanings, and it clearly becomes critical that we pin down the precise sense in a given context. Without such clarity, accounts of consciousness by different authors may diverge merely because they differ in their understanding of the term. This problem is certainly not new. In 1904 Perry pleaded, 'How can a term mean anything when it is employed to connote anything and everything, including its own negation?' (Cited in Forman, 1998, p. 13).[7]

From a metanalysis of works employing the term 'consciousness,' Baruš (1986–7) isolates three distinct clusters of meaning. He identifies *consciousness*$_1$ as referring to the registering, processing and acting upon information which occurs in a sufficiently humanlike biological system.[8] Baruš notes that, perhaps paradoxically, the organism need not be *aware* of such activity. This paradox is already anticipated in Perry's comment, quoted above (and see note 7). It is, perhaps, one of the most critical issues with which a nascent consciousness studies must come to terms.[9]

Baruš' second meaning of 'consciousness' is that of being aware of something, in the sense of having explicit knowledge of one's situation, mental states or actions. This is termed *consciousness$_2$*. Consciousness$_2$ thus incorporates *intentionality*, the concept introduced by Brentano (1838–1917) to signify that consciousness is always *about* something and affirms the objectivity of its content. Finally, Baruš identifies *consciousness$_3$*, which is direct awareness or consciousness without any content – the subjectivity or phenomenal quality which accompanies any mental act. It is argued by Forman that such *pure consciousness, consciousness without content*, is an experience associated with mystical states (see Forman, 1990 and contributors there). Although there is an ongoing debate amongst scholars of mystical literature as to whether claims about contentless consciousness should be taken at face value (see Chapter 3), 73 per cent of those attending a major conference on consciousness affirmed that 'It is possible for there to be consciousness in which there is awareness but no object of awareness'. Only 10 per cent denied this possibility outright (Baruš and Moore, 1998). The majority view seems to beg the question, however, of what is actually being recalled when someone claims to recall an experience of pure consciousness. Indeed, if there is no sense of self present, to whom did the experience 'belong', and who (or what) effects the subsequent recall? For Deikman (1982, 1996), there *is* a sense of self during such experience – but it is a self without attributes other than the power of observation itself, the *observing self*.

the observing self [handwritten margin note]

The fundamental distinction, applicable to conceptualizations of consciousness in most authors, is between the passive **phenomenal** quality of consciousness (its *is-ness*) and its active **informational** quality (its *about-ness*). As may be seen in Table 2.1, different authors have employed their own idiosyncratic terminology for this basic duality. There is some blurring of boundaries even in this basic distinction, since some authors take the phenomenal aspect of consciousness in the contentless sense (Forman; Baruš), whilst others define it in relation to contents being experienced (Farthing; Schooler). Perhaps the distinction is best characterized as one between experience itself (irrespective of whether or not contents are acknowledged) and integrative knowing (whereby the experienced contents are interpreted within a self-related context).

The informational quality of consciousness may be further classified by reference to the parameters of **accessibility** and **self-relatedness**. Bisiach (1988) maintains a division between what he terms C$_1$ (the 'phenomenal experience') and C$_2$ which 'refers to the access

TABLE 2.1 Various dichotomies in definitions of consciousness

Author	Phenomenal consciousness	Informational consciousness
Barušs (1986–7)	Consciousness₃	Consciousness₂
Bisiach (1988)	C_1 – phenomenal experience	C_2 - monitoring of internal representations
Block (1995)	Phenomenal consciousness	Access consciousness
Edelman (1992)	Primary consciousness – being mentally aware of things	Higher-order consciousness – conscious of being conscious
Farthing (1992)	Primary consciousness – direct experience of percepts and feelings	Reflective consciousness – thoughts about one's own conscious experience
Forman (1990)	Pure consciousness – contentless	
Lambie and Marcel (2002)	First-order phenomenal experience – what it's like	Second-order awareness – a kind of knowing by acquaintance
Lancaster (1993b)	Consciousness I – the 'within' to things	Consciousness II – access by 'I' to other mental events
Rao (1993)	Subject consciousness	Predicate-consciousness
Schooler (2002)	Basic consciousness – experience of perceptions, feelings, and non-reflective cognitions	Meta-consciousness – a re-representation of consciousness in which one interprets, describes, or otherwise characterizes the state of one's mind
Valentine (1999)	Phenomenal consciousness	Computational, functional information-processing consciousness

of parts or processes of a system to other of its parts or processes' (1988, p. 103). For Block (1995), this issue of access is sufficiently defining for him to coin the term *access-consciousness* to refer to that form of consciousness engaged when informational content is available. Access-consciousness refers to states in which representations of content can be drawn upon in order, for example, that they may be spoken about, or that they may become part of ongoing thought.[10] On the other hand, according to Block, a state is *phenomenal-conscious* if it has experiential properties.

If, however, we accept the integrity of Baruš' separation of *consciousness*$_1$ from *consciousness*$_2$ – implying that one may be 'unaware', as he puts it, of conscious material, then it is essential to realise that 'access' is not a universal qualifier of 'informational'. Both *consciousness*$_1$ and *consciousness*$_2$ concern informational content, but in the former case those contents may be inaccessible. Any potential confusion concerning this distinction between conscious contents of which we may be aware and those of which we remain unaware is reduced by adopting a more precise, operational understanding of this issue of accessibility. I have argued that the parameter of self-relatedness enters the picture here, since we need to specify **who** or **what** is doing the accessing of information (Lancaster, 1993b).[11] As the very words themselves imply, when I become conscious of something, then 'I' becomes part of the mental processes involved.[12] When I am not conscious, 'I' is absent from the picture. Indeed, the central distinction between phenomenal consciousness and informational consciousness can be reduced to that between 'consciousness' as an abstract noun and 'conscious' as an adjective. The mistake our language encourages us to make is that of thinking that one is just the adjectival form of the other. It is not: to be conscious implies a subject; consciousness does not. This is a crucial distinction. In general, when I use the unqualified noun 'consciousness' I mean to refer to the phenomenal quality itself; 'being conscious' necessarily implies a subject and an 'of', and is therefore the appropriate phrase for referring to the informational dimension of consciousness.

Using a phrase like 'I am conscious of the pen in my hand' carries the implication that a connection has been effected (**accessibility**) between the representation of **self** and that of the pen in my hand. These two parameters – accessibility and self – become the major focus for many of the questions which consciousness studies needs to address. As Harman (1995) notes in a commentary on Block's article, 'A substantive theory of consciousness necessarily involves a theory of what constitutes a self and of what constitutes access to that self' (p. 257). To return to Baruss' distinction between *consciousness*₁ and *consciousness*₂, these additional parameters might be introduced by suggesting that the former may, in principle, be capable of being accessed but is, in practice, incapable of being accessed by 'I'.

Each of these additional parameters becomes of critical importance in clarifying our approaches to consciousness. It might be thought that they are simply bipolar – that some content or other is either accessible or inaccessible, or that 'I' is either present or absent. Such is, however, decidedly not the case. Regarding the former parameter, there are numerous cases of mental content being present within the marginal region of the mind, which renders them neither fully accessible nor fully inaccessible. Regarding the relation of content to self, we find variations in the experiential sense of selfhood at different times. Relevant here is Buddhism's doctrine of *no-self*, suggesting that advanced meditative states involve no sense of 'I'. Seemingly at the other extreme are experiences of the All-Self (Krippner, 1999), where the sense of 'I' merges with that of an all-encompassing oneness of self. In later chapters these ideas will be explored more fully. For the moment I wish to stress that no single approach has a monopoly on the understanding of these parameters. Both have been extensively studied within phenomenological and spiritual traditions, as well as through research in the area of cognitive neuroscience.

Figure 2.1 illustrates the relationship between these parameters. Symbolically, the circle depicts consciousness, and the two parameters are depicted as two axes. I am suggesting that everything that comes within the orb of consciousness is capable of specification in terms of the two axes. Degree of accessibility is a parameter which attaches to informational content, whilst the parameter of 'self' connotes the condition of the person (or, indeed, creature) in the role of observer. The 'normal' state of consciousness allows slight modulations in the sense of 'I' (from 'I–' to 'I+') as well as variations in accessibility (up to the dotted region). For the present these are merely vague indications. Subsequent chapters illustrate in more detail the dependence of the state of consciousness on changes in self and in the level of information access. For now, it is sufficient to note that everyday 'mundane' consciousness is associated with a sense of 'I' which is experienced as the receiver of

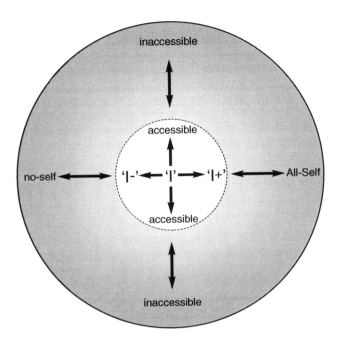

FIGURE 2.1 Parameters of consciousness. The vertical axis of accessibility refers to the informational content of the mind. The horizontal axis indicates that our experience of 'self' can vary. The centre of the circle defines the normal state of consciousness, in which the everyday sense of 'I' arises, with the accompanying sense of access to everyday content. The dotted inner circle indicates the normal range of fluctuation in our sense of 'I'.

impressions (*I see, hear*, and so on), director of conscious mentation (*I think*), instigator of conscious action (*I move my body*), and manager of memory (*I remember*). As will become clear below, there are reasons for doubting the accuracy of this simple introspective sense of 'I' as being the control centre of the mind.

To repeat, the primary distinction appears to be between consciousness itself and the processes involved when an observer becomes conscious of some content or other. It would, however, be misleading to concretize this distinction, as if to suggest that any explanations of the latter have no bearing on the 'hard' problem of consciousness. The value of the distinction lies in highlighting the importance of the two parameters of accessibility and self, as already mentioned, and encouraging methodologies for their elucidation. It does not follow, however, that because the 'hard' problem is concerned with the nature of consciousness itself, the study of these parameters of accessibility and self will remain tangential. On the contrary, as Pickering (1999) notes, the 'hard' and 'easy' problems often overlap to a significant extent. What should become clear through the chapters in Part II is that these parameters of accessibility and self are central to any serious approach to consciousness. Not only are they subject to study through the methods of cognitive neuroscience, but they also figure critically in the discourses of depth psychology and mysticism. They are terms that encourage an integrative approach.

Too often an unmovable wedge lodges between transpersonal approaches and those of mainstream psychology and neuroscience. Transpersonal theories frequently avoid the difficult confrontation with explanation, relying rather on classification of states of consciousness and their relative value in therapeutic or spiritual terms. Helminiak (1998) argues that Wilber's presentation, often regarded as something of a marker for transpersonal approaches, is 'strong in its *appreciation* of conscious experience but weak in its *account* of conscious experience, weak regarding knowledge, science, and explanation' (p. 262, italics original). Mainstream psychology and neuroscience, on the other hand, eschew any suggestion that spiritual or metaphysical insights might have a serious contribution to make to their subject matter. As should be evident by now, I believe this view to be misguided, and to hinder advancement in consciousness studies. By opening my examination of the approaches to consciousness in Part II with that associated with mysticism and the spiritual traditions, I shall begin to indicate the extent of their potential contribution to the debate. In subsequent chapters, the ways in which that contribution might become incorporated within an integrated discipline of consciousness studies will be explored.

Part II
Approaches to Consciousness

Chapter 3

Spiritual and Mystical Approaches:
1. Towards Emptiness

Transformation comes about only by passing through nothingness.

(Dov Baer, the Maggid of Mezeritch, cited in Matt, 1995, p. 87)

Principles and questions

By definition, an approach to consciousness that we may class as spiritual or mystical entails some notion of individual betterment. Individuals are seeking to achieve a temporary or permanent change in themselves – a transformation of consciousness, or a state of greater intimacy with the divine. However, our primary interest here is not in manuals of instruction – the kinds of practice offered to the potential seeker by different traditions – but in the insights into consciousness which inevitably accompany the teachings. Some of these are quite direct. Buddhism, in particular, includes within its corpus many texts that specifically address the processes of the mind. Others are less direct. The interest of Jewish or Islamic Sufi mystics is frequently focused on the mind of God, rather than on their own minds. Nevertheless, rich psychological insights ensue from this interest, for the mind of God and the human mind are viewed as related by correspondence. 'From the "I" of flesh and blood you may learn about the "I" of the Holy One, blessed be He,' runs a Jewish midrashic text.[1] The logical converse – that the human mind recapitulates the mind of God – is implicit in much kabbalistic literature. Insights into the divine mind – His thought, His creativity – illumine deep aspects of the human mind. Indeed, this notion of correspondence between humans and the divine becomes an explicit *isomorphism* between God and man, as Shokek observes:

> God and man are *isomorphic*, i.e., they share the same structure and are logically equivalent. This shared identity creates a powerful *intrinsic* quality between them: it means that God and man are identical not because they are dependent on the existence of some further, *extrinsic* thing, but rather because they are mutually dependent on one another.
>
> (Shokek, 2001, p. 6)

This mutual dependence makes man a partner to God in the perfection of creation, and God the partner to man in the perfection of self. This transformation myth will be discussed later, but for the moment I wish to emphasize the implications which this notion of isomorphism carries for our understanding of consciousness. It may broadly be asserted that whenever a mystic describes experiences of higher planes, features of ultimate reality, or the inner nature of the Godhead, the descriptions carry insights into the nature and potential of their own consciousness, whether this is made explicit or not (Lancaster, 2000c, p. 233). As I remarked in Chapter 1, it is hardly surprising that we can discern such insights into consciousness within these traditions, since transformation would be blind without knowledge.

A major recurring theme in the mystical literature concerns the encounter with *nothingness*. Whether we are concerned with the annihilation of the human 'I', with the mystical knowing of reality as a pure, contentless consciousness, or with the perceived quality of the divine as nothingness, it appears that an essential part of the mystical advance is some kind of de-conditioning from the normal associations that establish the parameters of consciousness. There is considerable debate about the extent of such de-conditioning in mystical states, and the consequent implications for our understanding of consciousness. For some, led by Forman (1990, 1998), the kinds of experience indicated here suggest that intentionality applies only to a derivative level of consciousness. According to this view, consciousness itself transcends the processing of information. But many remain sceptical of this notion of *contentless* consciousness, arguing instead that *all* conscious experience, even when seemingly characterized by emptiness, is necessarily conditioned and therefore contextual (for example Katz, 1978b). In this chapter I shall attempt to clarify the ramifications of this debate, and establish the lines of evidence that may lead us towards its resolution.

Additionally, mystical literature suggests different levels of consciousness. Corbin (1971/1978) uses the terms 'superconsciousness' and 'transconsciousness' to capture the Sufi understanding of higher states, and McGinn warns us against too readily dismissing such concepts:

> Beyond the merely discursive oppositions between the conscious and the unconscious, the personal and the impersonal, the mystics hold out the possibility of the transconscious and the suprapersonal. Many dismiss these claims as nonsense. The premise of our investigations is that this may be too hasty a solution.
>
> (McGinn, 1989, p. 192)

Kabbalistic texts refer to a 'preconsciousness' (Hurwitz, 1968; Scholem, 1975), which similarly connotes a level metaphysically higher than mundane human consciousness. The analysis of such higher states in this chapter will be expanded in Chapter 7. My interest lies in the characteristics of these higher levels, and how they might relate to the diverse states of consciousness which are identified in scientific psychology.

Finally, the inquiry will focus on those spiritual and religious teachings which directly address psychological processes and constructs relating to consciousness. The nature of self and its relation to consciousness constitutes a major topic in the literature of many spiritual traditions. In particular, Buddhism extends this interest into a detailed examination of the processes involved in perception and thought. What perspective is given to these psychological topics from the spiritual/mystical documents, and how might it inform the alternative approaches to be considered in subsequent chapters?

Answers to all these questions must be tempered through an understanding of method. The objectivity of science is transparent; that of introspection is open to challenge. As Wallace (2000) reminds us, the nineteenth-century introspectionist tradition petered out largely because its observations were inconsistent and/or unreliable. In attempting to bring introspection to an acceptable level of rigour for the fledgling psychological science, Wundt and his followers increasingly trivialized its scope. For instance, reaction times to stimuli became more important than the observations of subjective reactions to the stimuli. In arguing against the contemporary *taboo* on subjectivity, Wallace insists that effective methods for training in the skills of introspection do exist – but not among scientists. It is to the spiritual traditions that we must turn to find the requisite rigour of introspection harnessed in the pursuit of the meaningful features of experience.

Methods

The handmaid of knowledge is commentary. This holds for the spiritual traditions as much as it holds for science. The primary idea – be it a mathematical theory, a hypothesis confirmed by precise experiment, an introspection, or an elaboration of scriptural text – is subject to peer scrutiny. Commentary is to the world of knowledge as Darwinian selection is to the natural world. In evaluating any given idea we must be mindful of two stages – the idea's origin and its survival in the commentarial lion's den. The Darwinian parallel is especially instructive. The fossil record shows that an adaptation that might have aided survival in an ecological bubble, such as an isolated island, dies out when the degree of isolation is changed. Similarly, the historical record testifies that ideas current in spiritual 'bubbles' – cults and other isolated sects – die out when the forces sustaining their isolation crumble. Indeed, maintaining effective barriers to contact with the surrounding culture is a first step for leaders wishing to consolidate their power over cult followers. Leaving aside cults, it is significant that the boundaries between traditions have, to some extent, opened up over recent years. Increasingly, insights from one tradition are being evaluated in the light of those from others, making the commentarial edge even more incisive for those who are open to traditions beyond their own. Indeed, along with the comparative study of religion, transpersonal psychology has itself contributed significantly to this widening of the impact of commentary.

The ideas to be reviewed in this chapter have survived through hundreds of years of commentarial scrutiny. As Wilber (1979) correctly notes, such scrutiny is undertaken by those who have undergone appropriate training in the methods relevant to the insights. Just as a scientific thesis should be reviewed by someone sufficiently well practised in the scientific method to be equipped to highlight shortcomings, so a contemplative insight is routinely evaluated by those skilled in the methods of contemplation.

It might be objected that the validity of all those spiritual insights that have survived the commentarial process within their respective traditions is undermined by evident conflicts between the traditions. Ideas accepted within one long-standing tradition might be incompatible with those central to another. Indeed, the grim history of inter-religious conflicts seems to mitigate against the validity of the kinds of truth claims often found at the heart of the conflicts. Moreover, the birth of one religion from a 'parent' is generally attributable to the 'daughter' religion advocating a position at odds with the parent, as in the case of Buddhism's development from Hinduism, for example. Hinduism teaches that our best insight into ultimate reality comes through grasping the essential Self. All human conscious activity is a veneer through which this divine Self observes. Buddhism explicitly denies such a metaphysical Self. Its teaching of *no-self* insists that all traces of 'I' must be eradicated from the personality striving for *nirvana*.[2]

The question which must be answered is whether the diversity amongst the kinds of insights derived by mystics from contemplative, or other concentrative, methods annuls the validity of this whole approach for studying the nature of consciousness.[3] Perhaps predictably (otherwise, why would I devote two chapters to this approach?), I believe the answer to be an unequivocal 'no'. Although there are many significant details in the testimonies of mystics which are indeed difficult to reconcile with each other, there is sufficient of a common core to uphold their value for our study of consciousness. For Ferrer (2002), the common core concerns '*the overcoming of self-centeredness*, and thus a liberation from corresponding limiting perspectives and understandings' (p. 144, italics original). Spiritual and mystical teachings can reveal to us the ways in which self intrudes as a limiting factor in consciousness, together with insights into the form consciousness takes when such limitation is transcended. A slightly differently nuanced emphasis is given by Dupré (1989) when he suggests that the common feature in mystical testimonies involves a seeming shift in the centre of awareness from the self to 'a point beyond the self' (p. 9). Again, I am suggesting that such testimonies can be valuable in thinking about the nature of such a region beyond the self.

An integrated consciousness studies can introduce a further check on the validity of claims in this area. Our yardstick should be that any claims must be *compatible with data from other approaches*. This is not to say that we would require the same kind of observations from other approaches. Clearly, such a criterion would make nonsense of the idea of the value in different approaches in the first place. What the proposed yardstick does imply is that we should be able to integrate insights from mystical and spiritual areas with those from neuroscience and the other approaches. Indeed, not only should we be able to do this, but also advances in the discipline may be expected to arise when such integration itself yields further hypotheses for testing by one or more of the different approaches.

Spiritual claims about the role of self in consciousness, and the limitations it imposes, are indeed compatible with data from other approaches, as will be explored in future chapters. Moreover, whilst claims not immediately compatible with naturalism may be hard to reconcile with the other approaches, it does not follow that they are directly opposed by the data available from those approaches. Claims concerning ontological transcendence, for example, may not square with the *premises* of other approaches, but are not immediately contradicted by the fundamental observations. As we saw already, a neuroscientist such as Eccles can continue to hold to a supernatural view, even when armed with all the data available from the relevant branches of science. It is a matter of distinguishing evidence from belief.

The methodology associated with spiritual and mystical approaches is based on two complementary forms of training. First, the student is trained in the textual basis of the tradition. The vast majority of the world's mystical writings comprise comments or discussion of canonical, sacred texts and/or further commentary on the expositions of others. Participation in such dialogue demands a clear understanding of both the accepted meanings of sacred texts and the approaches to exegesis and commentary deemed legitimate to that tradition. As Sharf (1998) notes, psychological discussions frequently downplay this textual dimension in favour of the second aspect of training which involves issues of introspection and experience. Sharf is correct in insisting that this

bias constitutes a misrepresentation of the world's mystical literature. Invariably, the major figures in the traditions gained their
authority through mastery in this text-based knowledge, and not
through their access to exalted spiritual states.

Second, the student is trained in psychological processes, particularly those of will and attention. The ability voluntarily to focus
attention and maintain the focus in ways that would, without
training, be uncharacteristic of normal psychological functioning
(Deikman, 1966), is clearly fostered by meditative and other skills.
This training of the will is conterminous with that involved in the
first, text-based, form of training, which invariably requires the
student to master vast treatises. Many of these treatises require
considerable focus of attention, as when, for example, a convoluted argument unfolds over many pages. Mastery of religious
literature is a distinctive skill which may not simply equate with
mastery of other genres of writing. A stimulating example in the
context of a psychological inquiry is that of rabbinic literature, the
style of which has been viewed as anticipating many of the
hermeneutic features brought to our attention in a broader context
by Freud (Faur, 1986; Handelman, 1982). Study of rabbinic texts,
in the manner traditionally sanctioned, becomes a distinctive training of the mind. Not only does it involve the mastery over attention required in following long, convoluted arguments, but it also
facilitates a conscious grasp of the forms of logic which seem to
rule in the unconscious (Lancaster, 1993a; see below, Chapter 6).
Jewish mystics have invariably been steeped in mainstream
rabbinic literature, and their approach to mysticism takes on a
distinctively psychological flavour by dint of this idiosyncratic
rabbinic literary style.

Buddhist practices exemplify the approaches to training attention and will through meditation. Wallace (2000) distinguishes
two methods involving sustained attention: *vision-induced* and
imagination-induced. In the first of these, associated with the
Theravadin tradition, the meditator gazes at a physical object
'until an afterimage of it appears in the mind as clearly when the
eyes are shut as when they are open' (p. 104). The second method,
which Wallace illustrates from the Mahayana tradition, requires
an image to be created mentally. The image is progressively made
more vivid and held in the mind's eye for prolonged periods. The
ability to hold attention in ways such as these is the essence of
mindfulness. With continued practice, a stage is reached in which

'attention is focused single-pointedly, nonconceptually, and internally in the very quiescence of the mind' (p. 107).

Similarly, Brown's (1977) analysis of a Tibetan Buddhist school of meditation details the stages entailed in developing 'concentration' on visual objects and visualized images. In the case of a visual object, the practitioner gazes intently with half-open eyes, without distraction, and 'closely examines' the object. The meditative focus is subsequently extended to the other senses. Again, the goal of controlling the mind's natural tendency to wander is evident in the primary warning to the novice to guard against distraction. Brown emphasizes the effects of the concentrative practice on developing refinement in awareness of perceptual and thought processes, and of the distinctions between them. He conjectures that by means of these practices, those normal cognitive processes through which sensory images are perceived and further interpreted are slowed down. He suggests that the normal sequence of operations in such processes may even become reversed. Brown concludes that the meditator can develop extraordinary insight into these operations, especially those that are normally preconscious.

These principles of developing control over normally unruly features of the mind may be seen as central to the techniques employed across diverse spiritual traditions. The particular focus of attention may be culture-specific, and the spiritual goal may vary considerably in relation to the tradition's teachings, but the psychological objective of achieving a high level of focused attention and stabilization of mental forms remains the same. Such mastery over mental processes seems to play a critical role in relation to the transformational imperative of spiritual traditions. Moreover, insights that arise through this kind of spiritual training can be invaluable as an adjunct to the scientific study of consciousness. Wallace makes a forceful comparison:

> The role of meditative stabilization in the discipline of contemplation may be likened to the role of mathematics in the physical sciences. Without knowledge of mathematics and the ability to apply this knowledge in the study of the laws of nature, modern physical science would hardly have progressed as it has. Mathematics is indispensable not only for scientific understanding of the physical world but also for developing the necessary technology to further our knowledge and control of nature. Similarly, meditative stabilization is said to be indispensable for

gaining contemplative insight into the nature of physical and mental phenomena.

(Wallace, 2000, p. 104)

Insights gleaned through contemplative or concentrative practice, when validated through the tradition's commentarial tradition, contribute an essential ingredient to consciousness studies. They, and for Wallace *they alone*, can bring a valid framework for interpretation to whatever data may be gathered from third-person approaches. Those who attempt introspection without the benefit of the kind of training which is characteristic of contemplative and concentrative practice fail to observe the subtleties in fleeting, and peripheral, mental phenomena that constitute the bedrock of all theory about consciousness.

Support for this premise comes from studies which have examined the abilities of participants to detect rapid perceptual events. Using a test with brief single flashes of light and paired flashes, Forte, Brown and Dysart (1984–5) compared advanced meditators with non-meditating controls. By comparison with the control participants, meditators reported more detail, both about individual flashes and about the gap between pairs of flashes. For example, the meditators were able to describe successive moments of awareness which were not observed by the controls. Thus, one meditator, describing his response to a pair of flashes, stated, 'Now I see clearly the moment of recognition of the arising, the moment of passing, the gap, the moment of recognition of the second, etc.' (p. 329). The meditators were also more adept at distinguishing perceptual from thought processes. One meditator reflected that, 'The minuscule level of the flash happens separately from the cognitive elaborations. It's so tenuous' (p. 330).

Conclusions from a study such as this are problematic. Any one of a number of factors could confound the suggestion that prolonged meditation leads to heightened awareness of mental events. It may be that individuals more attuned to introspection in the first place are attracted to this kind of a meditative practice. They may be 'set' to detect the kinds of subtleties they report on account of their tradition's teachings; or there may be 'response bias' for similar reasons. The Forte *et al.* study attempted to answer such criticisms. For example, the authors note that that the particular tradition being followed by the meditators, a branch of Burmese Buddhism, makes a point of discouraging any preliminary teaching about the effects that may be expected to come about. Furthermore, the authors went some way in terms of experimental protocol to minimize confounding variables. Participants acting as controls were psychologists with knowledge of perceptual theory, who may therefore have been expected to have roughly equivalent expectancies to any the meditators may have had; and dummy trials were included as a control for response bias.

Other studies have found similar effects in advanced meditators compared to novice meditators, a finding that would seem to rule out the first objection concerning a greater tendency to introspection in those drawn to meditation in the first place. For example, Brown and Engler (1984) demonstrated that the longer the participant had been meditating, the greater the extent of deconstruction of perceptual and thought processes as indicated by responses on a Rorschach test. On balance, although it is notoriously difficult to overcome all possible experimental objections, a good case can be made for the view that training in mindfulness meditation develops insight into subtle features of consciousness not otherwise detected.

As I indicated earlier, we make a mistake if we envision the two spheres of training – the text-based and the meditative – as independent. Indeed, the fifth-century CE Buddhaghosa, whom Wallace cites in his exposition of the Theravadin account of vision-based practice, is one of the sages specifically mentioned by Sharf (1998) as gaining his authority through mastery of, and rigorous adherence to, sacred scripture. However, the point is stronger than this, since the very transformations that can bring about deeper insights into consciousness may arise through mystical engagement with sacred texts:

> [E]xegesis, as understood by the world's mystical communities, by the world's mystical personalities, is ... a primary form, a main channel, of mystical ascent; a basic source of spiritual energy; a performative mystical act with salient experiential – transformational – consequences.... To engage scripture, as the mystical adept engages it, is not only to participate in an intense dialogue with texts but also, and far more important, to reach out to, and sometimes even to feel and to touch ... those powers that lie at their origin.
>
> (Katz, 2000, p. 57)

It is for these reasons that a sharp demarcation cannot be upheld between the notion of introspection and that of *revelation*. In Table 1.1, I have included the term 'access to revelation' under the list of methods appropriate to the spiritual/mystical approach to consciousness. This appeal to a divine source of knowledge will surely strike many as bizarre, not only because of its theistic assumption, but also because it seems to remove the human input. By 'method' we generally have in mind something that we follow in a given approach – a set of parameters and procedures. Revelation, on the contrary, seems to connote our passivity in the face of a divine input. However, this is to miss the deeper meaning in the whole notion of revelation as understood in terms of mystical engagement with sacred, scriptural texts.

From her profound study of *Veda* and *Torah*, Holdrege (1996) captures the point: 'scripture is not a unidimensional textual phenomenon but is rather a multileveled cosmic reality that encompasses gross and subtle, mundane and supramundane dimensions' (p. 5). Insight into reality – which, because it is *divine* reality, includes that of consciousness and the mind – arises as the sacred text breathes wisdom into the mystic who is able to establish a full rapport with it. For the Jewish mystic, 'The Torah ... is ... not separate from the divine essence, not created in the strict sense of the word; rather, it is something that represents the secret life of God' (Scholem, 1960/1965, p. 41). And, as Holdrege writes, the Veda is 'the transcendent record of the structures of reality' (p. 228). Through their cognition of the Vedic hymns, the masters of this scripture, the *rsis*, 'have come to know everything in creation, gross and subtle, manifest and hidden, as clearly and vividly as one knows an object when one perceives it with ordinary perception' (p. 231).

The influential thirteenth-century Jewish kabbalist, Abraham Abulafia, equated the Torah with the Active Intellect, a transcendent sphere of mind. Mystical engagement with the Torah, as it were, *formats* the finite human mind in such a way as to enable it to receive an 'influx' from the higher sphere:

> The Torah is perfect for it makes the simple wise. And being sure testimony, it was given to us only in order to actualise one's potential intellect. Anyone whose intellect has emerged from *potentia* to *actu* is worthy of it being said that the Torah was given for his sake.
>
> (Cited in Idel, 1989b, p. 37, italics added)

Abulafia wrote about mystical techniques for achieving the goal of actualizing one's potential intellect, details of which I shall discuss in Chapter 7. For the moment, I simply wish to emphasize the link between hermeneutics and revelation indicated in Abulafia's 'way of prophecy', as he called it. Prising open the meanings of Torah by distinctive hermeneutic devices is identified with gaining access to the insights of revelation. In his analysis of the role of Active Imagination in Ibn Arabi's Islamic esotericism, Corbin (1958/1969) similarly asserts that prophecy is bound up with hermeneutics. More generally, Sells (1994) alludes to the apophatic mystery which 'is glimpsed only in the interstices of the text, in the tension between the saying and the unsaying' (p. 8). Very much a follower of Corbin's understanding of the spiritual imagination, Wolfson conveys the point clearly:

> The dichotomy posited by many scholars between exegesis and experience, interpretation and revelation, seems to me to be problematic. On the contrary, the connection between the process of textual interpretation (*midrash*) and prophetic states of consciousness or visionary experience – what one might call 'inspired exegesis' or 'pneumatic interpretation' – is found already in Psalm 119:18 and becomes pronounced in apocalyptic texts, the Qumran scrolls, and early Jewish mysticism.
> (Wolfson, 1994, p. 121)

Whilst the exegesis of scripture may seem tangential to an analysis of consciousness, its implicit experiential component renders it important. Dan insists that the distinctive feature of the early texts of Kabbalah is the role of experience in guiding their exegetical inferences:

> [Their authors] had deep within themselves the glimpse of supernal mystical truth, and then found a way to integrate a symbolical reflection of this truth within their exegetical works.
> (Dan, 1995, p. 24)

The point may be effectively illustrated from the following extract from *Sefer ha-Bahir*, generally considered the earliest text to introduce the major kabbalistic symbol system into Jewish mysticism:

> What is the meaning of, 'Lord, I heard your hearing,'[4] I feared' (*Habakkuk* 3:1)?.... Why did he say, 'I feared?' Because the ear resembles the [letter] *alef*,[5] and the *alef* is the first of all the

letters. Not only this, but the *alef* causes all the letters to exist. And the *alef* resembles the brain. Just as, in the case of the letter *alef*, when you bring it to mind you open your mouth, so with thought – when you think a thought to the infinite and bound-less.... What did he understand that he would fear? He under-stood the thought of The Holy One, blessed be He. Just as thought has no end, for a person can think and descend to the end of the world, so the ear has no end and is not satiated, as is written, 'The ear is not filled by hearing' (*Ecclesiastes* 1:8). What is the reason? Because the ear resembles the *alef*.

(Sefer ha-Bahir, 69, 70, 79)

While the passage overtly takes a midrashic, exegetical form, there seems little doubt that its dynamic derives from the experience of those who have delved into the nature of thought. What is the origin of thought? What form does any thought take prior to 'I' grasping it? The key to understanding this passage (in addition to the attributes of the letter *alef* explained in the note) seems to be a distinctive view of '*fear*'. It is a fear that arises from the decon-struction of hearing, from the void that paradoxically fills the emptiness left by the receding 'I'. The mystic arrives at the experi-ence of God's thought by embracing the silence behind his own, which resembles the opening of the mouth before sound arises from it.

This understanding of 'fear' may usefully be illustrated from one of the participants in Deikman's classic study of experimental meditation. Deikman instructed his participants to concentrate on a blue vase which was placed on a table opposite them. They were told not to analyze the vase, simply to try to see it as it 'exists in itself'. After three introductory sessions, this meditation was subse-quently performed for between 15 and 30 minutes on each occa-sion thereafter. Relevant to the issue of fear is the experience of one participant:

> She reported that a diffuse blue occupied the entire visual field and that she merged completely with that diffuseness. She had a sense of falling, of emptiness, of loneliness and isolation as if she were in a vacuum. Her sudden realization that there were absolutely no thoughts in her mind made her anxious and she *searched* for thoughts to bring herself back.

(Deikman, 1963, p. 337)

During an earlier session, she had described herself as practically merging with the vase, and reported that, 'I almost got scared to the point where I found myself bringing myself back in some way from it' (p. 334).

When the security of our known world is undermined by an attenuation of regular thoughts, then a fear of the unknown must be confronted. In the passage from the *Bahir*, the unknown source of thought becomes 'known' as the thought of God, but the fear remains on account of the boundlessness encountered.

Returning to the methodological point, our interest in such a passage does not lie in its exposition of the biblical verse, but in the experience which has evidently shaped the author's exegesis. The implication we can draw, namely that retracing, or reversing, the normal processes of hearing and thinking reveals an 'infinite and boundless' root thought indeed carries significance for our inquiry. For example, it has a significant bearing on our conceptualization of the relationship between conscious and preconscious activity. It is also worth noting that a degree of cross-cultural validation is evident in these ideas, since our understanding of this passage from the *Bahir* is commensurate with the awareness of a dissociation between perception and thought reported by the meditators in the Forte *et al.* study described above.

Finally, in this section on method, I should stress my own reversal of the typical psychological approach to religious states. I am not asking (at this juncture, at least) what is *causing* the state, be it a neural, cognitive, or psychoanalytic cause. Neither am I necessarily accepting a transcendent basis. My interest is in distilling those spiritual insights into consciousness which can complement and help clarify the observations of the other approaches.

The debate over pure consciousness

As Ferrer (2002) argues, the debate over pure consciousness is critical for the whole edifice of transpersonal psychology, since it has a key bearing on the kind of theory that underpins the topic. Much transpersonal theorising in the past has drawn from the *perennialist* view that a core of common truths underpins the diversity in spiritual teachings. Wilber, for example, holds that the aim of transpersonal psychology is to 'give a psychological presentation of the perennial philosophy and the Great Chain of Being' (cited in Ferrer, ibid, p. 72). A pinnacle of the common 'truth' is that the peak of human potential lies in directly experiencing a transcendent essence – the 'non-dual' source, unnameable yet unequivocally conscious. Describing the experience as one of pure, contentless consciousness not only seems, for many, to be true to the experience itself, but also has the great advantage of side-stepping the plethora of cultural labels which have been applied to the Ultimate – an important goal for most perennialists. It should be evident why this approach has proved popular for transpersonal psychology, since the universalistic claim has been a major part of the agenda of establishing a discipline which is able to transcend the particularities of religious doctrines.[6]

Nevertheless, the 'hermeneutic objection' (Nixon, 1999) to the idea of contentless consciousness is very real. The objection casts doubt over the claim that an experience may breach the bounds of the hermeneutic within which it is contextualized, a limitation which many would apply to both the genesis of the experience and its communication to others. The ensuing 'perennialist (or, *essentialist*) versus contextualist' debate – considered briefly below – may be difficult to resolve. Unlike Ferrer, my interest lies not so much in the implications of this fiery debate for transpersonal theory, but rather in the view of consciousness that emerges from the ashes of the debate.

Consciousness in the Samkhya-Yoga school

One reason for entertaining the possibility of pure consciousness arises from the view that consciousness amounts to a fundamental property, irreducible to other features of the universe such as energy or matter. On this view, my being conscious of the pen in my hand presumably depends on a range of perceptual and related processes which are somehow permeated with the fundamental quality of consciousness. Exactly how consciousness 'permeates' these brain events remains mysterious, since the question concerns the explanatory gap discussed earlier. If consciousness as a fundamental property is indeed irreducible to other phenomena, then, clearly, its cause cannot be identified with brain processes. Consciousness must be seen as *other* than the relevant brain processes. As already considered, such a view is held by several contemporary writers on consciousness, including Chalmers

(1996) and Griffin (2000). According to this formulation, the generation of consciousness is mysteriously bound up with the origins of the universe, in the same way as is the case for matter or energy.

The label 'pure' as applied to consciousness is entirely appropriate if consciousness is viewed as *other* in the foregoing sense. Of course, the postulation of consciousness as some kind of absolute does not depend on our ability to experience it as an absolute. The argument may simply be a logical solution to the hard problem. The label 'pure' takes on a philosophical meaning rather than an experiential connotation. There may be something about consciousness that transcends its contents, whether or not anyone could ever experience it as such. From this point of view, questioning the validity of so-called *pure consciousness events* (that is, experiences devoid of content; see Forman, 1990) need not compromise our understanding of consciousness as an absolute.

The mystical literature, on which the claims for pure consciousness are strongly based (see chapters in Forman, 1990, 1998), tends, however, to blend the philosophical with the experiential. Probably the most important school of thought that assigns an ontological reality to pure consciousness is that of *Samkhya-Yoga* in Hinduism. The oldest strands of Samkhya philosophy are lost; our major source comes in the later (third- or fourth-century CE) formulation of Isvarakrsna. Isvarakrsna posits a fundamental dualism between pure consciousness (*purusa*) and what may be best termed 'structuredness' (*prakrti*). The latter includes both physical and mental phenomena. Not only are there material realizations of *prakrti*, but *prakrti* is also manifested as the structured thoughts and images of the mind. As Schweizer (1993) points out, this is a radically different kind of dualism from that found in Cartesian philosophy, and avoids the problematic issue of how consciousness may be generated by structured matter. In the Samkhya view, *purusa* and *prakrti* are both primary realities, with the former responsible for our consciousness of mental content, much as a light (cf. *purusa*) would illuminate a translucent photographic negative (cf. *prakrti*).

The contemporaneous work of Patanjali established the practical methods (*yoga*) best suited to the soteriological dimension of Samkhya. This dimension is intrinsic to all Samkhya philosophy since an imperative towards liberation underpins the system of thought. The goal of both the knowledge system of Isvarakrsna and the yogic techniques of Patanjali is the realization of pure consciousness. Moreover, this is not simply a personal goal; a more cosmic end is envisaged:

> For the Samkhya system, it is not enough to say that matter functions in its various levels and forms: the evolutionary manifestation of *prakrti*... implies a purpose, a purpose that the material world, however complex, cannot supply. Matter is not conscious in itself; it has no sentient light in which to be seen. Without a conscious principle outside itself, it is blind, unknowing, and unknown.
>
> (Pflueger, 1998, p. 51)

The cosmic function of *prakrti* is to come to know that it itself is other than consciousness, and this can be achieved only through its manifestation in the human intellect. When all content disappears from the mind – indeed when mind itself disappears – yet pure consciousness remains, then the human task is achieved.

It is therefore evident that distancing Samkhya philosophy from the experience of pure consciousness would be untenable. The experience and the ideas are the warp and weft of the woven whole that is Samkhya. If the experience does not firmly imply what the system encourages the yogin to believe – that the only true consciousness is that of total emptiness – then the philosophical system is heavily compromised.

Pflueger is in no doubt that the ultimate experiences described are exactly what they are said to be – beyond any iota of constructed content:

> In the final analysis, the yogin gains everything (salvation) by losing every *thing*, deconstructing oneself as a *person* in favor of the nonlinguistic experience of *purusa*, an 'impersonhood' beyond any possibility of suffering, beyond any possibility of conception or construction. All the meditator's doing is undone: in the conscious silence apart from all objects of thought or perception, the meditator finds his or her innate nature to be simply consciousness itself.
>
> (Pflueger, 1998, p. 69)

The intellectual climate of postmodernism, however, casts a giant shadow over our inclination to take such statements of experience at face value. For Derrida, 'one cannot refer to the "real" except in *an interpretive experience*' (cited in Haney, 1998, p. 28). Katz (1978b) insists that the processes of mediation that we find at work in all our everyday experiences are equally to be found in mystical experience: *'There are NO pure (i.e., unmediated) experiences'* (p. 26, emphasis original). His concern is not simply with the difficulty of expressing the ineffable in language. It is the form of the experience itself which is, for Katz and others in this contextualist school, determined by the context given by the writings and teachings with which the mystic is familiar:

> Mystical reports do not merely indicate the postexperiential description of an unreportable experience in the language closest at hand. Rather, the experiences themselves are inescapably shaped by prior linguistic influences such that the lived experience conforms to a preexistent pattern that has been learned, then intended, and then actualized in the experiential reality of the mystic.
>
> (Katz, 1992b, p. 5)

Accordingly, the experience that convinces the yogin of the ontological reality of *purusa*, pure consciousness, is, for contextualists, merely a product of the supposition that such a reality exists. In a nutshell, contextualism is absolutely opposed to any form of absolutism.[7]

Katz asserts that:

> Properly understood, yoga, for example, is not an unconditioning or deconditioning of consciousness, but rather it is a reconditioning of consciousness, i.e., a substituting of one form of conditioned and/or contextual consciousness for another.
>
> (Katz, 1978b, p. 57)

Yet there can be no doubting the force of cross-cultural mystical literature that does seem to indicate the deconditioning at work. Katz may indeed be right that, as soon as an experience *gels*, then, to the extent that it is anything, it is already a product of mediation, and merely reflective of the tradition being followed. But is there no consciousness before the gelling? Might it not be the case that mystics are indeed pointing towards an essential, and universal, feature of mind, namely that an undifferentiated state of consciousness is encountered at the heart of the kinds of transformations in which they are interested? In the words of the Maggid of Mezeritch, quoted at the head of this chapter, 'Transformation comes about only by passing through nothingness.' Cultural factors may play strongly determining roles in relation to both the kinds of practices that mystics embrace and the nature of the transformed state itself. Yet as a transitional stage, an undifferentiated state may transcend cultural factors. The error of perennialism is that of promulgating the view that such a state of nothingness is the end goal of spiritual practice. In the majority of mystical writings, this is not the case. As Ferrer (2002) notes, experiences of this kind may comprise just 'the starting point of genuine spiritual inquiry' (p. 146).

The mystical literature alone may be insufficient to enable us to reach any firm conclusions here, since the polemical element in reports of mystical experience is invariably strong. However, the argument that experiential states can sometimes be totally devoid of content – states of pure consciousness – does not rest on mystical literature alone. We find seemingly spontaneous cases, in which experiences of total emptiness occur to those having no axe to grind in spiritual terms. In view of the absence of polemic, these cases undoubtedly lend extra weight to the argument for the psychological validity of some kind of contentless consciousness.

The psychology of pure consciousness

Sullivan (1995) is in little doubt about the validity of pure consciousness: 'the "pure consciousness" event has been repeatedly documented over many centuries and within different cultural contexts, so that its actual occurrence should be beyond reasonable dispute' (p. 55). He arrives at this conclusion following a literature review prompted by his own, spontaneous experience of pure consciousness. One of the reasons for ascribing validity to Sullivan's experience is the fact that it came 'out of the blue'. He had no basis for expecting such an experience. On the contrary, he informs us that, prior to the event, he had been of the opinion that there could be no such thing as contentless consciousness. He was not party to some religious or mystical teaching which could have seeded the idea of pure consciousness.[8] It would seem difficult to assert, therefore, that the experience he did have was conditioned.

Sullivan's experience came in the aftermath of an automobile accident. He describes coming round from a state he describes as one of 'nothingness':

> There was something, and the *something* was not the nothing. The nearest label for the something might possibly be 'awareness,' but that could be misleading, since any awareness I'd ever had before the accident was *my* awareness, my awareness of one thing or another.
> In contrast, this *something*, if it be called awareness, had no *I* as its *subject* and no content as its *object*. It just was.
> (Sullivan, 1995, p. 53)

Sullivan's main point is that such an experience is evidently genuine. '[H]ow was the *something-that-is-not-the-nothing* mediated by my cultural expectations...? In no way that I can see' (p. 57, italics original). This insight leads him to view consciousness and the information-processing functions of the brain as being independent.[9]

Clearly, there is considerable divergence between seeing pure consciousness as a kind of idling of the brain, and alternatively viewing it as a distinct ontological category, as in Samkhya-Yoga, for example. It is important to recognize that an assertion that experiences of pure consciousness possess psychological validity need not imply any acceptance of these kinds of ontological implications. For the present, then, let us simply recognize that the unpremeditated aspect of an experience such as Sullivan's is compelling evidence for its validity. And, importantly, his case is not unique. Hardy (1979) and Hay (1982) collected records of spiritual experiences from a wide range of respondents, some of whom reported experiences which were not at all in tune with their expectations. In a similar vein, Merkur (1989) reminds us that Catholic, Sufi and Jewish mystics have been known to *apologize* for some of the more extreme experiences they report having, indicating to him that the experiences were real. If they had *wanted* to have such experiences, why would they apologise? Evidently, therefore, the literature in which they had been immersed had not conditioned the aetiology of their experiences.

In the context of explicating William James' view of mysticism, Barnard gives a report of one of his own experiences which, again, seems to refute the contextualist argument, since his ability to interpret the experience only came some considerable time later:

When I was thirteen years old, I was walking to school in Gainesville, Florida, and without any apparent reason, I became obsessed with the idea of what would happen to me after my death. Throughout that day I attempted to visualize myself as not existing. I simply could not comprehend that my self-awareness would not exist in some form or another after my death. I kept trying, without success, to envision a simple blank nothingness. Later, I was returning home from school, walking on the hot pavement next to a stand of pine trees less than a block from my home, still brooding about what it would be like to die. Suddenly, without warning, something shifted inside. I felt lifted outside of myself, as if I had been expanded beyond my previous sense of self. In that exhilarating, and yet deeply peaceful moment, I felt as if I had been shaken awake. In a single, 'timeless' gestalt, I had a direct and powerful experience that I was not just that young teenage boy, but rather, that I was a surging, ecstatic, boundless state of consciousness.

(Barnard, 1997, pp. 127–8)

If anything, the relation to interpretation in this case is opposed to that argued by contextualists. Barnard claims that his experience prompted a long-term search for explanation: 'The "thatness" of the experience was always there, but this "thatness" was primarily operative as a goad prodding me to find some philosophical framework that could do justice to the inchoate content' (p. 128).

If the only experiences we are capable of were those predetermined by cultural expectations, the question must arise as to how anything *new* might arise at all. The observation that some experiences do seem to break out of the mould given by expectations allows for the possibility of diversity arising in society. In this sense, non-predetermined experiences in the psychological or mystical sphere may be akin to spontaneous mutations in the biological sphere. In their respective spheres, they are both vital for generating the diversity necessary for evolutionary forces to operate.

In arguing for the objectivity of the pure consciousness event, Forman offers one of his own experiences which occurred during a nine-month retreat on a neo-Advaitan path:

I had been meditating alone in my room all morning when someone knocked on my door. I heard the knock perfectly clearly, and upon hearing it I knew that, although there was no 'waking up' before hearing the knock, for some indeterminate length of time prior to the knocking I had not been aware of anything in particular. I had been awake but with no content for my consciousness.

(Forman, 1993, p. 708)

Such experiences lead Forman to adopt an analogy with radar. The radar system may be powered up and ready to respond to objects, even though there may be no objects for it to have contact with. 'Consciousness should be defined more precisely as that which is *capable of* responding to certain phenomena, responding not to radar waves but, say, sound waves coming through our auditory faculty' (p. 717).

The problem here is that consciousness is being defined in such a way as to grant validity to the very phenomenon for which Forman is claiming validity. If the force of the experience itself may not be adequate to convince a sceptic – and the hermeneutic objection is strong here, since Forman's experience was clearly fully in line with the teachings of the tradition he was following – why should this definitional manoeuvre be convincing? Moreover, Forman meets another potential objection by similarly incorporating the solution in his definition. I have in mind here the memory objection, that is, if there are no contents to the experience, what exactly is being remembered when Forman reports that he 'remembered' that he had been conscious but with no content? For Forman, 'To be conscious is to be able to remember' (p. 723), and therefore, if consciousness can be non-intentional, or 'pure', then, by definition, so can memory.

I have, in an earlier work (Lancaster, 1991), posited that a *pure memory process* may be at work during the kinds of mystical states which interest Forman. It should be noted, however, that this pure memory process was not posited as operating without content. I see it as an incessant dynamic, by means of which the relationships between active cognitive structures are determined and stored. The pure memory process underpins the generation of more personally-oriented associations that determine the individual's response in any given situation. While the personal aspect of memory activity may indeed be attenuated during the kinds of mystical state to which Forman refers, it may be that *preconscious* memory activity continues.

It is highly problematic to extract ourselves from the impasse of this debate over pure consciousness. It is imperative, however, to differentiate two distinct issues. The first concerns the academic debate over mysticism. To what extent is there such a thing as a core mystical experience which is an experience of pure consciousness? On balance, the evidence simply does not support this view. Indeed, the richness and diversity in the world's mystical literature is largely compromised by the view. There may, however, be a high degree of commonality in the *nothingness* experienced *en route* to whatever is deemed as the 'higher' state in a given tradition. Crucially, the experience that appears to be common amongst diverse traditions is not the goal, but the means to the goal.

The second issue is whether pure consciousness experiences occur, irrespective of their significance for mysticism. The answer to this second issue would seem to be a guarded 'yes', as illustrated by experiences such as those of Sullivan, Barnard and others. This answer is also supported by the above view of a commonality among states *en route* to the mystical goal of a given tradition. However, it is a hesitant 'yes' on account of the possibility that the apparent emptiness does not preclude there being some significant content-related activity at a preconscious level. While accepting that, on occasion, experiences may transcend predisposing ideas, I suggest that the 'purity' of the experience may not be all it seems. On the other hand, Nixon (1999) accepts the 'purity', but doubts that it has anything to do with consciousness, designating such experience as 'pure pre-conscious experience'. He suggests that prolonged meditation may bring about an 'atavistic return to the energetic source of all sensation and perception' (p. 264).

The confusion here may be resolved by distinguishing between the *experienceability* of whatever processing is occurring and the question of *content* itself. Normally, we experience the end result of the various processing stages that occur when attention is directed outwards (perception) or inwards (thought). For example, I am not conscious of the myriad computations taking place in my brain in response to ambient sounds stimulating the cochleae of my ears. But I am conscious of the words being spoken by the person with whom I am having a conversation. Here, my experience arises at the end-stage of the process, and we would generally refer to the earlier brain activity as *preconscious*. In this sense, processes are deemed preconscious if they occur prior to the later processes that actually give rise to experience. However, what if the view of preconscious activity as being prior to experience is actually misleading? Maybe a subset of those processes commonly designated as preconscious *are not intrinsically outside the realm of experience.*

At face value, such a proposal may sound self-contradictory, since consciousness is generally *identified* with experience. But, this is merely a matter of definitions. Suppose that many of the processes we typically class as 'preconscious' are not intrinsically pre-*conscious*, in the sense of being prior to experience. Instead, they might be defined as preceding an end-stage that *normally* gives rise to mundane consciousness. Under circumstances differing from the normal, including, for example, those mystical states under consideration here, the binding of experience to the end-stage associated with normal, or mundane, consciousness may be subject to change.

Looking in this way at the relationships between preconscious activity, experience and mundane consciousness, four possible scenarios emerge (Figure 3.1). The first scenario depicts the normal, 'everyday' situation, in which experience is restricted to the conscious end-stage. The content of preconscious activity is not experienced. The following three alternatives in the figure entail some degree of attenuation of the end-stage. The second scenario is simply one in which there is no experience, as in coma or non-dreaming sleep. The third scenario depicts a situation in which the experience attaching to the end-stage is still present, but in the absence of any of the content normally generated by the end-stage. This scenario is distinguished from the fourth in that the person is not experiencing any content-related activity of earlier processing stages. This third scenario gives rise to contentless experience: the person is awake and conscious, but their experience does not extend to whatever activity may be occurring preconsciously. Under the fourth possibility, the person experiences the earlier processing stages in some measure.[10] The figure depicts a reduced sense of 'I' in this fourth case, in accordance with reports of this kind of mystical experience. In effect, the situation illustrated according to this fourth scenario is one in which the individual becomes conscious of normally preconscious activity.

All this is vague. What are the parameters of events occurring during preconscious stages? What characterizes the 'end-stage'? What does it mean to say that the end-stage becomes 'attenuated'? Much detail remains to be painted in to the broad outline presented here – a challenge to be met in subsequent chapters. A key feature of the end-stage, to be discussed in detail in Chapter 5,

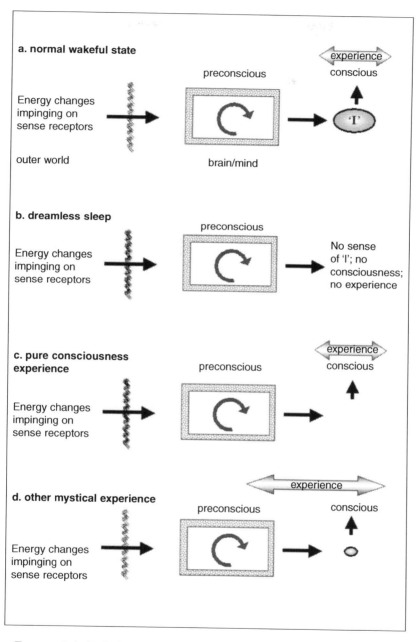

FIGURE 3.1 Relations between preconscious activity, experience and consciousness. See text for explanation.

is the postulated central role played by 'I' (as indicated in the figure). From both cognitive neuroscience and mysticism there is considerable evidence to suggest that the sense of 'I' as the focus of conscious mental events is actually constructed as the final stage in mundane states of consciousness (Lancaster, 1991, 1997a, 1997b, 2000c, 2001). Kihlstrom (1993) has similarly argued that consciousness of some event occurring in our inner or outer world depends on a link being established between the cognitive representation of the event and the representation of self. For Kihlstrom, 'I' becomes the touchstone of consciousness. However, when we bring the evidence of mystical literature into our analysis, it may be appropriate to regard 'I' as the touchstone of *mundane* consciousness only. Other forms of consciousness arise when the sense of 'I' changes, or, in the more extreme mystical states, disappears.

Whatever may be concluded about the validity of pure consciousness, it would appear incontrovertible that mystical states universally depend on attention being directed away from 'I', thereby attenuating the end-stage of perceptual or thought processes. In the instructional words of *The Cloud of Unknowing*, a classic of Christian mysticism:

> And therefore break down all witting [knowledge] and feeling of all manner of creatures; but most busily of thyself. For on the witting and the feeling of thyself hangeth witting and feeling of all other creatures.
>
> (Underhill, 1912, p. 179)[11]

On the stages of perception and thought

In the foregoing I have introduced the general notion of mental processes proceeding by stages, culminating in the generation of the sense of 'I'. This is not to imply that the end-stage implies *reflection* on self. In the case of visual perception, for example, the end-stage simply gives rise to the sense that *I am seeing* X, where X is the object in front of my eyes. I do not have to be *self-conscious* in order for 'I' to be implicitly active in a perceptual or thought process. It is simply there. 'I' is part of the whole process through which the visual entity is contextualized. The pen in my hand is not merely an elongated shape, nor is it merely a pen, but it is *my* pen in *my* hand, and part of the whole narrative of which *I* am the central player. The pen is where it is because *I* am using it to write down these crazy thoughts. The experience includes these elements not in a reflective fashion (although I can, of course, reflect on them, which is what I am doing now), but as immediate data of consciousness. It would be accurate to say that the end-stage gives rise to the capacity to reflect on self, but the 'I' it generates is not itself dependent on reflection.

The term '*end*-stage' may, perhaps, be a little misleading, since events can continue to be triggered in succession, as, for example, when I experience reflective thoughts concerning the object perceived. Nevertheless, we may conventionally recognize the end-stage of a perceptual process as being identified with the arrival of the formed image in consciousness. And, as suggested above, that stage may entail the forging of a link between the image and 'I' (or, in brain processing terms, between the neural representation of the object and the representation of self).

Both cognitive neuroscience and introspective spiritual traditions concern themselves with the stages of perceptual or thought processes. Detail of the relevant research in cognitive neuroscience will be presented in subsequent chapters; for the present I am emphasizing the contribution made by the spiritual traditions to the identification of the nature of preconscious activity in perception and thought. Later, I will focus on the complementarity between these approaches, for as we have seen, a meaningful theory of consciousness needs the support of both lines of evidence – the scientific and the introspective.

I mentioned above the idea of a *preconscious* as formulated in kabbalistic texts. Dov Baer, the Maggid of Mezeritch (1704–1742) appears to be the first to have used this term explicitly, although the central concept of a thought being formed prior to its arrival in human consciousness is present in earlier strata of Jewish mysticism (Scholem, 1975).[12] For Hurvitz (1968), the meaning of the Hebrew phrase translated here as 'preconscious' is, 'a kind of thinking, conceiving, or consciousness which preceded the actual thinking, conceiving, or consciousness of the moment' (p. 174). This aspect of mind is generally concealed from normal consciousness – a point underscored by Hurvitz's readiness to refer to it as unconscious. There is, however, more to this term than might be implied if we think of it only as a kind of 'cognitive preconscious' or 'psychoanalytic unconscious', for it refers also to a higher dimension of mind.

Spiritual advancement is viewed by the Maggid as requiring an *ascent* to the level of the preconscious, experienced as 'a creative pool of nothingness' (Matt, 1995, p. 87). In the Maggid's words: 'For thought requires a preconscious which is above the thought that thinks. Hence we find it written (*Job* 28:12) that "Wisdom comes from nothing"' (cited in Scholem, 1975, p. 355). Ultimately, the preconscious is understood as a sphere in the Godhead, whose activity is mirrored in the human psyche. It is designated as *Wisdom*, and is witnessed in those flashes of insight that bring knowledge that was previously concealed:

> Whatever exists in specific form has its roots in the universal, namely in the preconscious which is *hylic* in nature. As when a person has been pondering some matter and there suddenly falls into his mind an idea or aspect of knowledge, for this sudden illumination is drawn from the preconscious.
> (Maggid of Mezeritch, cited in Scholem, 1975, p. 354)

'Preconscious' or 'conscious'? Evidence from Abhidhamma

A discussion of stages in perceptual and thought processes is included in a part of the Pali canon of Theravadin Buddhism known as the *Abhidhamma* ('higher teaching'). Tradition holds that the Abhidhamma distils the insights into ultimate reality and the human condition originally gleaned by the Buddha during his enlightenment. The canonical form of the teaching is attributable to scholars of the third and second centuries BCE, and probably its most influential formulation is that written by Buddhaghosa in the fifth century CE. In accord with the central Buddhist teaching of *momentariness*, the Abhidhamma examines in intricate detail the constituent processes that make up all states of being.

The teaching of momentariness holds that the seeming continuity of matter and states of mind masks their real nature – which comprises chains of moments, each arising, briefly enduring, and decaying in succession. Successive moments arise by dint of their being conditioned by previous ones in the chain. A section of the Abhidhamma applies this theory in detail to perceptual and thought processes, which, accordingly, it views as comprising a number of fleeting, subsidiary stages. The 'moments' of the stages are normally so fast as to be undetectable in the untrained mind.

Before considering these stages in detail, I shall address a critical tension around their status in relation to consciousness. On the
one hand, the stages are envisaged as occurring very rapidly. Most
of the stages are viewed as being of only one moment's duration,
and billions of such moments are said to arise in the time of one
lightning flash! The whole process 'happens in an infinitesimal
part of time' (Narada, 1956/1975, p. 33). Indeed, as noted in
Chapter 1, Collins (1982) informs us that the commentators calculated a figure of 1/74,642 second per moment![13] The brevity of the
stages encourages me to think of them as *preconscious* in the
temporal sense of the term. They are stages occurring prior to the
'end-stage', as discussed earlier.

On the other hand, the stages are thought of as 'conscious' by
most commentators. In Pe Maung Tin's (1921) translation of
Buddhaghosa's classic, *Atthasalini*, the stages of perception are
referred to as 'kinds of consciousness'. According to Govinda
(1975), they are 'classes of consciousness', and for Rhys Davids
(1914), 'moments or flashes of consciousness'. Harvey (1995)
prefers the term 'discernment', but approves of Horner's 'discrim-
inative consciousness'. Cousins (1981) considers all the stages as
contributing to the 'process of consciousness', with each being
itself a consciousness element.

It is hardly surprising that we find this kind of diversity in translations of Pali terms, given that the shades of meaning in features
of mental process specified by the Abhidhamma frequently do not
have direct English equivalents. Pali is specialized for introspective
investigation in a way that English is not. The Pali term applied to
the various stages is *citta*, meaning momentary 'mind sets'
(Harvey, 1995). To the extent that each *citta* is a moment of watch-
ing, of knowing, then clearly it is also a moment of consciousness.

The Buddhist perspective is to be distinguished on this point
from the cognitive and neuropsychological. Velmans' (1999)
answer to his question, 'When does perception become conscious?'
epitomizes the perspective of cognitive psychology: 'only once
analysis is complete, and attended-to information is sufficiently
well integrated to be disseminated throughout the brain' (p. 561).
On this view, preconscious analysis is far from simplistic and is
able to extract complex levels of meaning in sensory stimuli. It is
difficult to imagine that the Abhidhamma is not dealing with these
kinds of analysis when it considers the stages in perception, all of
which are deemed to be *conscious*. This mismatch between the

perspectives of cognitive psychology and Buddhism is highly important, for it points to the critical difference between two major senses in which we use the term 'consciousness'.

In this context we must remember that the essential difference between Buddhism and cognitive neuroscience lies in the soteriological emphasis of the former. Whilst both are interested in specifying the micro-processes of mental functions, the reasons for the interest differ. Cognitive neuroscience is interested in the mind *as it is* (either in the mundane state, or as it operates defectively in pathological conditions). Buddhism, by contrast, inquires into what the mind *could* be, and its interest lies in the knowledge required for an individual to control and alter their mind, with the goal of achieving enlightenment. This requires the ability to control the early processes in perception, or thought, processes deemed *preconscious* by psychology. By the time the end-stage is reached, it is too late; the bias in the system has operated; one's prejudices have coloured the percept or thought.

Here we find the core difference between Buddhism and cognitive psychology, and this difference takes us back to the earlier discussions about transformation. The key to meaningful psychological change lies in the 'preconscious'. However, this very term tends to block such transformation for it implies that we cannot reach that part of ourselves. Possibly the most liberating step we can take is to grasp the *consciousness of preconscious states*. And the key to this step is the realization that the end-stage does not have a monopoly on consciousness. A specific form of *access-consciousness* is associated with the end-stage, in which the connection between the representation of 'I' and that of the object or event is the determining feature. I am conscious of the object to the extent that the neural representation of 'I' has access to that of the object. *Detachment* from 'I' may enable a more immediate consciousness of objects and events.

In accord with my earlier discussion (and see Figure 3.1), I suggest that the confusion is between 'experienceability' and the 'I'-related activity that characterizes mundane consciousness. From the Buddhist point of view, the end-stage gives rise to the 'conceit of I am' (Collins, 1982).[14] Harvey (1995) writes that in the unenlightened state, perceptual processing functions, 'to form a distorted interpretative model of reality: a model in which the "I am" conceit is a crucial reference point' (p. 247). The objective for Buddhism is to overcome the distortion of the model, to detach from 'I'. Central to this objective is the teaching of *anatta*, 'no-self', which conveys the idea that the sense we have of being (or 'having') a coherent and continuous self is an error, and one that lies very much at the heart of the unsatisfactoriness (*dukkha*) of life this side of *nirvana* ('enlightenment').

The no-self doctrine is summarized by Rahula (1967): 'What we call "I", or "being", is only a combination of physical and mental aggregates, which are working together interdependently in a flux of momentary change within the law of cause and effect' (p. 66). In the canonical *Milinda Panha*, the monk, Nagasena, conveys this point to King Melinda, by reference to his own name, describing it as, 'this designation, this conceptual term, a current appellation and a mere name'. Nagasena continues by remarking that, 'In ultimate reality, however, the person cannot be apprehended' (Conze, 1959, p. 149). Buddhagosa writes:

> For there is ill but none to feel it;
> For there is action but no doer;
> And there is peace, but no-one to enjoy it;
> A way there is, but no-one goes it.
>   (Cited in Pérez-Remón, 1980, p. 11)

While the denial of a metaphysical self, or soul, may be unique to Buddhism among the major religions, the notion of detachment from the empirical self (the immediate sense of 'I') is common across all spiritual teachings. This idea, that the 'I' is a barrier to more spiritually-effective forms of consciousness, is found in mystical texts from all the major religious traditions. In the Abhidhamma, detachment from 'I' is viewed as enabling the adept to control the normally automatic feeling reaction that takes place in the early stages of perception, and thereby to develop equanimity.

Equanimity is not only the prerequisite for further transformation, it is also central to the sharp observational skills that underpin the analysis of mental processes. My own approach to the nature of consciousness places considerable emphasis on these skills and their fruits, as depicted in the Abhidhamma texts. An understanding of the Abhidhamma's analysis of the stages of perception can cast considerable light on the nature of the psychological processes. It enables me to take the first steps towards the integrative theory of consciousness that I shall develop in future chapters.

The stages of perception in Abhidhamma

The Abhidhamma states that in a complete perceptual process there are seventeen moments of consciousness, grouped into a number of stages. During the first three moments, the mind's naturally pure state (*bhavanga*) is disturbed when a stimulus arrives at the 'sense door'. Following this, there is a turning towards the particular sense door stimulated (moment four – 'adverting'). In moment five, a sensory consciousness arises. In the case of visual perception, for example, this stage would be termed 'seeing.'[15] Such 'seeing' is not what we normally mean by the term, for there is no recognition of the object at this stage. It is characterized by a sense of contact between sense organ and sense object, and might be thought of as a consciousness that merely intimates that a formed entity has stimulated the eye. 'The subject sees a certain object, as to the nature of which it does not as yet *know* anything' (Aung, 1910/1972, p. 28, emphasis original). Harvey (1995) suggests that there is a 'bare awareness of a sensory object being present, plus the knowledge of which sense-modality it belongs to, and the discernment which discriminates the object into its basic parts or aspects' (p. 150).

The next three stages in the perceptual sequence – occupying moments six to eight – entail a more conceptual analysis of the input, by means of which the nature of the object giving rise to that input is clarified. The first of these stages is termed 'receiving', which may be understood as a receiving of the input by that faculty of mind which, in due course, will discriminate and cognize the sensory input. It is said to be characterized by a simple feeling tone, and may perhaps be best thought of as an initial sense of the 'flavour' conveyed by a given sense object, which at this stage is merely 'agreeable,' 'disagreeable' or 'neutral'.

'Receiving' is followed in moment seven by 'examining'. During this stage, the mind detects the marks of differentiation in the object. The function of *sanna*, 'cognition', is said to be strong during this stage. The linguistic element *sa-* implies 'linking', and the psychological function seems to entail an examination of the associations that the received entity give rise to. '*Sanna* is the activity of seeing-as: knowing something through the application of a specific perceptual label' (Harvey, 1995, pp. 141–2). By means of the examination, the nature of the object is assessed, but, as yet, there is no reaction to it. For Guenther (no date), consciousness at this stage has the 'nature of general inclusion' (p. 39), and therefore mistakes can be made, such as when a deer mistakes a scarecrow for a human. We should understand 'examining consciousness' as the function whereby one detects features in common across associated images, a necessary preliminary to establishing the identity of the stimulus that triggered the process in the first place.

The next stage – moment eight – is that of 'establishing,' which 'determines the nature of the mind's response to the object which has been identified' (Cousins, L. S. 1981, p. 33). As Aung suggests, during this stage the definitive properties of the object are separated from the surroundings, in order that the object might finally be apperceived in the ensuing stage. 'Establishing' is described as the 'gateway' to further perceptual reactions, since it determines the precise bias which will become dominant in the continuation of the mental process. It is important to realize that at no stage, up to and including this one of 'establishing', is the subject 'intelligently aware' (Aung, 1910/1972, p. 29) of the nature and character of the object.

From the moment of 'adverting' to that of 'establishing' the process is viewed as progressing automatically. By contrast, progress to the subsequent two stages is not inevitable, allowing for the possibility of so-called 'incomplete' cases, as indicated in Figure 3.2.

The next stage is referred to by the Pali term *javana*, which means 'running'. I will follow Rhys Davids in using this term untranslated, since no single English word adequately conveys its meaning.[16] Terms such as 'apperception' and 'impulsions' are often used, but are obscure. The term is evidently intended to convey the more active nature of the mind process engaged at this point. In fact, the *javana* thought process generally runs for seven moments of consciousness. The previous stage of 'establishing' is said to be characterized by a strong presence of drive. It is within the *javana* phase that this drive is consummated, and implicates potential actions likely to have future *karmic* consequences. In a useful analogy to the intake of food, 'establishing' is equated to smelling the food, while *javana* is the act of actually eating the food. *Javana* brings about the individual's conceptualization of the event or stimulus which began the process. 'At this stage ... the subject interprets the sensory impression, and fully appreciates the objective significance of his experience' (Aung, 1910/1972, p. 29).

moments of perceptual consciousness according to Abhidhamma

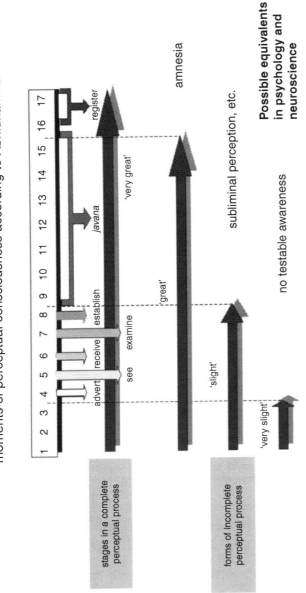

FIGURE 3.2 Perceptual stages identified in Abhidhamma texts. A complete process lasts 17 moments, as indicated in the upper illustration. The three incomplete cases recognized by the texts are depicted below. The stages are named for a visual example.

Javana is a critical stage for the individual's spiritual development, since it has the potential to lock in place habitual, 'unskilful' ways of perceiving and thinking. Buddhism calls on the individual to overcome such limitations in perception and thought. Moreover, in the unenlightened person, *javana* generates the sense of self as apparent subject of the perception, resulting in what to Buddhism is the 'conceit of "I am"' (Collins, 1982, p. 242).

According to the Abhidhamma, the perceptual process is completed with two final moments of 'registering'. Collins suggests that 'In modern terms, perhaps, one might interpret these two moments as the transition from a perception to the (short-term) memory of it; a transition necessary if the event is to be stored in (long-term) memory' (Collins, 1982, p. 243). Cousins points out that the precise meaning of the Pali term used here (*Tadarammana*) is 'having the same object' and that the stage, 'may perhaps be seen as fixing the conscious experience of the *javana* stage in the unconscious mind' (Cousins, L. S., 1981, p. 28). The notion of the whole *javana* reaction, including the sense of 'I' (in the spiritually undeveloped person) becoming fixed in memory, is a point of some importance. This notion will be discussed later in terms of the role of 'I' in memory (see Chapter 5). For the moment, let us simply note that the sense of self experienced at the time of perception is viewed as being stored together with the trace of whatever may have been perceived.

The function of each stage in the process is illustrated by various extended similes, an example being the following. A man is sleeping under a mango tree, with his head covered (moment 1). The wind rustles the branches, causing a mango fruit to fall, grazing the sleeping man's ear (moments 2 and 3). He is aroused from sleep by the sound (moment 4 – 'adverting'); removes his head covering and looks (moment 5 – 'sensation'); picks up the mango (moment 6 – 'receiving'); examines it by squeezing it (moment 7); and recognizes it as a mango by smelling it (moment 8 – 'establishing'). He eats it (moments 9 to 15 – *javana*); and savours the last morsels and the after-taste (moments 16 and 17 – 'registering').[17]

In addition to its description of the complete perceptual process, attributable to what is called a 'very great object', the Abhidhamma considers various incomplete cases, in which the process fails to reach moment 17. Three such cases are recognized (see Figure 3.2), two of which may be equated with known psychological conditions. The incomplete case labelled by the Abhidhamma as 'great', in which there is a failure to *register* the *javana* stage, would seem to relate directly to cases of amnesia. Here, there is no deficiency in perception per se, but subsequent memory for what has been perceived is compromised. The 'slight' case, which ends when the object is *established*, may be related to phenomena such as subliminal perception. Despite the nature of the sensory stimulus being established, it does not become incorporated into the normal conscious process dominated by the sense of 'I'. These postulated parallels to cases studied by cognitive neuroscience will be revisited in later chapters. For the moment, let me emphasize that the consciousness associated with the arising of 'I' (in Abhidhamma terms, arising through the *javana* moments in an untrained mind) should not be seen as the totality of consciousness. Material that may be inaccessible to 'I', and subliminal in such terms, may not intrinsically be outside of consciousness. Narada (1956/1975) makes it clear that, according to the Abhidhamma, we would be in error were we to assert that objects outside the sphere of focused attention, giving rise to incomplete processes, are perceived by the 'sub-consciousness' (p. 212). As indicated earlier, the processes such objects trigger are fully conscious, if not normally noticed.

Here, the issue of terminology raises its slippery head again. A crucial value in the Abhidhamma perspective is that of enabling us to recognize the cultural loading in our use of the term 'consciousness'. Quibbling over whether or not an image that has a 'subliminal' effect is best described as being processed 'subconsciously' will lead nowhere. It is only by penetrating into the processes involved that we can clarify the distinguishing features of different kinds of perception. As mentioned already, recognizing the relativity in the role played by 'I' may go some way to reconciling apparent tensions in terminological differences. Mainstream psychology has tended to become party to a kind of imperialism of self which has resulted in a somewhat monolithic view of consciousness. 'I' rules over its kingdom of consciousness, and any mental activity escaping its orb is simply ruled out from the conscious realm.

The approach of spiritual and mystical traditions casts doubt on the accuracy of this 'imperialistic' view of consciousness. And, as we shall see in future chapters, much of the neuroscientific and psychological evidence is supportive of the dethroning of self promulgated by spiritual and mystical teachings. The introspective Buddhist perspective examined in this last section provides a valuable, additional integrative framework for thinking about perception and consciousness. The stage model of perception enunciated in the Abhidhamma can usefully be related to the stages of processing as understood in both neuroscientific and psychological approaches. As will be seen, this integrative approach may offer an understanding of consciousness that is both defensible scientifically and meaningful in terms of the transformational goals of transpersonal psychology.

Chapter 4
Neurophysiological Approaches

Principles and questions

The neurophysiological approach to consciousness has much in common with that of cognitive neuropsychology (to be addressed in the next chapter). Indeed, I frequently refer to the whole area by the general term, 'cognitive neuroscience'. The connections include a strong adherence to the third-person form of the scientific method, and a reliance on demonstrations of brain activity to support postulates of the basis of consciousness. Nevertheless, the two approaches are sufficiently divided along one conceptual dimension for me to treat them in turn.

The neurophysiological approach focuses on the responses of individual neurones, whereas cognitive neuropsychology concerns itself more with brain systems and the psychological processes thought to arise from activity in those systems. Again, the distinction is not absolute, and both approaches draw on similar studies into brain function, including electrophysiological and imaging techniques such as PET or fMRI scans. The distinction between them is largely one of orientation. When it comes to consciousness, the neurophysiological approach is concerned with the properties of neurones, either singly or in groups, that are active in relation to a conscious state. The neurophysiological approach is largely a 'bottom-up' approach, which attempts to explain what it is about those properties that may give insight into consciousness. Cognitive neuropsychology, on the other hand, tends to focus on the distinctive psychological properties of conscious states, and only secondarily attempts to link these to specific brain systems. Baars

114

(1983, 1988) typifies the cognitive approach when he understands consciousness in terms of 'global workspace (GW) theory'. The role of consciousness in making information globally available to other systems is advanced as a logical (that is, psycho-logical) interpretation of a broad range of data. It is only as a secondary goal that the theory has been further fleshed out in terms of the putative brain systems involved (Newman and Baars, 1993). The value of the theory is not compromised by inadequacies in our understanding of its neural substrates: 'the abstract GW architecture can be realized in a number of different ways in the brain, and we do not know at this point which brain structures provide the best candidates' (Baars and McGovern, 1996, p. 89).

Clearly, a neurophysiologist, for whom the neural properties themselves would be of primary concern, could not have made this statement. The essential issue for the neurophysiological approach concerns the features of neural activity which appear to correlate with conscious activity. Note that the stress here is on correlation since the deeper question of why or how any feature of neural activity might be the *cause* of consciousness must effectively be side-stepped. The explanatory gap is not bridged by known neurophysiological parameters. Our search is for the *neural correlates of consciousness* (Metzinger, 2000).

The focus of the neurophysiological approach extends in two directions – to the sub-neural level and to the level of neural systems – and intersects with concepts drawn from modern physics and mathematics. Might the strange phenomena associated with the world of quantum mechanics open a door to consciousness at the micro level of neural components? At the other end of the scale, the mathematics of chaotic systems may provide a clue as to how consciousness enters into the behaviour of neural networks.

The challenge of the neurophysiological approach demands an understanding of the logic of neural communication. As we shall discover, the temporal domain of neural activity has proved critical for such an understanding. The evidence suggests that *phase synchrony* in the oscillatory electrical responses of groups of neurones provides something of a brain code whereby functional relationships between the neurones are signalled. It has been proposed that this 'code' itself constitutes the neural correlate of consciousness. My interest will focus on this proposal, and, specifically, on whether available evidence can support the idea that synchrony in neural responses may be a *necessary* and/or *sufficient* condition for consciousness.

In addition to the temporal properties of neural systems, their spatial organization is also of central concern for the neurophysiological approach to consciousness. It is increasingly clear that regions of the brain are specialized for specific psychological functions. To what extent might consciousness be considered as one such 'function'? Should we be searching for some kind of a 'consciousness centre' in a specific region of the brain?

So far, I have indicated the kinds of question that will arise in relation to the claims of those representing the neurophysiological approach to consciousness. My specific interest in the overarching transpersonal framework indicated in earlier chapters leads to a final set of questions. What relationship, if any, may be discerned between the *modus operandi* of neurophysiological systems active in conscious states and the kinds of insights we have noted from the mystical and spiritual approach? Are these realms simply too far apart to arrive at any meaningful answer? Clearly, I think not, since such relationships lie at the heart of my inquiry.

Neurophysiology meets quantum theory

> When the province of physical theory was extended to encompass microscopic phenomena, through the creation of quantum mechanics, the concept of consciousness came to the fore again: it was not possible to formulate the laws of quantum mechanics in a fully consistent way without reference to the consciousness.... The very study of the external world led to the conclusion that the content of the consciousness is an ultimate reality.
>
> (Wigner, 1972, pp. 133–4)

Quantum mechanics has radically challenged the view of reality implicit in everyday experience. Such experience generally encourages us to think of an objective world of material forms, each of which occupies a precise spatial locus and changes over time in defined continuous ways. Moreover, we take it for granted that the objective world exists, independently of ourselves, in a form analogous to that in which we experience it. All this is challenged by quantum mechanics.

The quantum perspective teaches us that, prior to an act of observation, the microelements of matter and their properties exist in a state of *superposition*. They cannot be described as waves or particles, but as probabilities of becoming either; they cannot be described as being in one locus or another, but as probabilities of ending up in one or the other. This perspective differs fundamentally from that of classical physics – and that of our everyday experience of the macro world of tables, chairs and other objects. For classical physics, an entity occupies a *discrete* position. The states adopted by such entities are best described as *either x or y*; not as *both x and y*. The more mysterious quantum perspective implies the latter – prior to an act of observation, both states are combined in superposition. Schrödinger, one of the pioneers of quantum mechanics, developed wave equations that indicate the potential state of a subatomic particle from the initial time of some particular event occurring until the time at which the particle is observed. The mathematical formulation of the particle's potential state is known as the *wave function*. Accordingly, at the time of observation there is said to be a *collapse of the wave function*. For example, prior to an act of observation, the wave function might describe a particle as being both inside *and* outside a box (that is, in probabilistic terms associated with each potential state). Clearly, however, when I observe the particle it is in an unambiguous position – it is, for example, unambiguously inside the box and not outside of it. The wave function has collapsed.

This brief description raises two points of interest. First, since 'observation' implies consciousness (that is, there can be no observation without an 'observer' in whom the events being observed reach consciousness), consciousness itself becomes an integral factor in the description of the physical world. From this viewpoint, a monist position that holds consciousness to be an *epiphenomenon* of matter cannot be sustained in our post-quantum world. More favoured by the implications of quantum theory are those participatory views that stress the fundamental integration between consciousness and matter. Second, the superposition of states pre-observation suggests a feature of preconscious processing. Consciousness is characterized by the presence of singular, discrete entities. I am conscious of the pen in my hand; and it is clearly a pen and not a pencil, or any other associated entity. I am similarly conscious of a thought to the effect that I could use a cup of coffee; and the thought is not jumbled with ideas of hunger or of fancying a glass of whisky.[1] However, the precision of the percepts and thoughts seems to arise only at the conscious level. Preconsciously, the possibilities in the just-forming image or

thought may be present in superposition. As I shall consider in
discussing the cognitive approach (Chapter 5), there is indeed good
evidence for such *multiplicity* in preconscious processing.
Consciousness demands the *either ... or* state; preconsciousness
may embrace the multiplicity in the *both ... and* state.

The major – and, as yet, unanswered – question in this discussion of observation and the physical world concerns the causal
sequence involved. Does consciousness cause the wave function to
collapse, or does the collapse of the wave function give rise to
consciousness? The first viewpoint, known as 'subjective reduction' or 'subjective collapse' (Penrose, 1997), may be traced to the
thinking of von Neumann in the 1930s, and was examined more
fully by Wigner in the 1960s. For Wigner (1972), it is the
observer's consciousness that determines the post-collapse state.
Wigner has been criticized for the dualist form of this argument,
since it seems to suggest that human consciousness stands *apart*
from the physical reality that it brings into actualization. He has
also been criticized for his anthropocentric emphasis. If human
consciousness can bring about the collapse, what about the
consciousness of other creatures? For Wigner, it seems that only
human consciousness has this property of instantiating physical
actuality, yet it is difficult to see why this should be the case. Moreover, if, as Wigner suggests, *my* consciousness gives rise to *my*
world, then how do I know that *your* world is the same as *my*
world? Indeed, it is for a similar reason that the *many-worlds* solution has been proposed for the conundrum posed by the collapse
of the wave function. According to this many-worlds interpretation, the electron-in-potential, that is, pre-collapse, both inside and
outside a box would be, post-collapse, inside the box in one world
and outside the box in another. Given the scale of events in our
universe and the enormous number of possibilities existing at any
given moment, the many-worlds solution must entail a myriad of
parallel universes. The sheer enormity of the proposed solution is
mind-boggling, and leads to much doubt as to its viability.

Returning to Wigner's view, the problems of dualism and
anthropocentrism become resolved if we conceive of consciousness, or the power of observation, as an intrinsic property of the
universe. My *individual* consciousness may simply be a part of a
larger consciousness (not limited to humans) that is ultimately
responsible for the collapse of the wave function. Although the
features of the world that I tend to perceive and to which I give

prominence may differ from those that you perceive, the world itself – brought into actualization by the collective drive to observation – is one and the same. Mindell (2000) argues that this collective power of observation derives from '*the tendency of nature to reflect upon herself*, to be aware, to lucidly notice otherwise invisible events' (p. 188, italics original).

The second viewpoint regarding the relation between the collapse of the wave function and consciousness assumes that the collapse occurs due to some intrinsic feature of the quantum state, and that consciousness is generated *by* the collapse. Penrose (1997) favours this view and names this 'objective reduction' or 'objective collapse'. He suggests that the pre-collapse state of superposition reaches a critical threshold at which it can no longer be sustained, due to the force of quantum gravity. Each possible state entails a distinct space–time curvature, and it is the juxtaposition of these that is unsustainable. The state therefore spontaneously collapses. Hameroff and Penrose (1996; see also Hameroff, 2001) argue that consciousness arises as a consequence of this objective reduction (OR) as it occurs in specific brain cell structures, known as *microtubules*. This theory may be classed as *pan-protopsychism*, in that it proposes that the fundamental potential for consciousness ('proto-consciousness') is a property of all pre-collapse quantum states. However, according to Hameroff and Penrose, only the microtubules in neurones are specialized to enable the proto-consciousness to become actualized as discrete conscious states. Although proto-consciousness is universal, consciousness and experience are not. For this reason, the theory differs from panpsychism or pan-experientialism.

Quantum events and synapses

All that has been written in the preceding section, with the exception of the reference to microtubules, has no direct relevance to the neurophysiological approach to consciousness. There has certainly been much speculation surrounding the possible relevance of quantum theory to consciousness, but our interest in this chapter is focused on those features of neurones, and their interconnections, that may advance our understanding of consciousness. Relevant theories, therefore, are those that propose neurophysiological sites for the occurrence of key quantum effects.

Beck and Eccles (1992) have advanced a model of quantum phenomena in the brain that is focused on synapses in the cerebral

cortex. Synapses are critical in the overall logic of neuronal function, since they are responsible for integrative action. Neurones
themselves, once triggered, have no 'choice' whether to conduct an
impulse or not. It is only in the balance of activation via synapses
that we can envisage any possibility of 'choice' within the system.
Of course, the notion of 'choice' here is necessarily vague, since it
is difficult to see how a physically determined system can offer the
potential for the kind of meaningful choice we intuitively associate
with free will and consciousness. Beck and Eccles specifically
invoke quantum phenomena at the pre-synaptic membrane in
order to attempt to accommodate the notion that choice, or
'mental intention', influences the physical system.

The problem here is that it is difficult to see exactly how the
proposed quantum events are, in fact, influenced by the mental
intent. The authors are correct in asserting that activation of a
synapse critically depends on the release of a neurotransmitter in the
kinds of micro quantities to which the principles of quantum
mechanics may apply. The difficulty of logically explaining how a
detached mind might pull the neural strings of the brain is, however,
not essentially eased by introducing probabilistic quantum terms.
The explanatory gap remains.

Beck and Eccles' proposed solution is grafted onto the interactive
dualist position espoused by Eccles (for instance, 1980, 1989). For
Eccles, the mind is autonomous but interacts with the brain via the
postulated quantum effects. More specifically, mind units, or
'psychons', interpenetrate neural units, or 'dendrons', effecting a
shift in the probability of release of the neurotransmitter in the
process of _exocytosis_. Exocytosis is the process whereby tiny
amounts of neurotransmitter are released from the presynaptic
membrane into the synaptic gap. It occurs when the membrane of
the neurotransmitter containers, or _vesicles_, fuses with the cell
membrane, thereby discharging their contents. This release of
neurotransmitter is the critical variable in the electrochemical activity of the brain, sine it determines the probability of response in the
postsynaptic cell. It is no exaggeration to suggest that the entire
course of brain activity ultimately hangs on all the myriad individual processes of exocytosis. There is therefore every reason to
consider exocytosis as central to speculation about the possible brain
dynamics relating to consciousness, as in Beck and Eccles' theory.

The theory proposes that quantum phenomena at the microsite
of the presynaptic membrane provide '_the chance_ for the mental

intention to select *by choice*' (Eccles, 1989, p. 191, italics original), whether or not a packet of neurotransmitter is released. The problem is that Eccles gives no convincing explanation of *how* such choice is effected. Beck (2001) discusses a possible *quantum trigger mechanism*, but there is still something of a missing link in establishing how alternative outcomes are determined. He suggests that the quantum trigger produces the potential for alternate outcomes, but it is left for the 'mind' to somehow choose the outcome.

It will be evident from these details that the theory comes under the category of 'subjective reduction', as detailed above. Consciousness, or the mind, is primary; whereas effects via quantum phenomena are secondary. In principle, the theory exemplifies the notion of the mind constituting a probabilistic field of some kind, an idea that has found expression in a number of theories of the mind-brain relationship (Libet, 1994; McFadden, 2002; Popper *et al.*, 1993).

Quantum events and microtubules

Hameroff and Penrose (1996) focus on microtubules for a variety of reasons. The microtubules form part of the sub-cellular skeleton – the *cytoskeleton* – responsible for many features of a cell's activities. In particular, in neurones they regulate and maintain the function of synapses, and therefore the above arguments for the role of synapses in the interface between consciousness and quantum phenomena apply equally to microtubules. Moreover, the authors argue that microtubules comprise an information-processing system *within* neurones. Protein sub-units of microtubules, compromising molecules of *tubulin*, may respond to intra-cellular excitation and function effectively as rapid switching devices. There is good reason to believe that information processing, albeit at a crude level, underlies the abilities of single-celled organisms to react to stimuli and learn appropriate responses. Given that, in this case, such processing clearly operates intra-cellularly, we should not rule out the potential for such intra-cellular processing within the brains of higher organisms. Such a possibility significantly increases the processing capacity of the brain by comparison with what would be available were computation to rely on synapses alone. Hameroff (2001) notes that conventional estimates of the human brain's computational level, based on neuronal processing via synapses, cite 10^{17} bit states per second. Were microtubules to be the fundamental processing elements, this estimate would rise to 10^{27} bit states per second.

However, the possible increase in processing capacity does not of itself have any bearing on the question of how consciousness arises. It is in relation to the postulated effects of quantum gravity on tubulin in the microtubules that Hameroff and Penrose arrive at their theory of consciousness. These are considered to constitute, as it were, the missing link between the micro and macro level, the former ruled by quantum logic and the latter by the logic of classical physics. Tubulin exists in at least two conformations (that is, molecular arrangements), α and β. The authors propose that *both* conformations are present during the pre-collapse stage of superposition. At the threshold for objective reduction, collapse of the wave function results in each molecule adopting a fixed alternative, either α or β. They propose that the phase during which the proteins exist in both conformations in superposition corresponds to the preconscious stage of information processing, and that the subsequent post-collapse condition is equated with the conscious stage.

The truly fundamental question in all this is whether quantum theory offers any kind of resolution to the explanatory gap. For the present, we have to reserve judgement on this question since there is no consensus amongst those well versed in quantum theory itself. It remains unclear as to how quantum phenomena may either cause (objective reduction), or be caused by (subjective reduction), consciousness at specific brain sites. Nevertheless, for many, there is something attractive, even reassuring, in the notion of a universal proto-consciousness somehow seeking its full actualization in consciousness. In its anthropocentric formulation, it is an idea that gives human beings a role on the widest stage of all. Goswami (1993) optimistically asserts that the 'brain-mind' is 'the place where the self-reference of the entire universe happens. *The universe is self-aware through us*' (p. 190, italics original). This echoes Jung's earlier assertion that the challenge of bringing unconscious contents into consciousness makes humankind the 'second creator of the world.... Human consciousness created objective existence and meaning, and man found his indispensable place in the great process of being' (Jung, 1963/1967, pp. 284–5). Reassuring, maybe ... but is there sufficient evidence?

The brain's code

Binding mechanisms

Over the past 15 years, the *binding question* has stimulated neuro-physiological research in areas relevant to consciousness studies. This question concerns the code whereby brain cells signal to each other that elements to which they are responding relate to a given object in the world. Consider Figure 4.1, which illustrates the manner in which visual neurones are thought to respond to visual stimuli. In the figure, the features of the woman are depicted as triggering the neurones represented by open circles, and those of the cat trigger the neurones represented by closed circles. The binding question asks how it is that the neurones become assembled into the correct groups. That is, how does the brain 'know' that a neurone responding to, say, an edge of the cat's tail should be grouped with one responding to a feature in the cat's leg, and not with a neurone responding to the woman's arm, and so on?

The answer to this question has come through research into the temporal relationships between the electrical activity of different neurones. As depicted in the figure, those neurones that are responding to features from a common object (for example, the cat) fire in phase synchrony with each other. The responses of these neurones are out of phase with the neurones responding to the features of a different object. Put simply, on the basis of this temporal code, the neurones align to signal the presence of objects in the outside world.

A considerable body of research underpins this schematic depiction of *binding* in neural systems. A research group led by Wolf Singer began to generate the evidence in the late 1980s. An initial study, for example, demonstrated that cells in the visual region of the brain responded in phase if, and only if, they were being triggered by features deriving from the same visual object (Gray *et al.*, 1989). As I commented in a work published at that time (Lancaster, 1991), these pioneering studies suggested the basis of a major feature of the brain's code. Subsequent studies have indicated that this kind of phase synchrony, in what is known as the gamma band (30 to 80Hz) of resonance frequency, signals relationships between neurones within and across all sensory modalities, and is strongly implicated when connections are being established between a current sensory input and related

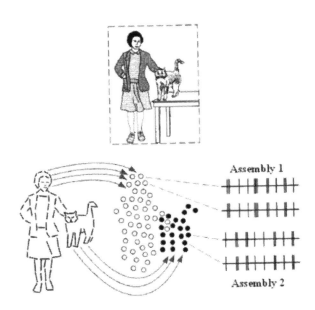

FIGURE 4.1 Diagram to illustrate the suggested role for neuronal synchronization in binding. It is assumed that objects are represented in the visual cortex by assemblies of synchronously firing neurones. In this example, the woman and her cat would each be represented by one such assembly (indicated by open and filled symbols, respectively). These assemblies comprise neurones which detect specific features of visual objects (such as, for instance, the orientation of contour segments) within their receptive fields (lower left). The relationship between the features can then be encoded by the temporal correlation among these neurones (lower right). The model assumes that neurones which are part of the same assembly fire in synchrony, whereas no consistent temporal relation is found between cells belonging to different object representations.
Reproduced from Engel *et al.* (1997), with permission of Oxford University Press.

representations in memory (for recent reviews, see Engel and Singer, 2001; Singer, 1999, 2000).

What is of primary interest for our present discussion is the proposal that such neural binding may underlie consciousness itself (Crick and Koch, 1990; Engel and Singer, 2001). This hypothesis derives from circumstantial evidence to the effect that binding and consciousness share key parameters, and from specific evidence concerning the patterns of neural synchrony which relate to animal awareness.

The circumstantial evidence largely derives from two ideas: the relationship between consciousness and attention and the supposed unity of consciousness. There can be little argument with the proposition that attention is directly related to consciousness. As William James asserted over a century ago, whatever is attended to becomes the focus of consciousness. So, for Crick and Koch, mechanisms underpinning attention are likely also to be implicated in consciousness. Niebur, Hsiao and Johnson (2002) point out that many studies have shown that attentional selection of an input to the brain is specifically signalled by mechanisms of synchrony. However, despite Crick and Koch's enthusiasm for proposing neural binding as the presumed basis of consciousness, it does not directly follow from the evidence gathered by Niebur *et al.* that synchrony is the *vehicle* of consciousness. As Damasio (2000) writes, 'Attention is as necessary for consciousness to occur as having images is. But attention is not sufficient for consciousness to occur, and is not the same as consciousness' (p. 113). The most that may be asserted is that synchrony may play a critical role in the brain's ability to control what enters consciousness.

The second part of the circumstantial case for the hypothesis that consciousness depends on neuronal binding arises from the supposed unity of consciousness. This idea derives from the introspective assertion that we do not experience consciousness as being in any way fractionated. An object always appears single and unified in consciousness, which may suggest that the same processes that give rise to that unitary quality in the percept also give rise to consciousness itself. As Crick and Koch argue, the binding of neuronal activities triggered by the object does not serve to add any specific information to that already given by the activation of the neurones themselves. Their proposal is that the binding serves to generate what is actually additional to the features – consciousness. And, of course, such an argument is not restricted to a particular percept, but extends to embrace the idea of consciousness as a whole. The hallmark of consciousness, so they assert, is precisely this sense of unity. I am one and continuous, and my conscious life is unified.

Unfortunately, there are reasons for doubting this confidence in the unitary nature of consciousness. As noted in Chapter 3, the introspective tradition in Buddhism casts considerable doubt on the substance behind this sense of a unified self at the centre of a unified consciousness. Moreover, the evidence of cognitive neuroscience is itself equivocal on this point. As discussed in Chapter 1, Zeki and Bartels (1999), drawing from a wide grasp of research in cognitive neuroscience, question the belief in the unity of consciousness, stating that 'this unity is not at all apparent to us' (p. 237).

In any case, circumstantial evidence alone is clearly inadequate for a substantive theory of consciousness. Such evidence is, however, supplemented by experimental work on animals. We cannot know directly whether an animal is conscious or not, so conclusions from this work depend on assuming parallels between humans and animals. The critical studies examine neural activity in circumstances paralleling those in which a human would experience no visual awareness. Two specific scenarios have been studied. In one, the animal has an *amblyopic* eye, roughly paralleling a squint or lazy eye in the human case. In the human case, the visual input from the lazy eye is suppressed and remains outside of visual awareness. The second scenario involves *binocular rivalry*, a situation in which each eye is presented with a different image. Again, in the human parallel, one of the two images is suppressed such that only the image from one of the eyes reaches visual awareness. In both scenarios, the studies on animals have recorded the neural activity to both the suppressed and the non-suppressed images. The results indicated that both images gave rise to activity in individual neurones, but that phase synchrony was present only for those neurones responding to the non-suppressed image. The fact that individual neurones responded to the suppressed image implies that these responses on their own were not correlated with the presence of consciousness. It was evidently the presence of phase synchrony that differentiated between the two images, suggesting that such synchrony somehow correlates with the visual signals reaching consciousness. These, and similar studies, are reviewed by Engel and Singer (2001), who conclude that neuronal binding mechanisms constitute a critical component of the neural correlate of consciousness.

There are major grounds, however, for doubting the simple conclusion that phase synchrony provides a mechanism for consciousness. First, many studies on animals demonstrating phase synchrony among groups of neurones have been conducted under anaesthetic. Indeed, a recent study (Vanderwolf, 2000) found that the amplitude of neural activity in the gamma band was higher during the anaesthetized state than during the normal waking state. It appears, therefore, that phase synchrony is just as much present in the absence of consciousness as it is when the animal is conscious.[2]

Second, studies on humans have cast doubt on the simplistic linking of the presence of phase synchrony with consciousness. Revonsuo *et al.* (1997) demonstrated that increased activity in the gamma band occurs some 300 to 500 ms (milliseconds) prior to a visual stimulus entering awareness. They recorded EEG activity while participants were viewing a random dot stereogram. In this form of stereogram each eye is presented with only a meaningless array of dots. However, the two 'random' arrays have been carefully structured such that a three-dimensional figure will be perceived when the images from the left and right eyes are fused in the brain. In effect, a random dot stereogram is a rather more sophisticated version of the 'magic eye' type of pictures that most people have seen. As with the magic eye pictures, it takes some time before one is able to perceive the 'hidden' image. Revonsuo *et al.* computed the power in the gamma band during the time that participants were attempting to perceive the three-dimensional hidden image. As already mentioned, an increase in power occurred not when the percept was seen, but up to half a second beforehand. From this study it seems that phase synchrony (presumed to be indicated by the increased power in the gamma band) is connected with the construction of the unified percept, but not with consciousness of it. Phase synchrony may be *necessary* for consciousness of the visual input, but not *sufficient* in itself for consciousness.

Levels of binding?

Revonsuo (1999) rightly points out that there is some confusion in current discussions on the subject of binding. In an approach that bears some similarities with my own, he recognizes that there are three different levels to which the binding problem applies. It is important to recognize the differences in the nature of the questions being asked at each level, and in the explanatory structures relevant to each. Most importantly, he reminds us that answers to the questions pertaining to one, or even two, of the levels may give only the semblance of an answer to the third. The first level is that of neural mechanisms, where the problem concerns the integration of single neurone activity into functional groups. At the second level, that of cognitive mechanisms, the problem is to understand how the results of a multitude of distributed modular processes are integrated and unified. How, that is, does the cognitive system generate unified images in perception and memory? Revonsuo's third level concerns the phenomenal unity of consciousness. Features at this level may not immediately map onto those at lower levels. For example, although it is true that I am conscious of particular unified objects and thoughts, the primary quality of my consciousness is that of presence, and of an ongoing holistic inter-course between my body, my self and my world. It remains unclear as to why neural binding might give rise to that sense of presence.

In fact, a yet broader perspective may be introduced by considering the fourth level I introduced in Chapter 1. Are there spiritual and mystical connotations of binding and resonance? In fact, the idea of resonance as a fundamental property of the cosmos is one that truly transcends the particularities of diverse traditions. For example, it finds expression in the Pythagorean view of sound as a primary quality underlying harmony and proportion in the universe. Pythagoras even claimed to have heard the 'harmony of the spheres', although not with normal hearing. In this cosmic sense, sound is the primary resonance that maintains the cosmos. A Vedic source tells us that *vāc*, a term that comes to mean 'speech' but conveys more deeply the communicative essence of sound, 'is the imperishable one, the firstborn of the cosmic order, the mother of the Vedas, the navel of immortality' (Holdrege, 1996, p. 48). The *Zohar* sees in the first word of Genesis, *bereshit*, an anagram of *shir ta'ev* 'a song of desire', enabling it to suggest that the whole of creation is a resonant song, mirrored and expanded by that of the angels in the heavenly hierarchy (*Zohar Hadash, Bereshit*, 5d).[3]

We may perhaps think of phase synchrony in neural systems as merely one level of this grandiose scheme. It would constitute a particular expression of a more universal role for resonance in bringing about alignment, or unification, within systems. From this point of view, phase synchrony does not cause consciousness, but it constitutes the code which enables the brain to engage with the consciousness which pervades the whole. The seeming unity of phenomenal consciousness is but a reflection of the unity of the whole, or, from a theistic point of view, of God.

Central to our understanding of the physical nature of the universe is the governing principle of entropy – indicating that dissipation and the tendency to disorder is fundamental. A useful global perspective on consciousness may involve viewing it as the complement to entropy. Consciousness reflects a drive to *coherence*, equally as fundamental as that of entropy. Phase synchrony in neural systems may be understood to be an expression of this drive as it operates within the brain. At the other end of the scale, mystics seek a higher degree of coherence through 'cosmic consciousness'. At all levels, the drive is evident as a dynamic towards alignment with larger structures, achieved through some form of resonance. The neurone becomes part of an assembly, unified by synchronous activation. At the cognitive level, the mental representation of some entity becomes situated within a larger scale ordering of reality – an egocentric map of the world. And, at the mystical level, the self seeks to annul itself by merging with the universal All-Self. This mystical goal is frequently depicted as a resonance of some kind between the individual human and the cosmic essences. The 'harmony of the spheres' is not simply referring to some kind of symbolic inter-planetary note of accord, but depicts the human potential for engagement through resonance with the cosmos. The microcosm becomes *tuned* to the macrocosm through resonance. In most spiritual traditions, the *breath* provides a key focus for experiencing this sense of a rhythmic connection to a larger-scale presence. 'Breath is the basis of the world above and the world below' (*Zohar* 2 59a), and it is through the rhythm of breathing that we can know, at a deep level, the rhythm of creation.

Von der Malsberg (1997) regards coherence as the defining feature of consciousness. He proposes that the greater the degree of coherence across regions of the brain, the 'higher' the state of consciousness. Von der Malsberg's use of the term 'higher' in this context means more alert, more focused, and, of course, more coherent. A state of 'highest consciousness', as he puts it, would be characterized by global order throughout the mind and brain. The studies of phase synchrony have been limited for technical reasons to relatively small-scale groupings of neurones. Von der Malsberg's scheme is broader in scale, envisaging whole brain systems phase-locked to each other, thereby making organized information available throughout the brain. Again, the picture is readily extrapolated to one that would sit easily with the more mystical outlook on reality. The resonance responsible, in von der Malsberg's theory, for global coordination within the brain might extend to realms beyond the brain. Van Lommel (2002) has suggested that the brain resembles 'a kind of receiver (interface) for consciousness and memories, like TV, radio or mobile telephone'. Were such a view substantiated, intra-cerebral phase locking could be envisaged as a physical correlate of a more fundamental 'tuning in' which operates at non-physical levels.

Van Lommel arrived at his speculation following a study of near-death experiences (NDEs) amongst cardiac arrest patients (van Lommel *et al.*, 2001). A number of these patients reported having NDEs during periods when their EEG recordings were flat, indicating that the brain was apparently not functioning. Parallels may be drawn with cases of NDEs in the blind studied by Ring and Cooper (1999). These authors drew attention to two critical observations. The first was that many of the blind individuals studied, even those who had been blind from birth, asserted that they were able to 'see' during the experience. The second crucial observation was that in some cases such 'sight' seemed to give information that could not have been gleaned through normal means. Regarding the first observation, it has to be recognized that the claim of having 'seen' does not of itself imply that *visual* perception occurred. There may have been a kind of preconscious mixing of the senses, a suggestion to which I will return later in Chapter 5. It is the second observation that is most relevant here, for it led the authors to conceive of some kind of extra-sensory awareness along the lines van Lommel proposes. Ring and Cooper assert that their evidence points towards there being a *transcendent* source of consciousness.

I shall return later, in Chapter 8, to arguments relating to the possible transcendent origin of consciousness. For now, my interest lies in the provocative parallel between what science can reveal about the brain code and more mystical notions of resonance and binding operating at a level beyond the brain (Lancaster, 1999). A potent symbol of binding is that of the *knot*, which takes on transcendental significance in a number of spiritual and mystical traditions (Eliade, 1952/1991). The thirteenth-century Jewish mystic, Abraham Abulafia, draws extensively on the symbolism of knots to expound his distinctive form of language mysticism. From his study of Abulafia's works, Idel (1988a) has concluded that 'the process of loosening and tying is identified with enlightenment'

(p. 136). The knots that have to be untied are those binding us to objects of this world – perhaps equating to the role of neural binding in identifying and categorizing images. The re-tying entails establishing connection to the highest level, that of the divine:

> Man is [tied] in knots of world, year and soul in which he is tied in nature, and if he unties the knots from himself, he may cleave to Him who is above them.... Therefore, when he becomes accustomed to the [meditative way of] separateness, he will strengthen [his] seclusion and connectedness [to the divine] and know how to unify the Name [of God].
>
> (Abulafia, cited in Idel, 1988a, p. 135, translation amended slightly)

The detail of Abulafia's distinctive approach to language in his mystical practice will occupy us in Chapter 7. Suffice it to suggest here that the knot symbolism serves to illustrate the way in which the ego is enmeshed with *schemata*, or psychological structures, that comprise our knowledge of the mundane world. Untying these knots from these worldly schemata, and re-tying them in relation to the divine Name, may equate to a psychological process of embedding our cognitive processes in a higher, less restrictive context.[4] Our psychological world is structured and conditioned most powerfully by language, and the quest to transcend the limitations of that structure may be realized by working with the very instrument of its conditioning – language. As Idel remarks, Abulafia's approach represents 'an attempt to transcend [language] by deconstructing language as a communicative instrument ... which ... would lead the mystic beyond the normal state of consciousness' (Idel, 1989b, p. xi).

Re-entry...

The neural system that gives rise to neural phase synchrony must involve a dynamic interaction between 'higher' and 'lower' levels in the processing hierarchy. Phase synchrony has been recorded amongst neurones in the first levels of the visual cortex in the brain. It is logical to assume that their temporal alignment comes about only after neurones higher in the processing system have generated the hypothesis that the responses of those first-level neurones should be attributed to a unified object.[5] As I conceptualized it in an earlier work (Lancaster, 1991), we may envisage that the lower neurones signal to higher regions that a specific set of features is present in the array in front of the eyes. The higher level, where memory readout operates, suggests that this set of features may indicate that such-and-such an object – a pen, for example – is present.[6] The higher level modulates the lower level activity in an attempt to ascertain whether the incoming signals could indeed match those associated with a pen. Such modulation is presumably what is observed as phase synchrony. That is, the matching of lower to higher levels is signalled when phase synchrony is achieved.

The sequence of events presumed to be involved in this way is modelled in Figure 4.2 (see also, Lancaster, 1991, p. 44). The stages may best be understood when thinking about the way we perceive under unclear conditions. For example, when seeing something in the distance at night we may become mindful of the stages involved: first, we detect the basic elements of the object; second, we find ourselves checking what those elements might comprise – maybe it's a cat, or perhaps a bush blowing in the wind; and, third, we check back in relation to the proposed object – does the way in which the elements are moving match what I know of a cat's pattern of movement and so on? Under clearer conditions, the 'stages' become indistinct, for recognition happens so quickly. Nevertheless, we may presume that perceptual recognition of the object comes about through a similar sequence of stages.[7] To take the example in Figure 4.2, if the pen were clearly visible, and the situation in which I am seeing it would naturally have led me to expect to see a pen, we may envisage that the oscillatory responses of input neurones and higher-order memory neurones would align practically immediately.[8] A meaningful, resonant pattern would rapidly be established.

Grossberg (1999) has proposed a model with many similarities to the foregoing. His *adaptive resonance theory* (ART) proposes that all conscious states are resonant states of the brain. Brain resonance is considered to result from the matching of data between *bottom-up* and *top-down* processing. Bottom-up processing (equivalent to the left-hand stages in Figure 4.2) establishes the categories relating to the input, and top-down processing (equivalent to the right-hand stages in Figure 4.2) filters the learned expectations connected with the categories. Grossberg proposes that if a mismatch results between these two processing streams, a memory search for a different, and potentially more appropriate, category

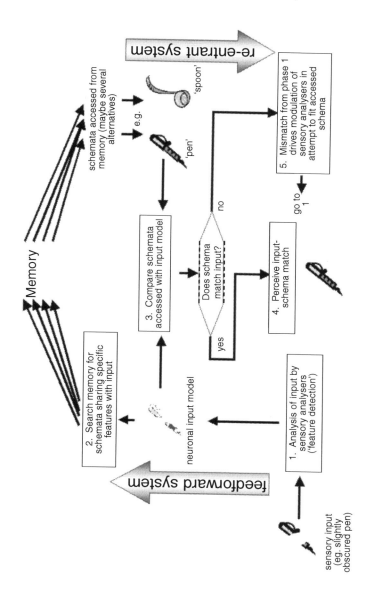

FIGURE 4.2 A psycho-physiological model of stages in perception (based on Lancaster, 1991; see text)

is initiated. The model depicted in Figure 4.2 makes the same proposal (for detail, see Lancaster, 1991). My model assumes that modulation of sensory analyzers resulting from a mismatch (stage 5) will eventuate in a second iteration of stage 2, that is, a renewed search of the memory for schemata sharing features with the input model.

Evidence supporting these models comes from several sources. First, the models explain a wealth of psychological data related to perception – data that imply, as Wittgenstein emphasized, that 'seeing is seeing as' (Gregory, 1990). Many classic psychological studies demonstrate that expectancy plays a determining role in what we see or hear. When people are shown playing cards in which the colours have been changed (hearts and diamonds in black, clubs and spades in red), they generally fail to perceive the error. Children from poor backgrounds overestimate the size of coins by comparison with richer children. And what we see when shown an ambiguous figure can be influenced by a prior word or picture selected to emphasize one of the two alternatives in the figure. These kinds of demonstrations indicate the role of interpretation in the act of perception, but they do not of themselves rule out a more unidirectional perceptual process than that suggested by the above models. The data are compatible with a theory suggesting that the interpretative process may come at the end of a one-way, hierarchical perceptual system.

However, reasons for rejecting such a one-way view of perception, in favour of the more interactive scheme depicted in Figure 4.2, may be found in the evidence derived from studies of the neuroanatomy and the physiology of perceptual systems. These studies strongly oppose the conception of the system as being one-way, or *feedforward* only. Rather they emphasize the role of *re-entrance*. What characterizes brain systems is their interactive nature whereby neurones from 'higher' areas project back onto the 'lower' regions – forming re-entrant pathways. This pattern is present throughout the sensory systems: the retina and cochlear, for example, receive *efferent* fibres from the brain as well as sending *afferent* fibres to the brain. The feedforward system of fibres emerging from the sense organ relays in the thalamus in the mid-brain, before projecting further fibres from the thalamus onward to the cortex (in the case of vision, for example, to the visual regions at the back of the brain). Yet, there are, in fact, more fibres projecting in the opposite direction – from the cortical visual regions back to the thalamus. Similarly, those areas to which V1 – the first region of visual cortex to receive the feedforward signals – projects also send re-entrant fibres back to V1. Overall, the neuroanatomical arrangement:

> [c]onstitutes a powerful means by which a target [higher] area not only can influence the outputs of currently active cells in the source [lower] area but also can selectively sensitize or inhibit other neighboring cells to modulate future incoming signals.
>
> (Di Lollo *et al.*, 2000)

In fact, this highly interactive pattern in the connectivity of neural systems suggests why the binding problem had been such a conundrum in the first place. It had been thought that we would find the neural basis for perception of objects at the highest levels in what were conceived as being primarily feedforward systems. The specific site representing the endpoint of a processing stream would constitute some kind of 'object recognition device'. The problem was that no locations of this kind could be found. Despite extensive mapping of brain regions involved in sensory systems, especially those concerned with vision, nothing remotely resembling a *terminus* could be identified (Zeki and Bartels, 1999). There is no place where it all comes together and where the 'higher level' interpretation and perceptual recognition might occur. The binding problem arose historically due to the frustrated quest to find such pinnacles of the presumed hierarchical system. It was only when the overemphasis on the spatial dimension (that is, searching exclusively for a brain locus) was replaced by interest in the interactive spatial and temporal aspects of brain function that the brain code began to be realistically deciphered. Today, as Llinás (1993) puts it, 'brain function is conceived as anatomically dispersed over specific sensory and motor maps, but bound together by time, in the sense of being capable of temporal resonance' (p. 49).

The re-entrant pathways have been shown to bring about the kind of modulation of feature analyzing systems that was predicted in my 1991 model. For example, Sillito *et al.* (1994) demonstrated that neurones in the LGN, the visual relay nucleus in the thalamus, alter their responsivity to visual features following activation of re-entrant fibres from the visual cortex. Similarly, the selectivity of V1 neurones is altered by the modulating influence of re-entrant fibres from higher regions in the visual processing pathways (Lamme, 2001). As Sillito *et al.* argue, the re-entrant system seems to function in establishing the accuracy of perceptual 'hypotheses' determined at the higher level. Confirmation that the hypotheses fit the sensory data comes about via synchronization in the firing patterns at the various levels in the system.

A final source of evidence to back up the models emphasizing the role of re-entrance in perception is drawn from computer simulations. Grossberg and his colleagues (for review, see Grossberg, 1999) have run computer simulations to test the predictions of ART. The simulations successfully demonstrated that the postulated interactions between bottom-up and top-down processes in attempting to secure a match between input data and 'expectancies' can indeed generate resonant states. Edelman and his colleagues have also run successful computer simulations, supporting his contention that re-entrance brings about object recognition through binding of widespread brain regions into resonant states. As Edelman and Tononi (2000) state, the simulations support the view that 'integration is achieved not in any place but by a coherent *process*' (p. 144, italics original).

This combination of evidence drawn from three sources – psychological observations, the anatomical and physiological specification of neural perceptual pathways, and artificial simulations – gives powerful backing to the proposed role of re-entrant systems in perception. Feedforward systems generate the raw possibilities ('neuronal input model' in the terminology of Figure 4.2) upon which memory-related activity generates hypothesized matches. Re-entrant systems bring about modulations of the feedforward signal processing to establish whether or not the hypothesized memory readout actually does match the current input array. A successful match is indicated when the systems involved achieve a resonant state.

Re-entrance and consciousness

Edelman (1989; see also Edelman and Tononi, 2000; Tononi and Edelman, 1998) is persuaded of the key role played by re-entrance in the neural process necessary for what he refers to as *primary* consciousness. Primary consciousness is the immediate consciousness of events, and is distinguished from higher-order consciousness, which entails a sense of self and the ability to reflect on past and future events. However, it remains somewhat obscure why resonant states, and activity of re-entrant systems in general, should result in consciousness. How do these activities bridge the explanatory gap?

Edelman and Tononi (2000) are aware that there is a problem in simply ascribing consciousness to a specific brain site. They rightly ask, 'How could having a specific location in the brain, firing in a particular mode or at a particular frequency, or expressing a particular biochemical compound or gene, endow a neuron with the remarkable property of giving rise to consciousness?' (p. 146). However, are they correct in limiting the problem to those theories that regard consciousness as dependent on activity in a particular *location* – a neurone or specific brain site? They seem to be asserting that the *temporal* approach – stressing the role of re-entrant systems in achieving resonant states – side-steps the problem. Surely, however, the logic of questioning arguments for a *spatial* basis for consciousness applies equally to arguments proposing a more distributed and *temporal* basis in the brain. Indeed, to the extent that consciousness is viewed as having a specifically cerebral cause, proposals such as those advanced by Edelman and by Grossberg remain basically of a *spatial* nature. The 'locus' for consciousness may not be a 'specific location in the brain', but it *is* a specific location – the brain.

We cannot expect the neurophysiological approach to go beyond its accepted subject matter, however. Edelman's arguments for positioning re-entrance at the centre of a consciousness-generating neural system are reminiscent of those we saw earlier about phase synchrony and consciousness in general. Consciousness is basically integrative, unified and coherent, as is the neural system operating through the dynamic of re-entrance. Conscious states are able to differentiate between huge numbers of possible meanings in the input array. The sheer physical limitation on the number of neurones in the brain means that a spatially-based intra-cerebral system would not be capable of such achievements. However, temporal binding across widespread neuronal groups is thought to offer significantly increased potential. Finally, Edelman stresses the speed with which integration needs to operate, again proposing that the re-entrance system provides the necessary ability to integrate across wide regions rapidly.

Llinás (for instance, 1993; see also Llinás *et al.*, 1998) adduces a further reason for viewing re-entrant systems as responsible for generating consciousness. Like Edelman, his interest lies in the integrative loops (that is, feedforward and re-entrant systems) between the thalamus and cortex. He recorded a 40Hz oscillation across the brain during both waking and dreaming (REM) states, but not during non-REM sleep (Llinás and Ribary, 1993). Since consciousness is present during the first two states, but not the third, Llinás concludes that the 40Hz resonance is significantly related to consciousness. What he calls the 'thalamocortical resonant column' becomes the critical feature of the brain's functional architecture responsible for the generation of consciousness. He likens the thalamocortical system to a consciousness-generating machine. During the waking state, consciousness is connected through the senses to the environment; during the dream state, it is connected to the inner world. In both states, however, the 'machine' generates consciousness as a means for representing the reality of the images – the reality of the outer world during waking, and, in the dream state, the reality of the dream world.

Further evidence of the importance of re-entrant systems for consciousness comes from studies of the timing of activity in the brain following exposure of visual stimuli (Lamme and Roelfsema, 2000; Walsh and Cowey, 1998). In monkeys, neurones in area V1 begin to respond about 40 ms following onset of a visual stimulus, and continue to be active for some time. An area of the cortex responsible for aspects of higher-level processing, the inferotemporal cortex (IT), is triggered some 80 to 150 ms after stimulus onset. By using transcranial magnetic stimulation (TMS), which inhibits normal ongoing activity in the region to which it is applied, we have been able to study the time course of sensory and perceptual events. TMS applied to the area of V1 up to 50 ms after stimulus onset caused disruption in the subject's perception of the stimulus. The reason is not difficult to understand: such TMS presumably interferes with the feedforward signals, rendering perception impossible. What is more striking, and relevant to my discussion, is that TMS administered between 80 and 120 ms after stimulus onset also disrupted perception. These data might be explained by suggesting that the re-entrant pathway from IT to V1 becomes active during the 80 to 120 ms time window.

The point is illustrated in Figure 4.3. The foregoing data suggest that the feedforward system causes activity in V1 between 40 and 80 ms. Any disruption of V1 activity up to 50 ms effectively erases the input. The further effects are interpreted in the figure by assuming that perception of the stimulus requires a matching

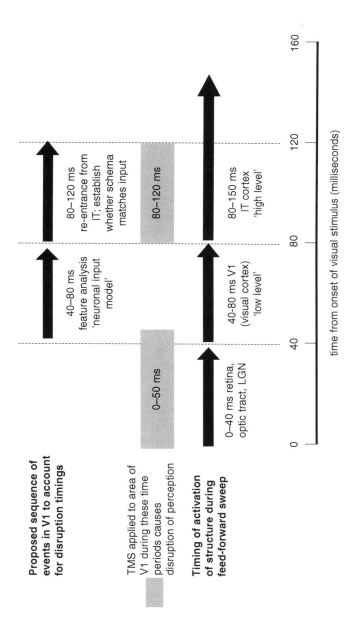

Proposed sequence of events in V1 to account for disruption timings

80–120 ms re-entrance from IT; establish whether schema matches input

40–80 ms feature analysis 'neuronal input model'

80–120 ms

0–50 ms

TMS applied to area of V1 during these time periods causes disruption of perception

Timing of activation of structure during feed-forward sweep

0–40 ms retina, optic tract, LGN

40-80 ms V1 (visual cortex) 'low level'

80–150 ms IT cortex 'high level'

time from onset of visual stimulus (milliseconds)

0   40   80   120   160

FIGURE 4.3 Time course of activation of visual structures and effects of TMS applied to area of V1

process, as described in the models discussed above. The matching process is effected via the re-entrant pathway from IT occurring at time 80–120 ms. TMS applied to V1 during this time period would disrupt the input, with the consequence that the system would be trying to effect a match with an input that is no longer present. Again, disruption during this time period would result in the stimulus failing to reach consciousness, *if we assume that consciousness is specifically tied to the matching process*. Finally, we must assume that TMS applied between 50 and 80 ms arrives too late to obliterate the initial generation of the 'neuronal input model', but too early to disrupt the matching to the reconstituted input after 80 ms.

A study by Supèr, Spekreijse and Lamme (2001) offers support for these ideas about the time course of visual activity in the brain. They recorded activity from V1 in monkeys under two conditions, one in which the monkey was aware of the stimulus triggering the V1 activity and one in which the monkey was unaware of the stimulus. Whether or not the monkey was aware of the stimulus was indicated by its eye movements – it had been trained to move its eyes speedily to a target when detected. On this basis, the authors assumed that trials resulting in visual awareness could be differentiated from those without awareness by determining whether or not appropriate eye movements occurred. The important results were that activity in V1 was identical between the two conditions up to approximately 60 ms, but after about 100 ms awareness made a difference – giving a larger response in V1. This pattern of results could be explained by assuming that awareness depends on the re-entrant input to V1 from a higher visual area, arriving at about 100 ms post-stimulus.

These lines of physiological evidence are not yet conclusive, but there is a growing consensus that the re-entrant system is critical for consciousness. Lamme and Roelfsema suggest that 'the feedforward sweep of information processing is mainly involved in pre-attentive, unconscious vision, whereas recurrent [re-entrant] processing is required for attentive vision and visual awareness' (2000, p. 577).

To move from the intricacies of millisecond and millimetre precision in these studies to the more global speculations of mysticism may seem like a move from the sublime to the ridiculous. But take it I will, for it is only by viewing these neurophysiological observations within a more global perspective that I think any headway on the hard problem of consciousness may be made. Again, despite the elegant demonstration of a seminal role for re-entrant systems, the explanatory gap remains. What is it about re-entrance that may advance our inquiry into consciousness?

A reflexive leap

[Y]ou only have to make the light circulate: that is the deepest and most wondrous secret.... [A]s soon as the light is circulating, heaven and earth, mountains and rivers, are all circulating with it at the same time.

(Wilhelm, 1962, pp. 22 and 33)

The above is from a Taoist text, the *Secret of the Golden Flower*. The text informs us that the golden flower is the light, and is 'the true energy of the transcendent great One' (p. 21). The text describes a mystical practice that seems to have considerable relevance to our discussion of re-entrance. The key to this practice is the 'backward-flowing method':

In the midst of primal transformation, the radiance of the light is the determining thing. In the physical world it is the sun; in man, the eye. The radiation and dissipation of spiritual consciousness is chiefly brought about when it is directed outward (flows downward). Therefore the Way of the Golden Flower depends wholly on the backward-flowing method.

(Wilhelm, 1962, p. 31)

One dimension of the 'backward-flowing method' entails conservation of seed, as in tantric practices. The outward flow of sexual energy is to be constrained, the energy being directed instead inwards and transformed. But the *Golden Flower* text is clearly focused on what seems to be construed as a parallel to the control of sexual energy – the energy pervading the senses. 'The seed is ... the light in crystallized form' (p. 40). When one strikes the correct balance between outward-directed, and inward-directed, vision, the light is seen and its circulation commences. The text explains that, in the appropriate meditative state, the eyes should be focused on the tip of the nose in order to encourage the desired balance – neither fully engaged with the outer world nor cut off from it entirely.

Zimmer proposes some physiological underpinnings of a practice such as this as follows:

> In seeing, hearing, smell, touch, etc., the specific stimulus is transmitted centripetally from the peripheral organs, the eye, ear, etc., to the higher centres in the brain and finally to consciousness. In the production of optical, acoustical, and other hallucinations, one must learn to transmit the specific energy in the reverse direction from the higher brain centres to the periphery.
> (Zimmer, 1960, p. 51)

But as our consideration of more recent research into perception has indicated, even normal seeing and so on entails both centripetal (feedforward) and centrifugal (re-entrant) activity. The view of a one-way, centripetal, route to consciousness is fundamentally flawed. What I believe is conveyed by the *Secret of the Golden Flower* is the role of the centrifugal pathways in consciousness itself. Given the dynamic two-way nature of our perceptual systems, understanding the basis of imagery and hallucinations is relatively straightforward. Whether I become aware of a percept of the outer world, or of an image that I know to be internally generated, or of a hallucination, is a matter of the *balance* in the system together with a marker of my *belief* in the source of the image (Lancaster, 1991). The practice of the 'circulating light' seems to entail a kind of controlled activation of re-entrant processes in vision, distilling their activity down to what is effectively the core visual experience, that of light itself.

Hunt (1984) understands the mystical experience of light as the result of a 'turning around' of the normal process of perception. The mystic becomes aware of the more primitive aspects of cognitive processes which are normally obscured in a full perceptual or thought process. In mystical states, normally preconscious processes become available to consciousness (see Chapter 3 and Figure 3.1). Hunt proposes that light is the experience of the abstract unity behind the cross modal form of schemata. The schema depicting a pen, for example, is not a structure dependent on vision alone; rather it condenses all my experience with pens into a multi-modal conglomerate of 'pen-ness'. Hunt argues that the mystic experience of light is one in which the most primitive aspect of the schema – its *noetic* quality devoid of any form – is activated. Translating this into the more neurophysiological terms

I have been considering, I am led to propose that the mystical experience of light arises when re-entrant pathways are activated without the intention of matching any specific form. Resonance in this case derives from the matching of a formless input to a schema void of content. This is reminiscent of Goethe's proposal that, 'the inner light ... emerge[s] to meet the outer light' (cited in Zajonc, 1993, p. 205).

In summary, we may speculate that these mystical ideas reinforce the view emerging from neurophysiological research that resonance between feedforward and re-entrant systems is a critical pre-requisite for consciousness. 'Backward flow' may refer to the shift in the balance achieved between the feedforward and re-entrant systems. In the non-mystical, 'normal' flow case, the driving force of perception derives from the sensory input, and the subject becomes conscious of the object when the re-entrant path effects the appropriate match. Under the 'backward flow' condition, on the other hand, the re-entrant path is operative in a manner less constrained by activity in the feedforward limb. Its mystical fruit is 'light', a term frequently synonymous with, or otherwise symbolic of, consciousness.

Neuroscience can provide evidence that resonance involving re-entrant pathways is likely to be necessary for consciousness of the external world. On its own, however, it is unlikely to furnish understanding of *why* this should be. What is this 'light', and what may be the broader significance of the reflexive basis of its generation?

The light is manifestly considered to encapsulate a holistic dimension of the world. This is clear from the *Golden Flower* text cited above, 'as soon as the light is circulating, heaven and earth, mountains and rivers, are all circulating with it at the same time'. Bohm's (1980) postulate of a holistic implicate order from which the explicate order of things and minds unfolds may be helpful here. Bohm considers consciousness to be a property of the implicate order. As it unfolds into the explicate order, it becomes actualized as experience of some specific entity or feeling; but in its primary state, it is holistic. Accordingly, we might identify the circulating light with the closest we can come to experiencing the holistic, implicate order. In mystical works, light universally carries the suggestion of *spiritual* presence, intimating that some 'higher', more inclusive dimension to things is being experienced. 'The Holy One, blessed be He is entirely light', states a midrash.[9] Wolfson

(1994) insists that this is not 'a merely theological axiom, devoid of any experiential component. On the contrary, the Presence is so characterized because it is through the phenomenon of light that the divine is rendered accessible to human experience' (p. 44).

This last idea is, I think, critical, and is worth expressing more generally. We are dealing here with a process whereby a higher actuality is 'rendered accessible' to a lower actuality. Whether we conceive of this in terms of the implicate order unfolding into the explicate, or of the divine becoming revealed to the human, the same principle is involved. And this principle may provide us with a useful approach to consciousness itself: consciousness may be understood as *the consequence of a higher actuality penetrating the domain of a lower.*

> Come and see. Through the impulse from below is awakened an impulse above, and through the impulse from above there is awakened a yet higher impulse, until the impulse reaches the place where the lamp is to be lit and it is lit ... and all the worlds receive blessing from it.
>
> (*Zohar* 1:244a)

As we noted in Chapter 1, a pillar of esoteric traditions holds that there is an ultimate correspondence between levels in creation. If, as the above extract implies, there is a principle whereby a 'lower impulse' awakens the 'higher', then we should expect to see its ramifications at all levels. This principle – which, it should be noted, is one of the most central in the whole of Kabbalah – primarily depicts the dialogue between earthly and heavenly realms, as in prayer. However, its application to the re-entrant paradigm examined above certainly accords with the tenor of kabbalistic speculation (Lancaster, in press). A number of kabbalistic texts refer to 'levels' of the brain, or the different 'brains' operative at successive levels of emanation from the Godhead. The nature of the dynamic interactions that operate between these levels is a major theme in kabbalistic literature, and the re-entrant paradigm fits aptly within this cosmic picture. The statement that the 'bottom-up impulse' awakens 'top-down influences' seems a pretty accurate description of the microcosmic state of affairs discussed above in relation to re-entrant pathways.

What, then, is the 'top-down influence' that is awakened? In the text's own terms it is light and 'blessing'. With regard to 'blessing', the essential concept is precisely that of a higher influence descending to a lower level. The Hebrew, *berakhah* ('blessing'), is related to *bereikhah*, a 'pool', and quite specifically a pool situated at a higher level than the village which it supplies with water; a 'cistern' in its original meaning. I would, accordingly, see more than a slight connection between this notion of light and blessing spreading through the worlds and my above formulation of consciousness as a higher actuality penetrating the domain of a lower. Again, in the symbolic language of the *Zohar*, the 'supernal brain' pours its influence into the 'inferior brain'.

With this excursion into mystical regions we seem to have wandered far from the neurophysiological approach, not least because terms such as 'higher' and 'lower' are difficult to define. Nevertheless, the above formulation may indeed be relevant to our earlier discussion of re-entrant systems. The key point about the re-entrant pathway is that it conveys readout from memory (see Figure 4.2). The pathway is the agent for bringing whatever is accessed at the cognitive level into the domain of the physical, or neurophysiological, sphere. However, there is no less of an explanatory gap in this context of cognition and the brain than there is with consciousness. How does *meaning* arise from mechanism? It seems to me that the 'higher' regions that are accessed by neural systems cannot themselves be merely neural. Indeed, as suggested by the above passage from the *Zohar*, there may be further levels in this interactive hierarchy. In these terms, the interaction between 'lower' and 'higher' regions of the human brain may be just the initiating step in a cascade of interactions reaching beyond the physical plane. At all levels, the same principles of operation apply: activation in the feedforward sweep, and receiving back via re-entrance. In this fashion, the brain would become a recipient of the twin 'blessings' of meaning and consciousness.

The foregoing assumes that memory cannot be reduced to the neurophysiological level, since it is presumed to be 'higher'. I define its status as being 'higher' than that of brain dynamics in two senses: first, memory is not simply the storage of data, as may operate in a computer, for example. Memory is concerned with meaning. This is an important point, to which I return below. Second, memory would be 'higher' if it were attributable to non-physical fields of some kind (Sheldrake, 1981, 1988). This, admittedly, is an unproven possibility, but the kinds of phenomena reported by Ring, mentioned above, and others (Lorimer 2001) should encourage us to keep an open mind.

The importance of *meaning* when thinking about consciousness is emphasized by Searle in his oft-quoted Chinese Room thought experiment.[10] In brief, Searle (1987, 1997) imagines being locked up in a room, and being required to act as a computer implementing a programme to answer questions in Chinese. He does not understand Chinese, but has a large repository of Chinese symbols (the database), and a rulebook written in English. He receives from outside the room questions posed in Chinese, which to him remain meaningless. But he is able to use the rulebook to select from his database of Chinese symbols appropriate responses, which he passes back to those outside the room. From the outside it appears that we have a convincing simulation of someone understanding Chinese, but of course there is no understanding inside the room, only a mechanism.

'The point of the story is to remind us of a conceptual truth that we knew all along; namely, that there is a distinction between manipulating the syntactical elements of languages and actually understanding the language at a semantic level' (Searle, 1987, p. 214). Searle's arguments have not gone unchallenged, but I see no reason to depart from his primary conclusion, and would extend the point to memory itself.[11] Memory is not an inert database, but is itself subject to processes such as indexing in relation to meaning.

Taking a global perspective on all this, we might envisage ourselves as an interface between the physical world and memory. The feedforward/re-entrant loop system ensures that the two realms are brought into relationship, that the world is invested with *meaning* and the presence of consciousness. This idea gives a spiritual twist to Velmans' (2000) *reflexive* theory of consciousness.

Velmans rejects a dualist position since he considers consciousness to be tied to brain activity. At the same time he insists on the irreducibility of first-person experiential properties of consciousness, asserting that they cannot be understood through third-person analysis of brain function. For Velmans, there is an essential complementarity between third-person accounts of those brain functions related to consciousness and first-person accounts of phenomenal experience. This complementarity is expressed through the *reflexive* projection of consciousness into the world.

In essence, the key to understanding Velmans' model depends on our answer to the question, *where is an experience?* As I look at the tree through my window, where exactly is my consciousness of the tree? In line with his emphasis on the value of first-person accounts, Velmans extrapolates from the clear fact that I experience the tree as being *out there*, in the world, to a theory of consciousness being reflexive. Since he identifies the contents of consciousness with experience, and, given that I clearly experience the tree as being in the world, the contents of consciousness themselves are *out there*, in the world. At the same time, for Velmans, consciousness is dependent on brain processes and must accordingly be *reflexively* projected into the world.

Although Velmans seems to recognize a global dimension to his theory when he writes that, 'we participate in a reflexive process whereby the universe experiences itself' (p. 233), it is not clear how this squares with his insistence on the *absolute* dependence of consciousness on brain processes. His rejection of any ontological notion of the *primacy* of consciousness is problematic (Lancaster, 2000a; Rao, 2002). As Rao puts it, 'Velmans appears to commit category mistakes when he attempts to resolve ontological issues by reducing them to epistemological concerns' (p. 64), and for this reason it remains unclear how the brain process itself generates first-person experience as he claims it does.

Harth (1993) refers to the dynamic interplay between the feed-forward and re-entrant pathways as the 'creative loop', for he rightly sees in it the basis of imagery and other creative aspects of what it is to be human. But perhaps this does not go far enough, for the interplay as it operates in the brain may be merely a sub-routine of what we might think of as a *cosmic loop*. The 'impulse from below' – stimuli entering the brain from the outer world – becomes the trigger for an influx of consciousness from a higher source. Through consciousness, the world, otherwise meaningless, is transformed into a world of meaning.

Chapter 5

Cognitive and Neuropsychological Approaches

Principles and questions

The term 'cognition' refers to *knowing*, and cognitive psychology is concerned with those processes of mind through which we know – perception, memory and thought, for example. Cognitive psychology has played a major role in the renewed interest in consciousness over the past 20 years or so. Its privileged position derives largely from its claim to harness the 'hard' techniques of experimental science in the study of the 'soft' conceptualization of processes of the mind.

It has clearly been demonstrated that cognitive processes (perception, and so on) can all function to some extent *with* or *without* consciousness. Scientific methods have been used to specify the differences between the cases: what exactly *changes* when consciousness is part of the aspect of cognition under study? The issue concerns the information-processing strategies that underlie subjective experience. How do they vary between conscious and nonconscious performance of some task? The cognitive approach shades into neuropsychology when the question is specifically extended to consideration of brain systems. The neuropsychology of consciousness asks, which brain systems (if any) are differentially activated when consciousness is, or is not, present? All these questions exemplify the method of *contrastive analysis*, which I discussed in Chapter 1.

Despite the evident power of the scientific method, we may ask whether the cognitive approach unduly *trivializes* the topic. There is much that cognitive psychology cannot be expected to achieve.

The cognitive parameters that appear to distinguish conscious from nonconscious processes involve issues such as the serial versus parallel nature of processing, or the speed of processing. Characteristically, the cognitive approach is focused on qualities such as these, which are either themselves readily measurable, or can be inferred from other, easily measurable, properties. The more fundamental questions, about qualia and the explanatory gap, for example, cannot be incorporated within the remit of cognitive science. Moreover, the cognitive approach is generally neutral, or even antagonistic, to any idea of a quest for personal transformation. Consciousness might be an effervescent 'added ingredient', but has no significance beyond its biological function (and exactly what that function might be may be hard to discern); it is the icing on the cake of nonconscious processing.

There is no space within cognitive science for a value-laden path of engaging with the hermeneutic of the unconscious, as in depth psychology. Indeed, Greenwald (1992) characterizes the 'unconscious' as revealed by cognitive science as being 'simple and dumb'.[1] It is simple since there is no evidence that nonconscious processing can engage in sophisticated analysis, and it is dumb in the sense that it appears to be able to handle only single words, or at the most simple phrases. This is, of course, a far cry from the rich kinds of aptitudes and abilities of the unconscious claimed by psychoanalysts or psychologically-oriented mystics. For Freud and Jung, for example, the unconscious is a realm of mental activity of a complexity way beyond anything demonstrated through the cognitive approach.

Despite this, there is much to learn from the cognitive approach. The approach has been primarily concerned with demonstrating the presence and extent of nonconscious processes, and investigating their role in the processing of information. Beyond the accumulation of data, the approach attempts to build logical models to advance the quest towards explanation. A process that can be effectively modelled is well on the way towards being explained. Over recent years, the approach has become strongly associated with those disciplines that have most to contribute to the substantiation of the models – artificial intelligence on the one hand and neuroscience on the other. Thus, as discussed in Chapter 4, a model might be supported by demonstrating that computer simulations actually achieve the outcomes predicted by the model (AI 'thought experiments') and/or by showing that the model is related to neural systems that actually operate in the predicted ways.

Of primary interest in my examination of the cognitive approach is the accuracy of Greenwald's characterization of the 'cognitive unconscious' as simple and dumb. Is this view itself perhaps something of a simplification? Might the experimental work in cognitive psychology indicate a more complex role for preconscious processing than Greenwald implies? And if so, what is it about normal consciousness that may operate to limit access to that complexity?

A core principle of cognitive science derives from its emphasis on *representation* (Gardner, 1987), itself largely a product of the rapport with ideas in AI. Reflecting on the *cognitive revolution* in which he played no small part, Miller describes its focus as 'the representational and computational capacities of the human mind and their structural and functional realization in the human brain' (2003, p. 144). The brain is thought to construct and manipulate representations of the external world and of the bodily and psychological self ('I'). Whilst such representations clearly must in some way involve neurones, the actual medium by means of which the representations are realized is not necessarily a primary concern for all cognitive psychologists. Those adopting the cognitive approach are mainly interested in the *logic* of representational systems. This core principle extends to the depiction of consciousness itself, which is viewed as representational by many of those for whom the cognitive approach is central (see works by Baars, Kihlstrom, Velmans and so on). The cognitive view generally holds that consciousness is always *of* something, and is to be understood as some kind of property of the representation of that something. Of course, this tenet frequently places advocates of the cognitive view at odds with those arguing that there can be states of pure consciousness (Chapter 3).

Cognitive psychology's interest in the neural systems that are presumed to actualize its models establishes its links with neuropsychology. Historically, neuropsychology was born in 1861 when Paul Broca reported on his post-mortem examination of the brain of an aphasic patient. He was able to assert a connection between a psychological state (the speech loss) and the centre for 'the motor images of words', in the brain region that came to bear his name. Of course, brain imaging techniques have vastly increased the reliability and precision in the identification of brain regions, but the principle of locating functional specialization remains the same.

Of especial note for our investigation into consciousness is 'the virtual epidemic of dissociations discovered by neuropsychologists whereby residual processing occurs in the absence of acknowledged awareness' (Weiskrantz, 1992, p. 2).[2] In a condition such as *blindsight*, to be examined below, patients appear to have no consciousness of visual material presented in a region of their visual field. Nevertheless, it has been unequivocally shown that they are able to respond to aspects of the 'unseen' visual material. There appears to be a *dissociation* between conscious and nonconscious visual processing. Research into such dissociations not only helps to specify the roles played in relation to consciousness by the various neural pathways, but also, as we shall see, offers valuable insights into the cognitive basis of consciousness.

The conscious access hypothesis

The global workspace

Baars first propounded his 'global workspace theory' in 1983. In various formulations since then, the basic tenets have remained, and the range of supporting evidence and proposed neurological foundations has developed considerably. Despite the interest in neurological evidence, however, the theory remains essentially an 'information-processing' account, in that it is concerned with how processing units gain access to the output of other units. In brief, consciousness is viewed as the means whereby such access is achieved.

The theory derives its central idea from the concept of a general problem-solving space in AI systems. Such a space functions by enabling sub-processors in the system to communicate their outputs to each other. Baars views the brain as containing a wide range of sub-processors, each of which is specialized for execution of some specific task. There are sub-processors for feature analysis, for face recognition, for comprehension of writing and so on. Each is highly specialized, achieving its allocated task through fast, efficient and automatic routines. Critically for the theory, the output of each sub-processor is not conscious. The global workspace gives the opportunity for integration amongst sub-processor outputs and for dissemination of information. Integration depends upon the 'packets' of information from individual sub-processors being introduced into the global workspace, where they become available as needed in relation to whatever specific problem is being addressed. Dissemination occurs via the 'broadcasting' of progress back to the individual sub-processors. Baars postulates that consciousness is a function of the global workspace itself and the broadcasting of information for which it is specialized. In comparison with the sub-processors, the workspace has a limited capacity. Consciousness, despite its broad integrative ability, can operate only sequentially and relatively slowly.

Baars has used various analogies to illustrate the theory. One analogy presents the global workspace as being like the podium at a conference. Experts might develop their ideas in specialized areas or meetings, but it is only when material is 'broadcast' from the podium that it can influence the whole conference. Another favoured analogy is that of a theatre. Much may go on offstage, but it is only the material onstage that reaches the audience. In both analogies, consciousness is associated with the focusing of content into one place and its being broadcast to all who might gain from it.

The theory neatly accounts for many observations about conscious versus nonconscious processing, and Baars (1996) confidently asserts that 'GW theory gives the most complete account to date of the interplay of conscious and unconscious processes in perception, imagery, action control, learning, attention, problem-solving and language' (p. 211). In a more recent article, Baars (2002) further notes that the theory's basic premise, that consciousness facilitates widespread access between otherwise independent brain functions, has been acknowledged by many researchers over the years since it was first developed, and is supported by much data arising from recent brain research.

Velmans (2000) criticizes the theory for its dehumanizing and mechanistic emphasis. There is no explanation of *why* activity in the global workspace should be conscious, merely an assertion that it is. As Velmans notes, simply *describing* the operational features of a hypothesized global workspace goes no way towards accounting for the proposed subjective experience of its contents.

The issue here is largely that of the explanatory gap, which I have already discussed. A further potential problem with the theory derives from its very strength – its broad applicability. The statement that consciousness is concerned with access of otherwise unconscious elements is practically a tautology. Is not the experiential accessing of content what we mean by 'consciousness'? All that seems to be added beyond this is a picture of the computational dynamics potentially involved. It is certainly possible, however, that the notion of access is correct but that the computational metaphor itself is misleading. We may note in this context, for example, that Penrose (1997) insists that a key property of consciousness is its *non*-computability.

Moreover, even if the notion of a global workspace of some kind is appropriate as a metaphor of consciousness, it may be too vague to be of much heuristic value. Baars seems to recognize this in his recent paper (2002) by situating the theory firmly within the framework of neuroscience. This manoeuvre appears to overcome the vagueness in a purely cognitive specification of the global workspace and its broadcasting of information. Nevertheless, consideration of the neurophysiological data claimed as evidence for the theory may suggest that Baars' approach is altogether too 'global'!

By way of illustration, consider the impressive array of research that Baars (2002) collates to indicate that more widespread brain regions are activated under conscious, in contrast to nonconscious, conditions. These data, he claims, give support to global workspace theory, since the more widespread areas associated with conscious processing presumably equate to a more *global* 'workspace'. This is fine as far as it goes, but it hardly seems surprising that the presence of consciousness is correlated with more widespread activity than that recorded when some activity occurs without consciousness. We would surely expect, on the basis of any brain-centred theory of consciousness, that becoming conscious of some event *adds* activity to that already occurring when processing was merely preconscious. What is of interest is not the bald fact that there is additional activity, but the nature of such activity, and what it suggests about the processes involved with consciousness.

The point may be exemplified by data relating to studies of visual masking. If a visual stimulus is rapidly followed by another, masking, stimulus, the subject reports no awareness of the original stimulus. The second stimulus has 'masked' the first. Despite this lack of awareness, it is clear from many studies that the original, masked stimulus (the 'prime') is processed to a reasonably high level within the visual system, since it can influence subsequent events. Thus, for example, the likelihood of a person seeing one version or another of an ambiguous picture is influenced by a masked image or word seen previously. Figure 5.1 illustrates this effect.

There has been a number of recent studies examining the brain areas active when a visual stimulus is, or is not, followed by a mask. Dehaene *et al.* (2001) found that non-masked stimuli (that is, stimuli that reach consciousness) produced higher levels of activity in those brain areas which were activated by masked (nonconscious) stimuli. Of more direct interest to the claims of Baars, the non-masked stimuli activated a wider range of areas. As indicated above, then, these data support global workspace theory – more 'global' areas are activated under the conscious condition. However, of considerably more interest than the bland equation of more widespread brain regions with a 'global work-space', is the consideration of what kind of processing strategy may be at work here. Dehaene *et al.* favour the kind of model I discussed in Chapter 4, namely one involving re-entrance. The data 'are consistent with theories that relate conscious perception to the top-down amplification of sensory information through synchronous co-activation of distant regions' (p. 757).

Indeed, the phenomenon of masking itself may be interpreted

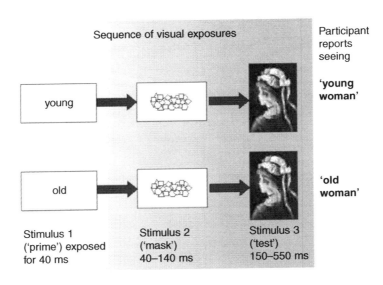

FIGURE 5.1 Typical sequence of stimuli in a study of priming using a masking stimulus

along the lines of re-entrant processing. Enns and Di Lollo (2000) survey a wide range of masking studies that have varied parameters either in the mask itself or in the attentional requirements placed on participants. The authors are led to the conclusion that masking occurs on account of a mismatch in signals between feed-forward and re-entrant pathways. According to this view, by the time the re-entrant signal engages with V1, the mask has obliterated all activity in V1 related to the original stimulus (Figure 5.2). It therefore becomes impossible for the re-entrant signal to find the match intended:

> Specifically, it is thought that the circuit actively searches for a match between a descending code, representing a perceptual hypothesis, and an ongoing pattern of low-level activity. When such a match occurs, the neural ensemble is 'locked' onto the stimulus.... By contrast, masking occurs when there is a mismatch between the re-entrant signal and ongoing activity at a lower level.
>
> (Enns and Di Lollo, 2000, p. 348)

Following the hypothesis that consciousness is introduced into information processing through the activity of re-entrant pathways, I construe the widespread activation of the brain recorded with non-masked stimuli somewhat differently than does Baars. The memory readout that generates the re-entrant activity is presumed to include a broad range of material contextually related to the original stimulus. If, for example, the stimulus were the word 'old', we might expect that memory readout would include, among other features, material related to emotional associations with ageing, maybe an image of an old relative, and/or symbolic associations such as 'valuable' or 'testament'. The attempted matching-to-input, enacted via re-entrant activity, which will have been triggered by such polymodal memory readout, would clearly cause activity in widespread brain regions, as observed. The interesting point about these proposals is not the 'workspace' idea itself, but the role that seems to be played by diverse associations to the stimulus. The broad range of associations in the memory readout does not reach consciousness. These remain *preconscious*. Consciousness arises through the actual matching process itself.[3]

I would suggest that the diverse associations triggered preconsciously by the input play a significant role in establishing the

Postulated brain events

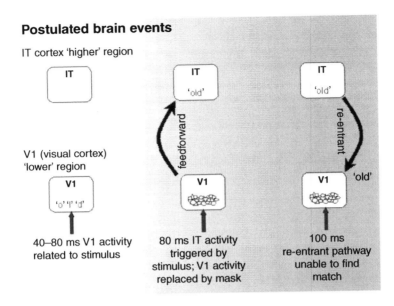

Stimulus sequence

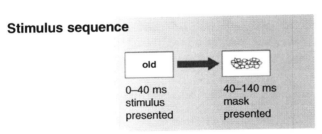

FIGURE 5.2 Postulated role of re-entrant pathways in masking (Adapted from Lamme, 2001)

meaning of the item perceived. A complex range of associations, such as the above examples in the case of the word 'old', are inevitably in the background of my sense of the word's meaning. This is an important point to which I shall return, for it relates critically to the depth-psychological level of explanation. For the moment, I have developed the point simply to indicate how the identification of consciousness with the global workspace may be correct as a general description, but lacks adequate penetration into the detail of the interactions between conscious and preconscious events that makes them interesting.

The role of self

A central feature of Baars' thinking about consciousness involves the role played by the self.[4] *Subjectivity*, the essential core of consciousness, 'corresponds to the sense of an observing self' (Baars, 1996, p. 212). Of course, this idea is not new. Baars cites Kant and James as major antecedents. Kant wrote that, 'It must be possible for the "I think" to accompany all of my (conscious) representations, for otherwise ... (they) would be nothing to me' (cited in Baars, 1996, p. 212). Jaspers developed Kant's thesis:

> Self-awareness is present in every psychic event. In the form of 'I think' it accompanies all perceptions, ideas and thoughts.... Every psychic manifestation, whether perception, bodily sensation, memory, idea, thought or feeling carries *this particular aspect of 'being mine'* of having an 'I'-quality, of 'personally belonging,' of it being one's own doing.
>
> (Jaspers, 1923/1963, p. 121, italics original)

Probably the most rigorous, and certainly the most influential, treatment of the role of 'I' in consciousness is found in the work of William James. In considering his ideas, we should note that he uses the term 'thought' to refer to all forms of what today we would call 'conscious processing'. Citing B. P. Browne, James (1890/1950) writes that 'The universal conscious fact is not "feelings and thoughts exist," but "I think" and "I feel"' (p. 226). Thoughts are given their place in consciousness by virtue of this fact, that they are owned, that they are personal, for, *'every thought is part of a personal consciousness'*. For James, 'I' is an overarching feature of consciousness.

James recognizes different aspects to selfhood – for example, the bodily, the social, and the spiritual. Writing of the 'self of all the other selves', the central core of selfhood, he notes that the other elements of our mental life seem 'to accrete round it and to belong to it' (p. 298). Moreover, self plays a critical role in memory, giving rise to the seminal sense that an event recalled is owned, that it happened in my past: 'Memory requires more than mere dating of a fact in the past. It must be dated in *my* past. In other words, I must think that I directly experienced its occurrence' (p. 650).

These ideas find expression in more contemporary, cognitive terms in my proposal that mundane consciousness might depend on the establishing of connections between the mental representation of 'I' (the *'I'-model*) and the representation of whatever it is that I am conscious of (Lancaster, 1991, 1993b, 1997a). Similarly, for Kihlstrom (1993, 1997; Kihlstrom *et al.*, 2000), what determines whether or not we become conscious of objects and events is the *linkage* between their cognitive representations:

> When a link is made between the mental representation of self and the mental representation of some object or event, then the percept, memory or thought enters into consciousness; when this link fails to be made, it does not.
>
> (Kihlstrom, 1993, p.152)

This linkage hypothesis is couched against the background of associative network models of cognition and memory. Mental activity is construed as the activation of constellations of connections in the 'working space' of the mind. The nodes in these constellations represent items of knowledge, and the connections between them stand for the associations through which the knowledge becomes actualized. Current goals would determine the precise flow of activation through the network.

Kihlstrom envisages the mental representation of self as a subset of the network:

> It consists of interconnected nodes representing my name; the names of people intimately associated with me; and my physical, demographic, and personality characteristics. Beyond these meaning-based representations, there may be links to perception-based representations of my face and body – quite literally, a self-image. In addition to this context-free knowledge about self, there is also autobiographical knowledge about specific experiences, thoughts, and actions that occurred at unique points in time and space.
>
> (Kihlstom, 1997, p. 453)

Activity in the network can proceed with or without contact with the self-node, that is, consciously or nonconsciously.

The idea that linkage to a self-representation is critical for consciousness needs to be distinguished from the concept of 'self-consciousness' as generally understood. Self-consciousness entails reflection on one's sense of self, including an examination of already enacted thoughts. That is not what is envisaged here. Rather, the postulated role of 'I' is central to the immediate, phenomenal presence of things. The proposal is that this sense of presence is vouchsafed in the everyday state of mind by virtue of the linkage between the 'I'-model and other representations. Metzinger (2000, 2003) has argued this point in terms of the role of the 'self-model' in consciousness. The phenomenal quality of interest is *pre-reflexive self intimacy*, which is:

> A very basic and seemingly spontaneous, effortless way of inner acquaintance, of 'being in touch with yourself,' a fundamental form of non-conceptual self-knowledge that precedes any higher forms of cognitive self-consciousness.
>
> (Metzinger, 2000, p. 295)

It is the *adhesiveness* of 'I' that parallels in a phenomenal sense the neurocognitive proposal that linkage between the 'I'-model and other representations plays a critical role in consciousness. 'Adhesiveness' is a term introduced by Ryle (1949) to capture the quality of 'I' being an ever-present accompaniment to experience. The sense of 'I' attaches to my experience just as my shadow attaches to my body. Glover (1988) similarly stresses adhesiveness as one of the defining features of 'I' (the others being elusiveness and irreducibility). Suppose, he argues, I had been in a car crash and woke in hospital with amnesia and a headache. I may have no recollection of earlier events, and be unable to recollect my past. I may not know my own name, or the identity of the relatives at my bedside. Yet, for all this, I would know that I was the one having the headache.

An antecedent for the general notion that 'I' plays this critical role in consciousness is found in the writings of the early twentieth-century French neurologist, Claparède. Claparède singles out the case of a densely amnesic patient of his, who showed a typical pattern of dissociation in memory. In the terms used by current psychology, she displayed *implicit* memory in the absence of *explicit* memory. That is, she was unable to recall any significant information after a delay of more than a few minutes (loss of explicit recall), but, as the following incident shows, a memory of events was retained in a form unavailable to conscious recall (preservation of implicit memory).

Claparède concealed a pin in his hand and pricked her finger when greeting her on a visit. This, evidently, caused her some pain. Claparède continues:

But when I again reached out for her hand, she pulled it back in a reflex action, not knowing why. When I asked for the reason, she said in a flurry, 'Doesn't one have the right to withdraw her hand?' and when I insisted, she said, 'Is there perhaps a pin hidden in your hand?' To the question, 'What makes you suspect me of wanting to stick you?,' she [replied], 'That was an idea that went through my mind', or she would explain, 'Sometimes pins are hidden in people's hands.' But never would she recognize the idea of sticking as a 'memory'.
      (Claparède, 1911/1950, cited in Kihlstrom, 1997, p. 456)

Claparède explains such behaviour by suggesting that 'everything happens as though the various events of life, however well associated to each other in the mind, were incapable of integration with *the me* itself' (cited in Kihlstrom *et al.*, 2000, p. 640).

There is a voluminous literature on neuropsychological dissociations between implicit (nonconscious) and explicit (conscious) processing. Careful testing has reinforced the view drawn from the above anecdote: the nonconscious performance of some task can be preserved when localized brain damage has interfered with the patient's ability to perform the task at will and in a conscious fashion. Moreover, in normal, non brain-damaged individuals, a similar range of dissociations is evident when experimental procedures ensure that key stimuli are presented nonconsciously. My proposals, and those advanced by Kihlstrom, concerning the representation of 'I' and its linkage to other representations, apply equally to both pathological and non-pathological cases. Access to 'I' is viewed as the primary determinant of mundane consciousness.

It is tempting to consider that, by means of this postulated role of linkage between neural models, consciousness has been 'demystified'. Of course, it has not. The hard problem of qualia and the explanatory gap remains. Consider Metzinger's (2000) assertion that *phenomenology* is an intrinsic property of the self-model that, as it were, infects other representations through contact. He presumes that, 'All representational states, which are being embedded into the currently active phenomenal self-model, gain the additional higher-order property of phenomenal mineness' (p. 292). But why should the 'higher-order property of phenomenal mineness' attach to the self-model in the first place? What is it about the self-model, or about a link being made between it and other representations that brings qualia into being?

One extreme position is to deny the existence of qualia. While Dennett (1991), for example, regards self as central to consciousness, calling it the 'center of narrative gravity', he regards qualia as illusory. 'There seems to be phenomenology.... But it does not follow from this undeniable, universally attested fact that there really is phenomenology' (p. 366).

A second answer entails stressing the *transparency* of representations. Transparency in this context refers to the fact that we are only ever conscious of what it is that a representation represents. The representation itself, by analogy, is like the glass in a window, and is therefore described as 'transparent'. We see the hills in the distance, not the window through which we are looking. Try as we might, we cannot know a representation. In those moments when we are most intensely aware of a perception, it is only ever the outer properties that fill our awareness. When captivated by the colour and scent of a rose, it would be absurd to suggest that we are somehow more intensely engaged with the representations of these properties than with the redness and the bouquet themselves. In the most sublime or ecstatic moments, it would be a strange philosopher indeed who would extol the beauty of the *representations*! No, we see *through* the representations, which are therefore characterized as *transparent*.

The principle extends more broadly. For example, blind people can *experience* through their sticks, and those who wear prostheses frequently develop a kind of awareness through them. This phenomenon has been studied more extensively using *sensory substitution* for the blind, in which a camera substitutes for the blind person's eye (Bach-y-Rita, 1972; see also Morgan, 1977). The pattern of luminance in the images transmitted by the camera is transformed into a related pattern of modulated pressure points relayed to the skin through an array of stimulators, for example on their back. With practice, and under conditions in which the patient has control of the camera, these blind individuals can begin to experience the image as being in the world, and no longer attached to their skin. They 'see' *through* their skin.

More generally still, we all can find ourselves fully engaged with a truly great movie. We are in the scene, not in the auditorium. We have a strong propensity to be 'out there', to be in the worldly narrative that is fabricated only partially on the basis of purely sensory data. And this propensity is undoubtedly a primary property of all perception.

But these very generalizations of the principle of transparency lead us to question the adequacy of claims that the principle accounts for phenomenology. Metzinger argues that it is the transparency in both the self-model and in the representations of the objects being perceived, that gives both the phenomenal sense of 'I' as agent, or perceiver, and the equally phenomenal sense of a known world. 'The phenomenal self is a virtual agent perceiving virtual objects in a virtual world' (2000, p. 300). Yet we have no solid grounds for assigning phenomenology on the basis of the transparency of representations. It is merely an assertion, a belief. [5]

We need to distinguish the basic properties of redundancy and projection from the 'seeing through' that transparency in its philosophical sense is supposed to explain. Take a scratch on the lens of my spectacles. Once it has been there for a while, I no longer see it. Indeed, careful studies have shown that a stabilized image on the retina rapidly fades from view. This is simply a feature of perception; the neural system rapidly habituates to non-changing sensory features. We 'see through' such features just as, in the philosophical sense, we are said to see through representations. Given the trivial nature of sensory habituation, it seems inconceivable that the analogous transparency of representations is the kind of property that might be elevated into the cause of phenomenality.[6]

The phenomenon of projection is critical. This is another basic and intrinsic feature of perception, the evolutionary significance of which is self-evident. We must be *in* the world to survive the world. Hence, given enough data, we can create a world, as in the case of virtual reality. If the data are sufficient, and sufficiently self-consistent, we will begin to live the narrative into which they adequately fit. There is no doubting the force of this primary motivation. Simply recognizing the primacy of projection does not, however, *explain* why projected contents are phenomenally experienced. There is still a missing link.

Interestingly, projection may be construed as a concomitant of the principle of re-entrance. As we have seen, the brain includes the hardware for the 'projection' of information from memory back onto the sensory input channels. Psychologically, this re-entrant loop enables the meaning of sensory information to become known in the act of perception. An essential component of such knowing entails placing the meaning where it belongs – in the world. If we accept as our primary premise that we become conscious by dint of activity in the re-entrant loop, as discussed in

Chapter 4, then projection becomes the further extension of consciousness into the world.[7]

From this point of view, the transparency is not a property of representations. Indeed, the search for a property of representations that can render them conscious was only triggered by the insistence that consciousness be defined in terms of representations in the first place. There is something deeply tautological about this!

Imbuing the glass in the metaphorical windowpane with a capacity to observe cannot extricate us from the problem. The fact that we are unable to *feel* our neurones hardly qualifies them with the ability to feel! No, the representations that enable the brain to model the world and the self are transparent, I suggest, because the *whole brain* itself is transparent. It constitutes the transparent agent of the interpenetration between the world and consciousness.

Memory and self

The 'I'-tag theory

As noted above, William James stressed the importance of the connection between memory and self. A memory must include the conviction that *I* experienced the event being recalled. We might imagine that, in the case of Claperède's patient, the memory of being pricked by a concealed pin existed in some 'ownerless' space in her mind. The memory was still influential on her actions and on her rationalization of those actions, whilst being unavailable to *her* – that is, to the representation of 'I' current in her mind. As Warnock (1987) argues, 'The image, if there is one, must be labelled not only "this belongs to the past" but also "it belongs to *my* past"' (p. 59).

I have proposed that this sense of ownership of memories entails a *tagging* system in memory. Memories are structured in association with the 'I'-model that was present at the time that the event was experienced. The term '*I'-tag* (Lancaster, 1991) refers to the function played by the 'I'-model associated in this way with specific memories. The 'I'-model acts as a *tag* on the other memories. Similar formulations have been advanced by Kihlstrom (1997), who refers to 'self-tokens', and Trehub (1991), using the term 'I-tokens'. In brief, the presence of 'I'-tags achieves two ends. First, it accounts for the sense of ownership stressed by James and

Warnock. Second, it is involved in the indexing of memories, allowing 'I' to play an active role in subsequent recall.

In order to explicate these two points, we need to consider further the nature of self. As ever, James is a valuable guide with whom to begin our consideration. In trying to define the central principle of selfhood, he notes that opinions differ:

> Some would say that it is a simple active substance, the soul, of which they are thus conscious; others, that it is nothing but a fiction, the imaginary being denoted by the pronoun I; and between these extremes of opinion all sorts of intermediaries would be found.
>
> (James, 1890/1950, p. 298)

In the 'I'-tag theory to be enunciated in this chapter, my reasoning tends towards the second view. 'I' is viewed as a construct, recreated from moment to moment in the mind.[8] The seeming continuity of 'I' is no more mysterious than the continuity we observe in fragmentary images, as in a movie. We *infer* the continuity that makes sense of the fragments. This is a more general expression of our earlier consideration of *'seeing as seeing as'*. We do not see the fragmentary shapes in front of us; we see birds and trees and so on. The mind rushes into an inference, *a meaningful interpretation* to explain the data of the senses. And 'I' may be understood within this context: it is the mind's most successful manoeuvre for increasing the sense of meaning (Lancaster, 1991). The mind synthesizes a narrative that fits the available information into a story that is structured around a logic of causation. And central to all the mind's narratives is the 'center of narrative gravity' (Dennett, 1991) itself, namely 'I'.

For cognitive neuroscience, 'I' is merely a representation, a model of the modelling system's own presumed coherence (Blackmore, 1986; Johnson-Laird, 1983, 1988; Oatley, 1988). Such thinking accords with the Buddhist material described in Chapter 3. Buddhism teaches that 'I' lacks substance and continuity, and is, indeed, merely a 'trick' of the mind.

Our view of psychological causation is modelled on what we learn about the world in general. All events have a cause, and if the cause is for some reason invisible, we tend to infer an absent cause. The same is true with regard to psychological causation. When the real cause of some behaviour is hidden, or unrecognized by us, our minds tend to impute some cause or other. Nisbett and Ross (1980) conducted a series of studies that clearly demonstrated this compulsion to attribute causes. In one, for example, the participants were required to choose a pair of stockings from a choice of four pairs. They were to select whichever they preferred. In actual fact the pairs were identical, and the factor determining the participants' choices reflected a position effect. The pair on the right was invariably the preferred choice. When questioned about their choices, however, participants strongly denied that position had any effect, suggesting rather that their choices were made on the basis of the stockings' characteristics, such as colour, sheerness and so on. It is evident that these confabulated explanations of the choices were functioning to reinforce the individual's sense of being in control, of making rational choices. The confabulations form part of the narrative of who they are and what they do – the narrative of 'I'.

That 'I' itself might be part of the confabulation is suggested from neurological cases. Sacks (1985) describes patients who appear to continually reinvent themselves in a drive to maintain credibility, presumably not only with the neurologist interviewing them, but also with themselves. This drive to construct a personal narrative identity is not easily dismissed as merely a peculiar feature of the neurological damage. Sacks sees it as an essential feature in the make-up of each one of us. The neurological damage simply renders it more apparent. Whereas normally the construction of 'I' is so seamless that we hardly realize that it occurs, in these patients, the construction becomes a struggle, and therefore very evident. Ramachandran and Blakeslee make much the same point:

> [T]he notion of a single unified self 'inhabiting' the brain may indeed be an illusion. Everything I have learned from the intensive study of both normal people and patients who have sustained damage to various parts of their brains points to an unsettling notion: that you create your own 'reality' from mere fragments of information.
>
> (Ramachandran and Blakeslee, 1999, pp. 227–8)

Through his research with split-brain patients, Gazzaniga (1988, 1997) has explored the compulsion to confabulate explanations and causes. A range of studies has demonstrated that the verbal left hemisphere of patients will offer seemingly rational explanations for their behaviour in cases where the behaviour was actually initiated by the right hemisphere. Being surgically separated from its right partner, the left hemisphere can have no 'knowledge' of the behaviour's true cause (which will have been some image or instruction presented only to the right hemisphere), yet it finds no difficulty in offering a confabulated cause. An example is the case of a patient to whose separated right hemisphere the word *walk* was presented. The patient had been primed to respond to command words and, accordingly, he began walking away from the testing area. On being asked his reason for walking, he (that is, his left hemisphere) answered that he was going into the house to get a 'Coke'.

Patients gave such confabulated explanations of their behaviour with a clear strength of conviction. It seems that, under conditions in which the *real* explanation for some behavioural or mental event is for some reason unavailable, a drive to construct a *purported* explanation is irresistible. Gazzaniga accounts for these observations by positing a specialized module of the left hemisphere, named by him the *interpreter*, which is dedicated to this function of generating explanations and interpretations:

> The interpreter considers all the outputs of the [brain's other] functional modules as soon as they are made and immediately constructs a hypothesis as to why particular actions occurred. In fact the interpreter need not be privy to why a particular module responded. None the less, it will take the behaviour at face value and fit the event into the large ongoing mental schema (belief system) that it has already constructed.
>
> (Gazzaniga, 1988, p. 219)

There seems little doubt that a central feature of this 'ongoing mental schema' is 'I'. As Gazzaniga notes, '[patients] view their responses as behaviours emanating from their own volitional selves' (ibid., pp. 233–4). Indeed, in a more recent study, Turk *et al.* (2002) have demonstrated that, in a split-brain patient, the left hemisphere shows a recognition bias for self, whereas the right hemisphere shows a bias for recognizing familiar others. This does not necessarily imply that the interpretative and self-recognition functions engage a unitary module. But I think we can reasonably presume that the two functions are bound up together. I have argued in more detail elsewhere (Lancaster, 1991) that there are good reasons for supposing that language is integral to both functions. The interpreter draws on a fundamental grammar that establishes 'I' as the first-person subject of the narrative it synthesizes. Whatever the precise cerebral mechanism, 'I' lies at the centre of the 'hypothesis as to why particular actions occurred'. 'I' itself is a hypothesis, one that brings a kind of final common path of unification into mental processing. It is the hypothesis of a unified subject of perceptions, thinker of thoughts, and instigator of actions. When Nisbett and Ross' participants explained their choices in terms of the characteristics of the stockings they selected, they were reinforcing their images of themselves as being in control. Their behaviour was thereby given a (fictional) controlling focus. Similarly, when the patient described by Gazzaniga explained his walking away from the test area, he was construing the situation as 'I' am thirsty and 'I' am going to get a Coke. The illusion of choice necessarily implicates 'I' as locus of control.

Gazzaniga identifies consciousness specifically with the output from the interpreter. He writes that:

[C]onsciousness ... is the elusive thread that runs through the story enabled in each of us by the interpreter as the result of its coordinating the behaviour of all the specialized systems that have evolved to enable human cognitive processes.

(Gazzaniga, 1997, pp. 72–3)

Again, the central character in the story is 'I', and we can view Gazzaniga's words as reinforcing the claim that 'I' is centrally involved in this key aspect of consciousness.

The 'I'-tag theory places 'I' not only as a crucial feature of mundane consciousness, but also as central to the organization of memory. As is axiomatic in all theories of memory, we may assume that association plays a critical role in the laying down of memories and their subsequent re-activation through recognition or recall. Any single element may function to trigger memories of items to which it was, or has become, associated. If a child experiences the sound 'pen' in association with the visual image of the pen itself, then he or she builds up an associative cognitive network in which the two are linked. Subsequently, the word 'pen' may trigger knowledge of pens, or the image of a pen may trigger the word. All this is obvious. The 'I'-tag theory simply recognizes that the 'I'-model takes on a superordinate role in this associative system.

All current representations enter memory in association with each other. The strength of the associations will depend on the frequency of pairings of given representations. The association between 'pen' and 'writing' is especially strong since these concepts are invariably present together in my mind. Consider the following, however. On one occasion I saw a butterfly land on my pen. The link between 'pen' and 'butterfly' is presumably weak since their pairing occurred only once (although the unexpectedness element in an event can also affect the associative strength). All this is basic, and well substantiated through research in memory. The 'I'-tag theory simply asserts that the one pairing that is probably stronger than any other is that between the pen and 'I'. That is, on virtually every occasion on which I see the pen, the 'I'-model will also be present in the mental workspace and connected to it.[9] It is effectively a tag attaching to the representation of the pen in memory.

In normal, non-pathological cases, the 'I'-model may display only relatively minor changes over time.[10] Consequently, the 'I'-tag associated with an activated memory effortlessly links into the current 'I'-model, giving rise to the sense of ownership of the memory, and the memory's presence in consciousness. But this may be slightly misleading, for it implies that there is an 'I'-model, as it were, present and waiting to make connections. Rather, I would envisage that at any given time, the 'I'-model is constructed on the basis of the 'I'-tags activated from memory. That is to say, all the events occurring in the moment – seeing the pen, hearing the music, seeing the wall of my study, and so on, are activating memories, each of which is associated with an 'I'-tag. The drive to construct 'I' draws on all currently active 'I'-tags.

This view of thousands of separate 'I'-tags being activated in any given moment needs to be further simplified. Again, assuming a non-pathological case, there will be considerable overlap in the 'I'-tags. It is probably best to conceive of them as sharing a common core, which effectively constitutes the continuity in a person's identity. A given 'I'-tag would include the common core, together with idiosyncratic aspects.[11] If a certain pen had been given to me by someone I love deeply, then its 'I'-tag would include the common core together with features of my sense of identity specifically bound up with that episode. For example, the 'I'-tag may include elements of *'I'-as-lover* that are completely absent from the psychological situation when I use a pen provided on the counter at my bank!

In actuality, then, in any given situation, we may envisage the common core amongst 'I'-tags as being strongly activated, and any distinctive 'I'-tag elements (attributable to shades of difference in 'I' at the time of experiencing particular objects or events) as only being activated to a lesser extent. This last point reflects our understanding of memory storage in general. Current theorizing, reflecting empirical data as well as computer parallels, views individual items as being stored in relation to generic templates. The individual item would include the template plus specific features. My armchair might be stored as chair + black + relax (hopefully!), and so on.

I have proposed that 'I'-tags play a key role in memory indexing (Lancaster, 1991; see also Teyler and DiScenna, 1986). The presence of appropriate 'I'-tags is viewed as being essential to normal conscious (explicit) recall. Consider the following example. I come through the door and absent-mindedly (= no sense of 'I' attaching to the action) place my keys in an unusual position, on top of the blue shelf, say. The next day, on needing to recall where the keys are, the relevant representation ('key on top of blue shelf') is simply unavailable to connect with my current 'I'-model. It may be present in the same kind of ownerless mental space as in Claparède's patient, but that does not help too much in my frantic search for the key! I may have to force a link by methodically rebuilding the 'I' connections, for example by trying to recollect what I did when I came in the previous day.

The 'I'-tag system may be viewed as a development from memory systems in other mammals, in which similar 'tagging' is thought to operate. Such tags would embody the animal's representation of itself in relation to its environment in whatever terms are employed (for example, spatial). Damasio (1999) suggests the term *protoself* to refer to the primitive basis of self that we share with other animals. He suggests that the animal constructs a model of itself through the operation of neural systems monitoring the state of the body in all its aspects. For Damasio, more complex notions of identity and personhood develop from the primitive protoself. Similarly, the 'I'-tag system is viewed as representing a development of pre-human memory indexing systems, only achievable with the development of explicit notions of selfhood. As MacPhail (1998) argues, despite demonstrations that some higher primates may possess rudimentary abilities to detect aspects of their own mirror images, there is no convincing evidence of anything like a 'self' in any nonhuman species. For MacPhail, the self is central to consciousness, and he therefore concludes that no animals are conscious in any meaningful sense of the term.[12]

Abhidhamma revisited

Following the discussion of the role of 'I'-tags in memory, and given the supposed transcendence of 'I' in enlightenment, we might wonder whether the Buddha perhaps had trouble remembering where he placed his keys.... Of course, renunciation of material things would probably render the issue of no consequence, so we need not trouble ourselves on his part for too long!

There is, however, a serious point to consider here. Interestingly, in response to my article about the 'I'-tag theory in relation to the Abhidhamma (Lancaster, 1997a), I received an email that made the following point:

> Anecdotal evidence suggests that your hypothesis about the 'I'-tag being involved in the 'access' consciousness is right. One of the endearing qualities of Suzuki Roshi, founder of the San Francisco Zen Center and a major force in bringing Soto Zen to the US, was his absentmindedness. Similarly, Kobin Chino Roshi, head of Jikoji Zen Center nearby, has a similar reputation. Also, I can attest from experience that after long meditation retreats, one tends to become more forgetful.

The logic here would be that any movement towards enlightenment has the effect of diminishing the presence of 'I', and accordingly, any role we may ascribe to 'I' in relation to memory would be compromised.

I am inclined to think that the goal of meditation entails *detachment* from 'I' rather then abolition of 'I'. We may envisage therefore that the input–output role proposed here for 'I' in relation to memory might continue, even in an 'enlightened' state.[13] Nevertheless, the value of dethroning 'I' in relation to this indexing role should not be overlooked. An inevitable implication of the 'I'-tag theory is a certain conservatism. Whilst the person is focused in 'I', items that may not readily have been incorporated within the orbit of 'I'-tags will remain inaccessible. This formulation approximates to the classic psychoanalytical view of the *unconscious*, a point to be explored further in Chapter 6. Detachment from 'I' may allow richer access to contents of the mind, even though, paradoxically, such access may not be available to recall from the normal 'I' (see the discussion below on 'I' and state dependence). Figure 5.3 schematically illustrates this concept.

In Chapter 4, the symbolic value of knots was considered in relation to Abulafia's system of language mysticism. Abulafia's primary aim was to untie the knots from worldly matters and rebind them in relation to the letters of God's Name. In Chapter 7, I shall be discussing in more detail the practices employed to this end. However, in passing, I note here a point of relevance to this issue of accessibility, explored more fully elsewhere (Lancaster, 2001). As in any storage system, a library for example,

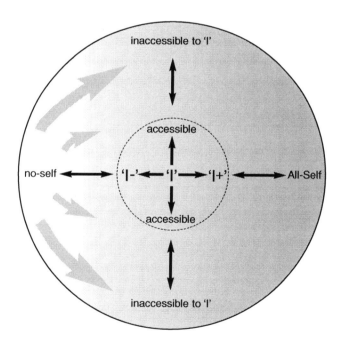

FIGURE 5.3 Parameters of consciousness: perpective of 'no-self'. The vertical axis of accessibility refers to the informational content of the mind. The horizontal axis indicates that our experience of 'self' can vary. See FIGURE 2.1. Accessibility may be increased by detachment from 'I', with the centre of gravity shifting towards 'no-self'.

accessibility in memory will be limited by the scope of the indexing system. It seems likely that the untying of schemata from 'I'
and the retying of them to the mystic's representation of God (that
is, via His Name) potentially achieves a shift in the scale of the
index. The tagging system would be transferred from one focused
in the small world of 'I' to one focused in the infinite divine world.
While this may seem a somewhat fanciful notion, it is predicated
on a very basic fact – that the kind of mystic we are considering
here had a deeply engrained belief in the transcendence and omnis-
cience of the divine. For the kabbalist, God in His essence is *ayin*,
a nothingness that embraces everything (Matt, 1995). The principal goal of this kind of mysticism requires detachment from 'I' and
attachment to God. Again, the point is very schematically illustrated in Figure 5.4, where it is assumed that there has been a shift
to the 'All-Self', the deepest root of the soul united with God.[14]

The 'I'-tag theory marries two complementary sources of information: research data from cognitive neuroscience and introspective data from mysticism. As far as the latter is concerned, the
Theravadin Abhidhamma material discussed in Chapter 3 has
provided a framework for the theory's consideration of the
processes involved in perception, as illustrated in Figure 5.5.

The stage of *seeing* is related to the initial feedforward processes
of feature detection. As discussed in Chapter 4, it is envisaged that
the presence of distinctive features of the input array is signalled by
the responses of the hierarchy of analyzers in V1 and the other
regions of the visual cortex. This generates the neuronal input
model, which interacts with the memory system. These interactions
are presumed to come about through the phase synchrony in neural
systems discussed in Chapter 4. In Figure 5.5, the hexagonal grey
shape depicts the neuronal input model, with other grey shapes indicating representations with which it is associated. The three stages
following that of seeing are all aspects of memory readout and the
matching process described earlier.

The stage of *receiving* corresponds to the response in the
memory system triggered as soon as the input model forms. Interestingly, the emphasis placed by the Abhidhamma on the role of
feeling in this stage relates to what we know of the basic operation
of memory, since feeling and mood seem to be primary drivers of
memory function. Next, the input model activates, through neural
resonance, the various schemata with which it accords. The Abhidhamma term, *examine*, is appropriate here since it is those

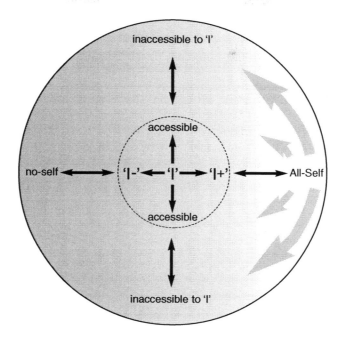

FIGURE 5.4 Parameters of consciousness: perspective of 'All-Self'. The vertical axis of accessibility refers to the informational content of the mind. The horizontal axis indicates that our experience of 'self' can vary. See FIGURE 2.1. Accessibility may be increased by detachment from 'I', with the centre of gravity shifting towards the 'All-Self'.

schemata which have associative links with the strongest match to the input model that are envisaged to be activated. As we saw in Chapter 3, it is this *examination* of associations that seems to be what is implied in the Abhidhamma texts. Finally in this memory-focused triad of stages, the identity of the object is *established* through the matching process, which involves re-entrant fibres interacting with the feedforward system.

I identify the *javana* stage with the procedures whereby the matched image becomes incorporated into the individual's ongoing narrative of meaning. 'I' is generated in this stage since, under mundane conditions, it is the essential centre of the narrative.[15] The *javana* process is likely to involve the brain module identified by Gazzaniga as the left hemisphere 'interpreter'. The figure assumes that a pen is at the focus of attention, but, clearly, the

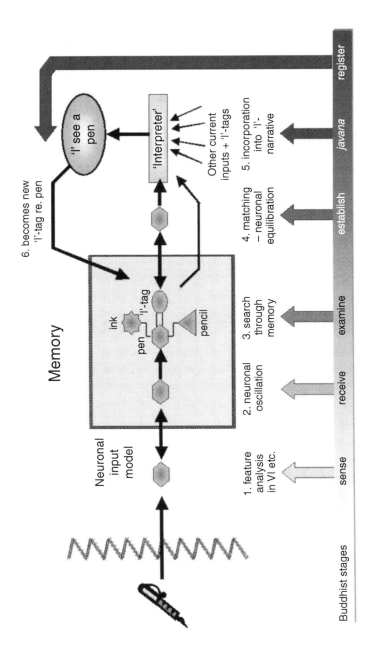

FIGURE 5.5 'I'-tag theory in relation to the stages of perception in the Abhidhamma system

constructed narrative will incorporate a wider range of material than that triggered by this specific object (hence, 'other current inputs' in the figure).

Finally, the *register* stage results in the updating of memory on the basis of the output from the *javana* stage. This will generally involve updating of 'I'-tags. However, it may be envisaged that detachment from 'I' (perhaps through appropriate spiritual practice), could lead to an attenuation of the emphasis on 'I'-tags. In Buddhist terms, attenuation of the 'conceit of I am', coupled with control over the determinants of the *javana* reaction itself (as encouraged in the Abhidhamma texts), would change the character of memory. There would be a weakening of the associative strength in the relevant 'I'-tags. The effect would be cumulative, since any weakening of the 'I'-tag associations would itself lower the immediacy of the sense of 'I' in the constructed narrative, leading to further attenuation of 'I'-tags, and so on. As discussed above, this could be expected to result in increased access to contents outside the orbit of those that are normally 'I'-tagged, together with correspondingly poorer access to items strongly associated with the habitual 'I'.

A theory is only as good as the evidence available to support it. What evidence can support the 'I'-tag theory and its predictions? At the outset, I would draw attention to the degree of integration the theory achieves between contemporary research in cognitive neuroscience and insights from an introspective system that many would regard as amongst the most sophisticated to have been developed. But I turn now to supporting psychological evidence for two of the important features of the 'I'-tag theory. First, I shall examine evidence to support the role ascribed to 'I' in memory; and, second, I shall consider in more detail the role assigned to associations (the stage of *examine*) in the theory.

'I' and memory readout

It has repeatedly been demonstrated that information actively related in some way to 'I' is better remembered than non-'I'-related information. Rogers, Kuiper and Kirker (1977) coined the term *self-reference effect* to describe this phenomenon. In their study, participants were required to remember lists of words. Under one condition, they were asked whether each word described themselves. This strategy of requiring participants to think of the words in relation to themselves gave a significant advantage in recall by comparison with that achieved using other encoding strategies. The authors assume that the self acts as a 'superordinate schema', facilitating encoding and recall of the information.

The self-reference effect is a robust phenomenon, observable across a wide range of different experimental conditions. For example, the effect is maintained with a range of different kinds of materials to be remembered, and with a variety of different techniques for creating the reference to 'I' (for example, using imagery instead of self-directed questions). In a meta-analysis of the self-reference effect in memory, Symons and Johnson (1997) argue that the effect is largely attributable to the role of self in creating matching conditions between the stages of encoding (learning) and retrieval. Self, in this sense, becomes the stable element between the two stages. The self enables greater elaboration and higher organization in the processing of items to be remembered, both of which give increased memory efficiency.

These conclusions are in agreement with what we would expect on the basis of the 'I'-tag theory. The self-reference effect is consistent with my analysis of the role 'I' plays as a kind of indexing agent in memory; as a 'superordinate schema' it enables the correct addresses to be located at recall. Although the theory holds that 'I' is a construct that may not be fully consistent over time, in normal, non-pathological, cases its level of variation is unlikely to detract from the efficient indexing evident from studies of the self-reference effect.

If it is indeed the case that 'I' plays this central role in relation to memory, then we might expect to find that our ability to recall early childhood memories is affected by the developmental course of the sense of 'I'. We all display *infantile amnesia*, the inability to remember beyond some cut-off point in our childhood. Is there evidence that the cut-off point relates to the age below which 'I' had not yet developed?

From extensive reviews of the literature in developmental psychology, as well as a consideration of the time course through which key brain structures develop,[16] Howe and Courage (1993, 1997) note that the 'cognitive self' begins to play a crucial role in the organization of memory from around 18 to 24 months. Studies leading to this conclusion have examined a variety of indicators of the development of the cognitive self. These include signs of self-consciousness, such as shy smiling or gaze aversion when an infant is confronted with a picture of themselves; first-person pointing, that is, pointing to a photo of themselves from a selection; and the comprehension and use of self-referent pronouns, such as 'I' and 'me'. The signs of self-consciousness are observed from about 18 months, and comprehension of self-referent pronouns, from about 22 months. Regarding the ability to recall childhood memories, a wide range of studies has examined the age of adults' earliest memories. Whilst there is some variation in results, Howe and Courage (1993) find 'solid evidence from most studies that memories are available for many individuals from the age of two years' (p. 315).

The similarity in the two ages (that is, of earliest memories and of the development of the cognitive self) encourages the authors to conclude that it is the sense of self that serves as the catalyst for the onset of autobiographical memories. Interestingly, memory function itself is present from, and before, birth. From their review of a wide range of studies, Howe and Courage (1993) assert that 'the basic "hardware" for perception, learning, and memory must be in place and functioning at (or before) birth' (p. 311). It is specifically the ability to access autobiographical memories that is compromised by the absence of the cognitive self at ages below two years. This leaves open the possibility that strategies for bypassing 'I' (as, for example, in states of detachment, or through techniques of free association, etc.) could reveal a potential for a non-'I'-focused connection to early childhood memories. Howe, Courage and Peterson pose a provocative question as the title of their 1994 paper: 'How can I remember when "I" wasn't there?' The foregoing suggests a possible answer: recall might be enabled by engaging in some technique – spriritual or therapeutic – to loosen the knots binding the memory to 'I'. These speculations anticipate the approach of depth psychology, to be examined in Chapter 6.

The picture solidly emerging from both the self-reference effect in memory and the time course of infantile amnesia implicates 'I' in memory function. The conclusion is strengthened from work on memory in cases of dissociative identity disorder (DID) and the state dependent effect in memory.

The presence of an amnesic barrier between *alter* personalities in cases of multiple personality was a defining feature from the earliest period of their study. Classically, one or more of the alters had no recollection of the others. In the nineteenth century, Janet elaborated the role of memory in dissociation, emphasizing that a patient might be cured only through a process that addressed the traumatic memories at the root of the dissociation. These memories had to be either 'removed' or otherwise transformed so as to be integrated into the patient's ego.

More recent studies have assessed experimentally the extent to which material learnt by a DID patient in one identity state might be accessible from their alter state. Such studies are relevant to the 'I'-tag theory when we assume that incompatibility between constructions of 'I' is the root cause of DID. Identity state 'I_1' is sufficiently distinct from 'I_2' that it is unable to connect with 'I'-tags deriving from 'I_2'. This contrasts with the 'normal' scenario in which successive constructions of 'I' have sufficient common ground to allow them to connect with most, if not all, 'I'-tags.

Nissen *et al.* (1988) tested one DID patient for both implicit and explicit memory across identity states. The procedure simply involved presenting to-be-remembered material when one of the identities (we will refer to this as 'I_1') was to the fore, then testing for appropriate recall following a delay during which a psychiatrist brought forward a different identity ('I_2'). The pattern of results indicated that the amnesia across identities was not absolute. In the case of explicit memory, simple material could be recalled by 'I_2' whereas hard material could not. In fact, results with the simple material may have reflected guesswork rather than memory. For example, after word pairs such as NORTH–SOUTH had been learnt by 'I_1', 'I_2' was asked to recall what had paired NORTH. Clearly, a simple guess by 'I_2' could have achieved the correct result. The standard inter-identity amnesia was evident with the more difficult pairings, such as SCHOOL–GROCERY.

Implicit memory was tested in a variety of ways. Overall, it appeared that simple, semantically-empty, material did pass between the identities. For example, one test required the patient to respond to flashing lights presented in a repeating sequence. The nature of the sequence was not explained. In this situation, participants will normally increase their speed of response as they implicitly learn the sequence. In the study, the speed of response times increased when the sequence had been presented to a different identity. Knowledge of the sequence had evidently been able to pass between the identities. Similarly, tests involving memory for unknown faces or simple words showed evidence of transfer across identities. When, however, the material was more complex, requiring semantic analysis, no evidence of transfer was found. For example, 'I_2' showed no evidence of greater understanding of a story which had already been presented to 'I_1'. The authors stressed that the critical variable seemed to be the extent to which *interpretation* of material was required. Where to-be-remembered material required no interpretation, it passed between identities; when recall was dependent on making sense of the material, it was restricted to the identity that had generated the interpretation.

This conclusion was largely confirmed in a larger scale study by Eich *et al.* (1997). Material that passed between identities was characterized as 'strongly data driven, allow[ing] for only one correct response, and *leav[ing] little room for identity-specific interpretive processes to operate*' (p. 421, italics added). As Dorahy (2001) comments in a recent review, it is not the distinction between implicit and explicit memory that determines what passes between the identities. Rather, the critical factor is the level of processing to which the material is subjected. This is consonant with my comments relating to the self-reference effect in memory – 'I' represents a superordinate schema for processing of information. Moreover, as I have suggested, 'I' is actually a part of the interpretation itself. We may envisage, for example, that when a DID patient hears a story, their understanding of it engages their own sense of 'I' in a contextualizing interpretation. No wonder, therefore, that when that specific 'I' is no longer present, their grasp of the story reverts to the level to be expected had they not heard it before.

This brings us to the evidence from study of the *state-dependent memory effect*. The essence of this effect is that recall is dependent on the degree of congruence between a person's state at the time of recall and their state at the time when the material was originally learnt. For example, people who are intoxicated at the time of hearing some item of information may not recall it subsequently when sober, yet it can 'pop' back into the mind when they are intoxicated again. Multiple personality, or DID as it is known today, may be understood in terms of these state-dependent processes (see also Bowers, 1984; Lancaster, 1991; Putnam, 1994). The argument hinges on the suggestion that it is the nature of the 'I'-model at any given time that is the critical aspect of the state. Recall will be facilitated to the extent that the 'I'-model is congruent between the time of learning and that of recall. Of course, a given 'state' is a complex amalgam of all the various factors, internal and external, impinging on the person at that time. The effects of a psychoactive drug, for example, may include both external (context, presence of others, and so on) and internal (chemical interactions in the brain) components. Given the arguments above about the construction of 'I' from 'I'-tags, it would follow that drugs of this kind would alter significantly the state of 'I' by comparison with the normal state. Indeed, I would argue that it is this alteration in 'I' which constitutes the essence of what we mean when we speak of 'altered states of consciousness'.

It is difficult to disentangle the variety of factors that may be determining state-dependent effects. In particular, the suggestion that 'I' may vary between the time of learning and the time of recall is often overlooked, perhaps because it does not directly accord with simple introspection. It *seems* that 'I' is a fixed point, as it were. Nevertheless, the consensus from both spiritual and scientific sources questions this simple introspection, as we have seen.

It has been suggested that *mood* may be responsible for mediating the kinds of memory effects under consideration. Thus, for example, in a range of studies, Eich and colleagues have demonstrated that manipulation of mood can influence memory. In a typical study, participants were coaxed into a happy or sad mood by using carefully chosen music and appropriate suggestions. When they were in the given mood, participants were required to generate memories related to words presented to them. Subsequently (for instance, two days later), they were again coaxed into a mood and tested for recall of the memories. Results indicated higher recall for congruent mood states (for a review of these studies, see Eich *et al.*, 1997; Eich and Schooler, 2000).

The mood-dependent effect only holds, however, when the material to be recalled is autobiographical. In Eich's study, for example, the list of words given at time 1 was used as a trigger for participants to generate memories from their *personal past*. Clearly, these memories will have had 'I' as a central referent. It was the ability to recall these events that became critical at time 2, which raises the distinct possibility that the 'I' dimension was just as influential – if not more influential – than the mood dimension. Certainly, the relation between these kinds of memory effects and those observed with DID patients becomes clearer when we recognize the powerful relation between identity ('I') and mood. Bower (1994) summarizes much research by noting that 'a temporary mood-shift can dramatically influence ... self-descriptions, [and] self-image' (p. 275). Indeed, most observers of DID emphasize that emotional trauma is at the root of the condition. The construction of separate identities may be seen as an adaptation to the demands of incompatible emotions.

When attempting to explain the studies of state-dependence in memory, it is difficult to distinguish the effects of mood changes from effects which may be attributable to changes in the 'I'-model. Preliminary data from research I have been conducting with Nuttall, however, suggests that state-dependent memory effects may occur in the absence of any changes in mood. These studies took advantage of the observation that meditation can give rise to alterations in the sense of self. Participants were required to meditate (M) or simply relax (R) prior to generating autobiographical memories. Several days later, following a second period of meditation or relaxation, they were asked to recall the memories. Congruent conditions (MM or RR) gave rise to higher levels of recall than did incongruent conditions (MR or RM), even though ratings of mood indicated no changes across the conditions.

There may therefore be some circumstances in which memory effects are bound up more with the state of 'I' than with mood per se. The point in relation to the 'I'-tag theory is that changes in 'I' *do* have implications for memory function. The areas of research considered here – the self-reference effect, infantile amnesia, memory in DID patients, and state-dependent effects – would seem to cohere around the central premise of interest. 'I' plays a major role in the laying down and subsequent recall of memories. The 'I'-tag theory provides an operational view of how this might come about.

Sparks from the rock

> In Rabbi Ishmael's School it was taught: '…And like a hammer that shatters the rock' (*Jeremiah* 23:29). Just as this hammer produces many sparks, so also may one Biblical verse convey many meanings.
>
> (Talmud, *Sanhedrin* 34a)

The theory portrayed in Figure 5.5 suggests that, during the process of perception, multiple associations with the target image are activated. As discussed already, the 'I'-tag is conceived as a major component of this stage of activation. Equally important for our consideration of consciousness is the multiplicity entailed in target-related activations. The above image of sparks flying from the rock might be seen as highly apposite to events triggered when the neuronal input model impinges on the memory process. As all the ramifications of the specific input pattern are activated, there must be a blaze of activity. Writing about the rabbinic approach to interpreting scripture (to which the above extract relates), Handelman (1982) notes that, 'multiple meanings ... are inherent in every event, for every event is full of reverberations, references, and patterns of identity that can be infinitely extended' (p. 37). It is my contention that these multiple meanings derive from the multiplicity in memory activation which occurs preconsciously during the stage labelled 'examine' in the 'I'-tag theory.

This analogy between a scriptural allusion and an important feature of preconscious processing is not trivial. I will argue more fully in Chapter 6 that access to the multiplicity in preconscious activity is a principle feature of 'spiritual' or 'mystical' states. A text is deemed *sacred* when it is subject to the belief that it contains within it an infinity of meaning. The mystic's primary goal in engaging with the text is to somehow embrace that infinity. In religions including Hinduism, Judaism and Islam, the sacredness of scripture is bound up with the sacred language in which it is written. Here again, it is the multiplicity within the meaning of the language that underwrites this sacred and numinous dimension. As Dan writes, 'The most important aspect of the concept of a divine language, encompassing eternal truth, is the infinity of meaning of language.... [I]f language is a divine expression, it must represent the infinity of God' (1995, p. 11).

As far as preconscious processing is concerned, there is considerable evidence for the kind of multiple activation of representations depicted in the 'I'-tag theory. In a now classic study of subliminal perception, Marcel (1980) demonstrated that images that do not reach a level of conscious recognition activate multiple meanings. The key elements of the study are illustrated in Figure 5.6. The study focused on participants' responses to polysemous words such as *palm*. In the sequence of presentations, the participant first saw a word designed to induce a context biased to one of the word's meanings (for example, 'hand'). Next, the polysemous word was presented, under one of two conditions. Under one condition the word was presented *subliminally*, and under the other, *supraliminally* (below and above the threshold for conscious recognition respectively). Finally, Marcel determined the participant's speed of

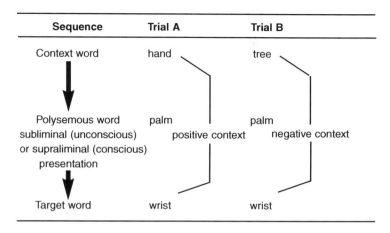

Sequence	Trial A	Trial B
Context word	hand	tree
Polysemous word subliminal (unconscious) or supraliminal (conscious) presentation	palm positive context	palm negative context
Target word	wrist	wrist

FIGURE 5.6 Experiment of Marcel (1980) illustrating the preconscious activation of multiple meanings of a polysemous word

response to a target word, either positively (trial A), or negatively (trial B), related to the context. When the polysemous word had been presented supraliminally, the results indicated faster response times for trial A than trial B. However, under the condition of subliminal presentation, there was no difference in response times between the two trials. Marcel interprets these data by assuming that the subliminal presentation activated both meanings of 'palm' equally, irrespective of the context. When, on the other hand, 'palm' was exposed supraliminally, the participant became conscious of the meaning related to the context, and any other activated meanings were inhibited.

Extrapolating from studies such as this to the normal course of events in perception, we may presume that a sensory stimulus activates multiple meanings preconsciously. By the time that the dominant meaning (that is, the object or event eventually perceived) reaches consciousness, all the other meanings become inhibited. Although the other meanings may continue to influence *unconscious* processing (see Chapter 6), they do not reach the conscious stream. In the terms of Figure 5.5, the multiple meanings are inhibited at the stage in which a match is achieved for the dominant representation.

It is important to stress that the preconscious activation relates to the *meaning* of a stimulus, and not simply to structural or other physical features. This conclusion may be reinforced by the results of an interesting study by Groeger (1988). The study used a dichotic listening paradigm, that is, different spoken messages were simultaneously presented to the participant's left and right ears. Under this paradigm, the participant can attend to only one ear at a time. In one experiment, the sentence 'She looked _____ in her new coat' was played to the ear to which the participant was attending. Included also to this ear was a choice of two words to complete the blank: 'smug' or 'cosy'. At the same time, the word 'snug' was presented to the non-attended ear, either at the threshold level for hearing or subliminally. The pattern of choices made by participants in order to complete the sentence suggests the role that meaning may play preconsciously in perceptual processing. When the word 'snug' was presented at threshold, participants tended to select 'smug' to complete the sentence, which suggests that the choice was made on the basis of a direct comparison of sound ('snug' sounds like 'smug'). In contrast to this, however, when 'snug' was presented below threshold, the word 'cosy' was the preferred choice, seemingly on the basis of the analysis of meaning ('snug' means something like 'cosy'). The result suggests that a word preconsciously activates other words related semantically. These semantic associations seem to have been attenuated when a specific, conscious connection (that is, 'smug') was established.

The multiplicity of preconscious activation may be more extensive than these studies imply. In this context, the phenomenon of *synaesthesia* is of particular interest. This is a condition in which bizarre sensory interconnections influence perception. A person experiencing synaesthesia (a *synaesthete*) may see a colour when hearing a particular word, for example, or experience a tactile sensation when tasting something.[17] Whilst most people can experience a degree of cross-sensory imagery, as, for example, when imaging a scene whilst listening to a strongly evocative piece of music, synaesthesia is distinctive in being a sensory rather than a conceptual phenomenon. A synaesthete who sees specific colours when hearing a letter, for example, will see the colour as an automatic concomitant of the sound, and it will appear to be 'out there', in the world, just like a normal perceptual experience. He or she does not *choose* to see the colour, just as a non-synaesthete would not choose to see or not see a scene in front of their eyes.

Several authors propose that the basis of synaesthesia involves polymodal interactions that are also a feature of normal perception and thinking (for instance, Cytowic, 1995, 2002; Grossenbacher and Lovelace, 2001). The distinctive feature in synaesthesia is that an aspect of the polymodal connections breaks through into consciousness. If this is the case, then the study of synaesthesia can give us valuable insight into the nature of these normally preconscious processes. The evidence from work by Marcel and others, suggesting that multiple representations are activated preconsciously, supports this view of synaesthesia.

The activation of hand-like meanings as well as tree-like meanings in response to the word 'palm' may indicate just the tip of the iceberg as far as the stage of 'examine' is concerned. A provocative image that I have drawn from a Jewish mystical text is that of the 'wheel of associations' to a given sensory input (Lancaster, 1991, 2000c; see also below, Chapter 7). In the preconscious, the reverberations set in motion by the neuronal input model may be as extensive as the ripples emanating from a stone dropped in a large pool. Moreover, the 'ripples' may not be only of an intellectual nature. Cytowic considers that emotion plays a major role in the interactions that come to the fore in synaesthesia:

> Synesthesia is emotional. The experience is accompanied by a sense of certitude (the 'this is it' feeling) and a conviction that what synesthetes perceive is real and valid. This accompaniment brings to mind that transitory change in self-awareness that is known as ecstasy. Ecstasy is any passion by which the thoughts are absorbed and in which the mind is for a time lost. In *The Varieties of Religious Experience*, William James spoke of ecstasy's four qualities of ineffability, passivity, noesis, and transience. These same qualities are shared by synesthesia.
>
> (Cytowic, 1995, para. 4.14)

Cytowic argues that emotional tone plays a major role in the normally preconscious links that determine our responses to the stimuli around us. He suggests that the limbic system, a subcortical region of the brain concerned with affect, is involved in the events of synaesthesia. Although a controversial suggestion, Cytowic claims that a number of lines of evidence support it.[18] For example, temporal lobe epileptics, who suffer abnormal discharges affecting the limbic system, may describe synaesthetic experiences at the time of their seizures. Moreover, psychoactive drugs, which also sometimes trigger synaesthetic experiences, are known to enhance the activity in pathways to the limbic system. In addition to citing specific evidence of this kind, Cytowic (1993) points more broadly to the role of feeling in creative uses of synaesthesia-like art forms. Poetry, for example, may involve a kind of *synaesthesia-in-action*, in which feeling drives the cross-connections implicit in many graphic metaphors.

One of the major theories positing a cortical, rather than subcortical, basis for synaesthesia implicates the re-entrant pathways, discussed above. Consider as an example the case of a synaesthete experiencing a colour in response to seeing a digit. Smilek *et al.*, (2001) suggest that the effect comes about when the re-entrant pathway from the posterior inferior temporal cortex interacts with the feedforward sweep in a 'lower' area known as V4, a region of the cortex which is responsible for initial colour analysis of visual stimuli. Grossenbacher and Lovelace (2001) similarly favour an explanation in these terms. They note that electrophysiological studies have indicated that electrical responses in synaesthetes and non-synaesthete controls are identical for the first 200 ms following presentation of a stimulus. This time course suggests to the authors that the difference lies in the activation of the re-entrant pathways. Normally, when a 'match' is achieved to the primary stimulus (for example, a visually presented letter), any further re-entrant activity is inhibited. The person sees the letter and nothing else. In the case of synaesthesia, it would seem that the match fails to trigger inhibition of the associated colour activity. The colour activity is projected back to the lower visual areas (probably V4) and, like all other activity 'winning through' to the re-entrant matching stage, is subjectively projected outwards into the world. The colour becomes a meaningful and conscious attribute of the concrete entity in the world.

This very brief excursion into the fascinating world of synaesthesia has served two purposes. First, it enables us to envisage the rich extent of the reverberations to ongoing input processing that normally operates preconsciously. Second, it further reinforces the thesis presented above that re-entrant processing is central to an understanding of consciousness.

Both of these ideas receive further support from the study of the intriguing syndrome of blindsight.

Neuropsychological dissociations of consciousness: blindsight

Neurology and phenomenology of blindsight

One of the major factors in the growth of scientific interest in consciousness from the 1970s onwards was the recognition that a number of neurological syndromes could best be characterized in terms of a dissociation between conscious and nonconscious processing. As we saw earlier in the case of Claparède's amnesia patients, this was not new. What was new, however, was the sheer range of syndromes that were being recognized as having this distinctive feature of dissociation (for reviews, see Milner and Rugg, 1992; Rossetti and Revonsuo, 2000). I shall discuss here one syndrome only, that of blindsight, and focus specifically on those features of the syndrome that advance our discussion of consciousness.

The term 'blindsight' was coined by Weiskrantz, and refers to the paradoxical finding that, when tested appropriately, patients who are apparently blind over one half of their visual field can display abilities that reveal residual visual functions. These visual abilities remain outside of reportable awareness, being, to all intents and purposes, nonconscious (Weiskrantz, 1986, 1997).[19]

The region damaged in these patients is V1, the primary visual receiving area in the cortex. Blindsight is only in evidence when a whole half of V1 is lost (due to surgery or wounding). This results in a *hemianopic* field, that is, a half-field of vision for which there is no reportable awareness of visual stimuli.

The residual, nonconscious visual abilities are dependent on visual pathways that bypass the damaged area. The major pathway to the various visual regions of the cortex passes through the lateral geniculate nucleus (LGN) in the thalamus to area V1 in the cortex, from where it projects eventually to 'higher' areas. This pathway is therefore compromised in blindsight sufferers since, on the affected side of the brain, V1 is no longer able to relay the signals. However, a minority of fibres from LGN project directly to areas beyond V1, and there is also a minor pathway that takes a subcortical route from the retina, before sending fibres to many of the cortical regions sustaining visual activity. In blindsight, then, an input to the visual regions beyond V1 is still present, albeit reduced. This input is evidently responsible for residual visual abilities. The interesting question for our purposes is why does consciousness seem to depend on the first cortical area, V1, being intact?

There are two major streams of visual activity in the cortex. The dorsal (upper) stream extends from V1 to the parietal cortex. This stream is fast and thought to be concerned with spatial aspects of the visual scene, including movement and action. The ventral (lower) stream leads from V1 to the temporal region, and is slow by comparison with the dorsal stream. This ventral stream seems to be more concerned with object recognition. We know from animal studies that both streams are affected by damage to V1, but the impact of this damage on the dorsal stream is much less than that on the ventral. The inferotemporal cortex (ventral stream), for example, is typically silenced when V1 is damaged, whereas regions of the parietal cortex still respond to visual input. This already suggests that the detail analyzed in the dorsal stream (for example, concerning movement) may be maintained to some degree in blindsight, but that the ability to recognize objects – the domain of the ventral stream – would be lost. This accords with features of the phenomenology of blindsight, as we will now consider. A possible basis for the differential contribution of the streams to awareness will be considered further in the next section.

When blindsight patients were first studied they were somewhat reluctant to respond to an experimenter's coaxing to state what they might be 'seeing' in their blind field. They had to be encouraged to guess. It turned out that such guesses were correct for a number of features of the visual stimuli, at levels significantly above chance. For example, patients were able to indicate accurately where a light had been flashed, or the direction of movement in the case of a moving light. The patient whom Weiskrantz originally studied was able to signal correctly whether an 'O' or an 'X' had been presented. In all cases, patients seemed to have no immediate visual awareness of the stimuli; they were not *seeing*. Somewhat more advanced ability with regard to shape perception was demonstrated by Marcel (1998), who also showed that patients made nonconscious use of words presented in the blind field. When, for example, the word RIVER was exposed in the blind field, patients subsequently understood the word BANK, which was presented auditorily and in the intact visual field, as the bank of a river. In other words, the word in the blind field must have been analyzed to the level of its meaning, since it clearly influenced processing of the subsequent ambiguous word. There is also evidence that emotional information can be extracted from visual stimuli in the blind field. De Gelder *et al.* (1999) found that a patient could respond to the emotional expression in a face presented in the blind field.

Explanations of blindsight

The above summary indicates the range of skills that are performed nonconsciously in blindsight patients. In itself, this list is not especially dramatic since there is evidence that many, even quite sophisticated, abilities are conducted without consciousness in both normals and a range of neurological patients (Velmans, 1991). What makes blindsight particularly interesting is the window that it provides into explanation. The challenge is to understand what exactly is missing in these patients, in both neural and psychological terms. Presumably, whatever is missing will be the element that normally underpins our ability to be conscious of the visual processing.

Clearly, what is missing in neural terms is area V1 of the cortex. However, V1 itself is unlikely to be the principal candidate as a correlate of visual consciousness, because the analysis it performs on visual information is relatively simple. Following earlier suggestions by Edelman (1992), Lamme (2001) proposes that the significant feature missing in these patients might be the interaction between the re-entrant pathway and the feedforward sweep in V1.[20] Under this proposal, blindsight would be explained as follows. The input to higher visual regions due to the pathways outside of V1 must be sufficient to enable the visual analysis necessary for the kinds of skills observed in these patients. However, the analysis is degraded by comparison with normal. Despite its degraded form, the visual analysis is presumed to be adequate to trigger a memory search of the kind discussed earlier in relation to Figure 4.2. The degraded quality of the input will mean that the search is, at best, somewhat compromised. Nevertheless, the search activates relevant representations, and eventuates in the kinds of successful 'guesses' which characterize blindsight. However, when it comes to the attempt to find a match between any memory readout and the neuronal input model, the re-entrant pathways can only draw a blank, as it were, from V1. If this proposal were correct, then it would lend further support to the contention that the stage of matching memory readout to neuronal input model is critical for conscious perception.

In relation to the two visual streams in the cortex, brain-imaging studies suggest that the dorsal (parietal) stream is responsible for residual visual abilities in blindsight. Milner and Goodale (1995) argue that this stream is primarily concerned with the visual control of action, and suggest ways in which preserved abilities in blindsight might relate to such a general function. The ventral (inferotemporal) pathway is attenuated in blindsight patients, consistent with Milner and Goodale's view that this pathway is concerned with object recognition and provides the contents for visual consciousness. Given that the inferotemporal region is thought to be critical for the memory readout necessary for object recognition, this understanding of the two streams is consistent with the re-entrant theory discussed above. The memory search, compromised already by the absence of information normally provided by the ventral stream, fails to eventuate in a match with feedforward activity.

Taking a more psychological stance, Weiskrantz (1997) argues that in order for visual material to enter consciousness, it is subjected to a *commentary system*. We do not become conscious of the immediate results of visual analysis, rather we are conscious of the commentary to which they lead: 'The ability to make a commentary is what is meant by being aware and what gives rise to it' (p. 229). Commentary *keys*, the basis on which a person is able to acknowledge that some event occurred, are 'the *sine qua non* of consciousness of a sensory event' (p. 203). The commentary allows further elaboration of the visual material – its meaning and contextualization. Noting that this general function of elaboration and contextualization occurs in higher animals as well as humans, Weiskrantz stresses that the commentary system is not necessarily verbal. However, it is likely to be critical for language development.

Weiskrantz's commentary system may be equated with the system discussed above, whereby material is incorporated into the 'I'-centred narrative. Becoming conscious of some object is to be understood in terms of the 'I' engaging with the representation of the object. The 'narrative' *is* the 'commentary'. This is not to argue that blindsight is uniquely human (which it clearly is not). As discussed earlier, 'I' takes over the role which more primitive self-orientating markers play in non-humans.

The two perspectives I have examined on blindsight, the neural and the psychological, are readily integrated. My proposal is that the re-entrant system is the means through which the 'commentary' is actualized. The commentary/narrative does not exist in some kind of a dualistically detached higher region of processing space, as it were. It is essentially a product of memory readout fully enmeshing with sensory analysis.

There are three principal questions that arise from this consideration of blindsight in relation to consciousness. First, what is the nature of the commentary? Second, what is the status of material prior to its incorporation in the commentary? And third, if the commentary is critical for consciousness, as Weiskrantz suggests, then how and why does it generate qualia?

The third question takes us back to the explanatory gap. As should be clear by now, I see no answer, not even a germinal one, to the question from a solely neuroscientific perspective, and am of the opinion that some essential core of consciousness is transcendent to the physical machinery of the brain. The first question has largely been answered already. In humans, the commentary incorporates material into a narrative in which *meaning* takes centre stage, and which establishes 'I' as the focus of meaning. 'I' is established *post hoc* as being the thinker of thoughts, perceiver of perceptions, and instigator of actions. Consideration of the second question relates to my earlier discussion in Chapter 3 about the status of normally preconscious material. There I proposed that a distinction needs to be made between 'experienceability' and accessibility by 'I'. Terminological difficulty plagues this issue on account of the inconsistent way in which the term 'consciousness' is applied. I will clarify the whole question more fully in Chapter 6. Here, I wish to consider the question specifically in relation to blindsight.

Natsoulas (1999) criticizes Weiskrantz for his assumption that blindsight patients have no visual awareness of material presented in their blind field. His own view is that, 'blindsight patients do have visual experience ... but are deficient in their awareness of the visual experience' (p. 160). For Natsoulas, experience is one thing, but awareness of the experience is another.

Blindsight patients certainly have experiences related to the visual material presented in the blind field. But Weiskrantz insists that these are not *visual* experiences. On the basis both of my own conversations with one of the patients frequently studied (GY), and of the transcripts of Weiskrantz's interviews with his patients, I think that he is correct. GY reports, for example, that he 'got a movement' when a light had been moving in the blind field;

another patient states that he had a 'feeling' that a stimulus was 'smooth' (when 'O' was presented) or 'jagged' (X). In GY's own words, however, 'You don't actually ever sense anything or see anything.... It's more an awareness but you don't *see* it' (Weiskrantz, 1997, p. 144, italics original). It seems to me that these experiences point towards a stage of processing that is poly-modal and strongly connected with feeling. The parallel with synaesthesia is noteworthy. Whilst synaesthesia is profoundly different from blindsight, in that synaesthetic experience is sensory and projected into the world, both syndromes emphasize the poly-modal and emotional processes activated prior to the match between memory readout and sensory input. I have frequently referred to this stage as 'preconscious'. The time has come, however, to revisit the conundrum of preconsciousness. This is one of my tasks in Chapter 6.

This long chapter has built on the foundations laid in Chapter 4 about the function of re-entrant pathways. There is a significant and growing consensus that these pathways hold the key for understanding the complex interactions between perception and memory. The consensus is that re-entrant activity functions to establish a meaningful link between memory readout and sensory activity. Moreover, consciousness appears to be intimately connected with activity in these pathways. My own view is that we cannot account for the explanatory gap in this way. But to disre-gard the growing consensus for this reason would be like ignoring our understanding of the universe on the grounds that we cannot grasp the initiation of the Big Bang. The origin of qualia is merely one aspect of the mystery of consciousness. The dynamics of the conscious–unconscious interactions that define our inner lives is one of the more accessible dimensions of the mystery. And the ideas raised in neurocognitive terms about the importance of multiple, polymodal associations to a sensory input, together with the role of 'I', significantly enhance our grasp of those dynamics.

Chapter 6

The Approach of Depth Psychology

The preconscious state ... is nevertheless something peculiar....
The evidence for this is the fact that large portions of the ego,
and particularly of the super-ego, which cannot be denied the
characteristic of preconsciousness, none the less remain for the
most part unconscious in the phenomenological sense of the
word. We do not know why this must be so. We shall attempt
presently to attack the problem of the true nature of the
preconscious.

(Freud, 1940/1964, pp. 162–3)

The Unconscious is not unconscious, only the Conscious is
unconscious of what the Unconscious is conscious of.

(Jeffrey, 1986, p. 275)

If by 'conscious' one means what I have called 'sensation
consciousness' (states with phenomenality) ... then these
sensation experiences [in blindsight] are conscious, not unconscious. It is only if the question means 'conscious' in the sense of
introspection that the states in question are unconscious.

(Nelkin, 1993, p. 430)

Principles and questions

Unfortunately, Freud never had the chance 'to attack the problem
of the true nature of the preconscious'. *An Outline of Psychoanalysis*, from which the above extract comes, was published

193

posthumously. The *Outline* was the last of Freud's major writings on psychoanalysis. We do, however, know something of 'the problem': the hard boundaries that Freud had proposed in his topographical model of the mind between the conscious, the preconscious, and the unconscious simply could not be made to work. Despite rejecting any notion of an *'unconscious consciousness'* in 1915 (Freud, 1915/1950, p. 103), he came close to it in his 1923 reworking of psychoanalytic theory, when positing an ego that has both conscious and unconscious components. In the above extract from his last major work, the tension is focused on the preconscious. According to his own earlier definition, preconscious contents have free access to consciousness. Yet here, in his swansong, he seems haunted by the inadequacy of the definition.

In Chapter 1, I raised the question of the relationship between the 'preconscious' as understood by depth psychology and the notion of 'preconscious processing' found in cognitive neuroscience. Are these ideas compatible? In a general sense, the answer is clearly 'yes', since both approaches use the term 'preconscious' to convey the idea of material being *outside* of consciousness, yet potentially able to reach consciousness.[1] There are, however, important distinctions between the two approaches. Freud's model is topographical: preconscious contents occupy a *region* of the mind distinct from contents that are conscious or unconscious. Cognitive neuroscience uses the term in a more temporal sense: processes that are preconscious precede the arrival of a stage of processing which is identified with consciousness. As I also noted in Chapter 1, a further critical distinction arises in relation to the possibility of therapeutic, or spiritual, transformation. Preconscious processing is thought by many post-Freudians to be a necessary stage in the integration of repressed mental contents. In this sense, the preconscious is a region of the mind in which prolonged psychological 'work' is said to occur. For cognitive neuroscience, on the other hand, processes deemed to be preconscious are thought of as largely automatic and of short duration. Indeed, any notion of transformation, in the therapeutic or spiritual sense, is deemed largely illusory.

A major question concerns the potential for integration among these approaches. Might ideas advanced in the arena of depth psychology receive backing from research in cognitive neuroscience? This question typifies my interest in the relationships among all the approaches under examination. In the case under consideration here, both depth psychology and cognitive neuroscience have much to gain from dialogue. The methods of depth psychology are open to criticism, yet the scientific basis of cognitive neuroscience means that its data are of unquestionable power. The evidence for preconscious processing as understood by cognitive neuroscience is unassailable. The question is whether such evidence can offer some authorization to the more psychodynamic view of the preconscious. In the other direction, the issue concerns the 'soulless' framework in the approach of cognitive neuroscience. Can we vitalize its models by imbuing them with the transformational spark of depth psychology?

Central to further discussion of the preconscious is the question as to how 'unknown' or 'unknowable' are its contents. Even phrasing the question in this way emphasizes the distinction between the approaches, since cognitive neuroscientists would think of preconscious *processes* rather than *contents*. But, the fact is that in both areas the same problem plagues our understanding. As the extract quoted at the head of this chapter illustrates, Freud came to think that the psychoanalytic preconscious is not fully knowable. The problem for Freud, however, was that his own definition of the preconscious in his earlier writings held that the contents of the preconscious were knowable. The preconscious had been conceived as a region of the psyche not subject to any kind of resistance; its contents could freely enter consciousness.

The extract from Jeffrey at the head of this chapter presents a position clearly at odds with that of Freud. Even the *unconscious* (never mind the preconscious) is not, in principle, unknowable. For Jeffrey, it is simply a question of accessibility: one mental domain may become unavailable for access by another, but the essential consciousness of the domain is unassailable. The third extract, from Nelkin, asserts that inconsistencies in the use of the term 'unconscious' may be attributable to different emphases in our definitions of consciousness. A state or process may be 'conscious' or 'unconscious', depending upon the *dimension* of consciousness at issue.

The critical feature that leads most of us to construe a state as 'unconscious' is its unavailability to introspection. Nelkin argues that such a state may, nevertheless, be phenomenal (cf. my earlier term, *experienceable*). Accordingly, if phenomenality were taken as the critical feature in distinguishing between what is, and what is not, 'conscious', a state regarded by most as 'unconscious' might be accurately described as 'conscious'.

To some extent, any confusion here is down to the question of terminology, which I have already discussed in Chapter 2. However, the psychoanalytic approach, which is the topic of the present chapter, necessitates some further consideration of the issues. There are two fundamental concepts that convey the essence of Freud's approach to the unconscious. Neither is adequately explored through the definitional manoeuvres of Nelkin and others. The first of these fundamental concepts is Freud's insistence that the term 'unconscious' applies to states and processes that are *mental*, as opposed to being purely physiological. The unconscious is a realm of the *mind*. The second of Freud's seminal ideas concerns the *dynamic* of the unconscious. The unconscious is not merely a realm of mind that occupies, as it were, a separate region from that of the conscious mind. The two are actually distinct in terms of the form of thinking that characterizes them.

As I shall explore later in this chapter, both these ideas were highly controversial. For example, contemporaries of Freud, including Pierre Janet and William James, took him to task for the suggestion that mental contents in seemingly healthy-minded individuals, could be *un*conscious. Whilst such might be the case in clearly disturbed, pathological cases, the very notion of unconscious mental contents in each one of us, as Freud's model proposed, was viewed with derision. I shall argue that underlying these tensions lies a fundamental conflict of *worldview*. The issue is larger than might be implied by suggesting that it is simply a matter of terminology.

The battle between the two worldviews, Freud's on the one hand and that of his detractors on the other, is not only of historical interest. Recently, for example, Searle (1992) has taken up Janet's mantle by criticizing the idea that any mental processes might be nonconscious. For Searle, some brain processes give rise to conscious mental content whilst others do not. There is no third category of nonconscious mental content. 'There are brute, blind neurophysiological processes and there is consciousness, but there is nothing else' (p. 228).

What kind of evidence is relevant to the challenge we face in resolving the debate between Freud and his detractors, both old and new? Given that recent research has led to the concept of a *cognitive unconscious* (Kihlstrom, 1987), we might suppose that the data of cognitive neuroscience would be compelling. However, as stressed at the outset, different *levels* in our approaches to consciousness demand different kinds of explanations and different methods of study. Applying the methods of cognitive neuroscience gives rise to a vision of the unconscious that is distinctly impoverished by comparison with that postulated by Freud and other depth psychologists. Does this mean that we must abandon the richer psychodynamic unconscious? The answer to this question will fundamentally depend on the extent to which we accept the validity of the methods used by depth psychologists, and resist granting an effective hegemony to the methods of cognitive neuroscience.

Why should we resist granting hegemony to cognitive neuroscience? There are two kinds of answers to the question. First, there is the concern that it mechanizes what it is to be a human being. Many people feel that there is more to us than the mere raw processing of data. Our lives are concerned with *meaning*, and there is no adequate explanation of how neural systems could possibly generate meaning at any level. A set of neurones may be triggered by the presence of an object in front of my eyes, but we have no idea why the result should be that I experience a meaningful object. It becomes even more problematic to understand how the really important experiences in our lives could be reduced to the types of analysis that are offered by cognitive neuroscience. The second kind of answer is less emotive. It simply states that cognitive neuroscience has been unable to explain the root cause of consciousness. It has not bridged the explanatory gap, and seems *in principle unable to do so*.

In fact, these two answers are two sides of the same coin. The core of consciousness concerns *meaning*. *Meaning* is precisely the subject matter of depth psychology, and the approach of depth psychology draws fundamentally on a methodology which is specifically focused in meaning, namely *hermeneutics*. As I discussed in Chapter 5, cognitive neuroscience may suggest that we live a kind of constructed narrative; but its methods are not directed towards understanding the narrative itself. If your interest lies in the content of that narrative and the reasons why it takes the form it does, then a hermeneutic approach is required. Only such an approach can indicate the differing planes on which the narrative exists, emphasizing unconscious, preconscious and conscious elements. The approach of depth psychology has value alongside more scientific approaches quite simply because it enriches our lives.

Blindsight revisited

Nelkin (1993, 1996) argues that phenomenal consciousness is preserved in cases of blindsight. This contentious claim depends, first, on his understanding of the nature of consciousness, and second, on his distinctive reading of the results from research with blindsight patients.

Nelkin attributes three *dimensions* to consciousness:

1. Phenomenality. As discussed already, this refers to the most essential aspect of consciousness, namely the presence of qualia, the raw stuff of experience.
2. Intentionality. This connotes the *aboutness* of consciousness, that is, the fact that experiences are centred on meaning. In this sense, a conscious experience is always about something. For Nelkin, intentionality is attributable to a certain kind of representation that has *aspectuality*. This means that the representation captures a specific aspect of whatever it represents. To give an example: the representation that you, the reader, may be generating in relation to the page currently in front of your eyes is aspectualized in terms of the meaning of the words. If you are reading, but thinking of something entirely separate, any representation will not be aspectualized in that way. We all know that this happens: you can read for half an hour, and realize that nothing of the content actually went in![2]

    Such aspectualized representations are propositional, that is, they comprise the knowledge that has been built up around whatever is being represented. Nelkin (1996) emphasizes the centrality of the propositional aspect by referring to this dimension of consciousness as 'propositional-attitude consciousness'.
3. Introspectibility. In this sense, a state is conscious if I am able to reflect upon it. Introspectibility may be equated with accessibility, as I have been using the term. In his 1996 book, Nelkin prefers to use 'apperception' to convey this dimension of consciousness. The term 'apperception' was coined by Leibniz to indicate the upper level in a hierarchy of perceptions, a level characterized by clearness of the perceived entities. During the nineteenth century, the term came to be used to describe the grasping by one mental system of the output from another. Nelkin adapts this historical usage, giving apperceptive

consciousness the status of a higher level than the preceding two dimensions. Apperceptive consciousness comprises 'proposition-like representations of either of the former states [phenomenal or intentional consciousness]' (1996, p. 8).

Nelkin supports the distinction between these dimensions both on philosophical grounds and in terms of psychological dissociations. A clear example of the latter would be the case of masked, or subliminal, perception. In paradigmatic research of this kind, individuals have no knowledge that a masked word has been presented; yet their subsequent perception or behaviour provides evidence that the word had been processed to a significant level (Figure 5.1). In cases such as this, it may be stated that dissociation between introspectibility and intentional consciousness has occurred. The meaning of the word has evidently been determined, implying the presence of intentional consciousness, but there is no access to the representation of that meaning – there is no apperceptive consciousness. In the terms developed in Chapter 5, I would argue that, in a case such as this, no link could be constructed between the representation of the word and that of 'I'.

So far this is fairly straightforward and non-contentious. Nelkin's more contentious proposal is that phenomenal consciousness can become dissociated from the second two dimensions of consciousness. This would imply that a person is phenomenally conscious of some entity but has *no means of knowing* that he or she is conscious in that sense. Nelkin (1993) tries to capture the point using the image of 'unintrospected phenomenality ... lurking in the shadows' (p. 427).

How could we know if such a possibility were real? What could convince us that qualia were present even though the individual 'having' them could not know it? How might we demonstrate that what appears to be unconsciousness (dimensions 2 and 3 above) is actually consciousness (dimension 1)?

There are no simple answers to these questions. I am, however, attracted to Nelkin's proposal. Before considering Nelkin's own evidence, let me explore the reasons why I think the proposed dissociation has merit. The first reason is that it avoids the idea of an absolute gap between those brain states that are, and those that are not, conscious. As Nelkin (1996) puts it, 'C2 [apperceptive consciousness] does not create phenomenal states where none existed before' (p. 180). Phenomenality is 'less of a dangler and less of a mystery' (ibid). Of course, a problem remains as to where phenomenal consciousness comes from.[3] There is still a mystery. But we do not have to search for the specific 'magical' addition at the end-stage of perceptual and other brain processes.

The second reason for entertaining the possibility of phenomenality in the absence of other dimensions of consciousness relates to my earlier discussions of mysticism and altered states. Specific states might be understood in terms of the distinctive pattern of dissociation occurring between the three dimensions. Experiences of 'nothingness' might be understood as exemplifying the case of phenomenal consciousness in the absence of both the other dimensions. A mystical state in which divine attributes are directly grasped may be 'preconscious' in the sense of being devoid of the normal access associated with the end-stage, but 'conscious' in terms of phenomenality and intentionality.

Overall, the challenge is to build a terminology that is sufficiently robust to allow serious exploration of the breadth found in diverse conscious states. At the same time, the terminology needs to be supportable in terms of the known brain processes and psychological phenomena relating to conscious states. We seek a terminology that can be operationally defined.

Nelkin's proposal that consciousness comprises three dimensions, each of which can stand alone or in association with one or both of the others, presents itself as a logical possibility. As noted in Chapter 2, many authors have arrived at very similar threefold definitions of consciousness. On this basis, the proposal carries introspective validity. Regarding the notion of dissociation, there is a solid history to the idea that aspects of consciousness which are normally integrated can become dissociated from each other (Hilgard, 1977; Janet, 1889; Perry and Laurence, 1984). The concept of dissociation has clinical value in explaining conditions such as DID or post-traumatic stress disorder (Van der Kolk, 1994). The concept is also current in contemporary thinking about dissociations between implicit, and explicit, processing (see Chapter 5).

The real question for Nelkin, however, is not whether the threefold division itself is reasonable, nor whether dissociation has explanatory value. The question is whether we can point to any states in which phenomenal consciousness is uniquely present, unaccompanied by the other dimensions of consciousness.

Nelkin claims support for his position from research which suggests that blindsight patients can discriminate colour hues in the blind field. Stoerig and Cowey (1989, 1992) demonstrated that blindsight patients could discriminate between light of different wavelengths presented in the blind field, even though they felt themselves to be merely guessing. As with normally-sighted patients, these patients' sensitivity was not uniform across all wavelengths, but was heightened for wavelengths corresponding to recognizable colours. Their performance reflected peaks in sensitivity, for example, in regions of the spectral sensitivity curves corresponding to 'red' or 'blue'. Nelkin argues that this observation suggests that the patients' performance depended on the hue of the colour, rather than on the more mechanical concept of the light's wavelength.

Here we have the contentious heart of Nelkin's claim. 'Blue' or 'red' are qualia; they are not mechanical properties. If the light's 'blueness' or 'redness' formed the basis on which the patients signalled their responses, then it indeed suggests the presence of phenomenal consciousness. Notwithstanding the fact that patients were unable to 'know' what they 'knew', in the sense that both intentionality and apperceptive consciousness were absent, the qualia themselves were the basis for the observed result.

Stoerig (1997) challenges Nelkin's conclusions. She doubts that blindsight patients were responding on the basis of colour hue rather than wavelength. The fact that there may be peaks in sensitivity corresponding to colour qualia is not in itself evidence that qualia were present. Physiological sensitivity to specific wavelengths of light may be the primary factor which determines the patients' choices. The fact that these choices corresponded with known colours does not imply that the colour qualia were present. The physiological system itself may be specialized in order to enhance responses to specific wavelengths.

This argument is intractable, since it is difficult to conceive of evidence that would distinguish the two positions. Stoerig accepts the theoretical position:

> It is in principle possible that the loss of apperception and conscious access is the primary deficit of blindsight; if you lose all access, you could still have phenomenal images, but you would not have any means to use them, let alone report them to others.
>
> (Stoerig, 1997, p. 231)

But she rightly adds that we cannot penetrate into a person's mind to see whether they might have inaccessible phenomenal images, because we have no means of directly accessing someone else's phenomenal experience.

There is an impasse here. The route of direct empirical support for Nelkin's position seems, for the present, to be something of a cul-de-sac. Nevertheless, this need not detract from the theory's philosophical integrity. Stoerig cannot *disprove* the theory; she can only question the basis of the suggested proof drawn from the neurological literature. As Nelkin contends, 'The best reason for maintaining the dissociability thesis will be if the large-scale theory that incorporates it is the best theory of consciousness that we have' (pp. 181–2). As will become clear, I think that a version of Nelkin's thesis may indeed provide us with the best theory of consciousness for the present.

The hermeneutic unconscious

On the possibility of unconscious mental events

In a work first published in 1923, Freud wrote a comment that might be seen as a direct rejoinder to these, much later, ideas of Nelkin: 'a consciousness of which one knows nothing seems to me a good deal more absurd than something mental that is unconscious' (1923/1961, p. 16). Evidently, the possibility that some mental contents might be conscious, but inaccessible, was already a live issue during the development of psychoanalysis. To whom was this rejoinder directed in Freud's own day?

Among Freud's critics were a number of highly influential writers who doubted that any *mental* events could be unconscious. William James (1890/1950) had written that the very idea 'is the sovereign means for believing what one likes in psychology and of turning what might become a science into a tumbling-ground for whimsies' (p. 163). He marshalled objections to each of ten purported proofs of the existence of unconscious mental states. The gist of these objections is that supposed unconscious events may merely be physiological in nature, and therefore not 'mental', or that such events may have been fleetingly conscious, but then rapidly forgotten.[4]

A second possible target of Freud's comment was the French neurologist, Pierre Janet. In 1889, ten years before Freud first published his major ideas about the unconscious, Janet had introduced the concept of *dissociation* to explain abnormal states. Janet argued that under hypnosis, for example, memories might become split off – dissociated – from the main focus of personality. However, unlike Freud, he considered that all activity occurs within the *field* of consciousness. Janet was the first to use the term 'subconscious', meaning that some mental events occur beneath the personality's immediate grasp. Nevertheless, in normal, non-pathological, cases all such events are capable of integration within the field of consciousness. They are not unconscious.

Both James and Janet distinguished between events that are 'merely' physiological and those that are mental. They regarded the former as unconscious in the trivial sense that they are simply mechanical. The great divide between Freud and his critics arises in thinking about states and processes of the mind.[5] For both Janet and James, the terms 'mental' or 'mind' were effectively synonymous with 'conscious'. Any intimation of 'unconscious-ness' as signalled by people's behaviour, was attributed to grada-tions in consciousness and/or divisions within the conscious sphere. The French tradition along these lines was particularly strong. For example, writing of dissociated elements in the mind, Binet (1896) emphasized that 'a consciousness never ceases to accompany these elements' (p. 348), even though the elements may be outside the sphere to which the ego has access. In the terms I used in the previous section, we may interpret Binet and Janet as holding that phenomenality and intentionality may be present although accessibility by the ego is not.

For Freud, 'mental' did not equate to 'conscious'. He described two distinct mental systems, only one of which is conscious. The unconscious system is the evolutionary older of the two systems, and is driven by the *pleasure principle*. The second system, that of the conscious mind, is the subjective dimension of the outwardly-directed perceptual activity of the brain. The consciousness system is motivated by the reality principle. In his *Project for a Scientific Psychology*, an early treatment of the theory, Freud explicitly distinguished his view from those theories that held consciousness to be the subjective side of *all* mental (that is, psychic) events. None of his later formulations changed this fundamental axiom.

Moreover, for Freud, the unconscious sphere proceeds in terms of its own distinctive logic *all the time*, even in normal, non-neurotic cases. The ever-present unconscious, with its own distinctive dynamic, is part of our normal make-up. Clearly, the Freudian position contrasts fundamentally with the French school exemplified by Janet and Binet, for whom any nonconscious activity in normal individuals is either *bodily*, that is, physiological, or *in process of becoming conscious*. In this sense, the French school is closer to the modern perspective of cognitive psychology, a point well understood by Hilgard (1977), who coined the term 'neodissociation' for his updated revision of Janet's theory.

The cognitive orientation in modern psychology stresses the computer metaphor of information processing. As noted in Chapter 5, for example, Baars' concept of the 'global workspace', and its role in making information accessible to other processing units, derives from computer science. The landscape of cognitive science is peppered with terms, such as 'central processing unit' or 'pattern recognition devices', whose original provenance was within IT. This emphasis on the computer parallel has played no small role in the resurgence of thinking about dissociation and the modularity of the brain and cognitive systems. Hilgard's neodissociaton theory gave shape to these developments. He identifies the 'executive ego' as being the 'central control structure' which sits atop an array of modular 'cognitive control structures'. Dissociation will be evident in a case where the output of a particular cognitive control structure bypasses the executive ego. In effect, Hilgard's proposals assert the hegemony of the computer-dominated approach of cognitive science over the more human-centred, therapeutic approaches in the clinical sphere.

As Kunzendorf and McGlinchey-Berroth (1997–8) argue, the computer metaphor encourages us to think of brain processes as quantitative, paralleling the quantitative and automatic processes in a computer. They consider that the metaphor leads us to view the quantitative brain processes as necessarily being pre- or unconscious, since the parallel machine processes comprise merely mechanical routines. The authors note that this line of reasoning concludes in our thinking of consciousness in dualistic or epiphenomenal terms. Consciousness is a mysterious added ingredient, somehow apart from the quantitative brain processes, but interacting with them (Cartesian dualism). Or it is viewed as being inconsequential to the processes of the brain (epiphenomenalism).

Kunzendorf's (for instance, 2000) preferred solution rejects the computer metaphor, holding instead that subjective experience is an intrinsic aspect of certain brain processes that determine the source from which images derive. Accordingly, these brain processes are thought to constitute a *self-conscious source-monitoring mechanism*. The mental images are never nonconscious. They are the subjective aspect of the decision made by the source-monitoring mechanism. If, for example, an image had been caused by sensory activity, and the source-monitoring system correctly determines that the image was attributable to the outside world, then the image would be a *percept*. If, on the other hand, I were fantasizing about the ideal dessert, an image of the crêpes (or whatever!) is determined as deriving from an internal source. Kunzendorf's theory is supported by data from his research into subliminal perception. These demonstrated that an image formed following exposure of a subliminal stimulus is *not* intrinsically unconscious. Rather, the image is misconstrued by the source-monitoring system as having been internally generated. The subject makes a misattribution as to the source of the conscious image.

The theories of Hilgard and Kunzendorf exemplify recent elaborations of the position adopted by Janet, which questioned Freud's view that some mental processes are unconscious. The theories articulate the notion that mental processes are predicated on preliminary, physiological (that is, non-mental) ones, and that all mental activity is conscious in some form. For Kunzendorf, there may be a misattribution, resulting in an image being subjectively dismissed for not being a percept, but the mental image itself is never unconscious.

Thus far, I have focused on only one of the fundamental propositions that Freud put forward, namely, his insistence that some mental activity is unconscious. I shall revisit the conclusion to which the above discussion seems to be moving – namely, that Freud was wrong in asserting this first proposition – following consideration of the second proposition. To anticipate, I believe that the second proposition – that the motivation and style of the unconscious thought process is distinct from that of the conscious mind – is difficult to reject. While cognitive neuroscience might not have reason to view the proposition sympathetically, there is a wealth of material in the therapeutic and spiritual traditions that seems to support it. Given a degree of support for the second proposition, I shall argue that it becomes impossible to sustain opposition to the first.

Dimensions of consciousness in the 'I'-tag theory

The sequential nature of the stages of the 'I'-tag theory developed in Chapter 5 tends towards the Kunzendorf–Janet type of model.

The processes depicted in the theory are either 'merely' physiological, or en route to becoming fully conscious. However, the picture is more complex when two key factors are introduced. First, recognizing that there are different dimensions of consciousness introduces the possibility that a stage which lacks consciousness on one dimension may nevertheless be conscious on another. Second, the function of the stage involving a memory search may be more extensive than is suggested by the narrow vision of it as a preliminary to matching the target image. As will be discussed below, the activation of memory images, triggered by the neuronal input model, seems to be more elaborate than is immediately implied by thinking of it as simply establishing the literal identity of a given input. In brief, I propose that the memory search gives rise to a distinct *stream* of mental activity, the logic of which approximates that ascribed by Freud to the unconscious thought process.

Figure 6.1 illustrates my proposals for relating various dimensions of consciousness to the stages of the 'I'-tag theory. The terminology involves a slight adaptation of that used by Nelkin, introduced above.

The first stage, that of feature analysis, is devoid of any conscious dimension. Feedforward neural activity is driven by the energy imparted by the external world onto the sensory systems in the first place. The responses of the feature analyzers are purely mechanical.

I postulate that phenomenal consciousness and intentionality are introduced into the brain's information processing by the activity of re-entrant processes. This proposal is in accord with the recent research that has been examined over Chapters 4 and 5. **Phenomenality** arises by dint of the feedforward activity intersecting with memory systems. As intimated already, I do not envisage that the brain processes themselves generate phenomenality. The feedforward activity engages a 'higher actuality' whose essential character is phenomenality.[6]

Intentionality has a dual connotation. It refers both to the specification of some entity and to the *movement towards something* (May, 1965). As May points out, this duality is evident in the two ways we use the word 'mean' in everyday English. The phrase, 'I meant the dark suit', implies a specification of an item. On the other hand, 'I meant to wake early, but forgot to set the alarm', conveys a movement towards something.[7] I assume that both connotations are implicated in the operation of memory. Activated

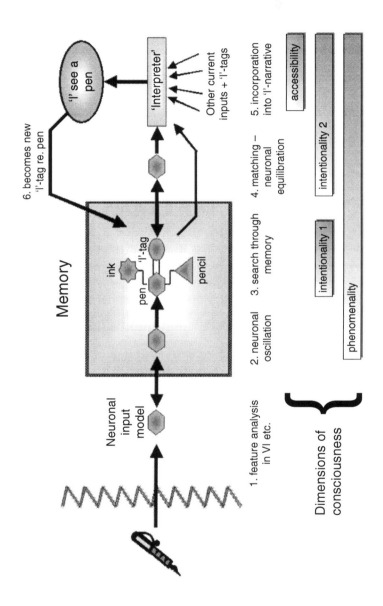

FIGURE 6.1 'I'-tag theory: dimensions of consciousness

representations are meaningful in the first sense, that is, they specify the entities which are represented. The sequence of activations
through the memory system is intentional in the second sense: the
sequence is moving towards something. However, neither connotation should be thought of as independent of the other. They are
two sides of the one coin: there can be no specification of an
entity's meaning other than in terms of the direction in which the
memory process is moving.

This is, of course, where Freud's major insight is critical.
He recognized two streams, each with its distinctive intentionality.
The unconscious stream, named the *primary process*, is irrational,
symbolic, and directed towards wish fulfilment. The conscious
stream, the *secondary process*, is rational and reality-orientated.
Leaving aside the question of unconsciousness itself, I would
include an adapted form of these two streams in the 'I'-tag theory,
using the terms *Intentionality 1* and *Intentionality 2*. **Intentionality 2** arises at the stage of establishing the identity of the object
through matching of input and memory readout. The essence of
this matching process is the drive to connect memory readout to
the world of the senses, the hallmark of *reality orientation*. **Intentionality 1** is associated with the memory activity that is not part
of the matching function in this way. Whilst I have reservations in
linking it with wish fulfilment in the rigid Freudian sense, its hallmark is indeed the kind of symbolic, non-rational processes of
association to which Freud drew attention. As I elaborate later in
this chapter, I envisage Intentionality 1 as giving rise to its own
distinctive stream of activity.

The two forms of intentionality correspond to two motivations
in the memory process. We may think of these as expansive and
limiting respectively. Intentionality 1 is expansive; it brings about
activation of the diverse ramifications of meaning that may be
discerned in the input. Evidence for this process derives from studies revealing that multiple meanings of a sensory input are activated preconsciously, as reviewed in Chapter 5. Intentionality 2 is
limiting, in that it functions to inhibit the activations that gain
access to the matching process in the stage following the memory
search.

Finally, **accessibility** (that is, 'access-consciousness', or Nelkin's
'introspectibility') arises when the matched object or event
becomes incorporated into the 'I'-narrative. Generally, it is only
Intentionality 2 that becomes incorporated in the narrative. The

'I'-model exerts further inhibitory influence on the expression of diverse ramifications in the narrative. As I shall explore in Chapter 7, however, therapeutic techniques, such as visualization or free association, as well as spiritual and mystical practices, may lead to aspects of Intentionality 1 becoming expressed in this final stage.

The critical consideration in relation to the approach of depth psychology concerns the validity of Intentionality 1. The debate surrounding the possibility of mental events being unconscious, which I have considered above, is secondary to this question of the validity of Intentionality 1. Disagreements over the unconsciousness of mental states and processes may largely be a matter of differing emphases being placed on one or other of the dimensions of consciousness. As I shall discuss below, this debate may fundamentally be a question of *worldview*. However, should Freud's concept of the primary process of thought – reformulated here as Intentionality 1 – be proved false, then the Freudian edifice would certainly collapse.

I referred above to research in cognitive psychology, which suggests that multiple representations of meaning are activated preconsciously. This evidence touches on an aspect of Intentionality 1, but it cannot be claimed that it fully substantiates the kind of dynamic motivation that is envisaged. The validity of Intentionality 1 rests not on research in cognitive science or neuroscience, but on the evidence drawn from its own level – that of hermeneutics.

Separating the levels

Woody and Phillips (1995) helpfully address the confusion surrounding the different ways in which the term 'unconscious' is typically used in contemporary literature. They recognize three distinct meanings of the term. First there is the *neurological unconscious*. This refers to the neurophysiological underpinnings of our experience. As they remark, this use of the term 'unconscious' tends to be confusing, since it bears no relation to the *psychodynamic unconscious*, which, following Freud, is the 'type' of unconscious that has entered the popular vocabulary.

Woody and Phillips go on to draw a distinction between two further uses of the term 'unconscious': the *cognitive unconscious* and the *psychodynamic unconscious*. The latter refers to the kind of unconscious to which Freud and others draw attention. Whilst they may disagree on details of its dynamic, all depth psychologists agree that the psychodynamic unconscious is ever-present and complex, which distinguishes it from the cognitive unconscious. Woody and Phillips' principal argument is that the kind of research that underpins our understanding of the cognitive unconscious is intrinsically unable to provide us with insight into the psychodynamic unconscious. Cognitive research essentially asks the wrong questions; a different approach is required.

The requisite approach involves the discipline of *hermeneutics*, since it is through the challenge to understand ourselves and our minds via the logic of interpretation that the psychodynamic unconscious emerges. The psychodynamic unconscious cannot be found through neurological or cognitive examination. The appropriate parallel to the tradition of psychoanalytic interpretation is that found in textual traditions. Here, the term 'hermeneutics' refers to the accepted interpretative mode that may legitimately be applied to the text. The text's various levels of meaning become revealed when we apply the appropriate hermeneutic. Similarly, interpretation of the overt phenomena of the human mind reveals the deeper features of that mind, without which interpretation would be irrelevant. The psychodynamic unconscious is the necessary condition for making sense of the interpretation of humans as complex psychological beings, just as acceptance of meaning beyond the surface level of the text legitimizes literary, or scriptural, hermeneutics.

None of this applies to our reasons for postulating a cognitive unconscious, the basis of which is found in the assumption of cognitive mechanisms directly leading towards a conscious end-stage of processing. According to Woody and Phillips, therefore, our increasing understanding of the cognitive unconscious can play no role in the quest to grasp the psychodynamic unconscious. For the same reasons, any suggestions by cognitive scientists that their research questions the 'reality' of the psychodynamic unconscious should be regarded with suspicion:

> [T]he psychodynamic unconscious is an artefact of the process of interpretation and self-interpretation whereby human beings knit their experiences together into networks of meaning. No doubt these interpretative relationships are realized by neurological processes and interact with cognition. But the dynamics of meaning-relations revealed in psychotherapy must not be confused with either the causal relations to be sought in

neurophysiology nor the relatively simple and low-level processing characteristic of the cognitive unconscious.

(Woody and Phillips, 1995, p. 127)

Hermeneutics is the science of interpretation. This was Freud's milieu *par excellence*. His work is characterized by the most penetrating insight into the complex mental gymnastics that may have lain beneath some individual expression – an overt remark, a dream image, or a work of art, for example. Whether or not his final conclusions are 'right', we tend to enjoy the game he allows us to play. This is a key feature of the lasting legacy of Freud. Freud's place in our cultural history is not primarily due to his introduction of a therapeutic practice. He was responsible for a foundational shift that gave us licence to embrace a daring hermeneutic imperative. The twin features of his work underpinning this shift are the recognition of an intentionality separate from that associated with the conscious mind, and the emphasis he placed on the role sexuality plays in that separate intentionality.

Woody and Phillips are, to my mind, correct in reminding us of the distinctiveness of what I will refer to as the *hermeneutic unconscious*. As they assert, its importance lies in the recognition that it contributes to the vision of what it is to be fully human. The imperative towards self-understanding is somehow diminished when the hermeneutic unconscious is excluded from our model of the mind.[8] To put it another way, without the hermeneutic unconscious we would be merely two-dimensional beings. I use the term 'hermeneutic unconscious' since, as Freud suggests, the unconscious itself is the hermeneutic heart of the mind. The slippages of meaning it generates, the motivated associations and concealing blinds, these are the very core of a mind given to interpretation. In the concealment is the interpretation....

A question of worldview

[P]sycho-analysis cannot accept the identity of the conscious and the mental.... The question whether we are to make the psychical coincide with the conscious or make it extend further sounds like an empty dispute about words; yet I can assure you that the hypothesis of there being unconscious mental processes paves the way to a decisive new orientation in the world and in science.

(Freud, 1916–17/1963, p. 22)

Freud in historical context

The above extract makes clear that Freud viewed the clash with critics such as Janet as being of more significance than I have considered thus far. Why should the issue of the unconsciousness of mental events 'pave the way to a decisive new orientation'?

This question is answered when we recognize the philosophical impact of Freud's propositions. In introducing one of his major essays, *The Unconscious*, Freud touches on the philosophical issue:

[T]he conventional identification of the mental with the conscious is thoroughly impractical. It breaks up all mental continuity, plunges us into the insoluble difficulties of psychophysical parallelism, is open to the reproach that without any manifest grounds it overestimates the part played by consciousness, and finally it forces us prematurely to retire from the territory of psychological research without being able to offer us any compensation elsewhere.

(Freud, 1915/1950, p. 100)

In order to fill the gaps in mental continuity, Freud insisted that unconscious mental events must be recognized. As Panhuysen notes, this move fundamentally challenged the Cartesian dualism that had previously dominated intellectual discourse in these areas. He writes that if it is indeed the case 'that the content of representations continues to work unconsciously as well [as consciously]', then:

[C]onsciousness and mind can no longer be regarded as one and the same. Psychic processes can be both conscious and unconscious. For this reason the Cartesian criterion for the demarcation of mind and matter, according to which unconscious processes take place in the material arena, is untenable.

(Panhuysen, 1998, p. 29)

Whyte (1962) explains why the particular form of dualism articulated by Descartes acted as a historical trigger to ideas of an unconscious dimension to the mind. By identifying mind, or thought, solely with 'I' ('I think, therefore I am'), Descartes had excluded other features of mind not so readily incorporated within the orb of 'I'. Whyte suggests that this bias mitigated, for example, against the kinds of intimations of thought and knowledge outside of 'I' that had, for centuries, been suggested by mystics. It also failed to allow for any understanding of the psychopathological cases that interested Freud. Descartes' exaltation of the conscious ego led to a historical reaction, a pendulum swing towards recognition of thought that is not 'I'-related, namely unconscious thought.

Cartesian dualism brought about the need for the idea of the unconscious to emerge. Prior to Freud, that need was taking shape in ideas about processes of the mind that are unconscious before they reach consciousness as a kind of consummation. But this could not answer the need, since the dualism is still effectively present: consciousness is the icing on the unconscious cake. Moreover, many denied the unconsciousness in such a picture. Mind processes were subconscious (James) or co-conscious (Prince) or dissociated (Janet), but not *unconscious*. What was needed was a view of a mental unconscious that fully interpenetrated the realm of the body. It was only Freud who genuinely toppled Descartes. Why?

Freud and anti-Semitism: 'the Jewish science'

[H]ow impossible it is to dispute the personal significance upon world-history of individual great men.

(Freud, 1939/1964, p. 52)

A telling comment of Freud's may be found in a criticism directed towards Janet in a paper on the history of the psychoanalytic movement that Freud wrote in 1914. Janet had mockingly suggested that Freud's insistence on a sexual basis to neuroses arose due to a feature of the mores in Vienna, the city where Freud had developed his theories.

We have all heard of the interesting attempt to explain psychoanalysis as a product of the peculiar character of Vienna as a city; as recently as 1913 Janet did not disdain to employ this argument, although he himself is undoubtedly proud of being a Parisian. This inspiration runs as follows: psychoanalysis, so far as it consists of the assertion that the neuroses are traceable to disturbances in the

sexual life, could only have come to birth in a town like Vienna –
in an atmosphere of sensuality and immorality foreign to other
cities – and it simply contains a reflection, a projection into theory,
as it were, of these peculiar Viennese conditions. Now honestly, I
am no local patriot; but this theory about psychoanalysis always
seems to be quite exceptionally stupid, so stupid, in fact, that I
have sometimes been inclined to suppose that the reproach of
being a citizen of Vienna is only a euphemistic substitute for
another reproach which no one would care to put forward openly.
(Freud, 1914/1949, p. 325)

To anyone who has more than a passing acquaintance with Freud's
life and writing style, the 'other reproach' is clearly that of anti-
Semitism (Gay, 1988). Janet's recourse to innuendo over the
atmosphere of Vienna revealed to Freud a deeper anti-Semitic
thrust in his polemic.

Freud was haunted by anti-Semitism throughout his life, and, as
a number of recent authors have stressed, a major feature of his
work was directed to understanding its aetiology. The characterization of psychoanalysis as 'the Jewish science' by those antithetical to
Freud was itself intended as a slur. It may, paradoxically, be accurate
in ways not overtly intended, as will be considered below. Such is the
way of history that the derogatory casting of psychoanalysis as the
Jewish science became, in 1977, 'a title of honour'. Freud's daughter, Anna, used this phrase on the occasion of the founding of the
Sigmund Freud Professorship at the Hebrew University of Jerusalem.

The potent and engrained anti-Semitism of Vienna has been fully
documented (Billig, 1997; Diller, 1991; Gay, 1988). It played a
major role in Freud's career development, for his decision to study
medicine was made only when his preferred path, that of law, was
thwarted by the anti-Semitic stance of the legal profession. The path
Freud took in his last years was similarly dominated by anti-Semitism, this time in the form of Nazism. In 1938, Freud had to flee his
beloved Vienna for London. At the end of his career, he poignantly
lamented in a letter to the English publication, *Time and Tide* (26
November 1938):

I came to Vienna as a child of four years from a small town in
Moravia. After 78 years, including more than half a century of
strenuous work I had to leave my home, saw the Scientific Society
I had founded dissolved, our institutions destroyed, our Printing

Press (Verlag) taken over by the invaders, the books I had published confiscated and reduced to pulp, my children expelled from their professions.
(Accessed www.loc.gov/exhibits/freud/images/vc008374.jpg on 8 November 2003.)

This is not the place for an extensive analysis of the influence of anti-Semitism on the direction taken by Freud's career. However, in order to understand the significance of the hermeneutic unconscious for any complete theory of consciousness, I suggest that a grasp of the Jewish roots of psychoanalysis is necessary. Bernstein (1998) speculates that Freud's intended lasting legacy to his fellow psychoanalysts was to emphasize that psychoanalysis represented a development of the distinctively Jewish blend of intellectuality and spirituality that had its origins in Mosaic monotheism. Bernstein considers that this intention underlies Freud's choice of reading for an address given on his behalf to the International Psychoanalytical Congress in 1938, the year before his death. Although he was too ill himself to attend, he chose a section of his last major work, *Moses and Monotheism*, to be read out. The section describes the way in which the Mosaic revolution introduced '*Der Fortschritt in der Geistigkeit*', a phrase that is difficult to convey fully in translation. Freud seems to be intending to convey a move away from magic and superstition, and towards a form of intellectual quest that, nevertheless, does not lose contact with spirituality. Bernstein suggests that Freud regarded this subtle blend of the spiritual with the intellectual as representing the achievement of Judaism at its best. Psychoanalysis was a means for perpetuating this achievement without the 'contamination' of faith and superstition.[9]

Freud was clearly a man possessed, certainly as far as completion of his work on Moses was concerned. The study of Moses, wrote Freud, 'tormented me like an unlaid ghost'. Of Moses he wrote that, 'The man and what I wanted to make of him pursue me everywhere'. Indeed, he confided that the historical roots of the Moses story had 'pursued me throughout the whole of my life'.[10]

Analysis of *Moses and Monotheism* reveals something of the motivations behind the whole edifice of psychoanalysis. In an imagined monologue with Freud, Yerushalmi puts it clearly:

I think that in your innermost heart you believed that psychoanalysis is itself a further, if not final, metamorphosed extension

of Judaism, divested of its illusory religious forms but retaining
its essential monotheistic characteristics, at least as you understood and described them. In short, I think you believed that just
as you are a godless Jew, psychoanalysis is a godless Judaism.

(Yerushalmi, 1991, p. 99)

Moreover, Freud seems to have produced his analysis of Moses
and the origins of Judaism with the specific, if somewhat
concealed, aim of dispelling the roots of anti-Semitism. In Freud's
version, Moses is viewed as an Egyptian dedicated to a monotheistic tradition which had been born in Egypt. When this tradition
grew out of favour in Egypt itself, Moses attempted to perpetuate
its tenets by teaching them to a group (the 'Children of Israel') that
he led away from Egypt. In the desert, however, the group rose up
in rebellion and murdered their leader. According to Freud, this
primal murder became repressed, but returns in various concealed
ways in the biblical narrative. Critically for Freud's understanding
of the relation between Christianity and Judaism, traces of the
primal murder theme return also in the tenets and practices of
Christianity.

   Freud's thesis hardly stands up to critical analysis, and the book
has been ridiculed for its poor scholarship. However, whatever the
status of the historical picture Freud paints, we may discern in the
book a creditable picture of his view of anti-Semitism. The most
historically insidious and psychologically potent accusation
against Jews has been that of their guilt as killers of Christ; the
Jews have the blood of 'God' on their hands. At a stroke, Freud
dispelled the authenticity and psychological force of the claim. The
primal killing was that of Moses, and since both Jews and Christians alike claim heritage from his 'tribe', then, to the extent that
any guilt could attach to the crime, both Jews and Christians are
implicated. The original title of Freud's book makes a further
point, which is lost in the English translation. The German is *Der
Mann Moses und die Monotheistische Religion*. Moses was man
('*Der Mann*'), not God. There is no deicide.

   Whilst this analysis of Freud's treatment of Moses offers considerable insight into Freud's motives, I am inclined to think that the
major thrust of psychoanalysis in relation to the tension between
Christianity and Judaism lies more in the notion of sacred texts
and hermeneutics than in the supposed origins of Moses and
monotheism. The sacred scripture of Judaism is dual: the *Written*

Torah and the *Oral Torah*.[11] Rabbinic Judaism repeatedly stresses the essential unity between these two. For example, the revelation at Mount Sinai itself is regarded as comprising both *Torot*.[12] Even the oral teachings throughout all future generations are described as being an integral part of the original divine revelation. The *Oral Torah* comprises the means for deciphering the written text, having, at its core, the rules for interpreting the *Written Torah*. As Handelman (1982) demonstrates, these rules accord with the 'rules' Freud established for deciphering the output of the unconscious mind. 'For both Freud and the Rabbis, interpretation was the pre-eminent mode of knowing' (p.151), and analogous techniques inform their respective logic of interpretation.[13] The hermeneutic rules deal with the legitimate methods for reading associations into the text, be it the text of the Torah or that of the mind. While the associations may not be present on the surface, they constitute an integral part of the totality known through the interpretative method. In the case of the Rabbis, such rules are required for the reason that the written text is viewed as multi-leveled; they bring order into what might otherwise seem like an interpretative 'free-for-all'. Psychoanalysis attempted to inject a similar order into the quest to decipher the human 'text'.[14]

The path of rabbinic Judaism is one of continually seeking the reasons for manifest words or actions. The *Written Torah* conveys a surface of stories and commands; the oral tradition (*Oral Torah*) seeks to penetrate beneath the surface to the concealed content. It is similar at the level of praxis: practising Jews perpetuate a way of life to which they are heirs, and may spend a lifetime uncovering ever deeper reasons for their religiously-prescribed actions. The 'given' is subject to continual analysis.

The parallel here with psychoanalysis is not vague, but incredibly precise. In *The Psychopathology of Everyday Life* (1904/1966), Freud collates numerous examples of the ways in which slips of the tongue or unintended actions reveal unconscious motivations. Indeed, as he makes clear, his distinctive approach is precisely to be found in the assumption of meaningful motivations within seeming accidents of speech and action. The motivation, and the meaning of the words or actions, may be brought to consciousness only through searching analysis of a kind analogous to that which Freud's Orthodox co-religionists apply to sacred text and religiously-prescribed actions.

Christianity canonized the written biblical text but rejected the oral tradition. Freud's input to healing the rift between Christianity and Judaism may, with hindsight, be seen to lie in the reintroduction of an oral tradition appropriate to the challenges of a post-religious age. Psychoanalysis is to the text of the human mind, and indeed to cultural products in general, as the oral tradition in Judaism is to the text of the Torah.[15]

Against this background, it becomes possible to elaborate the statement made above to the effect that it is Freud who heals the rift implicit in Cartesian dualism. Descartes' dualism is nothing other than the dualism intrinsic to Christianity cast in philosophical guise. Paul's rejection of the body as a medium of spirituality, recorded in the New Testament, eventuates in Descartes' glorification of the 'I', and the mechanistic view of the body accompanying it. By demonstrating that the dynamics of a *mental* realm were intimately bound up with the body (that is, via sexuality), Freud displaced dualism. Indeed, I suspect that this was the fundamental reason why Freud stuck so tenaciously to his theory of the sexual nature of the libido, even when disciples such as Adler and Jung challenged it.

Rejection of the body parallels rejection of the *Oral Torah*, for it is the *Oral Torah* that plugs the spiritual dimension into the everyday bodily and physical realm. As the *Oral Torah* itself insists, the realm of active spiritual endeavour is here 'on earth' not 'in heaven'.[16]

Of what relevance is all this to the contemporary interest in consciousness? After all, we appear to be living in a post-religious age, and Judaism, one of the two religions under discussion, might be thought to be of trivial influence given the number of its affiliates worldwide. The fact is, however, that European culture, dominated as it was by Christian thought, has been inevitably burdened by its own rejected and repressed contents. The interpenetration of spirit and matter in our worldly realm, as portrayed in rabbinic Judaism, was a central feature of these repressed contents. Descartes' dualism is the classic philosophical product of the worldview of Christianity, and is consequently a clear expression of the gross inability to integrate these repressed contents. Just as Freud taught that we must integrate our individual repressed contents in order to achieve psychological health, so too does cultural 'health' depend on an integration of repressed *cultural* contents. All contemporary debate about consciousness is necessarily grounded in the philosophical currents forged in Christian

Europe. The anti-Semitism that was of such significance to Freud, was a product of the repressed content of the dominant worldview (Cohn, 1970; Lancaster, 1993a).

In relation to consciousness studies in our day, the repressed has returned to haunt us in our quest to understand the embodiment of mind. In our post-Freudian age, we are beginning to embrace a new worldview, one in which the interaction between spirit and world, mind and matter is becoming paramount. The rise of consciousness studies over recent years is itself the measure of that shift in worldview. I think there can be little doubt that Freud recognized the deeper meaning of psychoanalysis in terms of these historical and cultural currents, and that it was for this reason that he thought his development of the new approach heralded a 'decisive new orientation in the world and in science'.

Vesey (1964) rightly notes that, in the historical development of our concept of mind, 'the one central theme is provided by the Cartesian notion of substance' (p. 12). Descartes removed any notion of soul from substance. And when Janet insisted on the identity of mind and consciousness he was subtly perpetuating the Cartesian divide. The corollary of substance having no soul is that mind can only be conscious.

Freud insists on the unconscious roots of meaning and thereby resurrects (if I might use the word) the soul of the world. In Christian Europe there were effectively two expressions of dualism: the separation of the transcendent God from the world, and the separation of 'I'-consciousness from the body. The idea of the psychodynamic unconscious pricks the bubble of the second, paving the way for today's emphasis on the embodiment of consciousness and its scientific study.

Two mental streams

To recapitulate, there are grounds from several sources for us to accept Freud's key postulates, and to recognize the importance for contemporary work on consciousness of the shift in worldview which he instigated. For Freud, the unconscious is driven by sexuality; its operative mode is that of the primary process – symbolic, non-linguistic, devoid of a time sense, and not reality-orientated. All this contrasts with the conscious mind, whose secondary process thought is rational, reality-oriented and verbal, and whose motivation is towards the acceptable norms of the social world. It is only on account of the complex role played by the unconscious mental dynamic that we need a process of hermeneutic analysis to understand humans. If the non-conscious mental activity were different only in level, but not in kind, from conscious activity there would be no need of a hermeneutical psychological tradition.

In relation to the 'I'-tag theory, I have suggested above that a complete picture of the processes involved requires us to incorporate a psychodynamic dimension into the 'search' stage. As discussed already, the question as to whether or not we view this dynamic as unconscious involves consideration of the dimensions of consciousness. I believe that this, in turn, becomes a cultural issue. Whyte (1962) makes the point that the realm we generally designate as 'unconscious' is the more general of the two realms of the mind, and that, 'it is unsatisfactory to define the more general by a negative: unconscious' (p. 183). This realm is not only the more inclusive of the two, but, as Whyte argues, is also the source of inspiration and spiritual knowing. For this reason, Whyte may be correct to criticize our use of a negative to describe it. However, I am inclined to think that the terminology would not have taken such a firm hold had it not been responding to some chord in our culture. In any case, the terminology is here to stay (at least for the foreseeable future), and I will, accordingly, continue to refer to the dynamic level of mind as the 'hermeneutic unconscious'.

The way to extricate ourselves from the terminological confusion is through the kind of operational approach that I have adopted. The 'I'-tag theory may be found to be lacking in detail, but I believe that its analysis of the stages involved in conscious processes offers a way forward in consciousness studies. In the terms given earlier, phenomenality arises with the interaction between feedforward neural activity and the sphere of memory. The hermeneutic unconscious engages this phenomenality in the operation of Intentionality 1. Phenomenality is subsequently imparted to the processes concerned with Intentionality 2 in establishing reality-oriented meaning. Finally, the 'I'-narrative takes on the dimension of access-consciousness, which, again, is imbued with the original phenomenality.

The diagrams I have used inevitably give a rather static picture of the 'I'-tag theory. A single diagram cannot do justice to what must be a complex interaction of events. At the very least, the situation could never be static, since expectations will already have activated the relevant representations. If the object in front of my eyes is a pen, then the preceding circumstance of, say, needing a writing implement to write down an idea, will have activated pen-related representations before the pen even enters my sphere of vision. From a neuroscientific perspective, Crick and Koch capture the point by referring to the 'penumbra' of the neural correlate of consciousness (NCC):

> [F]iring [of the NCC] will influence many neurons that are not part of the NCC. These we call the 'penumbra'. The penumbra consists of both synaptic effects and also firing rates. The penumbra is not the result of just the sum of the effects of each essential node separately, but the effects of that NCC as a whole. This penumbra includes past associations of NCC neurons, the expected consequences of the NCC, movements (or at least possible plans for movement) associated with NCC neurons, and so on. For example, a hammer represented in the NCC is likely to influence plans for hammering.
>
> (Crick and Koch, 2003, p. 124)

The same two questions that were pivotal for the controversy over Freud's model of the mind apply similarly to this concept of a penumbra. The first question asked whether the realm of mental events is to be exclusively identified with consciousness. The second addressed the logic of mental events: is there evidence for the existence of a stream of mental activity whose logic is radically distinct from that of the immediately-known realm of mind?

According to our earlier discussion, Freud would answer 'no' to the first question, and 'yes' to the second. The penumbra may possess unconscious mental qualities, and the unconscious processes have their own distinctive, hermeneutic logic. In line with the approach of cognitive neuroscience, Crick and Koch's answer would seem to be 'no' to the first question, and 'no' to the second.[17] My answer is a qualified 'yes' to both questions. As far as the first question is concerned, I hold that the penumbra includes the dimensions of phenomenality and Intentionality 1, but lacks those of Intentionality 2 and accessibility by 'I'. In relation to the second question, it will be clear from my earlier discussion of Intentionality 1 that the penumbra includes activations of a symbolic associational nature. If, to draw on Crick and Koch's example, a hammer is represented in the focus of consciousness, the penumbra will include reverberations around images of symbolically related items. For example, in addition to the direct associations of nails, the penumbra might include animal associations (*claw*-hammer), sexual connotations ('*banging*' in the vernacular), and so on. The point is that the penumbra is not merely a short-lived, passive response to the item forming in the centre of access-consciousness. It is also part of an ongoing dynamic, which takes its own distinctive (and motivated) course, and is only temporally linked to the item.

Memory operates according to the fundamental logic of resonance and association. My earlier term, the 'pure memory process', captures the impersonal basis of this logic (Lancaster, 1991). Clearly, the kinds of associations that fill the penumbra will not be purely impersonal. As intimated above, these associations will carry deep, for example Freudian, connotations. I shall, accordingly, refer to the memory activity responsible for the penumbra as the 'deep memory process' (DMP). The DMP, then, gives rise to memory images based on principles of similarity and symbolic meaning, which carry deep significance for a given individual. DMP activity generates a stream of mentation which is largely distinct from that of the 'I'-focused narrative. A subset of the images in the DMP stream will be incorporated in the 'I'-narrative stream. For example, a neuronal input model in relation to a pen may be expected to give rise to a variety of associated memory images, as indicated above. A subset of these – namely, those images that are logically and directly related to the pen – is successful in the matching process discussed earlier, and enters the 'I'-narrative stream. However, the majority of memory representations triggered by the DMP will remain outside the 'I'-narrative stream. These might include a broad range of associations, for example, to the colour of the pen, to the word 'pen', to the shape of the pen, and so on.

The DMP stream and the 'I'-narrative stream are separate in the sense that they are both ongoing synchronously, each according to its distinctive form of logic. The DMP stream is associated with Intentionality 1; the 'I'-narrative stream, with Intentionality 2. Despite the difference in intentionality, the two streams clearly interact. As already mentioned, a subset of images in the DMP stream enters the 'I'-narrative stream in the normal perceptual matching process. In addition, associations thrown up in the DMP stream may influence the 'I'-narrative stream, as in the classic Freudian slip scenario.

In the reverse direction, as pointed out in Chapter 5, the 'I'-model active at the time that some object or event is experienced in the 'I'-narrative stream, becomes part of the storage network associated with the object or event. In future activations, this 'I'-tag will have a constraining influence on the DMP activity. The DMP stream opens to the possibilities of diverse associations, a critical operation underpinning creativity. The 'I'-narrative stream narrows down the possibilities according to the constraints of reality orientation and social conformity.

Figure 6.2 illustrates the two streams. It presents a hypothetical sequence of events that might occur following a decision to jot down some notes in planning a piece of writing. Each, seemingly frozen, instant is depicted in the form of the earlier figures (that is, 5.5; 6.1), which apply whether the stimulus is a sensory event or a thought. Thus, for example, the first instant (in sequence from the top) depicts the thought, 'I am planning the outline of the piece of writing', whereas the fourth depicts the percept, 'I see the pen', as in the earlier figures. The DMP stream may be seen to comprise the stage of 'searching through memory' depicted in the earlier figures. Enlargements of this stage are given at the left of the figure. They illustrate the kinds of associations that may be activated in the DMP stream. For reasons of space, only three enlargements of the five instants are included. Again, the static form of the diagram makes it difficult to indicate the dynamic nature of the streams. In particular, the DMP stream has its own ongoing life, as it were. It is influenced by current sensory inputs, but proceeds independently.

As should be clear, the two streams correspond closely to Freud's 'unconscious' and 'conscious' systems. However, both streams are phenomenally conscious, and both are intentional, in the distinctive ways discussed above. Only the 'I'-narrative stream carries the additional dimension of accessibility (by 'I'). The value of the approach I have adopted lies in its integration of cognitive and psychodynamic concepts. The 'I'-tag theory provides an operational framework for incorporating the kinds of effects proposed by classical psychodynamic theories.

Experimental evidence

Despite my appeal to the value of hermeneutics and the cultural niche of Freudian theory, the question of evidence cannot be easily

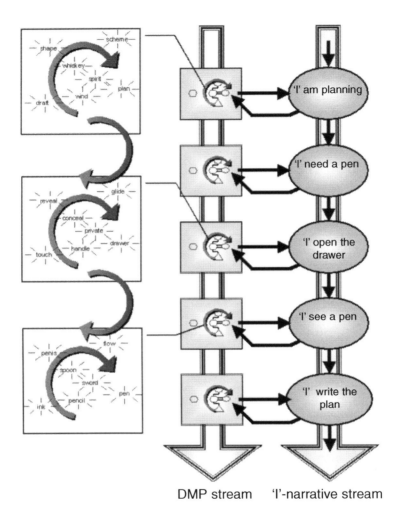

DMP stream   'I'-narrative stream

FIGURE 6.2 Two streams of mentation (See text for explanation)

waved away. In closing this chapter, I shall briefly review experimental evidence that lends support to some of the key tenets of psychoanalysis.

Solms (1997; Solms and Turnbull, 2002) finds support for Freud's ideas on dreams from recent research that specifies the areas of the brain which are implicated in the initiation and control of dreaming. Freud's critical insight into dreaming concerns his distinction between the *manifest*, and the *latent*, dream content.

Two brain areas with key roles in the control of dreaming have been identified, and, according to Solms, each seems to be specialized for one of the two Freudian aspects. This first area deals with visual processing, and Solms suggests that it is involved in the visual form taken by the *manifest* content of dreams. The second area includes connections from diverse areas to the limbic system. The limbic system is thought to generate emotional tone and plays an important role in memory functions. Following Panksepp (1998), Solms characterizes this second dream area as the brain's *seeking* system. This area is responsible for the behaviour whereby an organism seeks out the means to fulfil its drives. Solms emphasizes the relation between such functions and the Freudian concept of *libido*. Since the libido determines the *latent* content of dreams, Solms speculates that this dream area of the brain is responsible for the latent motivations underpinning a dream's visual content. Solms' major point is that the unfolding picture of neurological function seems to be consistent with the fundamental analysis of dreaming that Freud developed through the phenomenological data available to him.

As noted in Chapter 5, the cognitive support for psychoanalytic ideas has generally been considered weak. In characterizing the cognitive unconscious as 'simple and dumb', Greenwald (1992) effectively removes the carpet from beneath the major premise on which all depth psychology is based. However, Shevrin (2000) finds reason to challenge Greenwald's assertion. Shevrin reports on several studies which, using techniques of subliminal presentation, point to the reality of a psychologically complex and causative unconscious. Shevrin's research has demonstrated that the brain discriminates between subliminally presented words which are either positively, or negatively, emotionally toned. This observation implies that the unconscious has the capacity to generate affect, as psychodynamic theory suggests.

In a further study, Shevrin addressed the assumptions of psychoanalysis more directly. Clinicians were asked to specify words or short phrases that seemed to be indicative of unconscious conflicts in patients undergoing analysis. For example, one patient was unable to consciously realize the extent of the ambivalent feelings that he seemed to harbour towards a close friend. On the basis of their analysis of transcripts from therapeutic sessions, clinicians surmised that, at the root of his problems lay a profound, unconscious fear of the friend. Source material for this diagnosis included a dream which involved the patient being stabbed. One of the phrases the clinicians specified for Shevrin's study, therefore, was 'Stab me'. The chosen words and phrases were then presented to the patient to whom they related under two conditions: one subliminal and one supraliminal. All the patients' brain responses to the words were then compared with their responses to pleasant words. Results indicated that, when the words were presented supraliminally, brain responses were identical, whether the words were clinically active or merely pleasant. Differences emerged, however, when the words were presented subliminally. The pattern of results suggested that patients were indeed detecting the significance of the words at an unconscious level. Shevrin suggests that, under the condition of supraliminal presentation only, an inhibitory process (repression?) was kicking in. Shevrin's work lends some support to psychoanalytic ideas of unconscious motivation and repression. Interestingly, his results also seem to affirm the validity of the clinicians' judgement.

Despite research of this kind, there is no real consensus on the validity of the claims made by depth psychology. It is worth repeating the point made by Woody and Phillips that this kind of experimental research is, at best, of tangential relevance only. As remarked earlier, the relevance of the idea of a psychodynamic unconscious lies in its usefulness in helping us understand the deeper nature of what it is to be human, especially in terms of psychological hermeneutics. The focus of Chapter 7 will extend my discussion of hermeneutics by examining its expression in language mysticism. As I shall argue, the practices found within these schools of mysticism strongly suggest the presence of a spiritually important, psychological associative system, largely distinct from the normal 'I'-narrative stream. While this system may not equate to the Freudian unconscious in all regards, its distinctive hermeneutic logic bears key hallmarks of the Freudian primary process, and may be cited in further support of the claims of depth psychology.

Chapter 7

Spiritual and Mystical Approaches
2. Towards Fullness

[T]he concept of infinity of meaning transforms the Torah from a socially motivated document into a tool employed by mystics for the sake of their own self-perfection.

(Idel, 2002, p. 91)

Language mysticism

The 'unknown' in psychology and religion

The whole idea that some form of unknown realm is an active participant in our lives is pivotal in relating insights from depth psychology to those found in religious traditions. Religions have universally posited a transcendent dimension, concealed within the manifest appearance of things and operative beneath the surface of our minds. Clearly, in theistic traditions, behind all levels of concealment lies the being of God, the transcendent source. The psychodynamic unconscious is similarly concealed from the immediate grasp of the mind, but is nevertheless highly influential in our lives. Despite his attitude of antipathy to most formulations of religion, Freud's insistence that the unconscious is mental, rather than merely physiological, is critical here, for it legitimizes the potential spiritual function of the unconscious. It would be absurd to think of a deeper, spiritual level of being as rigidly mechanical.

The post-Freudian 'spiritualization' of the unconscious owes much to Jung's postulate of a *collective unconscious*. Jung accommodated the religious view that the concealed dimension is present in the physical, as well as in the mental, realms. For Jung, mental and physical events are fundamentally interrelated, since the collective psyche finds expression in both. It is for this reason, for example, that Jung felt that 'physical' events could be intrinsically meaningful, as in his concept of *synchronicity*.

Parallels between the constructs of depth psychology and those of religion apply both to the manner through which the concealed realm influences us and to the potential for spiritual transformation. The concealed realm is, in some sense, 'inhabited' with entities that influence activities at the surface level. In religious terminology, the concealed realm (for example, 'heaven') is inhabited by *beings* (for example, 'angels') whose function it is to communicate from that realm to the revealed one (for example, 'earth'). Similarly, in Jung's formulation, the 'unseen' collective unconscious is inhabited by *archetypes* that function to transmit higher knowledge (the 'numinous') to consciousness. As far as the transformational arena is concerned, religion encourages the individual to *transcend* the seen realm by gaining knowledge of the higher, concealed level. For Jung, the *transcendent function* brings about transformation through its propensity to impart knowledge of a 'higher' image from the union of two opposites, each of which is immediately grasped in the conscious (lower) mind.[1]

These putative relationships between the constructs of depth psychology and those of religion inevitably raise the ontological question. Indeed, the very term 'construct' is hardly appropriate in the religious sphere, where entities such as 'heaven', 'angels', and, of course, 'God' would not be considered to be constructs at all, but *real*. While a fuller treatment of this question must wait until Chapter 8, I raise it here since it substantially impacts on the present chapter's aims. I intend to consider the potential of the 'I'-tag theory for explaining certain mystical states. To the extent that the terms of reference I have used in developing the theory have been physiological and psychological, such explanations will appear *reductive*. However, the potential for psychological theories to contribute to *non-reductive* explanations must also be recognized. Neurological and psychological details may provide us with a framework for understanding mystical states, without necessarily constituting a full explanation.

As William James argued, the neurological and psychological dynamics associated with mystical states may represent the *conditions* necessary for access to the higher, supernatural, source of the mystical phenomena:

[I]f there be higher spiritual agencies that can directly touch us, the psychological condition of their doing so might be our possession of a subconscious region which alone should yield access to them. The hubbub of the waking life *might* close a door which in the dreamy Subliminal might remain ajar or open.

(James, 1902/1960, p. 242, italics original)

Psychology may offer an important contribution to understanding details of what James refers to here as 'the Subliminal'. Transpersonal psychology in particular can address the conditions under which the sacred may enter an individual's life, but, as Wolfson (1994) rightly reminds us, psychology 'cannot *account* for ... the appearance of the sacred' (p. 118, italics added).

The above-mentioned duality between two levels, one 'seen' and one 'unseen', hardly suffices to capture the mystical concept of an ultimately unknowable essence of the divine. Mystical teachings suggest that at least three levels should be distinguished: the immediately known ('conscious'), the content-bearing unknown ('unconscious'), and the fully unknowable – 'that secret which is not perceived or known' (*Zohar*, for example, 2:239a). Whilst Jung argued that there is an unknowable core to the unconscious, his insistence on its immanent, psychological nature somewhat distances him from the testimony of mystics.

A further contentious issue for the seeming parallel between psychodynamic and religious concepts concerns *revelation*. It goes without saying that religions view revelation as deriving from a transcendent source. This marks their distinction from the naturalistic orientation of depth psychology. A tension remains, however, even when we leave this metaphysical point to one side. Mystical conceptions of revelation carry connotations that do not sit easily with the psychoanalytic idea of unconscious contents being 'revealed' to consciousness.

The pioneers of depth psychology seem to have viewed their therapeutic mission as being the permanent illumination of previously unconscious contents. The mystical traditions, on the other hand, envisage a more dynamic interplay between concealing and revealing. For example, when the *Zohar* states that 'Everything is concealed and revealed' (2:230b), it has in mind an ongoing *two-way* dynamic. Revelation of secrets can only occur in a manner that results in their re-concealment. Paradox is the path to enlightenment. Katz notes a similar approach in the work of the Christian mystic, Meister Eckhart:

> For Eckhart, the Bible is a book of secrets, and the key to understanding it is an awareness that it reveals ultimate truths while concealing them and conceals them while revealing them. In commenting on it ... he wishes to convey the unconveyable by speaking of X and then denying X, leaving some trace of the meaning of X while not describing X.
>
> (Katz, 2000, p. 44)

There is an echo of this principle in the English word 'recover'. Some object, having at one time been lost, has now been found. That which became concealed is now revealed, but the revealing is only evidenced in the *re-covering*. The re*veal*ing is itself of necessity a re-*veil*ing. Take the case of recovery from illness. What is it that is re-covered if someone recovers his or her health? Surely, in our language we have a hint that the vital principle itself is essentially concealed when all is as it should be.

In Sufism, this teaching is conveyed using the symbol of the *veil* in a more systematic fashion. The paradoxical nearness and distancing perpetrated by the veil serves to convey the relation of the finite human mind to the 'Real', the realm of God's infinite essence. 'The Real becomes manifest by being veiled, so He is the Manifest/the Veiled', writes ibn Arabi (cited in Chittick, 1999, pp. 81–2). Whilst a major veil over the Real is the human self, even obliteration of the self as achieved through Sufi practice cannot, for ibn Arabi, remove the veiling of reality. The veil amounts to an ontological necessity.

Chittick explores the paradoxical meaning of the veil throughout the cryptic writings of the tenth-century al-Niffari:

> [God] said to me: Your veil is everything I make manifest, your veil is everything I keep secret, your veil is everything I affirm, your veil is everything I obliterate, and your veil is what I unveil, just as your veil is what I curtain.
>
> (Chittick, 1999, cited p. 73)

The mystic's path cannot lead beyond the veil. Rather, it is a path of recognizing the vital dynamic that inevitably accompanies the divine in all His manifest forms. Even union with God can arise only when God Himself removes the veils of knowing and self-hood. Moreover, whatever remains present in the mystical state is yet a further veil. '[I]n the last analysis, to emerge from one veil is to enter into another veil' (p. 77).

There is no emerging into full light, as if the covering could be totally thrown off. Rather, the mystical goal is one of consciously engaging with the inner working of creation, where the *concealing–revealing–concealing* dynamic operates. As Webb and Sells (1995) note, it is difficult to integrate the approach of early depth psychologists such as Freud, or Jung, with this aspect of mystical teachings. Webb and Sells argue that the more recent approaches of Lacan and Bion, by comparison, seem to resonate well with this mystical perspective. According to Bion (1988), 'The real is never gathered in, but glimpsed via activity, in movement' (p. 199). Bion designates what he calls the 'ultimate reality' by the letter 'O', thereby indicating the emptiness at its heart. It is 'represented by terms such as the ultimate reality, the absolute truth, the godhead, the infinite, the thing-in-itself' (p. 26). And it is ever present beneath the psychoanalytic practice. Bion's recognition that 'O … can "become" but it cannot be "known"' (p. 26), places the real in the same category as the ineffable source of emanation, as conceived in mysticism.

Webb and Sells (1995) stress that in the approach of Lacan and Bion, psychoanalysis is no longer directed to the goal of healing. It is no longer the 'talking cure'. 'Lacan and Bion do not envision psychoanalysis as an enterprise for healers, and they view the real as something beyond the unconscious even if the unconscious is an avenue to it.... [T]he unconscious is the pathway to the real' (pp. 201–2). With the work of Lacan and Bion, then, some of the more spiritual roots of psychoanalysis have come to the fore.

Language in psychoanalysis and religion

It is reported that, when asked by a young psychoanalyst for advice in developing competence, the influential post-Freudian psychoanalyst, Jacques Lacan, answered, 'Do crossword puzzles!' (Lacan, 1966/1977, p. 56). Indeed, one of Lacan's central axioms is that the unconscious is structured as a language. It is hardly surprising therefore that he would encourage a facility with linguistic puzzles for enhancing a therapist's insight into the ways of the unconscious.

Lacan equates the two features that Freud regarded as central to the primary-process logic of the unconscious, namely, *condensation* and *displacement*, with the linguistic forms of metaphor and metonymy respectively (Skelton, 1995). Condensation refers to the way in which 'a similarity of any sort between two elements of the unconscious material ... is taken as an opportunity for creating a third, which is a composite or compromise idea' (Freud, 1904/1966, pp. 58–9). The parallel with language is found in the role metaphor plays in the evolution of words and phrases, and is well illustrated by the psychological impact of puns. Displacement, on the other hand, may be illustrated by cases of forgetting, where Freud observed that substitute memories could arise on the basis of associations that have been established to repressed material. This parallels metonymy, which refers to the substitution of attribute words for the primary object intended, as when 'crown' is used for 'king'.

The pun is central to the hermeneutic unconscious. Consider the following incident involving a man breaking a match when lighting a cigarette. An innocent enough event; yet this occurred whilst the man was in conversation with a woman who had just separated from her husband, and occasioned the man unthinkingly to blurt out, 'It's such a pain when your first match breaks....' It seems evident in retrospect that unconscious processes had both motivated the clumsy attempt at striking the match and led to the verbal innuendo. The hermeneutic unconscious condenses the meanings of 'match' beneath the surface of the encounter. But the condensation is not restricted to this idiosyncratic incident; we may presume that it was an active feature in the evolution of the word 'match' in the first place. In its meaning of a stick that makes fire, 'match' refers to the bringing together of two substances. Movement between them causes the substance on the stick to ignite. The 'Freudian' (that is, sexual) interpretation needs no elaboration. The point is that echoes of linguistic evolution continue to pervade our actions and verbal repertoire. In the aphorism of Thass-Thienemann (1968), 'Language reveals not the prehistory of material things, but the prehistory of the human mind' (p. 65).

For psychoanalysis, understanding the substructure of our language can be both revealing and ultimately transformational. This applies in regard both to personal matters and to the more historical dimension conveyed by Thass-Thienemann. The more insight we can develop into the concealed motivations behind our personal, perhaps idiosyncratic, use of language, the more we are able to bring the unconscious motivations to consciousness. For Freud (1933/1964), this was the transformational goal of psychoanalysis: 'Where id was there ego shall be' (p. 80).

Yet language also points towards that which is not. For Lacan (1966/1977), the word is 'a presence made of absence' (p. 65). Language lies at the root of the *conceal–reveal–conceal* dynamic by virtue of its ability to bring to mind some entity that is no longer present before us. But in this, language merely points towards the essential otherness which is, for Lacan, the discourse of the unconscious. The Cartesian 'I think therefore I am' becomes a Lacanian 'I think where I am not, therefore I am where I do not think' (p. 166). As this aphorism implies, for Lacan, the practice of psychoanalysis becomes directed towards the unfolding of otherness, not the grasping of some ideal self.

The Lacanian emphasis on language recapitulates the role of language in scriptural traditions, and his emphasis on the importance of using psychoanalysis to actively engage with otherness, resonates with traditions of language mysticism. In Chapter 6, I emphasized the Jewish background to the development of psychoanalysis. The interactive worldview central to rabbinic Judaism provided the milieu from which Freud developed his anti-Cartesian stance. With Lacan's emphasis on language, a second critical feature of the rabbinic worldview comes to the fore. The Rabbis regarded the polyvalence of scriptural language as an essential basis for all their teachings, and ultimately as the medium through which any encounter with the divine is achievable.[2] It would be difficult to argue that Freud had not been influenced in his psychological stance by the complex rabbinic attitude to language that permeated his religious heritage.[3]

One example will suffice to illustrate the ways in which linguistic associations serve to convey deeper teachings throughout rabbinic literature. The midrash on *Genesis* opens with a discourse based on a verse in the book of *Proverbs*. Wisdom, personified as the author of the verse, recalls the primordial time prior to manifest creation: 'Then I was by Him, like a little child; and I was daily His delight, rejoicing always before Him' (*Proverbs* 8:30). The intent of the midrash is to establish that the Torah is itself primordial, identified with primordial wisdom. This intent is realized through scrutiny of the word '*amon*', translated here as 'little child'. The midrash examines a variety of meanings of several words linguistically associated with the original '*amon*', including 'tutor', 'master-craftsman', 'covered', 'hidden', 'great', 'artisan', before arriving at its intended conclusion:

> The Torah declares: I was the instrument that the Holy One, blessed be He, used when He practised His craft. It is customary that when a king of flesh and blood builds a palace, he does not build it himself but he hires an architect; even the architect does not build it solely from his head, but he uses plans and blueprints in order to know how to lay the rooms and to arrange the doors. So too, the Holy One, blessed be He, looked into the Torah and created the world. And so the Torah said: 'By means of [i.e., the Hebrew letter, *bet*, a particle conventionally translated as 'in'] a beginning, God created the heavens and the earth,' and the word 'a beginning' always alludes to the Torah, as Scripture says, 'The Lord created me at the beginning of His way' (Proverbs 8:22).
>
> (*Midrash, Genesis Rabba* 1:1)

The associations establish the parameters of the argument. The surface reading, namely that of the child playing innocently with a parental figure, is revealed as a screen to the deeper connotation of the 'master-craftsman', or *architect*, uncovering the plan of creation in front of God. By locating this key teaching within the orbit of the multiple meanings of the sacred text, the teaching is given its authoritative standing. The authorization given by dint of the teaching's associative connections to the scriptural text is bolstered by two further factors. The first is the status of the teacher; and the second is the intrinsic logic of the teaching and the extent to which it fits into the overall rabbinic worldview. But it is the appeal to the multiplicity of meaning that is of most interest in psychological terms. Effectively, the rabbinic method entails continually situating ideas, teachings and laws in the context of the multiplicity of the sacred text.

Language and the unknown

Commentary on scripture plays a double-edged role. On the one hand, it reveals particular meanings that may have been latent in the text. On the other hand, precisely by emphasizing particular meanings, it compromises the multiplicity of meaning that characterizes sacred scripture. A move to deny that fluidity of meaning is tantamount to idolatry: 'As soon as the [divine] attributes are "known" (perceived as objects by a subject other than them) they harden into idols' (Sells, 1994, p. 212). Guarding the multiplicity of meaning within the scriptural text is paramount.

At bottom, it is this conception of the multiplicity of meaning attaching to the sacred text that legitimizes any appeal to its supposed divinity. As Katz (2000) remarks, 'the master text that is appealed to has inexhaustible levels of meaning.... Precisely because the text is God's Word (Logos, *aql*, *sruti*, or Torah), it carries the inherent possibility, even the necessity, of multiple meanings' (p. 17).[4] I suggest that it is this multiplicity of meaning that introduces a psychological element into the exegetical and mystical approaches to scriptural language.

The multiplicity of meaning in the Koran is reflected in Ibn Arabi's insistence that no two readings of the Koran should be the same:

> When meaning repeats itself for someone who is reciting the Qur'an, he has not recited it as it should be recited. This is proof of his ignorance. But when someone's knowledge is increased through his recitation, and when he acquires a new judgement with each reading, he is the reciter who, in his own existence, follows God.
>
> (Cited in Chittick, 2000, p. 154)

Regarding the Torah, I cited in Chapter 5 the Talmudic axiom that a biblical verse conveys multiple meanings. This notion of a 'polysemic abundance from God' (Yadin, 2003, p. 2) is central to rabbinic hermeneutics. The mediaeval kabbalists went further in recognizing an infinity of meanings in the Torah (Idel, 1986, 2002). This conception derives primarily from the explicit identification between God and Torah: 'Since God has neither beginning nor end, no limit at all, so also His Perfect Torah ... has, from our perspective, neither limit nor end' (anonymous, cited in Idel, 1986, p. 148).

The multiplicity found within the sacred text points in two directions simultaneously. One direction is towards the text's source, that is, the divine, and the other is towards the human mind. Unlike the multiplicity of textual meaning advocated in contemporary deconstructionism, the mystic offers us a vision of oneness at the base of the sacred text. It is on account of the infinite essence of the divine source that the sacred text must display multiplicity in its manifestation. Just as white light splits into a multiple spectrum, so multiplicity of meaning is the consequence of the infinite manifesting within a finite textual form. In the other direction, that of the mind, the multiplicity in the text is the realm of encounter between the human and the divine. In aspiring to connect with the infinite, the human mind plunders the mystical plurality of the text.

This point is well illustrated by the following, cryptic kabbalistic analysis:

> We learnt, 'It is the honour of God to conceal a word' (*Proverbs* 25:2). What is a 'word' As it is said, 'The head of your word is truth' (*Psalm* 119:160); and 'The honour of kings is to probe a word' (*Proverbs* 25:2). What is a 'word'? As is written, '[Apples of gold in settings of silver is] a word fitly [Hebrew *of'nav*] spoken' (*Proverbs* 25:11). Do not read 'fitly' [*of'nav*] but 'its wheel' [*ofanav*], as in 'My presence will go' (*Exodus* 33:14).
>
> (*Sefer ha-Bahir*, 33)

I shall discuss the intent of this passage in some detail in the next section. I quote it here simply for the insight it gives into this notion of a human–divine encounter via the multiple meanings of a sacred text. 'Truth' – intimating the infinite essence – is concealed in words. The mystic – the 'king' in the text – probes the words to unlock the hidden meanings. The medium of encounter is the 'wheel' of language, by which is meant the nexus of richly interconnected, associated meanings that are unlocked by the mystic's grasp of linguistic processes.

Language is, of course, the primary medium of all communication. To the extent that mystics have attempted to communicate their profound insights into the transcendent, their language becomes a *language of unsaying*, in Sells' (1994) evocative phrase. In such use of language, paradoxes, seeming contradictions, and apparent logical gaps may be the primary vehicles for conveying what is effectively unsayable through the normative use of language (Lancaster, 2000b). For example, Eckhart preached:

> I wanted nothing, I longed for nothing, for I was an empty being. But when I went out from my own free will and received my created being, then I had a 'God,' for before there were any creatures, God was not 'God,' but he was what he was.
>
> (Cited in Cousins, 1990, p. 68)

Eckhart therefore prayed to God, 'that we may be free of "God"'. The mystic path entails recovering the void that precedes any form whatsoever. The God that Eckhart sought is beyond the 'God' identified with attributes. The use of inverted commas can hardly detract from the difficulty Eckhart faced in trying to convey his sense of the profound nothingness of the transcendent. His language is a potent language of unsaying.

In addition to its communicative function, language plays an internal cognitive role. Not only are words central in much of our thinking, but also language has been shown to influence perceptual processes. The way we organize the sensory world is bound up with the linguistic categories available. More than this, language is critically involved in the construction of self (Bruner, 1997). Bruner argues that self arises as a narrative construction which binds our past into our present. The continuity of self is nothing other than this narrative. From the beginnings of self in early child-hood and through the whole of adult life language plays this seminal role. Bruner notes, for example, how the bedtime soliloquies of a girl he and colleagues studied between her second and third birthdays seemed to develop in tandem with her sense of self: 'It became plain to us in the course of this lengthy study that the act of self-accounting – at least, short-term accounting – is acquired almost with the acquisition of language itself' (p. 156).

In the terms I have used above, Bruner's analysis suggests that language is critically implicated in constructing the '*I*'-*narrative stream*. Given that mysticism strongly promotes a path of detachment from 'I', language becomes a hindrance to the goals of mysticism. The role played by language in constructing and maintaining the 'I'-narrative stream is therefore often opposed in mystical practice. As Hayes (1997) writes, 'Enlightenment is achieved in the *letting go* of language' (p. 580). Yet this gloss fails to recognize the mystical use of language itself, which may be found in all scriptural traditions (Katz, 1992a, 2000). Where language is deliberately used in ways intended to open the mystic to 'higher meaning', the same detachment may require not a letting go of language, but a distinctive embrace of the potential-ities in language. Here we are dealing with a mysticism of *full-ness*, in certain respects distinct from that of *emptiness*, examined in Chapter 3.[5]

Cousins reminds us of the centrality of these two terms for all theological discourse:

[F]ullness and emptiness are the ultimate religious categories: experiential, metaphysical, theological and mystical. In all realms, the issues point ultimately to these two categories: in the spiritual journey, techniques of contemplation, the epistemology of our knowledge of God, the metaphysics of being and non-being, and the nature of God himself.

(Cousins, E. H., 1981, p. 60)

For Cousins, the questions at the heart of mysticism may be stripped to these bare essentials: 'Is God the dark abyss or the fullness of radiating light? Is he the silent ground or the fire of love?' (p. 60).

Cousins singles out the thirteenth-century Franciscan, Bonaventure, as representative of the path of fullness. The importance of language for this path is explicit in Bonaventure's theology, for he asserts that language holds the key to knowledge of God. All features in creation are expressions of God's language. Creatures are His nouns; their energy, His verbs; their interrelations, His propositions and conjunctions. Grammar defines the created world. Indeed, for Bonaventura, 'at its very apex and center – on the level of the Absolute – reality is linguistic' (Cousins, 1992, p. 241).

Both the mysticism of emptiness and that of fullness have important contributions to make to the psychology of consciousness. As noted in Chapter 3, it has been claimed that the experience of emptiness suggests that consciousness need not be intentional, that it may be pure, or contentless. The language mysticism under examination in this chapter also contributes to our understanding of consciousness. As will be discussed below, it contributes significantly to our understanding of the associative processes operating in perception and thought. In psychological terms, the practices of language mysticism may be understood as deconstructing the role language normally plays in sustaining the habitual 'I'-narrative. Further than this, the practices may encourage a greater knowledge of the preconscious determinants of meaning than is available in ordinary states of consciousness. The 'fullness' of the mystical state is a consequence of the mystic gaining access to the multiplicity of associations normally inaccessible in the preconscious.

I use the term 'language mysticism' to refer to traditions in which the mystic *regards language as an active vehicle for pursuing the goal of personal transformation and/or engaging with the divine*. Invariably this entails exegetical approaches to a sacred text regarded as veiling the infinite. It is in this sense, for example, that Fishbane (2000) understands the *Zohar* as encouraging 'the spiritual transformation of the exegete *through exegesis*' (p. 105, italics original). Such exegesis is not merely an intellectual pursuit, in the normal sense of the word. Exegesis becomes a vehicle for the mystic to engage with the divine spheres that are themselves concealed within the text.

Language mysticism also includes traditions in which distinctive techniques are used to supplement exegesis in pursuit of the goal of transformation and/or engaging with the divine. *Mantras* or *koans* exemplify linguistic elements harnessed for purposes of transformation. Their habitual semantic functions are largely irrelevant to this use of language in mysticism. By giving his student a *koan*:

> [T]he master is seeking to revolutionize the student's consciousness, particularly in the context of meditation – when consciousness is particularly sensitive – such that it breaks free and transcends the regulative categories of knowing and thereby is opened up to new forms of awareness.
>
> (Katz, 1992b, p. 6)

Similarly, a mantra is not intended as an expressive linguistic element. The famous mantra *Aum* encapsulates an order of language function clearly distinct from normal semantics, since it includes in itself the very principles of transformation which constitute the meditator's goal. In '*Aum*' each letter depicts a progression in the state of consciousness, with the sound as a whole depicting the ultimate state, that of *Atman*, the universal Self.

The essential complementarity between the mysticism of fullness and that of emptiness is graphically illustrated by kabbalistic traditions on the symbolism of the 'black fire' and 'white fire', which are mystically viewed as constituting the Torah. The overt writing on the scroll, comprising inked letters on a blank parchment, is mystically construed as a reflection of the higher essence of the Torah, said to be written in black fire on white fire (see Rojtman, 1998). This teaching emphasizes the role of both the letters and the spaces as agents of meaning. The letters convey the fullness of meaning associated with exegesis, and the spaces intimate the essential emptiness that complements the exegetical imagination.

Far from being merely the absence of letters, the spaces become a key to many of the mysteries. Idel draws attention to a sixteenth-century kabbalist, Rabbi David ibn Avi Zimra, for whom 'the whiteness of the parchment that encompasses all the letters from within and without includes a certain allusion' (cited in Idel, 2002, p. 58). As Idel explains, the allusion is to the infinite divine essence, which, analogously to the white space of the parchment, encompasses all things, and could never be contained within the finitude of the black letters.

Thus, the mysticism of emptiness associated with the white spaces is complemented by that of fullness implied by the letters. As will be discussed in the next section, the corpus of Kabbalah includes complex mystical practices that were designed to fill the mind with seemingly bizarre combinations of letters and other linguistic elements. Such practices were viewed as granting the mystic access to the highest spheres of divine creative activity. For all their complexity, however, these practices also acknowledge the nothingness at the root of the letters. A mysticism of fullness never annuls that of emptiness, just as the black letters could have no existence without the white spaces.

Idel (ibid) suggests that the peculiar extent to which language mysticism developed within Judaism owes much to the absence of other vehicles of expression. During Judaism's long exilic period, the absence of a geographical centre, combined with the prohibition on visual images, meant that language became imbued with a distinctive numinous depth and complexity. Language not only became the medium of exegesis, but was also viewed as the dynamo of the inner workings of creation. A mystic might enter into these inner mysteries of creation by emulating God's own use of linguistic elements in creation. In the elaboration of the complex linguistic practices directed to such imitation of God's creativity, I suggest that we find distinctive evidence of the inner processes of consciousness.

The wheel of language

Twenty-two foundation letters. He [God] placed them in a wheel, like a wall with 231 gates. The wheel revolves forwards and backwards.... How? He permuted them, weighed them, and transformed them. *Alef* with them all and all of them with *alef*; *bet* with them all and all of them with *bet*. They continue in cycles and exist in 231 gates. Thus, all that is formed and all that is spoken derives from one Name.

(Sefer Yetsirah 2:4–5)

The *Sefer Yetsirah* is a cryptic text, generally dated to some time between the first and fifth centuries CE. It lies at the core of the tradition of language mysticism in Judaism. The above extract describes the manner in which God is said to have employed the letters of the Hebrew alphabet in creation. Everything in creation is formed by means of a process involving permutations of letters. The 231 gates allude to the number of two-letter combinations (without reversals) generated from the entire set of 22 letters in the alphabet, of which *alef* is the first letter and *bet*, the second. A useful modern analogy may be found in our conception that the elements of DNA are permuted into forms which generate characteristics when expressed biologically.

At the same time as indicating God's own techniques of formation, the *Sefer Yetsirah* may be read as an instruction manual of mystical practice. For the mystic, emulation of God's arcane linguistic practice becomes the means for engaging with Him, since God is known through imitation of His ways. Thus, for example, the *Sefer Yetsirah*'s list of actions whereby God effected His creative 'letter-working', becomes a template for a sequence of stages in the mystic's concentrative practice. God is described as having 'engraved [the letters], He carved them, He weighed them, He transformed them, He permuted them, and He formed [everything] with them' (2:2). According to one interpretation, this sequence presents a guide to visualization practice, starting with establishing the outline of a letter in the mind's eye ('engraving'), proceeding to strengthen its mental form so that it might blaze in 'black fire' ('carve'), and so on (Kaplan, 1990).

This tradition of language mysticism incorporates a pronounced emphasis on wheel-related imagery. As was briefly mentioned in the previous section, such imagery gives a clue to the psychological role of association in the tradition's practices. The 'wheel' hints at both the structural nexus of interconnected meanings and the mental process required to access them. The desired mental state is one in which ideas are 'rolled around' to bring less immediate associations to consciousness. In the above extract from the *Sefer Yetsirah*, it is stated that the creative process depends on a *wheel of the letters* which 'revolves back and forth'. According to

Abulafia, whose language mysticism derives in large measure from the tradition conveyed in the *Sefer Yetsirah*, the practice focuses especially on the letters of the various names of God: 'And begin by combining this Name, namely Y-H-V-H, at the beginning alone, and examine all its combinations and move it and turn it about like a wheel returning around, front and back, like a scroll' (cited in Idel, 1988a, p. 21).

As will be discussed later in this chapter, Abulafia's practice included several features well known for inducing alterations of consciousness. These included fasting, breath control, ritualized physical movements, and visualization, all of which are found in diverse mystical practices. The distinctive feature in his practice was undoubtedly the intense linguistic activity. This entailed decomposing words into their constituent letters, which would then be permuted according to strict rules in highly complex patterns. As Scholem points out, Abulafia's practice entailed developing associations in a controlled meditative state:

> In fact this is nothing else than a very remarkable method of using associations as a way of meditation. It is not wholly the 'free play of association' as known to psychoanalysis; rather it is the way of passing from one association to another determined by certain rules which are, however, sufficiently lax.
>
> (Scholem, 1941/1961, p. 135)

Abulafia instructed his pupils to 'revolve the languages until they return to their prime material state' (cited in Idel, 1989b, p. 10). The meaning attaching to individual words would be deconstructed by this device of returning them to their elemental letters; the 'knots' binding the soul would be loosed. Such *deconstruction* was a preliminary phase to *reconstruction* of the letters specifically in combination with those of the various divine Names. The role played by the Name of God in the practice was, again, highly structured within a paradoxically free-flowing framework. The Name of God is, as Scholem (1941/1961) notes, 'the real and ... the peculiarly Jewish object of mystical contemplation' (p. 133).

Abulafia equated the wheel of the letters with the *Active Intellect*, a term introduced by the Aristotelian philosophy that informed much mediaeval Islamic and Jewish speculative thought.[6] In the sequence of celestial intelligences emanated from God, the Active Intellect functioned as intermediary between the divine and the human spheres. Abulafia's system was directed towards achieving mystical union with the Active Intellect through imitating its mode of operation. The letter-working and hermeneutic activity that Abulafia taught was viewed as emulating the linguistic operations of the Active Intellect.

Earlier I quoted from the *Bahir* a passage in which the mystic is encouraged to enter into the wheel of a word's meaning:

> What is a 'word'? As is written, '[Apples of gold in settings of silver is] A word fitly [Hebrew *of'nav*] spoken' (*Proverbs* 25:11). Do not read 'fitly' [*of'nav*] but 'its wheel' [*ofanav*], as in 'My presence will go' (*Exodus* 33:14).[7]

The mystic is enjoined not to be satisfied with a word's immediate meaning. The path to the 'apples of gold' requires accessing the wheel of meanings to which any given word relates. In characteristic fashion, the instruction itself is conveyed via the very technique it encourages. The vowel-less form of Hebrew scripture means that the word generally translated as 'fitly' could be articulated differently, giving the word meaning 'its wheel'. The reading of a scriptural text becomes 'fitting' to the extent that its words are elaborated in terms of their 'wheels of associations' and subtleties of meaning.

The reference to *Exodus* 33:14 adds an important dimension.[8] The allusion is simple enough etymologically, since the Hebrew words for 'presence' and 'wheel' have letters in common. But the author seems to be alluding to a deeper connection. The Exodus passage describes God's intention to reveal His presence to Moses. It represents the pinnacle of all the individual human-divine encounters portrayed in the Hebrew Bible. As the biblical commentators emphasize, the reference is to God in His very essence. Nachmanides (1194–1270), the most influential of the more mystically-oriented Jewish exegetes, states that the verse intimates that God is agreeing to Moses' request that He reveal the details of His Name to him. By including this reference in order to illuminate the cited paragraph's interest in the wheel of language, the *Bahir* seems to be drawing a connection between the hermeneutic approach to the multiplicity of the text and the more arcane understanding of letter permutation as a feature of the divine Name. Indeed, Nachmanides himself points to the basis of this connection when he states in the introduction to his commentary that the Torah consists wholly of divine Names. This is his understanding of the writing of 'black fire on white fire'. The conventional form of the Torah, consisting of commandments and stories, is merely derivative. The mystic, then, employs the derivative level in order to ascend to the essential, mystical level.

Two levels of wheel imagery are being conjoined in these allusions. The *Bahir* overtly alludes to the 'wheel of a word', by which is meant the variety of meanings which may be elaborated by probing linguistic associations. Such activity is midrashic, and therefore primarily exoteric, in nature. But the second level in the allusion is esoteric, concerning, as it does, the 'wheel of the letters' as related to the Names of God.

In this way, the wheel imagery conjoins a relatively simple psychological observation with the more mystical understanding of the Names of God, and their use in the esoteric practices relating to the inner process of creation. Psychologically, the multiplicity of the scriptural text is probed by using the associative function of mind. As the exegete turns the wheel of language and meaning, possible interpretations are continually enriched by diverse associations. But the approach promoted by the *Sefer Yetsirah* extends the reach of the exegete to the wheel of *letters*, that is, to the sphere of the elemental forces of creation. This extension entails, as Idel (2002) notes in relation to Abulafia's work, 'a transition from a limited state of consciousness to a larger one' (p. 90).

In psychological terms, the emphasis on wheel-related imagery may be understood as highlighting the associative faculty of mind. 'Rolling around' letters and words relates to a free-flowing state of mind through which creative ideas may arise. The cognitive approach explored in Chapter 5 has provided evidence that multiple meanings are activated preconsciously, that is, prior to the end-stage of normal perceptual and thought processes. In terms of the 'I'-tag theory, the 'wheel of language and meaning' may be applied to the stage labelled 'examine' in relation to the Abhidhamma terminology discussed above (Figure 5.5). The emphasis on this stage, both through associative exegesis and by the more distinctive practices of language mysticism, may be viewed as shifting the focus away from the end-stage ('I'-narrative stream) and towards the normally preconscious activity (deep memory process stream). Figure 7.1 illustrates the shift envisaged. Whereas figures in previous chapters have depicted a perceptual process triggered by a sensory stimulus, Figure 7.1 illustrates a more contemplative process of thought. The 'stimulus' in this case may be words of the

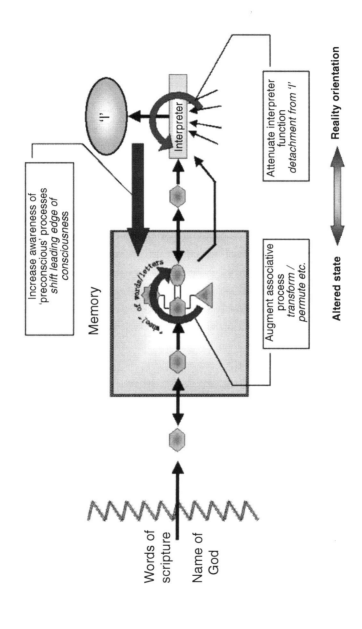

FIGURE 7.1 'I'-tag theory: proposed effects of language mysticism

sacred text, or the Names of God. Despite this difference in the kind of stimulus triggering the process, the basic stages involved are the same. The novel element introduced in Figure 7.1, by comparison with earlier figures, concerns the shift envisaged to be occurring towards the normally preconscious stage represented by the 'wheel of words/letters'. As indicated in the figure, this is a shift away from the 'reality orientation' attaching to the 'I'-narrative stream. The shift brings about an altered state of consciousness.

Familiarity with rabbinic texts is likely to seed the importance of the 'wheel of words and meanings', but would not in itself result in the kind of change in consciousness depicted in Figure 7.1. Such transformation will depend on the other features of the mystical practices mentioned above, such as breath control and visualization, in combination with the letter-working itself. Nevertheless, exoteric familiarity with the 'wheel of words and meanings' undoubtedly sensitizes the potential mystic to the more arcane work connected with the 'wheel of the letters' and the Names of God.

Figure 7.1 envisages a shift in the focus of attention away from the 'I'-narrative stream and towards that of the deep memory process. There are two possible routes through which this shift might be achieved. One route would entail attenuation of the emphasis on 'I' during the end-stage. The other involves augmenting awareness of the associative stage. Both of these are likely to be involved in most mystical traditions, but different practices may emphasize one over the other. Attenuation of 'I' features prominently, for example, in many Buddhist practices, whereas the elevation of language to divine status in Judaism favours augmenting the 'wheel' of associations, as in midrash and kabbalistic practice.

Language and synaesthesia

This notion that mystical practice can shift the focus of attention to cognitively more primitive stages is supported by Hunt's (1984) detailed analysis of altered states of consciousness. Hunt argues that mystical and other altered states may be understood in terms of a 'turning around' onto earlier stages in cognitive processes, stages that are normally 'masked' (that is, not available to introspection). Of paramount importance in understanding mystical states are those early cognitive processes that involve synaesthetic associations of the kind I have discussed in Chapter 5. Like Cytowic (1993), Hunt considers that synaesthesia is a product of an early stage of perceptual processing, which, in normal, non-synaesthetic individuals, is preconscious. As discussed in Chapter 5, synaesthesia only comes about in rare individuals when this, normally preconscious, stage is abnormally prolonged into consciousness. Hunt's argument is that mystics gain access to this early stage of information processing. The 'insight' typically experienced in mystical states derives from this basic level of cross-modal intelligence. Hunt suggests that the mystical sense of knowing more than would normally (that is, rationally) be known is attributable to the inclusiveness and openness of these synaesthetic, or cross-modal, connections.

Of particular interest to my discussion of language mysticism is the connection Hunt makes between these kinds of mystical synaesthesias and language. The metaphorical function is central to all language, and synaesthesia is the most concrete expression of metaphor. Language clearly depends on linkages being forged across different sense modalities, for otherwise a word could not encompass experiences that are essentially polymodal. Take the word 'cat', for example. The word would be ineffective were it to depict only the visual image of cats and not the sound they make, or the texture of their fur, and so on. It is for this reason that Hunt argues that 'complex synaesthesias *are* the "deep structure" of language' (p. 505, italics original). They constitute the bedrock out of which the communicative function of language arises.

A theory of the evolution of language advanced by Ramachandran and Hubbard (2001) includes a similar appeal to the role of synaesthesia. These authors assume that synaesthetic connections established the conditions necessary for language to evolve. Synaesthesia between sensory areas and the motor regions controlling vocalization, for example, would have enabled primitive vocalizations to capture sensory qualities directly, giving rise to the onomatopoeic dimension that is basic to language. Words such as *smooth* or *jagged* clearly bear a sound relation to their referents. Presumably, the evolution of language entailed a preliminary stage in which, to take this example, a smooth visual shape synaesthetically triggered a sound having a 'smooth' quality, whereas the sound associated with a jagged shape had a 'jagged' quality. A moment's reflection on a wide range of words will indicate that this relation between word sound and visual shape is extensive.

I earlier referred to Thass-Thienemann's (1968) insight that language reveals the pre-history of the human mind. Whilst the

onomatopoeia underpinning synaesthesia may pertain to perhaps
the oldest stratum of the mind, metaphor and metonymy similarly
unearth the profound underpinnings of the immediate sense of the
language we use. The meaning of single words, phrases, and even
whole conversations, is always greater than it appears, since the
wheel of language is active beneath the conscious surface – in both
speaker and listener – generating the associations that give context
and flavour to our utterances. Skelton (1995) reminds us of the
'hidden fact' that 'did we but know it we are always saying at least
two things at a time' (p. 173). Drawing on the earlier work of
Saussure and Merleau-Ponty, Abram (1996) emphasizes the
'webwork' of language (cf. my term 'wheel') whereby 'each term
has meaning only by virtue of its relation to other terms within the
system' (pp. 82–3). He continues,

> In English, for instance, the sounded word 'red' draws its precise
> meaning from its situation in a network of like-sounding terms,
> including, for instance, 'read', 'rod', 'reed', and 'raid', and in a
> whole complex of color terms, such as 'orange', 'yellow',
> 'purple,' 'brown'; as well as from its participation in a still wider
> nexus of related terms like 'blood', 'rose', 'sunset', 'fire', 'blush',
> 'angry', 'hot', each of which holds significance only in relation
> to a constellation of still other words, expanding thus outward
> to every term within the language.
>
> (Abram, 1996, p. 83)

Midrashic logic, exemplified by the earlier example of linkages
between 'little child', 'tutor', 'master-craftsman', 'covered',
'hidden', 'great', and 'artisan', illustrates the bringing-to-
consciousness of these normally preconscious connections.
Language mysticism goes further in exploiting the potential of an
altered state of consciousness to engage more fundamentally with
the process that underlies linguistic associations. As the link to
synaesthesia suggests, Jewish mystical practice adds an evolutionary dimension to the more normative midrashic-style verbal associations focused at the level of the words' semantic meanings.

  Where contemporary biology and psychology see evidence of
the evolutionary roots of language, the Jewish mystic sees echoes
of the primordial stirrings of creation. This is a direct concomitant
of the worldview of Jewish mysticism, in which language is
construed quite literally as the dynamo of creation. The potent

synaesthesias that underpin the evolution of language become, in this mystical framework, a feature of the mechanism of creation. For the mystic, the pre-history of the human mind is the pre-history of the work of creation. Hunt (1984) notes that the kinds of perceptual anomalies experienced in mystical states 'embody all the transformational operations of the "deep structure" of language – deletion, substitution, expansion, condensation, addition, and permutation' (pp. 473–4). These are, of course, precisely the kinds of operations that are central to both language mysticism and the Freudian primary process of thought. For the mystic, however, it is their resonance with the divine work of creation that is distinctive.

Expanded consciousness

As should be clear from the above discussion, I attribute the 'fullness' attaching to the forms of mysticism under consideration as being due, in psychological terms, to the richness of normally preconscious processing. In these cases there is an attenuation of the filtering out of multiple associations, which normally accompanies the generation of the 'I'-narrative stream. At the same time, in the state of 'fullness', there is a shift of attention towards the 'wheel' responsible for generating the associations. The mystic's consciousness is 'expanded' by dint of the amount and intensity of content. The mystic is flooded with inspirational material. It is this feature of his method that led Abulafia to designate it the *Path of Prophecy* in addition to the *Path of Names*. For Abulafia, language serves the prophetic function by aligning the human intellect with the Active Intellect. He writes that, 'the intent behind language is the discovery of the function of the Active Intellect, that makes human speech conform to the Divinity' (cited in Idel, 1989b, p. 22). When such a 'conformation' is achieved, the human mind is receptive to the outpouring of divine communication.

In this context, considerable tension arises between naturalistic and supernaturalistic approaches to understanding the basis of mystical knowledge. By describing the rich fount of material to which mystics become receptive as deriving from 'preconscious' processing, I am situating the explanation within a psychological, and therefore, naturalistic, framework. Clearly, this was not the mediaeval mystics' own framework. For them, the Active Intellect was the sphere aligning human intellect to the *divine*. As indicated already, Jewish mystics identified the Active Intellect with the wheel of letters used by God in creation. The *prophetic* state, which was the goal of Abulafia's mysticism, is one in which the mystic achieves union with the Active Intellect and is accordingly able to receive the influx from a transcendent level.

The important question of the value and limitations of *psychologization* will be further explored in Chapter 8. Let me note in passing here that the quest to explain mystical knowing within appropriate frameworks cannot be divorced from the urge towards the encounter with God. The works of Eckhart, one of the most eloquent advocates of the divine encounter, are largely devoted to an analysis of *intellect*, viewed as the vehicle of encounter. Indeed, his approach, like that of his Jewish contemporary, Abulafia, may best be characterized as 'intellectual mysticism' (Idel, 1988b). The intellectual imperative helps to avoid the tendency towards sentimentalizing mystical experience. Like Abulafia, Eckhart situates his mysticism firmly within the context of the Aristotelian explanatory framework current in his day. For example, the formulation that the desired state of divine union arises through an alignment between 'the Knower as subject and the Known as object and Knowledge itself as the relation' (cited in Kelley, 1977, p. 212) is found also throughout Islamic and Jewish sources of the time, and is a direct expression of the Aristotelianism that united the traditions.

There is some continuity between the mediaeval quest to explain mystical states in terms of Aristotelian constructs, and the interest, in our day, in explaining such states in relation to neurological and psychological structures. Where the latter are viewed as *fully* explaining the mystical state, the continuity is certainly stretched. But, in those formulations (for example, Newberg, d'Aquili and Rause, 2001) which leave open the possibility that the neurological and psychological structures are 'vehicles' for a higher reality, the continuity is strong. Certainly, the appeal to structures that are essentially 'non-denominational' does provide an element of continuity between the mediaeval period and our own (Lancaster, 2001).

Psychological explanations of mystical states inevitably emphasize the more general features of the states. A complete explanation will balance this with recognition of the distinctive elements in the given mystical tradition. Attempts to squeeze all features of mystical traditions into a straightjacket of universalism, as found in authors favouring perennialism, does not seem to me to lead to adequate explanations. The mediaeval authors, such as Abulafia, Ibn Arabi, and Eckhart, may usefully guide us in the art of explanations that integrate common structures with those that are distinctive to their own tradition.

Three key psychological principles have been identified that apply to all altered states of consciousness (Jaynes, 1976/1990; Tart, 1975, 2000). First, there has to be a pervasive *authorization*, which underpins the individual's intention and expectations, and gives legitimacy to the kind of alteration in state likely to occur. Second, a specific *induction procedure* must be employed, which triggers changes characteristic of trance-like states. Third, there needs to be a *cognitive restructuring* which functions to maintain the altered state itself. The cognitive restructuring may extend beyond the immediate duration of the altered state. Indeed, in meditative and other mystical states, a primary goal is to bring about long-term transformation. The important effects of meditation are not the short-term, perhaps pleasurable or relaxing, experiences that accompany performance of the practice itself. Of primary importance is the cognitive restructuring that leads to a changed view of the world.

In furthering my analysis of the expanded consciousness associated with language mysticism, I shall examine each of these three psychological principles in turn. My objective is twofold. In the first place, the psychological framework helps situate an approach such as Abulafia's in an explanatory context which has been validated through extensive research. Second, distinctive features in language mysticism can expand our understanding of the psychology of consciousness. In the same way that distortions of perception – as in the case of visual illusions, for example – have led to significant advances in the theory of perception, so too the distortions in normal language function evidenced in language mysticism may cast light on the role language plays in consciousness.

As should be evident from previous chapters, this emphasis on the two-way dynamic between psychology and mysticism exemplifies my approach to consciousness. The overall framework of the 'I'-tag theory has been derived from insights culled from the Abhidhamma's analysis of thought and perception. At the same time, detail about the processes involved in each of the individual stages has been given through research data at neurophysiological, cognitive, and depth-psychological levels. Consciousness studies demands a marriage of science and mysticism.

Authorization

Jaynes argues that alterations of consciousness require *archaic authorization* and a *collective cognitive imperative*. The collective cognitive imperative establishes the culturally agreed-on form that the altered state should take. The archaic authorization establishes that some person, or a deity, is responsible for controlling this state. In the case of hypnosis, for example, the person to be hypnotized will have expectations as to the nature of the trance, which will take the form of culturally-shared beliefs and ideas about likely outcomes. The person undergoing hypnosis is effectively prepared to hand over control to the hypnotist, who thereby takes on the authorization role.

In language mysticism, the cognitive imperative depends on the perceived divine origin of letters and language. In Islam, the letters of the Arabic alphabet are held to convey the secrets of the divine (Schimmel, 1975), and in classical Judaism, as we have seen, the Hebrew letters are agents of creation. In a Talmudic text, the advice given to a scribe is to 'be meticulous in your work, for it is the work of heaven; should you omit one single letter, or add one too many, you would thereby destroy the whole world' (Talmud, *Eruvin* 13a). As codified in the *Sefer Yetsirah*, the world comes into being through God's letter-working, and it can therefore be destroyed through improper actions with letters. Jewish mystics perceive themselves to be emulating God's own work of creation by engaging in the linguistic practices learned through study of the *Sefer Yetsirah* and other sources.

The authorization is clearly implicit in the cognitive imperative. The letter-working is perceived to be of divine authority, for it is 'the work of heaven'. The divine source of the practice is initially a matter of belief, but, as the practice develops, it may come to be an active feature of experience. This is well illustrated in the case of an anonymous pupil of Abulafia who left a valuable testimony of experiences gleaned through the practice of letter permuting and combining. He records that after some two months of regular practice, he seemed to be no longer 'in this world'. He continues: 'And behold, something resembling speech emerged from my heart and came to my lips and forced them to move' (Scholem, 1941/1961, p. 151). This was identified as the 'spirit of wisdom'. On reporting back to his teacher, the pupil is told that, 'My son, it is the Lord who must bestow such power upon you for such power is not within man's control'.

All mysticism of fullness involves a subtle balance between the control asserted by the mystic and a more submissive, or receptive, state through which the 'higher presence' is enabled to operate. Idel (2002) suggests that Abulafia assumes the existence of two stages in his practice, which may be distinguished on the basis of this change in the sense of perceived control. The relevant passage from Abulafia is worth quoting at length, for it conveys the general principles of the approach of disciplined association at the heart of his method:

> It is incumbent to revolve the entire Torah, which is [consists] in the names of the Holy One, blessed be He, and it is incumbent to innovate new wonders on each and every letter and on each and every word, from time to time. And it is incumbent to inquire into one word and connect it to another, and then leave the second and look for a third to connect it with [the first], and then another, sometimes at their middle, sometimes at their beginning, sometimes at their end, sometimes by their numbers and sometimes by their permutations, until he will exit from all his initial thoughts and will innovate other [sic], better than them, always one after another. And despite the fact that he does this while the holy name is sealed within his blood, he will not feel until it will move from its place and the blood will not run from his face by the attribute of judgment together with that of joy, he did not achieve anything from the prophetic comprehension. But it is known that when the Name, whose secret is in blood and ink, began to move within him, and he will feel it, as one who knows the place of a stone which is within him, he will then know that the knowledge of the Name acted in him, and it began to cause him to pass from potentiality to actuality.
>
> (Idel, 2002, cited p. 341)

The first part of the passage details the 'wheel' of associations that the mystic pursues amongst letters and words. The distinction between two stages in the practice comes later in the passage where a change becomes evident in the role played by the divine Name. In the first stage, the mystic does not 'feel' the Name; there are no intense physiological changes and there is no 'prophetic comprehension'. In the second stage, the Name 'moves' within the mystic, becoming the active force, which causes his intellect to align with the Active Intellect ('from potentiality to actuality'). In the first stage, the mystic is in control; in the second, the divine Name takes control and the mystic is simply in the role of receiver of divine influx.

Induction procedure

For Jaynes, the induction procedure involves a *narrowing* of consciousness. Again, to take the example of hypnosis, the hypnotist may instruct the client to focus on a single spot, to hear only their voice, and so on. Tart focuses more on the relative balance between *patterning* and *destabilizing* forces in the baseline state of consciousness. Normally, for example, a kind of constant checking for reality orientation comprises the major patterning force, holding us to a conventional state. An induction procedure will bring about an increase of destabilizing forces. For example, as part of the induction of a trance state, a hypnotist may suggest that an arm is levitating. If the client observes some movement upwards in the arm, the perceived concordance between the suggestion and their bodily reality functions to destabilize the normal state. The observation contravenes everyday reality orientation.

In Abulafia's method there are clearly features that relate to the induction of altered states. However, it is questionable whether the altered state is best described as a 'narrowing' of consciousness, as Jaynes suggests is generally the case. The intense *focusing* brought about by Abulafia's techniques is accompanied by a high level of complex conscious content. The mystic is intensively engaged with subtle nuances of words and letters, the shapes of letters, their numerical equivalents, and a host of other paralinguistic features. There is some tension between my use of the term 'fullness' to describe the altered state and Jaynes' notion of a 'narrowing' of consciousness. The choice of appropriate term may largely depend on whether it is being applied to the focusing or the ideation. The focus is certainly narrowed, but then so it is whenever one is intensively engaged in some task. The 'prophetic' state itself, however, would seem to entail an *expansion* in the level of ideation.

The features in Abulafia's techniques that seem to have played prominent roles in inducing an altered state are largely *somatic*. This accords with the above extract, in which the change between two stages of the practice is described in physiological terms. In the writings of Abulafia and others from this school of language mysticism, there are many references to bodily changes accompanying the prophetic state of consciousness. The hairs of the head become erect, the blood drains from the face, bodily limbs tremble, and there is a bodily feeling as if being anointed with oil.

The induction procedure includes fasting prior to the letter-working itself, and various other preliminaries such as lighting candles and wrapping oneself in the prayer shawl. By direct effect, or by psychological association, these may be expected to heighten the aura of expectancy. Physiological concomitants of the letter-working practice include breath control, visualizations, chanting, and ritualized head movements. The method is practised alone and at night.

Many of these features are similar to techniques found in other mystical practices, and they undoubtedly would have contributed to the generalized change in state. Some would have had direct physiological effects. Fasting and breath control, for example, are thought to induce alterations of consciousness as a consequence of the changes they cause in the levels of nutrients and oxygen reaching the brain (Persinger, 1987). Other features of the induction procedures may have enhanced a propensity towards synaesthesia, which, as discussed above, seems to be involved in reversing the normal flow of perceptual and other cognitive activity. The head movements, for example, corresponded kinaesthetically with the vowel sounds being chanted or visualized. Indeed, given that specific letters were associated with individual limbs, the whole body effectively became a vehicle for the esoteric letter-working.

As already discussed in the previous chapter, the emphasis on *embodiment* may be seen as a further expression of the anti-dualistic stance which characterizes the Jewish worldview. Just as the Rabbis viewed the physical world as the realm of spiritual encounter, so the mystics regarded the human body as comprising the esoteric principles that are enshrined in the Hebrew letters.[9] Abulafia writes:

> Know that all the limbs of your body are combined like that of the forms of the letters combined one with the other. Know also that when you combine them it is you who distinguish between the forms of the letters for in their prime-material state they are equal ... and with one sweep you can erase them all from a writing board. So too [with] all the moisture of your body and all of your limbs ... they all return to their prime-material state.
>
> (Cited in Idel, 1989b, p. 6)

Induction of the mystical state demands the dissolution of all self-related structure, as expressed through both the mind and the body. Abulafia's 'prime-material state' is a distinctive expression of the 'undifferentiated unity' that Stace (1961) sees as a goal of introverted mysticism. For Stace, a phase of the introverted mystical path entails 'the blotting out of the distinction between the "I" and the infinite unity in which it is sunk or merged' (p. 122). Perhaps reflecting his strong emphasis on Buddhism and Christian mysticism, Stace does not recognize the kind of bodily role that Abulafia portrays in this 'blotting out'. For Abulafia, the body should be fully engaged in the 'sweeping away' of differentiation. The letters themselves are the pivotal connection between all levels – that of the human body, that of the world and that of the divine.

The strong emphasis on embodiment in all the features of the induction procedure is noteworthy, and represents a further connection to depth psychology. The body is the expressive terrain of the unconscious, as Freud discerned in his studies of hysterical neuroses. The linchpin of Freud's insights into these neuroses was his recognition that bodily symptoms reveal unconscious complexes. Indeed, his implacable emphasis on the sexual nature of libido, the 'energy' of the unconscious, served to root the *psyche* in the *soma*.

Freud's insight into the pathological represents a potent complement to the Jewish mystic's vision of the sublime. In both, embodiment is central; and in both, progress towards the desired goal demands some form of associative practice. Freud's 'free association' uncovers the motivations behind surface contents; Abulafia's 'disciplined association' reveals the hidden thought process in the mind of God.

Cognitive reconstruction

> Read the entire Torah, both forwards and backwards, and spill the blood of the languages. Thus, the knowledge of the Name [of God] is above all wisdoms in quality and worth.
>
> (Abulafia, cited in Idel, 1989b, p. 27)

The phrase 'spill the blood of the languages' hardly suggests a sedate form of word association! As noted earlier, the intention was to reach the 'prime material state', a state in which words no longer conveyed any cognitive meaning. As suggested by Idel, the practice of language mysticism along Abulafian lines is likely to have resulted in a profound deconstruction of semantics. The prime matter is that of the letters in their primordial creative function. Like individual elements of the DNA code, they have no meaning until expressed through their combinations.

Given the role played by language in structuring and maintaining the self-model and its relation to the world, we may envisage the practice eventuating in a dissolution of psychological structure. As discussed in earlier chapters, Abulafia conveys this teaching by using the metaphor of *knots*:

> Man is [tied] in knots of world, year and soul [i.e., space, time and persona] in which he is tied in nature, and if he unties the knots from himself, he may cleave to He who is above them.
>
> (Cited in Idel, 1988a, p. 35)

The 'undifferentiated unity' to which Stace refers may aptly be captured in the image of schematic 'knots' being untied. But, for Abulafia, the aim is the *reconstruction of meaning*. For all that the permutations of words and letters brings a deconstruction of normal linguistic meaning, the elements are re-unified at a higher level through the all-encompassing divine Names. This aspect of his practice is designated by Abulafia, the 'path of the veritable essence of prophecy', the 'Holy of Holies' (Idel, 1989b, pp. 105, 101). The transcendence of self- and worldly-oriented language brings in its wake the power attaching to the higher integration. The mystic becomes magician or creator, for the Name is no mere appellation but, for Kabbalists, the very essence of the divine mystery: 'It is proper for those who walk on this path to produce ... a new universe' (ibid, p. 103). Idel suggests that, in this emphasis on the miraculous level of creation, the mystic is being likened to God Himself.

The reconstruction of meaning brought about through this kind of mysticism might be conceptualized psychologically in terms of the memory-indexing function discussed earlier. In Chapter 5, I suggested that 'I'-tags play a role as a form of indexing system in memory. All events that are experienced in the 'I'-narrative stream become stored in relation to the 'I' that was constituted at the time of experience. As discussed in detail above, we may envisage that these connections – 'I'-tags – are critical for both the activation of memories in their proper context, and for the sense of personal engagement that accompanies their activation. The memories are available to *me*, and carry the sense of belonging to *me*, as it were.

These functions characterize the mundane mind. What, then, of the mind trained through the practice of language mysticism? All the knots have been loosed – the strictures limiting memories to 'I' have been overcome. But it is not intended that untied threads of the mind be left in this unattached state. The imperative is to re-tie them, not to 'I', but to the Active Intellect, through the divine Names. We might formulate the intention as that of substituting 'I'-tags with linguistically-based 'God-tags', as it were. On these lines, Abulafia's system of language mysticism may be viewed as re-formatting the memory system in relation to a higher-order indexing system. Psychologically, the undifferentiated state is merely a transition to a globally more integrated one.

These are speculative thoughts. However, the idea is not as far-fetched as it seems. Leaving aside, for the moment, any supernatural elements in the goals of language mysticism, the basic consideration is that of effecting an increase in scale with regards to accessible memory. The accessibility of any storage system is limited by the scale of its index. And, ultimately, the accessibility of our memories is what defines us; the greater the scale, the greater we are.

To the Jewish mystic, the Name of God is certainly the key to broadening the scale of being. The Name is the cipher of the macrocosm. 'All that is formed and all that is spoken derives from one Name' (*Sefer Yetsirah* 2:5). The Name depicts the opening to the infinite within the finite, and a memory formatted around such a superordinate schema will bring about transcendence of the limited world of 'I'. It is indeed a 'new universe' that the mystic may create: one in which the centre of narrative gravity is no longer 'I' but rather the divine narrative of creation. Consciousness may be expanded, not only in the immediate sense of enriching the content of experience, but also in the more profound sense of re-aligning the foundations of memory.

Part III
Beyond Within

Chapter 8
Together Again

Overview

In the preceding chapters, my intention has been to enter into sufficient detail in order to distil the contribution that each relevant area may make towards an integrative theory of consciousness. It is only when equipped with such detail that we can begin to find the complementarity that currently exists between the different approaches. It is this complementarity in the data that is truly critical for any theory of consciousness which attempts to unify the approaches. Clearly, our confidence in such a theory will be enhanced when data from diverse approaches are mutually supportive.

In this brief overview I shall emphasize these areas of complementarity. Examination of the key points from each of the approaches will provide what might be thought of as building blocks towards an integrative theory.

Philosophical issues

The background discussed in Part I impinges on all the approaches. This concerns the specification and clarification of the various dimensions of consciousness, and the issues of causation and explanation. My approach to defining consciousness is similar to that advanced by Nelkin (1993), discussed in Chapter 6. The dimensions that an adequate theory of consciousness must explain are **phenomenality**, **intentionality**, and **accessibility**. A further key term is 'self'. Self is the *lens* of consciousness; it focuses the three dimensions in a given state. Normally, as the sense of 'I' in a mundane state of consciousness, self constrains accessibility. In an altered state, the scale of self has been changed, which brings about concomitant changes in the scale of accessibility. An expanded self means an expanded state of consciousness; a narrowed self gives rise to a restricted state.

A full explanation of any dimension of consciousness requires that we understand what causes it. Our approach to explanation is determined by the ontological stance we adopt, for only that which is deemed ontologically real can be imbued with the power of causation. Three primary orientations in the study of consciousness are evident. **Neurophysicalism** holds that consciousness arises through a *causal process at the physical level*, and that the only physical structure capable of generating consciousness is the *brain*.[1] Neurophysicalism is a species of *naturalism* in that the source of consciousness is considered to be an entity, or process, in the natural world. It is distinct from a second species of naturalism, which I refer to as **holophysicalism**.[2] Holophysicalism is the view that consciousness is a feature of the physical world as a whole. The source of consciousness is not the brain, although the brain may have a specific role to play in the 'shaping' of conscious contents. Both these naturalistic perspectives are distinct from **supernaturalism**, which sees the origin of one or more of the three dimensions of consciousness as deriving from a realm ontologically transcendent to the physical world.

The approaches to consciousness considered in Part II have provided data that allow further discussion of the various dimensions of consciousness. Any useful theory of consciousness must be grounded in these data. It is important to note that the relation between data and theory should not be muddled by the question of orientation. As I have stressed in earlier chapters, in the absence of definitive evidence, authors adopt a *belief* in one of the orientations. There are no grounds for unequivocally linking data from a given approach to a specific orientation. It is certainly the case, for example, that most cognitive neuroscientists are neurophysicalists. But this does not mean that the data from cognitive neuroscience cannot inform a theory which holds that one or more of the dimensions of consciousness derive from holistic natural, or supernatural, phenomena. The pursuit of consciousness is largely stymied by confusion between data and belief.

My review of the data from the various approaches considered in Part II suggested a number of features which may be expected to inform any theory of consciousness. However, none of the data can bridge the explanatory gap. We have to accept that there is a mystery surrounding phenomenality. This does not mean that the data cannot enable us to theorize about other dimensions of consciousness. The 'I'-tag theory, which I have elaborated over these pages, does precisely that. Its incorporation of neurophysiological, cognitive and psychodynamic data into a picture of the stages involved when events 'reach' consciousness is defensible irrespective of any considerations about phenomenality. The fact that I regard data from these three approaches as inadequate for explaining phenomenality does not detract from the integrity of the 'I'-tag theory's understanding of the stages themselves.

Complementarity across approaches to consciousness

My examination of the *spiritual/mystical approach 'towards emptiness'* stressed the debate surrounding the phenomenon of contentless consciousness. On balance, there seems to be reason to accept that some conscious experiences lack both a sense of 'I' and any intentionality in terms of meaningful images, be they percepts, memories, or thoughts. Given our reliance on first-person observations with regard to contentless consciousness, we cannot rule out the possibility that preconscious activity remains content-driven in these states. Nevertheless, from the experiential point of view, it appears that phenomenality is potentially dissociable from the other dimensions of consciousness.

The spiritual/mystical approach suggests, moreover, that such emptiness is not merely an interesting anomalous experience. It is central to the quest for transformation that motivates this whole approach. For theistic mystics, experiences of nothingness are to be understood as a necessary stage in the path to encountering God. The mystic is transformed specifically by 'passing through nothingness'.

The quest for transformation also motivates the intense introspection associated with mystical approaches. A prerequisite of transformation is a thorough grasp of what it is that has to be transformed. Indeed, disciplined introspective knowledge is already a sign of a mind undergoing transformation. For our purposes, the key point is that the spiritual traditions contribute a first-person understanding of consciousness that is at least the equal of those available from more philosophical and scientific approaches. Any theory of consciousness that flies in the face of such understanding should be regarded as suspect.

Complementarity between the spiritual/mystical approach and other approaches is especially prominent in the emphasis on the idea of *stages* in perceptual and thought processes. Stages that may have been grasped through introspective or exegetical mystical activity may be seen to relate to those proposed in relation to the third-person data of cognitive neuroscience, for example. Jewish mysticism contributes the idea of a preconscious that has both temporal and transformative implications. The temporal aspect is evident in the view that the *preconscious* precedes the mental activity that is accessible in the normal state of consciousness. The transformative implications follow from the teaching that the preconscious is a *higher*, divine, manifestation of mind. The mystic seeks to unify the self with this higher level.

Buddhism provides insight into the sequential operations that eventuate in a thought or percept. As will be clear from the earlier chapters, the operational analysis given in the Abhidhamma has shaped my understanding of the stages of perception. The 'I'-tag theory is largely a re-working of these stages as informed by the other approaches.

From the *neurophysiological approach* we learn about the brain mechanisms that integrate current sensory activity with memory. Sensory neurones are assembled into functional groups on the basis of phase synchrony, or resonance, in neural signals. This 'brain code' is able to determine levels of compatibility between the sensory analysis and memory readout. There is little evidence to support the proposal that the phase synchrony is a *direct* correlate of consciousness, but it seems to be a *necessary* correlate of the preconscious processing that may eventuate in consciousness.[3]

More specifically, the neurophysiological data suggest a highly interactive system, with *re-entrant pathways* playing an essential role in the equilibration between sensory data and memory readout. We may postulate a key role for these pathways in relation to *intentionality*, for it is only when sensory data are set in a context given by memory that they may be said to take on meaning.

The *cognitive and neuropsychological approaches* inform us about the content of preconscious activity, and about the transition between preconscious processing and access-consciousness. Preconscious processing is characterized by activation of multiple representations in memory readout. Most of these become inhibited when a perceptual process reaches its 'end-stage' of access-consciousness. The end-stage constitutes an *interpretative* process which establishes 'I' as a focus of cognitive activity. In practice, there is no definitive 'end-stage' since individual cognitive acts obviously fuse over time. 'I' becomes seemingly continuous since it is the one fixed point in the ongoing interactions between incoming activity and memory.

The defining feature of mundane consciousness is the linkage between 'I' and other representations. When we speak of a normal state of consciousness, what we mean is that the contents are *accessible to 'I'*. Variations in either the nature of 'I' or the level of accessibility of content will lead to altered states.

Cognitive and neuropsychological research also point to the role 'I' plays in relation to memory. The 'I'-tag theory incorporates this role by emphasizing that the linkage between the representation of some object or event and 'I' becomes stored in memory. The term "'I'-tag' specifically refers to this association between the representation of self and representations of other objects or events. The 'I'-tag is responsible for the critical sense of personal ownership of the memory. In addition, it plays an 'indexing' role in the memory system, since it enables a current construction of 'I' to activate other representations to which it connects by virtue of those representations' 'I'-tags. Indeed, this is the basic reason for thinking of it as a 'tag'.

These interpretations of data from cognitive and neuropsychological research lend further support to my understanding of the transformational imperative evident in the mystical approach. Concentrative practices may lead to a more detached view of 'I'. They encourage greater awareness of the constructive processes involved in the sense of self and in everyday cognitive processes. A goal of such practices is the realization that 'I' is a means to an end (as proposed here in relation to its indexing function, for example) and not the true centre of operations in the mind. Despite appearances to the contrary, 'I' is not the receiver of impressions, thinker of thoughts and instigator of actions.

The *approach of depth psychology* has informed my understanding of intentionality. The stage-based picture encouraged by neuroscientific and cognitive research is misleading if it encourages us to think of particular events as occurring in isolation. For example, perception of a given object (such as the pen used in the figures) will always be embedded in a broader context. This broader context entails two distinct streams of intentionality. The first is attributable to the preconscious activations of memory images, which I have termed the *deep memory process* (DMP) to distinguish it from the 'I'-based processing of the second stream. The DMP stream constitutes the equivalent in the operational terms of the 'I'-tag theory to the more topographical idea of the psychodynamic unconscious. The DMP stream is characterized by the diversity of associations to the originating stimulus. This diversity gives rise to the DMP stream's own distinctive hermeneutic, which entails irrational and symbolic relations between images. A potent historical precedent for understanding this hermeneutic is found in the 'midrashic logic' that underpins rabbinic Judaism's approach to sacred scripture.

The second stream of intentionality parallels the conscious system of the mind in the Freudian topographical model.[4] In terms of the 'I'-tag theory, this *'I'-narrative stream* incorporates the events and objects of thought and perception into an interpretative framework focused on 'I'.

The DMP stream is autonomously active; it has its own 'life'. Indeed, this observation underlies my use of the phrase 'deep memory process' and its conceptualization as a stream of processing. The autonomous dynamic of the DMP stream ('unconscious' in Freudian terms) is the critical insight deriving from the depth-psychological approach. Its autonomous activity is *additional* to its role as a preliminary to the 'I'-narrative stream. In the latter sense, the DMP gives shape to the meanings that are the lifeblood of the 'I'-narrative stream. When a percept or thought is gestating in the mind, the preliminary form ('neuronal input model') gives direction to the associative process that generates the DMP stream. The majority of the activated associations will remain 'unconscious' in the sense that they do not become the focus of the 'I'-narrative stream. Nevertheless, they exert a critical influence on the meaning of whatever does become the focus. For example, Freudian-type associations to a pen's shape and name (for instance, phallic associations), as well as more idiosyncratic connections, may colour my perception of the pen, without my being aware of their influence.

I argued in Chapter 7 that the sense of *fullness* experienced in many mystical states is attributable to the multiplicity of content in the DMP stream. There is an intimation of 'more' within the structure of experience. This kind of intimation has been seen as a hallmark of spirituality by many, including William James and Rudolph Otto. Many spiritual practices may be characterized as enabling increased access to the normally inaccessible contents within the DMP stream. The *spiritual/ mystical approach 'towards fullness'* is centred on this issue of the 'more' which lies beyond conscious experience. In theistic traditions, an intellectual sphere beyond the purely human mind is postulated as the source for this intimation of more. In the examples of mediaeval mysticism that I have explored, this intellectual sphere was identified with the Aristotelian concept of the *Active Intellect*. The Active Intellect was viewed as the source of inspirational content, and the sphere of mystical union with the divine.

Whilst the assumption of ontological transcendence implicit in the idea of the Active Intellect places it beyond the scope of conventional science, two features in particular enable some degree of contact with psychology. First, the fact that it was viewed as a realm of *intellect* (and not simply some nebulous transcendent existence) means that we may realistically entertain ideas of the relationship between normal human thought and that pertaining to the Active Intellect. Second, descriptions of the mystical practices that were viewed as bringing about an alignment between the human and divine intellectual spheres are highly psychological, since their concern is essentially with altered states of consciousness. In considering the extent to which data from different approaches may be complementary, these two features are clearly critical. In relation to both the intellectual activity of the Active Intellect and its role in bringing about an altered state, the appropriate psychological comparison is with preconscious activity. Both the Active Intellect and the processing style of the preconscious involve multiple dimensions of meaning, and both the Active Intellect and the preconscious are implicated in the search for transformative states of consciousness.

The dynamic of the DMP stream, which incessantly engenders multiple activations through its associative and hermeneutic logic, resonates with the Jewish mystic's vision of the Active Intellect. The Active Intellect is equated with the primordial Torah, source of all potential meanings and root of hermeneutic diversity. The Active Intellect is the divine power to confer form, as epitomized in the creative role of divine speech, recorded exoterically in *Genesis* ('And God said....'). The fundamental point of connection between the preconscious and the Active Intellect comes with the creative power each possesses. This creativity is not concerned solely with externals, as in problem-solving, or creative writing, for example. Fundamentally, the creativity of the DMP stream and that of the Active Intellect relates to the creation of the basic cognitive structures of the mind. The mystical vision of engaging with the primordial mysteries of creation may correspond to the psychological challenge of recreating the wellsprings of self.

The 'I'-tag theory enables us to conceptualize in psychological terms the effects of the practices associated with language mysticism. In essence, these effects derive from one central feature – namely, the aim of stretching the limits of the experienceable. We may envisage that in the concentrative mystical state, with its emphasis on the associative dynamic of the DMP, activity that is normally preconscious becomes accessible. A number of potential psychological benefits may ensue from this shift towards experiencing earlier stages in mental processes. The mind might become less limited by the tagging function normally associated with 'I', and therefore more open to the creative possibilities found in the context of multiple preconscious associations. Such an untying of the habitual, egocentric 'knots' that organize mental operations would be potentially transforming. We may envisage 'therapeutic' benefits arising from the fact that the world would no longer be viewed through egocentric lenses. There may be greater empathy with others, increased tolerance, higher creativity.

In the marketplace of spiritual practice, such transformations of personality may have considerable currency. Yet, without doubt, it is the taste of the transcendent that is the real oil for traditional practitioners of language mysticism. The practice is liberating, ultimately, because it aligns the human mind with the infinite unknowableness that is God.

In defence of the transcendent

> [T]he iconography of the transcendent cannot simply be waved away with some self-appointed authoritative hand.
> (Taylor, 1999b, p. 296)

Is it adequate to conceptualize the effects of spiritual practice in terms of potential transformations of personality alone? It may indeed be the case that the shift towards normally preconscious processes opens the mystic to the kind of change that may be described using psychological terminology. But the testimony of mystics themselves is invariably of something altogether different. 'Be wary that thou conceive not bodily that which is meant spiritually,' warns the author of *The Cloud of Unknowing*. And a purely naturalistic conception of the author's notion of 'spiritual' would hardly seem to suffice: 'The higher part of contemplation ... hangeth all wholly in this darkness and this cloud of unknowing; with a loving stirring and a blind beholding unto the naked being of God Himself only' (Underhill, 1912, pp. 234 and 86–7).

As noted above, Abulafia identified the wheel of the letters with the Active Intellect, a sphere imbued with the essence of the divine. His linguistic practices were directed towards achieving union with this sphere. Untying the knots from egocentric meaning was not an end in itself, but a preliminary to the binding of experience to the divine. The biblical sequence "'I, I, He'" (*Deuteronomy* 32:39), for example, is cited as representing the union of the 'supernal divine power' with the 'human power' (Idel, 1988c, p. 11).[5] The human 'I' and the divine 'I' fuse in the one power depicted by 'He'.

My analysis has suggested that the 'wheel' of language depicts the associative power at work in preconscious processing. Yet this idea pales somewhat in the face of the vision at the heart of all kabbalistic language mysticism, which identifies the wheel both with the primordial Torah and with the divine process of creation. The wheel is responsible for both the diversity of forms generated by God and the multiplicity of images in the human mind. A species of psychologization that compromises this equivalence may *explain away* as much as it explains.

Here we confront the central tension that has surfaced at key points in earlier chapters. What are the gains and losses associated with the endeavour to strip mysticism of the supernaturalism found at its heart? Is it possible to hold onto a psychologically viable tradition of spiritual transformation without embracing a view of a transcendent realm ontologically distinct from that of the human brain and the material universe as a whole? In short, is there, as Hick (1980) formulates it, 'well-grounded human belief that the Transcendent exists' (p. 434)?[6] Hick considers that claims made by mystics and others concerning the reality of the Transcendent pass a reasonable test on the grounds that (i) a significant number of such individuals have been sane and generally to be trusted; (ii) the claims are not substantially contradicted by scientific knowledge (they may be contradicted by scientism, but not by scientific knowledge); and (iii) the claims show a significant coherence across diverse times and places. The hypothesis that the Transcendent is real 'should be judged by its comprehensiveness, its internal consistency, and its adequacy to the data – in this case the data of the history of religions' (Hick, 2001, p. 192). On all counts, Hick finds reason to accept the hypothesis.

The question is raised here because I believe that it has profound implications for the mystery of phenomenality. If there is a void at the heart of things through which the Transcendent manifests, then why not accept, as the great spiritual traditions insist, that the Transcendent is ever present as the core of consciousness?

The answer to this last question will be clear: many would not accept such a step because it sets their work outside the discourse of scientific psychology. There can be no scientific validation of the Transcendent. Friedman (2002) argues forcefully that transpersonal psychology effectively stands or falls on this point. While he holds that the broader discipline of transpersonal studies may legitimately take an inclusive position with regard to the Transcendent, transpersonal psychology should not. In this way transpersonal psychology can maintain rapport with its sister disciplines in a scientific psychology.

From a diplomatic point of view, Friedman may be correct – it may be wise for those who see themselves as academic psychologists to refrain from speculation that would breach the recognized bounds of the discipline. However, I consider that such a stance downplays the importance of the *transformational face* of transpersonal psychology. Through the pages of this book I have emphasized the profound relationships we find between the transformational and the scientific faces of transpersonal psychology. The insights of mystics can give shape to our speculations about the roles played by neurocognitive processes in relation to consciousness. And in complementary fashion, the scientific data from cognitive neuroscience add substance to mystical notions of transformation. Recognition of the dynamic rapport between these two faces must lie at the heart of the discipline of transpersonal psychology.

But what if it were shown that acknowledgement of the Transcendent in some form is essential for the fullest realization of the transformational quest? Recognition of the rapport between the two faces would be strained unless such acknowledgement of the Transcendent were acceptable to those exploring the scientific face.

It is certainly the case that the spiritual sources I have used to set parameters for my exploration of the scientific face intrinsically acknowledge the Transcendent. The preconscious as conceived in Jewish mystical thought is unequivocally divine; the Abhidhamma assumes a logic of karma and rebirth which transcends physicalism. It might be argued, however, that the key insights on which I have drawn could stand alone; their validity need not depend on the belief system of which they formed a part. The question, then, concerns the legitimacy of extracting psychological concepts from these traditions without 'encumbering' ourselves with their authors' metaphysical assumptions.

As far as the transformational imperative is concerned, I find attempts to draw on the 'wisdom of the ancients', without being encumbered by the baggage that they were 'too primitive' to jettison deeply misleading. What if the 'baggage' is not superfluous to the practices they developed? What if our assumption of their primitiveness is pure conceit? Perhaps, in reaching for the key to consciousness we need the humility to recognize that, in Newton's words, 'we stand on the shoulders of giants'.

The question I have raised over acknowledgement of the Transcendent is essentially the same as that raised by Martin Buber in his criticism of Jung's psychologization of the divine. For Buber (1952/1988), God is an ontological reality whose existence goes beyond the psyche. The key to religious transformation, namely a genuine I–Thou relationship, is compromised when we adhere to Jung's religion of 'pure psychic immanence', as Buber called it (p. 84). It is the 'unincludable otherness of a being' which renders that being effective in bringing about transformation. Only when 'I renounce all claim to incorporating it in any way within me or making it a part of my soul, does it truly become a Thou for me' (p. 89). Buber's target is the *narcissism* that he considered to accompany the Jungian view of the self as the divine image in man. From a Jungian point of view, there is no need to posit contact with a sphere that is essentially 'other' in ontological terms when explaining personal transformation, or *individuation*. The Jungian encounter with archetypes and the realization of the self demand nothing beyond the psyche, which is ontologically part of the human realm.

Buber refutes Jung's defence that he (Jung) makes no metaphysical statements. To Jung's argument that he writes only as an empirical psychologist, Buber replies that Jung's writings reveal a view 'according to which God does not exist "absolutely"', that is,

independent of the human subject and beyond all human condition' (p. 81). For Buber, this *is* a metaphysical assertion – that God
has no absolute existence. Jung indulges in metaphysical speculation without accepting that he is so doing, which, for Buber, is
indefensible. More than this, when Jung asserts that metaphysical
statements derive from a primary psychic reality, Buber sees nothing but a vacuous truism. To be of any value, a statement must
reach beyond its immediate psychological reference. To cite a more
mundane example, when I make the statement that this pen exists,
the intention goes beyond the limited psychic reality of the pen.
Buber insists that psychological statements about archetypes, for
example, are inadequate if they are not pointing to their ontological status. Ultimately, the victim of Jung's approach to religion is
faith, and Buber castigates the great betrayal which is thereby
perpetrated.

Does any of this matter? If all I can know is that which exists
within the psyche, then Jung may be right in asserting that my
contact with the divine must be limited to this ontological sphere.
Anything else is, indeed, mere faith and speculation. And my path of
self-discovery may appear just as profound as any journey predicated
on a supposed ontological, transcendent being. Why introduce a
scientifically opaque term when we can continue to embrace a notion
of transcendence (with a lowercase 't') without it?

The issue here may usefully be framed within the traditional
context of *idolatry*. For Islam and Judaism, idolatry refers to the
imposition of any mental construction on the limitless. Despite all
the myriad forms that a mystic may experience, an attitude is to be
inculcated to the effect that there is always something unknowable
beyond the forms themselves. Yet in the profound opening-up of
the mind likely to be engendered by serious spiritual practice, there
is a potent inclination to 'lock on' to whatever is immediately
available and regarded as the source of the teaching. In the context
of new religious movements this can sometimes be the 'guru' or
cult leader, resulting in a powerful fixation. In nature mysticism,
the void may be filled by a sense of the powerful presence of the
universe in its sublime glory. While undoubtedly uplifting, this
vision remains constrained by its finitude, unless accompanied by
a sense of the Transcendent. In practical terms, language mysticism, for example, hinges on the mystic's faith that infinite wisdom
in some sense truly resides in the scriptural text. It is precisely this
that renders it 'sacred'. Without such faith, the goal is merely that

of deciphering the (human) author's limited intentions. It may be a scholarly goal, but is no longer mystical.

The mystic cultivates a distinctive attitude to the unknowable. When the Psalmist wrote, 'I will lift up my eyes to the hills; from where comes my help?' (121:1), the Jewish mystic understands that, 'From *ayin* – from *nothingness* – comes my help'.[7] Matt (1995) cites the great Sufi poet, Rumi as conveying the same message: 'The whole world has taken the wrong way, for they fear non-existence, while it is their refuge' (p. 104). Indeed, the very essence of Islam lies in its absolute conviction that all depends on submission. 'Not my will, but Thy will' would seem to be the uniting call of the monotheistic faiths. Locating the *Other*, to whom the mystic submits their will, within the framework of the self or the psyche deprives it of that quality of essential otherness that defines the encounter (Buber, 1952/1988).

This issue is certainly not of modern provenance only. It is cryptically addressed in Jewish sources dating from the first century, which are almost certainly connected with material preserved in the Dead Sea Scrolls. It is stated that four entered *Pardes* – paradise, meaning that they engaged in a mystical ascent – but only one of them emerged intact from their endeavours. That one was Rabbi Akiva, who gives the following warning: 'When you approach the pure marble stones, do not say, "Water! Water!"' (Talmud, *Hagiga* 14b). In this seemingly obscure utterance it seems that he is concerned that we should not mistake one ontological level for another. The simple visual allusion refers to a confusion of the superficial appearance of the watery surface with the true substance of the stones. But, of course, there is considerably more depth to this warning. The marble stones depict a metaphysical level associated with the inner workings of creation. It is higher than the level to which water relates, water being associated with the flowing quality of imagery ('formation'). 'Do not confuse the two!' warns Rabbi Akiva. As ever, a subtle allusion is conveyed in the cryptic use of Hebrew: the word for 'marble' has the connotation (if parsed slightly differently) of *existence*, or *being*.[8] We may then translate into modern idiom, 'When you reach the sphere of pure being, do not psychologize it!'

The importance of acknowledging the Transcendent is similarly depicted in the mystical reading of *Exodus* 18:17. The Children of Israel demand to know, 'Is the Lord among us or not?' What kind of a question is this, you might well ask, when, according to the narrative, the Lord has just sent plagues on their enemies, provided a pillar of fire for night-time reading, split the sea to reveal the royal road, rained food from heaven, and extracted water from a rock! The surface reading seems somewhat strained, to put it mildly. The mystical reading, however, recognizes that a deeper concern was being expressed:

> The explanation is as given by R. Shimon. They wished to know whether the divine manifestation which they had experienced was that of the Ancient One, the All-hidden One, the Transcendent, whose designation is *Ayin* (Nothingness), or of the Small Countenance, which is designated by the four-letter name ('Lord').
>
> (*Zohar* 2:64b)[9]

The 'children of Israel' doubted whether the immanent presence of the divine was truly accompanied by the transcendent divine essence. The significance of this doubt is intimated in the immediately following biblical verse: 'Then came Amalek and fought with the people' (*Exodus* 18:18). In Jewish thought, Amalek represents the archetypal spiritual antagonist, the force opposing spiritual advance; and the episode warns of the dangers of a moment's doubt as to the reality of the Transcendent.

Should we dismiss these warnings as pertaining to an outmoded theistic mysticism? Are they no more than admonitions for followers to stay within a dogmatic system of thought? I think not. I am inclined to the view that these directives arise from an experiential recognition of the importance of acknowledging the Transcendent. The transformational face of transpersonal psychology deploys practices that have been largely derived from religious traditions. They were never designed to function in a secular context, and acknowledgment of the Transcendent may be integral to the ways in which they might enable the highest forms of realization. Faith in the transcendent ground of being might just be the oil that allows the cogs to turn.

There can be no scientific proof of the Transcendent. That much is clear. This is the basis of Friedman's (2002) argument for removing the question from the domain of transpersonal psychology. The issue, however, is not whether or not we can prove the reality of the Transcendent, but *whether or not an attitude that acknowledges the Transcendent makes a difference*. Are spiritual practices more effective when set in the broad context of their traditions' view of the Transcendent? Now this is a fit question for transpersonal psychology. From my own experience, and that of the majority of people with whom I come into contact in the context of transpersonal psychology, the answer is 'yes'.[10]

This affirmative answer is consonant with the position at which William James arrived in the conclusion to his classic study of religious experience. The 'unseen region' into which the 'further limits of our being plunge' is real because it generates real effects:

> [T]he unseen region in question is not merely ideal, for it produces effects in this world. When we commune with it, work is actually done upon our finite personality.... But that which produces effects within another reality must be termed a reality itself, so I feel as if we had no philosophical excuse for calling the unseen or mystical world unreal.
>
> (James, 1902/1960, p. 491)

And lest there be any doubt as to his intent, he adds, 'God is the natural appellation, for us Christians at least, for the supreme reality'. While any specific formulation of the divine will inevitably be inadequate, recognition of an ineffable and transcendent core may not be an optional extra for anyone interested in spiritual transformation. 'The concept of the Real does do vital work,' as Hick (2001, p. 192) insists.

Grosso (2001) rightly remarks that 'if materialism is true, an air of humbug must hang over the transpersonal vision' (p. 116). As he asserts, on this scenario spiritual experience becomes a narcissistic illusion, 'perhaps useful, perhaps edifying, but at bottom a beguiling brain state devoid of transcendent import'. The alternative to this narcissistic illusion is to follow the testimony of the mystics. Writing of the 'data' that have been observed by those following a path of spiritual practice, Wilber (1996) asserts that, 'by far the most common interpretation of those who have seen this data is: you are face to face with the Divine' (pp. 219–20).

Where does this leave transpersonal psychology and consciousness studies? Earlier I referred to the two faces of transpersonal psychology, the transformational and the scientific. While the transformational quest does not require us to give up our critical faculties, we may need to suspend *dis*belief at the outset in order that spiritual practice may begin to generate the data that can

facilitate progression. As I have argued, there are grounds for
defending this suspension of disbelief. We have the testimony of
sane explorers of consciousness to encourage us to accept the
hypothesis of a transcendent reality, together with the general
adequacy of the hypothesis to the relevant data in the history of
religions. It is clearly not a scientific hypothesis in that it is not
falsifiable by the data available through objective measurement.
However, rather than squeeze transpersonal psychology into the
scientific worldview, it may be more appropriate simply to recognize that transpersonal psychology challenges the bounds of that
worldview. In particular, the quest for transformation may be
significantly enriched when we adopt a vantage point beyond the
scientific worldview. The hypothesis of some form of transcendent
core may be thought of as *utilitarian*, rather than scientific. It is a
hypothesis that can make a difference to our lives.

Transpersonal psychology should be concerned with the parameters that impinge on a transformational path. Recognition of the
Transcendent is one such parameter. More than this, the proper
interest of transpersonal psychology focuses on the structures and
processes that operate in relation to the encounter with the sacred.
This interest has been exemplified through my earlier discussion of
the mediaeval conception of the Active Intellect, and the ways in
which its functions might be operationalized in terms commensurate with contemporary neuroscience and psychology. The quest
towards union with such a divine sphere has always comprised
two limbs: the direct path of encounter through practice, and the
path of knowledge. The contemporary approaches that I have
examined have much to contribute to the path of knowledge.
Indeed, the 'I'-tag theory as a whole offers various significant
points of integration between the scientific, and the sacred,
approaches to mind. The divine qualities that mystics have
ascribed to the Active Intellect are certainly not compromised by
situating it within the context of preconscious processing. On the
contrary, a path frozen in terms of the concepts specific to a past
age is most certainly not a path of knowledge.

And what of consciousness? In proposing an integrative theory
of consciousness, I suggest that the linkage between the two faces
of transpersonal psychology is critical. *Given the reasonable
grounds for postulating the role of a transcendent reality in relation to the transformational face, I propose to accept that such a
transcendent dimension fills the elusive missing link in our under-*

standing of consciousness. That missing link pertains specifically to phenomenality. The proposal is, then, that the mystery of phenomenality derives from a transcendent origin.

In itself, this proposal is hardly new! It simply restates the cornerstone of spiritual belief that has resounded down the centuries. The distinctiveness comes with the context in which the proposal is made. The body of research examined in Chapters 4 and 5 has established that interactive neural dynamics and re-entrant processing are central to consciousness. When understood from the multi-levelled perspective that I have developed, the organizational principle of re-entrance has currency beyond the specifically neurophysiological data themselves. Ultimately, it is an expression of the interpenetration of levels in a unified hierarchy. The neural level feeds forwards to the cognitive level, where memory structures are activated. I conjecture that the cognitive level likewise feeds forward to activate complexes and archetypes at the level studied by depth psychology. From this level the feed-forward system ascends a stage further to 'awaken the impulse' at the transcendent level.

The re-entrant limb of this *cosmic loop* returns the 'light' of phenomenality to each of the different levels, thereby introducing the essential core of consciousness to each. I envisage that this re-entrant dynamic also kindles the specific expressions of selfhood appropriate to each level – observing self; archetypal self; 'I' and protoself.[11]

The broad sweep of this overview is given more detail by consideration of the other dimensions of consciousness – Intentionality 1, Intentionality 2 and accessibility. The 'I'-tag theory has specified the stages through which each of these dimensions comes to expression. Each dimension of consciousness is best understood from a given level amongst those that have provided the framework for my exploration of the approaches to consciousness. Depth psychology is equipped to investigate intentionality in ways that are closed to cognitive neuroscience. On the other hand, cognitive neuroscience can illuminate the question of accessibility. The foundation stone of the feed-forward – re-entrant principle derives from understanding the logic of the brain code, which is the distinctive preserve of neurophysiology.

Recognizing the demarcations in investigative approach and explanatory structures, as explored in Part I, is the key to any integrative theory of consciousness. Transpersonal psychology is the single discipline appropriately equipped to achieve the required integration. It should be evident that proposing a transcendent core to phenomenality does not deny to science its role in consciousness studies. On the contrary, it enables science to engage directly with the complexities of consciousness, without the embarrassment of the unscientific assumptions too frequently made about the cause of consciousness. The proposal of a transcendent core to phenomenality is a proposal for a revitalized sacred science that enables psychology to regain its vantage point on the soul.

As mentioned on a number of occasions throughout this book, all current theories of consciousness entail a leap of faith. Each has its particular strengths and weaknesses. Physicalist positions have the strength that no reality is posited other than that which we can subject to the rigours of scientific examination. But they cannot do more than proffer the hope that some kind of scientific breakthrough will eventually provide us with the full story of consciousness. Theirs is a faith in the power of science. Given the necessity of a leap of faith in addressing the mystery of consciousness, we must ask whether this is the kind of leap for which our culture is searching. Each will have their own answer, but my own sense is that terms such as 'purpose' and 'meaning' are key features of the quest, and that many seek a spiritually-satisfying understanding of consciousness. The theory which I have presented in this book meets the challenge by integrating the twin paths to knowledge that dignify human purpose, those of science and religious mysticism.

Notes

Chapter 1: The big picture

1   Here I follow Giller (2001) in translating the Aramaic *moha*, which literally means *brain*, as 'consciousness', since this term effectively captures in modern idiom the intent of the text.

2   The *Zohar* is universally recognized as the most influential text of Jewish mysticism. It first circulated in the thirteenth century, leading most scholars to date its authorship to this period. Within the Jewish tradition it is generally seen as recording mystical speculations from an earlier period, and is ascribed to a second-century author, Rabbi Shimon bar Yochai. The *Zohar* employs a complex system of imagery in its depiction of the inner workings of creation. The term in the extract quoted here, *Atika Kadisha* (Holy Ancient One), indicates the first proto-structural conformation of the divine being as it begins the process culminating in the 'In the beginning' (*Genesis* 1:1) of manifest creation.

Translations from the *Zohar* are by the author. Where appropriate, I have referred to extracts as presented in Tishby (1949/1989).

3   As will be discussed later, the term 'panpsychism' does not fully capture the range of views that comes under the umbrella of the belief that consciousness is a property of the physical world as a whole. I have therefore coined a new term to capture the essence of this perspective, namely '*holophysicalism*'. Physicalism holds that consciousness is generated by structures within the spatio-temporal, physical world, and the prefix '*holo*' ('whole') implies that consciousness is not limited to specific structures (such as brains).

4   The question of spatial metaphor in relation to consciousness is both interesting and problematic. Religious traditions generally adopt a spatial perspective whereby the physical realm is 'lower' than that of mind and consciousness. As discussed here, states of mind deemed closer to the divine origin of the mind are considered 'higher'. For cultural reasons, the spatial metaphor is powerfully engrained in our thinking about these matters. We should remember, however, that it is only a metaphor and implies no concrete implications.

5   I use the term 'depth psychology' to cover those approaches which stress that the psyche comprises both conscious and unconscious spheres, each having its own complex, dynamic processes (for

example, the approaches of *psychoanalysis, analytical psychology* and so on).

6　There has been considerable discussion over what exactly constitutes a transpersonal experience. In their review of the relevant literature up until 1991, Lajoie and Shapiro (1992) emphasized the presence of 'unitive, spiritual, and transcendent states of consciousness' (p. 91). However, the implicit metaphysical assumptions in this phrase have led some to propose alternative formulations less challenging to the ontological basis of scientific psychology. Thus, Walsh and Vaughan (1993) define transpersonal experiences as those 'in which the sense of identity or self extends beyond (trans.) the individual or personal to encompass wider aspects of humankind, life, psyche or cosmos' (p. 203). Both definitions implicitly emphasize the transformational value in the experience, a feature which is at odds with the overtly value-free analysis of the mind encouraged by scientific psychology.

7　The term 'Godhead' refers to that aspect of the divine that manifests itself through creation. The divine essence extends to a realm of complete *otherness* that can neither be known, nor conveyed in human language. In Jewish thought, the Godhead is knowable since it emanates principles that are known through their effects in the mind and in the world. The Godhead includes male and female elements that are not fully united until their union is perfected through human unification practices.

8　Brown (1977, p. 262) notes that prolonged meditation can bring about a subjectively sensed slowing down of mental operations, and argues that it is, accordingly, 'plausible' that meditators can observe normally very brief stages in the workings of their own minds.

9　The notable exception is Buddhism, which eschews notions of an eternal soul. Nevertheless, most scholars agree that Buddhism's central notion of *nirvana* depends on a concept of transcendence. Smart describes the concept of nirvana as 'an unutterable, indescribable transcendental state' (Smart, 2000, p. 236; see Lancaster, 2002).

10　The definitional feature of representational systems mentioned above, namely that the system is made to correspond to something other than itself, is not breached in this notion of a self-model. The system doing the representing is presumed to be within the brain, whereas the *self* being represented is the sense of the whole body, together with its history, feelings (Damasio, 1999), and sense of agency.

11　Jung made a point of emphasizing that the psyche is *real*, and seems to have meant this in an ontological sense. 'Psyche is reality par excellence' (Jung, 1951/1959, p. 66). Freud, on the other hand, held that his psychoanalytical constructs would eventually be explained in biological terms.

12   This ontological position opposes the contemporary view that chance determines the course of evolution. It would suggest that biological systems arose through the agency of a non-physical reality.

13   The classical problem with reductive explanation is that of deciding at which level to stop. Level 1 in Table 1.1 proposes that neural systems might explain psychological phenomena. Most reductive approaches to consciousness argue that we will indeed find our solutions at this level. However, it is evident that whatever is happening at such a level could, in turn, be analyzed further into neuronal, subcellular, molecular, atomic and sub-atomic levels of explanation. We need some basis for recognizing that each level presents its own dynamics, its own characteristics, which are not reducible.

14   I use the term 'holophysicalism' to refer to the view that consciousness is a feature of the physical world as a whole. See Chapter 8, note 2.

15   In his *Discourse on Metaphysics* of 1686, Leibniz writes in proposition XIV, 'it is most true that the perceptions and expressions of all substances intercorrespond.... It is God alone ... who is the cause of this correspondence in their phenomena and who brings it about that that which is particular to one, is also common to all, otherwise there would be no relation' (Wiener, 1951, p. 310). Leibniz was at pains to emphasize that different 'substances' do not causally interact in the manner suggested by Descartes and others. This view, which Leibniz himself admits 'seems strange', is generally dismissed today as a somewhat fanciful way of construing the relation between mind and body, namely as a non-interacting parallelism. For example, Leibniz's parallelism suggests that when I decide to type this word, my fingers move, not because my thought triggers my muscles but because the physical and mental worlds are in perfect alignment, as established by God in His act of creation. I am inclined to think that general dismissals of Leibniz's perspective found in textbooks on the mind–brain relationship are frequently inadequately informed, for they do not appreciate his *monadology*. For Leibniz, each substance, or *monad*, expresses the whole universe, and it is this intrinsic wholeness to all things which underlies the parallelism. In other words, the seeming bizarreness of Leibniz's parallelism comes about only on account of a failure to fully grasp its holism. Leibniz's approach to explaining perception holistically and non-mechanistically offers a valuable perspective for post-modern thinking about consciousness (see Marshall, 1992).

16   This is not to say that my framework may have no bearing on developmental aspects. Clearly, a spiritually-minded person would suggest that Level 4 represents a more advanced stage than Level 2, and so on. This is, however, irrelevant to my purposes. It is worth noting, in passing, that the hierarchical stage basis of Wilber's model

is the feature most subject to criticism. Moreover, a recent study of meditators with an average of 16 years' experience suggested that, while they recognize a meta-process of transformation in their lives, they have no sense of arrival points or discrete stages (Pearmain, 2001).

Chapter 2: A common purpose?

1   A case that serves well to illustrate this influence on neuroscience from society at large is that of hemispheric differences in function. The explosion of interest in this topic largely followed the pioneering suggestion of Levy-Agresti and Sperry (1968) that the brain housed complementary systems for analytical and holistic processing styles. While this suggestion was grounded in observations on split-brain patients, the exact formulation (particularly the notion of the 'holistic' style) derived more from currents in the cultural world. It seems likely that the movement towards diversity of expression and experience that grew from the early 1960s onwards provided the ground in which the schematization by Levy-Agresti and Sperry took root. Once mooted 'scientifically', the idea became strengthened in the cultural world – eventually generating a proverbial 'dichotomania' of distinct 'left brain' and 'right brain' functions. In a nutshell, an idea was seeded through currents in elements of the society at large, formulated and given authority by neuroscience, and subsequently picked up and amplified by society more broadly.
2   Flanagan's term 'natural method' emphasizes his view that the only legitimate form of causation is physical. Although the method draws on a wide variety of disciplines, it resists accommodating notions of non-physical causation as advocated by a minority of authors in disciplines such as anthropology or comparative religion.
3   It was generally believed in the Renaissance that the *Corpus Hermeticum* drew on Egyptian sources, which later influenced the Greek traditions, especially that of the Pythagoreans. Its ideas were therefore seen as predating Christianity. However, contemporary scholarship would date the *Corpus* to no earlier than the second century CE. The importance of kabbalistic texts lay in the fact that they confirmed that the Hermetic ideas were to be found in the hidden meanings in the Hebrew Bible, and consequently in sources viewed as legitimate for Christianity.

   One of the reasons for the importance of Renaissance magic lay in the Christian rejection of the structure of ritual commandments in Judaism which had taken on quasi-magical status within the kabbalistic framework. Since the early development of Christianity annulled the basis of Judaism's ritual practice, alternative means had to be found for attempting to effect communion between microcosm and macrocosm, as a means of influencing the divine. Jewish mystical sources had generally emphasized the role of normative religious practice in bringing about the desired goal of harmony in the macrocosmic–microcosmic system, promoting the divine order and triggering beneficial divine influence.

4   'Never' – or in this case 'forever' – is a dangerous word, and we can envisage science fiction scenarios where we might gain access to another's experience. If we could download an individual's memories to some kind of future super-computer and subsequently connect our own brain, we would, according to some (Goertzel, 1998; see also Wertheim, 1999), gain direct access to their experience. Nevertheless, for the present such scenarios remain exactly that, *fiction*, and it is difficult to see any intimations in our present science that would truly open up such possibilities.

5   The explanatory gap, more specifically, refers to the problem encountered when we draw on physical and functional properties of the brain in order to explain an experience. Levine (1983) argues that it is conceivable for the specific physical and/or functional properties normally associated with a given experience to occur without the experience happening at all. In other words, we can conceive of a creature (maybe artificially created) in which such physical and functional states are present, but which has no phenomenal experience. The mere fact that such a scenario is conceivable leads Levine to conclude that there is, indeed, a gap in our explanation – the total description of physical characteristics does not convey an explanation for phenomenal experience. This conclusion is analogous to that drawn by Jackson (1982) from his seminal thought experiment in which a neuroscientist (always known as 'Mary', following Jackson's lead) has grown up in a room totally devoid of colour. The neuroscience of her day is effectively complete, and she has total knowledge of all features of the brain relating to the processing of wavelength-based (that is, colour) information, together with all details of optics. Come the day when the door is unlocked and she ventures out into a colourful world, what has changed for her? As Jackson argues, she may have had all the information about colour prior to her excursion but she lacked the knowledge of what it is actually like to experience the visual impact of colour. The story has significant parallels to that of Plato's cave – again intended to illustrate the point that a 'higher' level of experience is needed in order to correctly conceive the nature of the 'lower' material.

6   Griffin (2000), following Whitehead, refers to this view as *panexperientialism* in order to distance himself from the view that all of

nature is conscious (*panpsychism*). For Griffin, an atom involves 'distinctively atomic occasions of experience' (p. 175), but is not conscious. We must ask whether this distinction is anything more than terminological. Much confusion has ensued from equating 'consciousness' with 'being conscious of something'. I interpret Griffin as saying that an atom instantiates experience but is not conscious of anything. But then, of what does its experience consist? In my view, there is indeed a fundamental and irreducible quality to experience. In line with the approach of *Samkya-Yoga*, to be discussed in Chapter 3, I would term this quality 'contentless consciousness'. This essential quality of consciousness is distinct from mind, which is characterized by its intentionality, or aboutness (mind always has structured contents). Of course, Griffin is free to term the fundamental quality 'experience', but the problem is that we have no clear referential parameters to clarify terminology. Beyond terminology is the ontological question – for Griffin, experience is ontologically a part of nature; for *Samkya* philosophy, consciousness is ultimately transcendent (Larson and Bhattacharya, 1987).

7   By referring to 'its own negation', Perry is concerned about the notion of consciousness being present within unconscious states: 'there is consciousness-stuff, and unconscious consciousness, called respectively mind-stuff for short, and unconscious physical states or subconsciousness to avoid a verbal contradiction' (cited in Forman, 1998, p. 13.). This is a very real conundrum, which I addressed in a previous work (1991) and will be considering further in Chapter 6. If we use the term 'consciousness' to refer to a fundamental quality which may accompany all mental activity, or which, in holophysicalist terms, pervades the whole universe, then it cannot be excluded from states closed to our introspection. In this sense, then, 'consciousness' is indeed present in the *unconscious*. While this construction is terminologically confusing, it is an unavoidable paradox on account of the way we generally use these terms. Recognizing the distinction between 'consciousness' in its *phenomenal* sense and in its *access* sense – to be discussed later in this chapter and in Chapter 6 – goes some way to resolving the paradox.

The problem is not of historical interest only. Schooler's (2002) proposals offer three 'levels of consciousness', the first of which is termed 'non-conscious.' The light metaphor may be instructive here. To call the lowest level of light 'darkness' seems reasonable enough – it may be thought of as the zero point on a scale. But if the real question concerns my ability to see, I may certainly still be seeing in pitch darkness – my eyes are open and I have phenomenal experience. It is just that the absence of light means that my seeing is a seeing of nothingness.

8   The phrase 'sufficiently humanlike biological system' is intended to exclude most animals and computers. Both these exclusions are contentious. Dawkins (1993) would ascribe consciousness (broadly equated with this sense of consciousness$_1$) to most, if not all, animals. According to her, an experiential aspect may be inferred when an organism prefers one state to another. Since even the simplest unicellular creature clearly moves away from aversive stimuli, Dawkins would presumably view it as conscious. Regarding non-biological systems, probably the majority of those engaged in artificial intelligence (AI) hold the *strong AI* position which would not exclude consciousness from silicon-based (or other non-biological computational) systems (see contributions to Ito, Miyashita and Rolls, 1997).

9   A host of difficulties arise at this point. I earlier emphasized the circularity involved when the term 'awareness' is used to define consciousness, yet here we have the notion of consciousness without awareness, implying that the two terms do indeed convey different meanings. Confusion reigns since Chalmers (1995), among others, would have the term 'consciousness' reserved for the phenomena of experience, and 'awareness' for the more cognitive aspects – which would seem to be diametrically opposed to Baruš' usage. Moreover, to take the human case (which would seem to be the only reasonable case to gauge), what does it mean to say that I am unaware (unconscious?) of content that in some sense is conscious? These fundamental issues will become resolved in later chapters when I have established more fully the stages involved in conscious processes.

10   The idea of *representation* is itself a cornerstone of cognitive neuroscience. Thus, perception may be assumed to involve sensory input interacting with past memories to generate representations of the objects or events which caused the sensory activation. I have argued that the potential to generate such representations is a defining feature of informational consciousness (Lancaster, 1991).

11   It is frequently asserted that *self-consciousness* constitutes a form of consciousness distinct from the informational form discussed already. Block (1995), for example, distinguishes *self-consciousness* from both *phenomenal-consciousness* and *access-consciousness*. In my view, the fundamental distinction is the one I have made between phenomenal consciousness ('consciousness as such', Rao, 1993) and all forms of informational, or structured, consciousness. The latter clearly changes according to the complexity of the structures involved, but there is no difference in kind according to whether or not self is amongst the represented items.

12   I deliberately use the designation 'I' with the third person verbal form. Although it may not scan especially smoothly, this usage

emphasizes that 'I' is itself a representation – essentially a structure which the mind generates as its 'centre of narrative gravity' (Dennett, 1991; and see Chapter 5). From the phenomenological point of view, I am the subject of my experiences. But the challenge to understand operationally what exactly is happening when an individual is indeed having experiences requires that we attempt to model the processes occurring. The manner in which 'I' enters into these processes is of critical importance, and my usage of the third person conveys this sense of our observing – from the outside – these processes. In a nutshell, I *am* but 'I' *is*.

Chapter 3: Spiritual and mystical approaches:
1. Towards emptiness

1   *Genesis Rabbah* 90:1; *Leviticus Rabbah* 24:9. The quote is given in the name of Rabbi Levi.

    Midrash refers to a corpus of Jewish literature, dating from the second to the twelfth centuries CE, and still of the utmost importance to the practice of Judaism today. The style of midrash is largely homiletical, and frequently draws on word play to derive a teaching from a scriptural passage. As will be discussed in later chapters, Jewish mysticism largely draws its intellectual roots from the midrashic imagination.

2   There is some debate as to whether or not the Vedic conception of Self is genuinely incompatible with Buddhism's teaching of no-self. It has been argued by many of the greatest scholars of Buddhism (including, amongst others, Conze, Humphreys and Suzuki), that the *no-self* teaching was polemical, that is, it was used to counteract particular tendencies in the Vedic world of the Buddha's day. It was not intended to deny totally the reality of an absolute Self, metaphysically distinct from the bodily oriented self ('empirical ego'). As Fontana (2000) reminds us, a classic of Buddhist literature asserts that, 'The Self is lord of self' (p. 202). Nevertheless, in a thorough study of the earliest sources, Harvey (1995) finds no evidence for this view. The attainment of nirvana depends on a stripping away of any 'I' quality whatsoever. The Hindu–Buddhist tension on this count might be resolved by supposing that the absolute Self carries no personalistic ('I') content. Nevertheless, at a purely linguistic level, the very word 'Self' appears to be problematic – it cannot have any meaning if stripped of its subject status. The essential tension is that between the theism of Hinduism and the atheism of Buddhism. The 'subjective' sense of Self in Hinduism pertains to *Brahman*, the transcendent deity. In distancing itself from the notion of a

transcendent deity, Buddhism necessarily denies the selfhood that might attach to any transpersonal level of being.

It is, of course, a central tenet of the perennialist view, adopted by many transpersonal psychologists, that the incompatibilities between traditions are relative only. Core teachings are viewed as converging around a unified vision of the ultimate truth. Ferrer has recently urged us to recognize the shortcomings of this idealistic vision:

> [T]ranspersonal scholars have generally overlooked the important developments in ... fields such as comparative mysticism, cross-cultural philosophy of religion, East–West hermeneutics, or interreligious dialogue, all of which started with universalistic assumptions and aspirations, but gradually moved to more dialogical, hermeneutic, and pluralistic approaches.... Had the transpersonal orientation been more in touch with these disciplines, it is probable that perennialism would have been questioned before and that transpersonalists would have felt more encouraged to explore alternative visions for understanding interreligious relations and the nature of spiritual phenomena.
>
> (Ferrer, 2002, p. 107)

3   The term 'concentrative' is preferred since it better covers the range of techniques found in mystical traditions. Some of the more active practices – involving, for example, complex movements, chants or other linguistic performances – hardly gel with the dictionary meaning of contemplative as 'meditative, thoughtful' (*Oxford English Dictionary*). All these practices, however, demand special training, not only in the specific activity used, but also in the ability to develop and sustain sufficient concentration.

4   The King James Version translates the Hebrew, *shima'khah* (lit. 'thy hearing'), as 'thy speech', which clearly makes more immediate sense. However, the mystical text is specifically interested in the closeness indicated by the idea of the mystic hearing God's *hearing*. Compare this with the *hadith* (traditional sayings attributed to Muhammad): 'When I [Allah] love my servant ... I become the hearing with which he hears, the seeing with which he sees, the hand with which he grasps'. Sells elaborates:

> For the Sufis, the condition indicated by this hadith cannot be attained as long as the Sufi is seeing, hearing, walking, touching, and speaking for and through himself. Through a quest for a life beyond egoism, through the ritual devotions of the Islamic *shari'a*, and through the supererogatory or free devotions of meditation,

vigils, fasting, and devotions the Sufi arrives at the taming or the 'passing away' of the ego-self. When the ego-self passes away, the divine sees, hears, walks, touches, and speaks, through the human faculties.... [T]he duality between the human and divine is transcended.

(Sells, 1994, p. 69)

5   *Alef* is the first letter in the Hebrew alphabet. Some of its other features take on profound symbolic meaning in the continuation of this text. One, it is a letter which is soundless, intimating the idea of the silent root of thought. Two, if an *alef* appears at the beginning of a word, despite its own soundlessness, the sound of its associated vowel is made (hence, 'you open your mouth'). In fact, in the case of a verb, such an *alef* at the beginning of a word generally indicates the first-person form. This may be relevant to the passage's interest in moving from human thought ('I') to God's thought. Three, its shape could be seen to resemble the undulations in both the ear lobe and the cortex of the brain. As already noted (Chapter 1, n1), the term 'brain' in kabbalistic writings has the connotation of 'consciousness' or, as here, 'thought'.

6   The supposed 'neutrality' of transpersonal theory is a feature that has come under sustained attack. The privileging of non-dual states devoid of theistic content in the schemes of Wilber and others reflects an attachment to certain Buddhist and Hindu Vedanta schools. As Adams (2002) notes, Wilber 'conveniently ignores' writers even from within these traditions whose emphasis differs from the non-dual one. We can ask, with Adams, 'On what basis can he [Wilber] affirm that the noetic content of the non-dual experience is somehow superior to the noetic content of the theistic awareness of a God that transcends the universe?' (p. 171).

It is inevitable that an *active*, participatory involvement with a given spiritual system will lead to greater knowledge of that system over others. My own bias towards kabbalistic sources in the present, and earlier, works reflects my engagement with Judaism and its mystical tradition. However, there is a critical distinction between an approach which seeks to extract features for further analysis, and the more evangelical one which encourages others to seek to develop their spirituality along given lines. This goes back to the point made in Chapter 1 concerning the two faces of transpersonal psychology. The face oriented towards guiding others in their aspirations to transformation can slide, all too easily, I believe, into something of a spiritual straightjacket. Moreover, as Hanegraaff (1998) forcefully argues, perennialism breeds a paradoxical intolerance to religious traditions, on account of the doctrinaire way in which its adherents can downplay those features – often of ultimate value to a practitioner of a given religion – which do not readily fit into the perennial scheme.

7   Here I have deliberately indicated a paradox in the contextualist position. As Forman and others have pointed out, contextualism suggests the relativity of all knowledge, implying that its own thesis cannot be afforded the status of a *universal* theory. On the other hand, the alternative *absolutist* position tends to be chauvinistic in its agenda of assimilating diverse views of the Ultimate into its own scheme, which has been derived primarily from Indian sources. In fact, the implication that *pure consciousness* is some kind of absolute may be somewhat misleading when taken in the context of Hinduism as a whole, for as Holdrege remarks,

> The dualistic perspective of Samkhya is generally subsumed within a monistic framework with a theistic cast: the deity that is deemed by a particular Purana [cosmological scheme] to be the ultimate reality is identified with Brahman and is described as encompassing and transcending both Purusa and Prakrti.
>
> (Holdrege, 1996, p. 99)

The debate between the two schools of thought – contextualist and absolutist – should be seen as one arising from broader tensions in post-modern society. Contextualism sits more comfortably with the pluralism of contemporary western society, which is generally suspicious of any idea of absolutes. It is, however, restrictive for one seeking transformation. Why invest in some form of disciplined practice when the best that may be gained is the substitution of one form of conditioning for another? Some degree of 'buying in' to an absolutist creed (such as one advocating an ultimate, non-dual source) may be necessary in order for the transformational juices to begin to flow. In more traditional language, this element of *faith* may be necessary for full engagement in a tradition's path.

8   In asserting that Sullivan had no reason to expect a pure consciousness event to occur I am, of course, dependent on his own testimony. There is the possibility – which seems unlikely to me – that some kind of expectancy towards pure consciousness had developed unconsciously prior to the event.

9   For Sullivan, the brain is the organ of both consciousness and information processing. His physicalist stance is not the issue of concern here. This stance is neither contradicted nor confirmed by acceptance of the genuineness of contentless experience.

In a commentary on Sullivan's paper, Binns (1995) makes the point that *preformative* processes may be involved, even in the case of an introspectively 'contentless' event. Perhaps a consciousness attaches to these processes, even though the content is in some way blocked from awareness. One might imagine this as a *tip of the tongue* type phenomenon writ large: the whole of mental content at a given time being just 'beyond' (or, perhaps more accurately in the case of preformative processes, just '*before*') the focus of one's mind. In this connection, James (1890/1950) pointed out that the seeming emptiness involved when we are trying to recall a forgotten name is no 'mere gap', for it is a gap that is intensely active. In a similar vein, Dainton (2002) has recently suggested that mystical experiences described as being contentless may, in fact, involve consciousness of an unusually simple kind, and that terms such as 'void', 'contentless', or 'pure' are merely the aptest way of recounting them. Both Binns and Dainton would assert that the consciousness present is attached to content, but that the content may be outside the normal sphere of awareness.

As a final rejoinder to this minimalist conception, it is worth noting that the Yoga literature describes stages experienced prior to the complete cessation of content, some of which resemble the kind of state Binns and Dainton seem to suggest. The question then presents itself as to why, if we can see some kind of accuracy in the descriptions of these pre-ultimate states, might we reject the accuracy of the final state, in which the texts are fundamentally interested.

10   This is not to say that *all* preconscious activity is potentially available to experience. Velmans (1999) suggests that a range of operations occurs prior to consciousness, including the initial transformation of stimuli into neural code, analysis of the coded signals, and the matching of these to stored memory traces. It seems highly unlikely that the initial preconscious phases are available to experience (although some Buddhist accounts, to be reviewed in the next section, might suggest otherwise). On the other hand, as Velmans remarks, the later preconscious activity includes 'sophisticated ... analysis and identification' (p. 557). It is these, more sophisticated, activities that I would regard as likely to form the content of awareness in the kinds of mystical states relating to this fourth scenario.

In Chapter 7 I shall discuss in detail the kinds of mystical experiences of 'fullness' that relate to this fourth scenario.

11   Some of the old English usage in this passage may need elucidation. The term 'creatures' refers to all created things, that is, all worldly entities. The term is not restricted, as modern usage would have it, to living beings. 'Witting' means *knowing*.

12   A literal translation of the Hebrew used here, *kadmut ha'sekhel*, would be 'former intellect'. I follow Hurvitz (1968) and Matt (1995) in substituting the term 'conscious' for 'intellect', given the overall context of the phrase as used by the Maggid. It must be

noted that no specific term for 'consciousness' was available in the original Hebrew.

13   Given that the Buddhist texts conceive of a full perceptual sequence as lasting for 17 moments, this figure would imply that a complete act of perception occupies less than one millisecond. Such a figure is readily discredited, especially since some 35 milliseconds minimum is taken for visual signals to reach V1, the first receiving area of the visual cortex (Lamme and Roelfsema, 2000). However, I do not think that this discredits the intent of the Abhidhamma authors. Surely, their time estimates were intended to emphasize the brevity of the stages, and, in particular, the fact that an untrained mind would not detect the stages.

     The question of how the authors themselves detected these stages is addressed by Rhys Davids (1914), who suggests that the moments might be 'indefinitely multiplied' (p. 183) when conditions are such that the perceptual process does not proceed in its normal automatic and rapid fashion. While it would be fanciful to imagine a monk (even if enlightened!) attending to processes occupying a fraction of a millisecond, it is not so difficult to grant some validity to observations made when meditation may have slowed, or isolated, aspects of the process. This would be analogous to our use of visual illusions, for example, to grasp aspects of processes normally occurring too rapidly for us to detect (Gregory, 1990).

14   I am referring here to the stage termed '*javana*', discussed below. In the Abhidhamma, this is not technically the end-stage, for it is followed by moments concerned with registering the percept in memory. However, it seems reasonable to regard it as equivalent to psychological descriptions of the end-stage in perception since these view storage in memory as subsequent to perception.

15   In the present discussion I employ the translations as given by L. S. Cousins (1981).

16   'I have spent many hours over *javana*, and am content to throw apperception [the term generally used] overboard for a better term, or for *javana*, untranslated' (Rhys Davids, in Aung, 1910/1972, p. 249).

17   This simile and its exposition may be found in Aung (1910/1972), p. 30; Collins (1982), p. 243; and Tin (1921), pp. 359–60.

Chapter 4: Neurophysiological approaches

1   This is not to deny that we can be unsure about which of two conscious thoughts to follow. Maybe I fancy a drink but cannot make up my mind between coffee or tea. The ambiguity lies in my

inability to decide between specific alternatives, not in the representation of the alternatives in my consciousness.

2   This somewhat begs the question as to the role of anaesthesia in relation to consciousness. Those who hold that consciousness is somehow generated by the brain, argue that anaesthetics interfere with the generative process, thereby abolishing, or attenuating, consciousness. Since the phase synchrony—consciousness hypothesis is clearly associated with this school of thought, Vanderwolf's data are indeed problematic. If, on the other hand, we view consciousness (or proto-consciousness) as a more fundamental, or universal, property (holophysicalism), it follows that, whatever the function of phase synchrony may be, it is not responsible for consciousness itself. As discussed later in the chapter, there are grounds for thinking that phase synchrony signals the *preconscious* identification of sensory meaning.

3   In transliteration this anagram may be clearer. The Hebrew for 'In the beginning' is *b/v-r-a-sh-y-t*; and 'a song of desire' is *sh-y-r t-a-b/v*. Recognition of the transcendental value ascribed to such word play in Jewish tradition is crucial to understanding the force of such an allusion:

> The opening of scripture from within radically transforms the grammaticality of the text: the ordinary connections between the letters of a word and between the words of a sentence are broken. These components now become extra-ordinary. Indeed, each letter has (virtual) anagrammatical significance; each word may encode numerous plays and possibilities; and each phrase has any number of potential correlations within Scripture.
>
> (Fishbane, 1998, p. 12)

I shall be considering the psychological basis of this view of scripture later in Chapters 6 and 7.

4   This idea will be developed in Chapter 7. For the moment it is worth stressing that the Name of God carries the mystical connotation of an infinite and all-embracing creative presence. Clearly, there would be nothing 'higher' about the substitution of one limiting entity (the ego) by another, equally restrictive structure, as in a sentimental and naïve, 'humanized' image of God.

5   It is convenient to use such language of decision- or hypothesis-making. This would be analogous to saying that a computer detected a sequence of letters as approximating to a given word, and 'decided' to correct it accordingly – an input of 'accordinlgy' becomes included in a file as 'accordingly', for example. Of course, there is no homunculus making a decision or generating hypotheses, it is simply a process of input-matching and response selection. So

too in the brain – despite the huge complexity in terms of neurone groups and possible image–object relations, it is simply a matter of the relative probabilities of a given input array matching a given perceptual memory schema.

6   We are here concerned with *preconscious* memory readout operating within the early phases of perceptual processes. It is obvious that any meaningful percept is dependent on memory interacting with sensory analysis prior to the image reaching consciousness. How else would I see the entity in front of my eyes as a meaningful object? In principle, the basis of memory is the same whatever the level at which it is operating: a current image activates a stored image through association in some form (which most likely involves resonance). The difference between this preconscious operation of memory in perception and the more everyday understanding of memory (as in 'I must remember where I placed my keys') concerns the question of who or what engages the process of access. In the latter case, 'I' is active in attempting to access the memory; in the former case, memory is being accessed prior to any 'I' connection being involved. In Chapter 5 these ideas will be examined further in relation to the cognitive approach to consciousness.

7   It seems likely that the value of the Buddhist analysis of perceptual stages, discussed in Chapter 3, is dependent on this presumed equivalence between the sequence of perceptual stages operating rapidly under normal conditions, and the more prolonged sequence under obscured conditions. The Buddhist sages were able to analyze the nature of the processes in a drawn-out case, and generalized from this to the normal, rapid case. Similar generalizations underpin recent psychological analyses of perception.

8   The role of expectancy is critical in short-circuiting the routines depicted in Figure 4.2. A considerable body of experimental evidence supports the importance of expectancy effects in perception, and these effects appear to work both forwards and backwards in time. It is readily demonstrated that, should a noise obscure the 'm' sound in the phrase, 'the cat sat on the mat', our hearing of the full phrase is not compromised. This illustrates *forward*-operating expectancy. More interestingly, *backward*-operating expectancy is illustrated by studies conducted by Warren (cited in Grossberg, 1999; see Warren, 1984 for review). If, for example, a noise is followed by 'eel is on the wagon', then the first word is heard as '*wheel*'. If, on the other hand, the noise were followed by 'eel is on the shoe', the first word is heard as '*heel*'. These observations do not seem to reflect a kind of post-hoc interpretation by the listener, but indicate the way the sounds are actually *heard*.

The diagrammatic representation of the 'neuronal input model' in Figure 4.2 cannot convey the complex of input analysis actually occurring at any moment in time. Clearly, the features of the pen, themselves extracted through a hierarchical process, would be embedded in a rich complex of multi-sensory activity and ongoing thought. It is this entire complex that is simplified as the 'dotty' depiction of the 'neuronal input model' in Figure 4.2. For a more complete treatment of the details of this model of perception and memory, see Lancaster, 1991.

9   *Numbers Rabbah* 15:7, and elsewhere.

10   In referring to Searle I should emphasize that his stance on consciousness diverges significantly from that being presented here, specifically in relation to the role of levels of explanation. Searle insists that consciousness is a *biological* phenomenon, and, while recognizing its *emergent* nature, considers that full understanding of the topic will arise as brain science develops:

> [W]e know as a matter of *fact* that brain processes cause consciousness. The fact that we do not have a theory that explains how it is possible that brain processes could cause consciousness is a challenge for philosophers and scientists. But it is by no means a challenge to the *fact* that brain processes do in fact cause consciousness.
>
> (Searle, 1998, p. 1938, italics added)

Unfortunately, as I have stressed throughout this book, the assertions that Searle makes certainly do not have the status of *facts*.

11   Velmans (2000) reviews a number of challenges to Searle's position. It has been proposed, for example, that a robot, able to interact fully with the world and programmed to develop in ways similar to those of childhood, would build up a system of *meaningful* representations of the world. Moreover, we could enable it to generate representations of itself as the indexical centre of its world. I agree with Velmans, however, in his view that any amount of complexity in a robotic system does not in and of itself imply that the robot would have first-person experience. As Velmans notes, 'a robot might have an executive system which operated on the basis of higher-order representations of itself and the world ... and *still not have anyone at home!*' (p. 93).

Chapter 5: Cognitive and neuropsychological approaches

1   In general I prefer to restrict the term 'unconscious' to the discourse of depth psychology. Each area has its legitimate *approach*, but to suggest that the 'unconscious' revealed through cognitive science

can be identified with that of psychoanalysis is misleading (Woody and Phillips, 1995). This issue will be examined in Chapter 6, but for the moment, it should be emphasized that the repeatability criterion of science restricts cognitive psychology to analysis of *preconscious* processing, that is, processes that would normally eventuate in consciousness. This must be distinguished from the notion of a realm of mind having its own *hermeneutic*, separate from that of consciousness. The methods used by cognitive science are generally unable to give strong evidence of such a realm. For some, this implies that the constructs of depth psychology are suspect; for others, that the methods are simply too limited.

2   I use the terms 'consciousness' and 'awareness' synonymously in this chapter. There is considerable confusion over these terms in the literature of cognitive neuroscience. As far as my use of terminology is concerned, if I am aware of an object, then I am conscious of it. There are indeed finer points of distinction to be made about what exactly is happening when I become aware/conscious of the object, and specifying these is of major concern (as we saw already in Chapter 4). However, these finer points need to be brought out through an operational understanding of the events involved, and are not well served by tighter use of terminology alone.

Weiskrantz's term '*acknowledged* awareness' emphasizes the active stance that a person takes in relation to material that, prior to acknowledgement, was preconscious. More detail of Weiskrantz's view of this active stance will be presented in the discussion of *blindsight* later in this chapter. The point to note at this juncture is that using the term 'awareness' as opposed to 'consciousness' in this context is not a result of a coherent strategy shared by all those working in cognitive neuroscience.

3   Some caution is needed here in assigning consciousness to the final matching process. In the general and mundane sense in which Baars understands the term 'consciousness' it is probably correct to think of it in relation to the final match that occurs. However, as already discussed in Chapter 3 especially in relation to the Buddhist view of perceptual processes, we should re-examine the distinction we readily make between conscious and preconscious processes (see below, Chapter 6). For the moment, I am merely pointing to the complex of associations that are activated by a sensory input, and am happy to class these in accordance with general psychological parlance as 'preconscious'.

4   The term 'self' is probably as slippery as is the term 'consciousness'. For Kant (1781/1968), our sense of 'selfhood' – the sense, that is, of being the subject of our thoughts and so on – is a surface appearance to that which in itself cannot be known. Transpersonal approaches have tended to presume a 'higher' or 'deeper' self of

some kind – a sense of *soul* – beyond the immediate sense of personal identity. In his postulate of a *self*, which is distinct from the *ego* and cannot be known in its entirety, Jung's approach might be thought of as transitional between Kant and the more contemporary transpersonal view. The cognitive approach eschews indemonstrable concepts such as that of a higher self, and its use of the term 'self' connotes only the immediate sense of identity.

Without necessarily inferring any ontological implications, I make a distinction between the expression of selfhood at the interface between the individual and their world (the *identity plane*: Lancaster, 1991) and that at the root of individual personhood – the 'deep', or 'higher', self. At the least, this distinction serves to emphasize the difference between the two narratives into which many of us embed ourselves, namely the mundane and the spiritual. I use terminology intended to reflect this distinction: the direct pronoun 'I' is used to convey the sense of immediate identity, leaving 'self' for the deeper, or spiritual narrative of selfhood. In citing the ideas of others, I use their terms. Thus, for example, Baars' 'self' equates to my 'I', and so on.

5   My argument here is against the validity of the notion of phenomenology being somehow caused by representations, which is the fundamental claim of those defining consciousness as representational states. The more fundamental question is, why do we have to search for the key to phenomenology in representations in the first place? The cognitive scientist and the cognitively-inspired philosopher define consciousness in terms of representations, and then have to employ a sleight of hand to account for a property of representations that itself yields phenomenology. This must be recognized for what it is – an article of faith. The core assumption of cognitive science, that one system somehow represents another, fits well with data from brain imaging studies and the like. I therefore have no difficulty with the assumption itself. Indeed, it underpins my notion of the 'I'-model and its role in perception. This is not, however, to accept that representation *in and of itself* gives phenomenology. I do not, for example, consider that representational systems in computers could generate subjectivity and qualia (for a detailed argument, see Lancaster, 1991).

6   It may be objected that the analogy is false; it is not a question of a perception of our representations fading rapidly – rather we *never* perceive them. But this is merely an assumption. It may be that an early stage of visual development specifically entails overcoming the propensity to be aware of the medium of vision – of the finger that points, as it were, rather than of the vision itself. Certainly, work with those blind from birth who have their optical system restored later in life through surgical means, shows that we have to learn to

see things as being 'out there', and not as attached to our eyes (Morgan, 1977).

7   In psychoanalytical terms, we are not thought to be conscious of all our projections, a constraint that superficially conflicts with the claim I am making that projection constitutes the outer limb of the re-entrant pathway responsible for consciousness. But this objection assumes that accessibility is the same as consciousness. The objection falls into the error of not recognizing the distinction between phenomenal- and access-consciousness, in the terms given by Block (1995). As discussed above, my approach holds that the phenomenal quality enters mental processing through the accessing of higher actualities. Feedforward activity becomes conscious when it is engaged by re-entrant pathways carrying memory readout. And such memory readout is what makes sensory material *meaningful*. Meaning is therefore also equated with consciousness. However, not all meaningful material is *accessible*. A subset only of this material is available to the 'I' (self-model) constellated at any given time. For psychoanalysis, there is the added assertion that some meaningful material is unable to link with 'I'; it is *repressed*. The paradox that such material may be conscious in terms of its meaningfulness, but unconscious in terms of the blockage to 'I' is one that will be explored further in Chapter 6.

8   This is not to imply that the former of James' alternatives – the 'soul' aspect of selfhood – is to be dismissed. He certainly concludes in his *Varieties of Religious Experience* (1902/1960) that the 'extra-marginal self' is continuous with 'an altogether other dimension of existence' (p. 490), which he identifies with God. As was discussed in Chapter 3 (note 3), many have suggested that even in Buddhism this notion of a deep Self has its place. Whether or not this is an accurate representation of the classical Buddhist sources, there can be no doubting its centrality for all other religions. My approach in this chapter, however, addresses the everyday interactions between memory and that 'I' which denotes the lower expression of selfhood.

The cognitive orientation adopted by both Metzinger ('self-models') and Kihlstrom ('self-tokens') precludes the existence of any kind of a 'higher' dimension to being, and hence the one word 'self' suffices. They may be correct, or they may be wrong. As will be evident from this book and others of my works, I am more inclined towards a transpersonal orientation that includes recognition of deeper, more spiritual, dimensions of being. This deeper level is beyond 'I' (although the quality of witnessing itself may be a feature of both levels). The validity of the 'I'-tag theory's analysis of the role of 'I' in memory is certainly not dependent on acceptance of any transpersonal orientation. The theory does, however, provide a basis for thinking about the claims made in most spiritual traditions about the limitations of 'I'.

9   It is worth repeating that the 'I'-model is present whether or not self-consciousness accompanies the mental events. As has been explained already, the 'I'-model is assumed to be present whenever I am conscious of some object or thought. The 'I'-tag is the memory storage element corresponding to the sense of oneself as subject that accompanies all normal consciousness more or less implicitly.

10   *Dissociative identity disorder* (DID), previously known as *multiple personality disorder*, constitutes the major pathological case in which the relative continuity of 'I' is compromised. Memory phenomena in such cases are discussed below.

11   This formulation differs from the classical suggestion of Kant (1781/1968) that 'the representation *"I think"* ... in all conscious-ness is one and the same' (p. 153). Again, in non-pathological circumstances, this kind of continuity characterizes the common core of 'I', as I have termed it. It is envisaged here, however, that the 'I'-tag will always include some idiosyncratic elements.

12   The re-entrant systems discussed earlier are certainly present in animals, suggesting that the contribution of these pathways to consciousness should not be viewed as restricted to humans alone. Nevertheless, the form of consciousness postulated here as being determined by access to the 'I'-model is distinctively human. In terms to be further discussed in Chapter 6, the animal may be *phenomenally* conscious, but lack introspectibility.

13   Detachment of *what* from *what*? might be the operative question. The clear implication of the notion of detachment from 'I' is that consciousness should not be defined solely in relation to the 'I'-model. In theistic contexts, detachment from 'I' is readily under-stood in terms of some form of merger with the Godhead. Consciousness experienced in this state is thought of by mystics as attaching to the divine Self. In non-theistic contexts, consciousness experienced during detachment is construed as devoid of any self-dimension. It is the pure consciousness associated with no-self.

14   Figure 2.1, on which these figures are based, was centred on the mundane sense of 'I' and its relation to accessible contents of the mind. The layout of the figure reflects this by placing 'I' in the centre of the circle. Since they are based on Figure 2.1, Figures 5.2 and 5.3 illustrate changes in the sense of self by depicting a deviation along the 'self' axis from this central point. Of course, the position of 'no-self' and 'All-Self' towards the edges of the circle is purely arbitrary. Indeed, in practice these two concepts of 'no-self' and the 'All-Self' may not be as distinct from one another as the figures imply. Both are concerned with an ability to grasp the circle as a whole. Perhaps a more accurate depiction would have the 'All-Self' *replacing* 'I' as

the centre of the circle, with the experience of 'no-self' corresponding to an erasure of the centre as a significant point of reference.

15 It is necessary to add the qualifier, 'under mundane conditions',
since the whole point of the Abhidhamma analysis is to recognize
what is meant by detachment from 'I' and how it might be achieved.
The object of the Buddhist path is to gain increasing control of the
stages prior to *javana*, in order that the 'conceit of I am' – normally
brought about during *javana* – is overcome.

16 There is considerable evidence to suggest that explicit memory
depends on the activity of a neural system involving the hippocampus and its connections to the inferotemporal cortex as well as
to more widespread cortical regions. Major structures of the
hippocampus itself are mature from birth and may be implicated
in the earliest forms of memory formation. However, the
hippocampal–inferotemporal cortex circuit develops more slowly
over the first three years of life, and its lack of maturity may be a
factor in childhood amnesia. MacPhail (1998) argues that three
factors come together in the first three years of life, with the
implication of causal relationships:

> [C]onscious access to the hippocampal-dependent system coin-
> cides with the development of language – which, of course, coin-
> cides with the development of the self-concept. Development of
> the self allows the child to obtain controlled access to the
> hippocampal (and now explicit) store, so that he or she may now
> deliberately recall, mull over, and 'daydream' about past events.
> (MacPhail, 1998, p. 173)

17 The word–colour form of synaesthesia (that involving a word generating a specific colour experience) is the most common. This is one
of several factors that led Ramachandran and Hubbard (2001) to
propose that synaesthetic connections play an important role in the
evolution of language. See Chapter 6.

18 The controversy over the neural basis of synaesthesia owes much to
problems in interpreting brain imaging studies. A PET study by
Paulesu *et al.* (1995) suggested that synaesthetes showed enhanced
activity in the cortex by comparison with non-synaesthetes.
However, Cytowic argues that this kind of imaging can be misleading, in terms both of the precision of the technique and of the logic
applied to the results. On the latter point, Cytowic insists that
synaesthesia is a complex integrated phenomenon, and that the kind
of 'snapshot' given by scanning can do no more than indicate areas
which may be involved in the more superficial aspects.

19 The assertion that blindsight patients are not conscious of visual
stimuli in the blind half-field has been challenged (Barbur *et al.*,

1993; see also Zeki and Bartels, 1999). The claim made by Barbur *et al.* is that a blindsight patient does have awareness of such visual material. The issue here is whether the awareness that the patient describes is indeed visual. Weiskrantz (1997) makes a robust defence of his view that there is no visual awareness of relevant stimuli in blindsight patients, arguing that whatever awareness is present, it is certainly not visual. For my purposes, as will become clear below, it is the non-visual and *synaesthesia-like* aspect of this awareness that is particularly interesting.

20   It is unlikely that activity in V1 is a necessary condition for all forms of visual consciousness. Nunn *et al.* (2002) studied the brain areas activated in word-colour synaesthesia. By comparison with non-synaesthetic controls, synaesthetes showed greater activation in the area known to be responsible for preliminary analysis of colour information in a visual input (V4/V8). Area V1, by contrast, showed no increase in activity. It follows that the distinctive colour experience in the synaesthetes is mediated by activity in V4/V8 and *not* V1. These data do not necessarily contradict the postulated role for re-entrant pathways in synaesthesia since V4/V8 could be the critical 'target' region for re-entrant activity in this case. This is not the preferred explanation of Nunn *et al.*, however. Noting that the increased activity in area V4/V8 was in the *left* hemisphere only, they suggest that abnormal *direct* connections between language areas and V4/V8 may be responsible for the synaesthetic colour experience. The evidence of this study alone, however, cannot indicate the precise sequence of neural events responsible. It might be, for example, that the bias to the left hemisphere arises subsequent to the feedforward sweep. The attempt to find a 'match' for word meanings via re-entrant pathways could selectively trigger connections to V4/V8 in the left hemisphere.

Chapter 6: The approach of depth psychology

1   In making this statement, I am following Freud's major definitions of 'preconsciousness'. Clearly, Freud's late and uncompleted revision – to which I have just referred – makes the issue more confused. The question of the potential 'knowability' of mental states is the main concern of this whole chapter, and any shortcoming in this opening statement is itself indicative of the scale of the problem to be addressed.

2   Nelkin considers that it takes an act of *will* for a representation to be aspectualized. The sense of meaningfulness that permeates our perceptual world arises through such an act of will. We are not

simply passively generating representations. This is an important point which enables Nelkin to distinguish the human situation from that of a computer, for example. The computer has no will and, consequently, is not conscious in the intentionality sense.

3   Nelkin suggests that phenomenal consciousness is associated with non-aspectualized representations. I have already expressed my reservations about linking consciousness to representation per se. Nelkin clearly wishes to see *all* dimensions of consciousness as products of brain function. As we have seen, there is no evidence to back up this proposal – it is the neurophysicalist's article of faith. My own view accepts Nelkin's arguments for the possibility that phenomenal consciousness may be present in the absence of other dimensions of consciousness. However, I regard phenomenal consciousness as deriving from beyond the brain.

4   A distinction must be drawn between James' rejection of an unconscious sphere of mental life and his advocacy of the importance of the *subconscious*. He recognized that states of consciousness other than the normal state play a significant role in our lives. He regarded religious experiences, for example, as evidence of the subconscious at work. The subconscious is not *un*conscious; it is not a sphere of mind completely locked away from our introspection. Rather, it comprises functions at the fringes of everyday consciousness, which are not normally noticed. Only when the 'hubbub of the waking life' (James, 1902/1960, p. 242) is stilled may the life of the subconscious be evident.

5   The word *psyche* tends to be preferred in psychoanalytically oriented literature. The Greek original, *psyche*, means 'soul', but most contemporary psychoanalysts use the term to mean 'mind' in general. Bettelheim insists that the connotations of 'psyche' as *soul* were important for Freud:

> By coining the term 'psychoanalysis' to describe his work, Freud wished to emphasize that by isolating and examining the neglected and hidden aspects of our souls we can acquaint ourselves with those aspects and understand the roles they play in our lives.
>
> (Bettelheim, 1985, p. 12)

When used in depth psychology, both terms, 'mind' and 'psyche', should be understood as comprising conscious and unconscious realms. However, a distinction is clearly evident, at least in the popular imagination, for 'psyche' continues to carry a more mysterious connotation. The 'mind' is more transparent, less mysterious than the 'psyche', and may therefore be construed as including only that which is itself transparent, namely consciousness. The whole question of where consciousness begins and ends, as it were, cannot be fully understood without grasping the powerful cultural and historical underpinnings to these issues, as will be discussed.

6   On account of this appeal to an ontologically transcendent source of phenomenality, the 'I'-tag theory is rendered nonscientific. However, the integrity of the theory as a whole stands on the assertion that different dimensions of consciousness arise at specific stages, as will be discussed. Only the dimension of phenomenality entails a mysterious leap beyond scientific data. It may be that phenomenality arises through some as yet undiscovered feature of the neural architecture. However, I am inclined towards the transcendent hypothesis since it integrates the theory with the data from religious mysticism, which itself carries a certain integrity. Arguments for some kind of transcendent dimension to consciousness will be raised more fully in Chapter 8. For the present, the following outline points are offered in defence of the hypothesis of a transcendent source of phenomenality:

1. There is no convincing scientific evidence to doubt it.
2. It offers a parsimonious solution to the conundrum of consciousness.
3. It enables a synthesis of the major knowledge systems that have been developed (that is, those based in science, psychology, philosophy and religion).
4. It derives from ideas bearing remarkable internal consistency over time and place.
5. It satisfies what many regard as a need to live a life imbued with higher purpose and meaning.

7   Freud's argument is that such forgetting is motivated. The example given here, therefore, indicates two intentions: one, to wake early, and the other, to oversleep. As is well known, Freud's interest was directed to the conflict between such motivations, and how it might be reduced therapeutically.

8   This argument is clearly *utilitarian* rather than scientific. A scientific argument would draw on observable evidence supporting the inference that a hermeneutic unconscious is present beneath the surface of the conscious mind. Freud claimed that the evidence of the case histories he presented was scientific in these terms. However, many would disagree with this assertion. As I have suggested, the studies which implicate multiple meanings beneath the conscious mind offer some, albeit limited, evidence of a more positivistic kind. Further scientific evidence will be reviewed briefly at the end of the chapter. However, such lines of evidence are by no means universally

accepted, and are hardly adequate to substantiate the postulate of a hermeneutic unconscious.

A utilitarian argument is one which asserts that, in a situation in which the scientific evidence is ambiguous, it is legitimate to consider the value to ourselves of a given postulate. In this case, I consider that our humanity is advanced by the postulate of a hermeneutic unconscious. Clearly, any unambiguous scientific refutation would give grounds for rejecting the postulate. For the present, no such unambiguous refutation has been forthcoming.

A utilitarian argument may also be applied in the case of the postulate that some form of transcendent reality underpins the phenomenal quality of consciousness (see above, note 6). Given that an 'as if' dimension inevitably accompanies all of human life (as for example, in the way that we accept the reality of the physical world despite the impossibility of definitive proof of such a reality), it might be asked whether some 'as if' constructs are more beneficial than others. Along these lines, we might argue in support of the postulate of a transcendent dimension to consciousness not only on the basis of appropriate nonscientific data (reports of mystics and the like), but also on the grounds of the postulate's value in promoting benefit to individuals and society as a whole. Acknowledgement of the transcendent may be seen as bringing refinement to the human moral sense and legitimizing the quest for self-perfection.

9   I would add that Freud's last words in the apparently unfinished *Outline of Psychoanalysis* also carry some significance in this regard. He quotes from Goethe's Faust:

> Was du ererbet von deinen Vatern hast,
> Erwirb es, um es zu besitzen
> [What thou hast inherited from thy fathers,
> acquire it to make it thine.]

One is tempted to think that this is exactly what Freud had done with his own heritage from his fathers. Moreover, his gloss on the lines from Goethe, with which his work closes, takes on further significance: 'In the establishment of the super-ego we have before us, as it were, an example of the way in which the present is changed into the past' (1940/1964, p. 207). Was Freud hinting that it was for others to link his science of psychoanalysis (present) with the rabbinic traditions of his fathers (past)?

10   All quotes from Bernstein (1998), pp. 23 and 25.

11   A simple definition of these terms identifies the *Written Torah* with the *Pentateuch*, and the *Oral Torah* with the traditions concerning its interpretation. These traditions came to be written down in the *Talmud, Midrash* and other rabbinic texts. A full grasp of the meaning

of 'Torah', however, needs to recognize the considerably more subtle and all-embracing ramifications of the term. For Judaism, Torah is the blueprint of creation, the world soul, and the very essence of God's thought (Lancaster, 1993a).

12   *Torot* is the plural of *Torah*.

13   The term 'the Rabbis' refers to the sages who shaped rabbinic Judaism by means of their input to the *Oral Torah*. The major period of this activity extended from the first century BCE to the fifth century CE.

14   Jewish belief and practice are predicated on an intense bond between the Torah and God. The multi-levelled 'truth' of the Torah becomes, in Jewish thought, the multi-levelled revelation of the divine being. To the extent that human being itself is merely a dimension of God's being, the link between the 'text' of the Torah and that of the human is evident:

> For centuries the Torah had been treated as a document so sacred that every letter, every nuance of style – even the size of the letters in the handwritten scroll – were regarded as having profound hidden meanings, which the mystic and the exegete interpreted in a manner strikingly like that of the psychoanalyst interpreting turns and vagaries of human expression. All that was needed was a transfer of subject matter from the text of the Torah to the 'text' of human behavior, a point not even novel in Jewish tradition.
>
> (Bakan, 1958, p. 252)

15   To emphasize the point, it is interesting to note that Freud seems to have identified himself with both Moses and Rabbi Yochanan ben Zakkai. Both figures are remarkable for their perpetuation of a line of tradition into a changed era, and it seems that Freud saw himself as following in their footsteps. In 70 CE, Rabbi ben Zakkai escaped the ashes of the Roman conquest of Jerusalem, and the destruction of the Second Temple, to establish a rabbinic academy on the coast of the Land of Israel. It was in this academy that the seeds of rabbinic Judaism were sown. The hermeneutic line that has dominated Jewish thought since that time was wrought through the work of this academy and its successors. All features of the Temple rites, which had fronted divine worship in the era ending with the Roman occupation, were sublimated and transformed into interpretative study and prayer. 'Rabban Johanon ben Zakkai, who sensed the approaching Destruction, began to prepare the people to live without Temple and sacrifices' (Urbach, 1969/1979, p. 666).

When Freud left Vienna under the tyranny of Nazi occupation, the parallel with Rabbi ben Zakkai was the one to which he referred:

> After the destruction of the Temple in Jerusalem by Titus, Rabbi Jochanan ben Zakai asked for permission to open a school at Yavneh for the study of the Torah. We are going to do the same. We, after all, are accustomed to our history and tradition, and some of us, by our personal experience, to being persecuted.
>
> (Cited in Handelman, 1982, p. 151)

In this statement, Freud seems to have recognized that he was on the eve of a new era (or maybe he thought it had already begun). His role would be not only to perpetuate what he regarded as the 'very essence' of Judaism into the new era, but also to overcome the primary block to its acceptance, namely anti-Semitism.

The seeds of the tension between Christianity and Judaism were, of course, also sown in the time of Rabbi ben Zakkai. Unlike what became rabbinic Judaism, the fledgling Christianity perpetuated the sacrificial orientation of the Temple culture by projecting it back, through the person of Jesus, onto God himself. I have argued (Lancaster, 1993a) that the divergence in these two approaches to perpetuating the Temple practice underlies most, if not all, forms of Christian-inspired anti-Semitism.

16 This is a theme repeatedly stressed in the primary compilation of oral teaching, the *Talmud*. Perhaps the most striking articulation of the theme comes in the discussion of 'Aknai's oven' (Talmud, *Bava Metsia* 59b). In brief, one of the rabbis, Eliezer, attempted to convince his fellows that his own ruling over the ritual status of a particular oven was correct. The Talmud records that he called on heaven to support him by a series of miracles, which duly occurred, culminating in a voice from heaven which declared, 'Rabbi Eliezer is correct in all details'. Despite this, his fellow rabbis continued to argue against him, since, as they put it, 'It is not in heaven' (*Deuteronomy* 30: 12), that is, the spiritual path with which they are concerned is under the jurisdiction of man, not God. The tale ends with a telling insight into the audacity of the Rabbis: Rabbi Nathan met Elijah and asked him, 'How then did the Holy One, blessed be He, react?' He replied: 'He laughed, and said, "My sons have defeated me, My sons have defeated me!"'

17 Crick and Koch propose that penumbra neurones are the site of unconscious priming. Evidently, therefore, they view the penumbra as unconscious. The term 'priming' generally implies a mechanical biasing of responses, which hardly equates to the kind of psychodynamic process proposed by Freud. We can detect the influence of the computer paradigm in Crick and Koch's view, for priming is seen as analogous to the kind of 'autocorrect' feature whereby the computer completes a word stem according to a simple, mechanical rule.

Chapter 7: Spiritual and mystical approaches:
2. Towards fullness

1   While the third that arises from the union of two opposites is
    'higher' in the sense that it intimates the self which is transcendent
    to the ego, Jung is careful to avoid any ontological implication: 'by
    "transcendent" I do not wish to designate any metaphysical quality'
    (Jung, 1921/1971, p. 610). Clearly this marks a point of distinction
    from the religious traditions. I shall return to the disputed meta-
    physical status of the *transcendent* in Chapter 8.

2   The polyvalence of scriptural Hebrew is a product of the vowel-less
    ('unpointed') form of the text. A single written word might give rise
    to a variety of differing spoken words ('oral tradition'), each with a
    different meaning. The rabbinic view of language is considerably
    more complex than this feature alone implies, however, since multi-
    plicity of meaning is predicated on the assumption of the divine
    essence of the written text (see below).

3   Yerushalmi (1991) collates evidence from several sources to argue
    for the importance that Jewish influences had on Freud's work. In
    terms of linguistic influence, of particular interest is the Hebrew
    inscription that Freud's father, Jakob, wrote in the Bible he gave his
    son on the latter's 35th birthday. The subtle form of the inscription
    suggests that Jakob had considerable understanding of rabbinic
    styles. As Yerushalmi argues, it would seem unlikely that Jakob
    would have written in this style (not to mention, in Hebrew) had he
    not known that Sigmund could relate to it.

4   Katz is referring to the sacred texts of Christianity, Islam, Hinduism
    and Judaism respectively. His point extends more widely into other
    mystical traditions and their reliance on scripture. Even in Zen, Katz
    notes, we find reverence for the sanctity of the *sūtras*.

5   The two forms of mysticism are sometimes distinguished by using
    the terms '*apophasis*' (speaking towards emptiness) and '*kataphasis*'
    (speaking towards fullness). As Sells (1994) notes, both these two
    categories are always to some extent present in mystical discourses.
    We can only distinguish mystical traditions as being relatively more
    oriented to one category or the other.

6   The identity of the wheel with its 231 gates and the Active Intellect
    is 'proved' through the cryptic logic known as *gematria*, whereby
    two or more phrases may be seen to display equivalence of meaning
    if their numerical values are equal. In this case, *Yesh ra'el* ('There are
    231' or 'Israel') = 541 = *sekhel ha-pu'al* ('Active Intellect'). *Gema-
    tria* depends on the fact that each Hebrew letter is also a number,
    alef = 1, *bet* = 2, and so on.

7   For full passage, see above p. 236.

8   The allusion to *Exodus* 33:14 is not found in the earliest manu-
      scripts of the Bahir (dated 1298), and may be a later addition. The
      allusion is included in the first printed edition (Amsterdam, 1651).
      See Abrams (1994).

9   A striking example of the principle of embodiment playing a central
      role in the world of Jewish mysticism is found in the case of the
      golem. The golem is an anthropoid said to be created by Jewish
      mystics as the high point of a magical ritual. The ritual is itself based
      on the same *Sefer Yetsirah* texts as those used in all other forms of
      language mysticism. The golem was 'brought to life' by means of the
      permuting of letters, each of which was embodied in the mystic's
      own body. A psychological approach might see the golem as a
      projection of a kind of magical enlivening taking place in the
      mystic's own sacred body (see Lancaster, 1997b, 1997c).

Chapter 8: Together again

1   For neurophysicalists, outstanding questions include how the brain
      generates consciousness, and *what* level of complexity is needed for a
      brain to generate consciousness. Similarly, a further question for phys-
      icalists in general is whether the 'hardware' need be biological. *Func-
      tionalists* regard the form of the hardware as inconsequential for the
      generation of consciousness. Consciousness is a product of the *func-
      tions* realized in the hardware. In the absence of substantial evidence,
      it remains somewhat arbitrary as to which, if any, non-human brains
      may be considered to generate consciousness, and whether an
      appropriately complex silicon-based 'brain' would be conscious.

2   'Holophysicalism' is my preferred term to include all the approaches
      that have been labelled with the prefix 'pan-' in previous chapters
      (panpsychism, pan-protopsychism, pan-experientialism). Although
      the shades of view expressed in these different terms are legitimate,
      they all come under the umbrella of a naturalistic approach that chal-
      lenges the hegemony of neuroscience in relation to consciousness.
      Accordingly a single, unifying term for these approaches is preferred.

3   As has been remarked in earlier chapters, the term 'preconscious'
      may be somewhat misleading, since those processes that precede
      normal, mundane consciousness may not be strictly *inexperience-
      able*. Mystical and other altered states involve experience of
      normally preconscious activity. The paradox is overcome by recog-
      nizing the differentiation amongst dimensions of consciousness.
      Preconscious processes are conscious in phenomenal and intentional
      terms, but nonconscious in terms of access from 'I'.

4   The distinction between the Freudian unconscious and conscious

realms of mind is to be understood in terms of intentionality and accessibility. I have argued that both the unconscious and the conscious are 'conscious' along the dimension of phenomenality. However, each has its distinctive intentionality, and, unlike the conscious, the Freudian unconscious is inaccessible to 'I'.

5   The translation is normally, 'I, [even] I, [am] He'. The brackets here indicate that the pronouns are juxtaposed in the original.

6   In view of my arguments in this chapter asserting some kind of reality to the Transcendent, I follow Hick in using an uppercase 'T'.

7   The original Hebrew, *me-ayin*, may be translated as 'from where?' or 'from nothingness'. The latter translation clearly suits the mystical imperative: '[*Me-ayin* means] from that place from which all higher and lower entities derive, and to which they aspire to return' (*Zohar* 2:83a).

8   The Hebrew for pillar is *Sh-Y-Sh*, pronounced '*shayish*'. The same three letters, with the initial *Sh* acting as a prefix would be '*she-yesh*', meaning 'which there is', or 'that which is real'.

9   The mystical reading hinges on the Hebrew construction of the biblical verse. If the intention of the verse were, 'Is the Lord among us or *not*?', it would typically have used a different term for the negative. The negative term actually used (*ayin*) gives the meaning, 'Is the Lord among us [together] *with nothingness*?' It is this nothingness that the *Zohar* understands to mean 'the Transcendent'.

10   Of course, subjectivity and individual bias are highly problematic variables in this context. Quantitative research in this area is fraught with problems – how can you manipulate 'faith' as a variable? A particular image of the divine, which is claimed by one person as expressing the root of their faith, might be nothing but a sentimental or idolatrous construct to another person who, nevertheless, claims to have faith. For these reasons, progress in addressing the issues raised here concerning attitudes to the transcendent is likely to depend on qualitative research (Braud and Anderson, 1998).

11   It should be clear that the hierarchical scheme presented here pertains specifically to human consciousness. In the case of animal 'consciousness', I would envisage the same principle operating, with feedforward activity at the neural level triggering a higher level which engenders phenomenality via re-entrance. In the case of animals, however, the expression of self is presumably limited to that of the protoself. Given the lack of 'I', it follows that the two dimensions of Intentionality 2 and accessibility must be absent from animal information processing. For this reason, it is questionable whether the term 'consciousness', without further qualification, has much value when applied to animals. The presence of phenomenality and a protoself does not constitute 'consciousness' in the normally-accepted sense of the word.

References

Abram, D. (1996). *The Spell of the Sensuous: Perception and Language in a More-than-Human World*. New York: Vintage Books.

Abrams, D. (1994). *The Book Bahir: An Edition Based on the Earliest Manuscripts*. Los Angeles: Cherub Press.

Adams, G. (2002). A theistic perspective on Ken Wilber's transpersonal psychology. *Journal of Contemporary Religion*, **17**, 165–79.

Aung, S. Z. (1910/1972). *Compendium of Philosophy*. Revised and edited by Mrs Rhys Davids. London: Pali Text Society.

Baars, B. J. (1983). Conscious contents provide the nervous system with coherent, global information. In: R. J. Davidson, G. E. Schwartz and D. Shapiro (eds), *Consciousness and Self-Regulation, Vol. 3*. New York: Plenum Press.

Baars, B. J. (1988). *A Cognitive Theory of Consciousness*. Cambridge: Cambridge University Press.

Baars, B. J. (1996). Understanding subjectivity: global workspace theory and the resurrection of the observing self. *Journal of Consciousness Studies*, **3**, 211–16.

Baars, B. J. (1997). *In the Theater of Consciousness: The Workspace of the Mind*. Oxford: Oxford University Press.

Baars, B. J. (2002). The conscious access hypothesis: origins and recent evidence. *Trends in Cognitive Sciences*, **6**, 47–52.

Baars, B. J. and McGovern, K. (1996). Cognitive views of consciousness: what are the facts? How can we explain them. In: M. Velmans (ed.), *The Science of Consciousness: Psychological, Neuropsychological and Clinical Reviews*. London: Routledge.

Bach-y-Rita, P. (1972). *Brain Mechanisms in Sensory Substitution*. New York: Academic Press.

Bakan, D. (1958). *Sigmund Freud and the Jewish Mystical Tradition*. Princeton, NJ: D. Van Nostrand.

Barbur, J. L., Watson, J. D. G., Frackowiak, R. S. J. and Zeki, S. (1993). Conscious visual perception without V1. *Brain*, **116**, 1293–302.

Barnard, G. W. (1997). *Exploring Unseen Worlds: William James and the Philosophy of Mysticism*. Albany, NY: State University of New York Press.

Baruss, I. (1986–7). Metanalysis of definitions of consciousness. *Imagination, Cognition, and Personality*, **6**, 321–9.

Baruss, I. (2001). The art of science: science of the future in light of alterations of consciousness. *Journal of Scientific Exploration*, **15**, 57–68.

Barušs, I. and Moore, R. J. (1998). Beliefs about consciousness and reality of participants at 'Tucson II'. *Journal of Consciousness Studies*, 5, 483–96.

Beck, F. (2001). Quantum brain dynamics and consciousness. In: P. van Loocke (ed.), *The Physical Nature of Consciousness*. Amsterdam: John Benjamins.

Beck, F. and Eccles, J. C. (1992). Quantum aspects of brain activity and the role of consciousness. *Proceedings of the National Academy of Sciences USA*, 89, 11357–61.

Bernstein, R. J. (1998). *Freud and the Legacy of Moses*. Cambridge: Cambridge University Press.

Bettelheim, B. (1985). *Freud and Man's Soul*. London: Fontana.

Billig, M. (1997). Freud and Dora: repressing an oppressed identity. *Theory, Culture and Society*, 14, 29–55.

Binet, A. (1896). *Alterations of Personality*, trans. H. G. Baldwin. New York: D. Appleton & Co.

Binns, P. (1995). Commentary on 'contentless consciousness'. *Philosophy, Psychiatry, Psychology*, 2, 61–3.

Bion, W. R. (1988). *Attention and Interpretation: A Scientific Approach to Insight in Psycho-Analysis and Groups*. London: Tavistock.

Bisiach, E. (1988). The (haunted) brain and consciousness. In: A. J. Marcel and E. Bisiach (eds), *Consciousness in Contemporary Science*. Oxford: Clarendon Press.

Blackmore, S. (1986). Who am I? Changing models of reality in meditation. In: G. Claxton (ed.), *Beyond Therapy: The Impact of Eastern Religions on Psychological Theory and Practice*. London: Wisdom Publications.

Block, N. (1995). On a confusion about a function of consciousness. *Behavioral and Brain Sciences*, 18, 227–87.

Block, N., Flanagan, O. and Guzeldere, G. (eds) (1997). Nature of consciousness: philosophical debates. Cambridge, MA: MIT Press.

Bogen, J. E. (1998). My developing understanding of Roger Wolcott Sperry's philosophy. *Neuropsychologia*, 36, 1089–96.

Bohm, D. (1980). *Wholeness and the Implicate Order*. London: Routledge & Kegan Paul.

Bower, G. (1994). Temporary emotional states act like multiple personalities. In: R. M. Klein and B. K. Doane (eds), *Psychological Concepts and Dissociative Disorders*. Hillsdale, NJ: Lawrence Erlbaum Associates.

Bowers, K. S. (1984). On being unconsciously influenced and informed. In: K. S. Bowers and D. Meichenbaum (eds), *The Unconscious Reconsidered*. New York: John Wiley & Sons.

Braud, W. G. and Anderson, R. (1998). *Transpersonal Research Methods for the Social Sciences: Honouring Human Experience*. Thousand Oaks, CA: Sage.

Brown, D. P. (1977). A model for the levels of concentrative meditation. *International Journal of Clinical and Experimental Hypnosis*, 25, 236–73.

Brown, D. and Engler, J. (1984). An outcome study of intensive mindfulness meditation. In: W. Muensterberger, L. B. Boyer and S. A. Grolnick (eds), *Psychoanalytic Study of Society, Vol. 10*. Hillsdale, NJ: Analytic Press.

Bruner, J. (1997). A narrative model of self-construction. In: J. G. Snodgrass and R. L. Thompson (eds), *The Self across Psychology: Self-Recognition, Self-Awareness, and the Self Concept*. New York: New York Academy of Sciences (Annals Vol. 818).

Buber, M. (1952/1988). *Eclipse of God: Studies in the Relation between Religion and Philosophy*. Atlantic Highlands, NJ: Humanities Press International.

Carrier, M. and Mittelstrass, J. (1991). *Mind, Brain, Behavior. The Mind–Body Problem and the Philosophy of Psychology*. Berlin: de Gruyter.

Chalmers, D. J. (1995). Facing up to the problem of consciousness. *Journal of Consciousness Studies*, 2, 200–19.

Chalmers, D. J. (1996). *The Conscious Mind: In Search of a Fundamental Theory*. Oxford: Oxford University Press.

Chamberlain, D. B. (1990). The expanding boundaries of memory. *Pre- and Peri-Natal Psychology Journal*, 4, 171–89.

Chittick, W. C. (1999). The paradox of the veil in Sufism. In: E. R. Wolfson (ed.), *Rending the Veil: Concealment and Secrecy in the History of Religions*. New York: Seven Bridges Press.

Chittick, W. C. (2000). Ibn al-Arabi's hermeneutics of mercy. In: S. T. Katz (ed.), *Mysticism and Sacred Scripture*. Oxford: Oxford University Press.

Churchland, P. (1989). *Neurophilosophy: Toward a Unified Science of the Mind/Brain*. Cambridge, MA: MIT Press.

Claparède, E. (1911/1950). Recognition and me-ness. In: D. Rapaport (ed.), *The Organization and Pathology of Thought: Selected Sources*. New York: Columbia University Press.

Claxton, G. (1996). Structure, strategy and self in the fabrication of conscious experience. *Journal of Consciousness Studies*, 3, 98–111.

Cohn, N. (1970). *The Pursuit of the Millennium: Revolutionary Millenarians and Mystical Anarchists of the Middle Ages*. Oxford: Oxford University Press.

Collins, S. (1982). *Selfless Persons: Imagery and Thought in Theravada Buddhism*. Cambridge: Cambridge University Press.

Conze, E. (1959). *Buddhist Scriptures*. Harmondsworth, UK: Penguin Books.

Corbin, H. (1958/1969). *Creative Imagination in the Sufism of Ibn Arabi*, trans. R. Manheim. Princeton, NJ: Princeton University Press.

Corbin, H. (1971/1978). *The Man of Light in Iranian Sufism.*, trans. N. Pearson. Boulder: Shambhala.

Corbin, H. (1976/1990). *Spiritual Body and Celestial Earth: From Mazdean Iran to Shi'ite Iran*, trans. N. Pearson. London: I. B. Tauris and Co.

Cornelissen, M. (ed.) (2001). *Consciousness and its Transformation: Papers Presented at the Second International Conference on Integral Psychology.* Pondicherry: Sri Aurobindo International Centre of Education.

Cousins, E. H. (1981). Fullness and emptiness in Bonaventure and Eckhart. *Dharma*, **6**, 59–68.

Cousins, E. H. (1990). The self and not-self in Christian mysticism: Augustine and Eckhart. In: R. E. Carter (ed.), *God the Self and Nothingness: Reflections Eastern and Western*. New York: Paragon House.

Cousins, E. H. (1992). Bonaventure's mysticism of language. In: S. T. Katz (ed.), *Mysticism and Language*. Oxford: Oxford University Press.

Cousins, L. S. (1981). The Patthana and the development of the Theravadin Abhidhamma. *Journal of the Pali Text Society*, **9**, 22–46.

Crick, F. (1994). *The Astonishing Hypothesis: The Scientific Search for the Soul*. London: Simon & Schuster.

Crick, F. and Koch, C. (1990). Towards a neurobiological theory of consciousness. *Seminars in The Neurosciences*, **2**, 263–75.

Crick, F. and Koch, C. (2003). A framework for consciousness. *Nature Neuroscience*, **6**, 119–26.

Cytowic, R. E. (1993). *The Man who Tasted Shapes*. New York: Warner.

Cytowic, R. E. (1995). Synaesthesia: phenomenology and neuropsychology – a review of current knowledge. *Psyche*, **2**.
URL: http://psyche.cs.monash.edu.au/v2/psyche-2-10-cytowic.html

Cytowic, R. E. (2002). *Synesthesia: A Union of the Senses*. 2nd edn. Cambridge, MA: MIT Press.

Dainton, B. (2002). The gaze of consciousness. *Journal of Consciousness Studies*, **9**, 31–48.

Damasio, A. R. (1999). *The Feeling of What Happens: Body and Emotion in the Making of Consciousness*. London: Heinemann.

Damasio, A. R. (2000). A neurobiology for consciousness. In: T. Metzinger (ed.), *Neural Correlates of Consciousness: Empirical and Conceptual Questions*. Cambridge, MA: MIT Press.

Dan, J. (1995). The language of the mystics in medieval Germany. In: K. E. Grözinger and J. Dan (eds), *Mysticism, Magic and Kabbalah in Ashkenazi Judaism*. Berlin: Walter de Gruyter.

Dan, J. (ed.) (1997). *The Christian Kabbalah: Jewish Mystical Books and their Christian Interpreters*. Cambridge, MA: Harvard University Press.

d'Aquili, E. G. and Newberg, A. B. (1993). Religious and mystical states: a neuropsychological model. *Zygon: Journal of Religion and Science*, **28**, 177–200.

d'Aquili, E. G. and Newberg, A. B. (1999). *The Mystical Mind: Probing the Biology of Religious Experience*. Minneapolis: Fortress Press.

Dawkins, M. S. (1993). *Through our Eyes Only: The Search for Animal Consciousness*. Oxford: W. H. Freeman.

de Gelder, B., Vroomen, J., Pourtois, G. and Weiskrantz, L. (1999). Non-conscious recognition of affect in the absence of striate cortex. *Neuroreport*, **10**, 1–5.

Dehaene, S., Naccache, L., Cohen, L., Le Bihan, D., Mangin, J.-F., Poline, J.-B. and Rivière, D. (2001). Cerebral mechanisms of word masking and unconscious repetition priming. *Nature Neuroscience*, **4**, 752–8.

Deikman, A. J. (1963). Experimental meditation. *Journal of Nervous and Mental Disease*, **136**, 329–43.

Deikman, A. J. (1966). Deautomatization and the mystic experience. *Psychiatry*, **29**, 324–38.

Deikman, A. J. (1982). *The Observing Self: Mysticism and Psychotherapy*. Boston: Beacon Press.

Deikman, A. J. (1996). 'I' equals awareness. *Journal of Consciousness Studies*, **3**, 350–56.

Dennett, D. C. (1991). *Consciousness Explained*. Harmondsworth, UK: Penguin.

Dennett, D. (1997). Consciousness in human and robot minds. In: M. Ito, Y. Miyashita and E. T. Rolls (eds), *Cognition, Computation, and Consciousness*. Oxford: Oxford University Press.

Diller, J. V. (1991). *Freud's Jewish Identity: A Case Study in the Impact of Ethnicity*. London and Toronto: Associated University Presses.

Di Lollo. V., Enns, J. T. and Rensink, R. A. (2000). Competition for consciousness among visual events: the psychophysics of re-entrant visual processes. *Journal of Experimental Psychology: General*, **129**, 481–507.

Dorahy, M. J. (2001). Dissociative identity disorder and memory dysfunction: the current state of experimental research and its future directions. *Clinical Psychology Review*, **21**, 771–95.

Dupré, L. (1989). Unio mystica: the state and the experience. In: M. Idel and B. McGinn (eds), *Mystical Union and Monotheistic Faith: An Ecumenical Dialogue*. NY: Macmillan.

Eccles, J. C. (1980). *The Human Psyche*. Berlin/Heidelberg/New York: Springer.

Eccles, J. C. (1989). *Evolution of the Brain: Creation of the Self*. London: Routledge.

Edelman, G. M. (1989). *The Remembered Present*. New York: Basic Books.

Edelman, G. M. (1992). *Bright Air, Brilliant Fire: On the Matter of the Mind*. London: Allen Lane/Penguin Press.

Edelman, G. M. and Tononi, G. (2000). Reentry and the dynamic core: neural correlates of conscious experience. In: T. Metzinger (ed.), *Neural*

Correlates of Consciousness: Empirical and Conceptual Questions.
Cambridge, MA: MIT Press.

Eich, E. (1995). Searching for mood dependent memory. *Psychological Science*, **6**, 67–75.

Eich, E., Macaulay, D., Loewenstein, R. J. and Dihle, P. H. (1997). Memory, amnesia, and dissociative identity disorder. *Psychological Science*, **8**, 417–22.

Eich, E. and Schooler, J. W. (2000). Cognition/emotion interactions. In: E. Eich, J. F. Kihlstrom, G. H. Bower, J. P. Forgas and P. M. Niedenthal (eds), *Cognition and Emotion*. Oxford: Oxford University Press.

Eliade, M. (1952/1991). *Images and Symbols: Studies in Religious Symbolism*, trans. P. Mairet. Princeton, NJ: Princeton University Press.

Engel, A. K., Roelfsema, P. R., Fries, P., Brecht, M. and Singer, W. (1997). Role of the temporal domain for response selection and perceptual binding. *Cerebral Cortex*, **7**, 571–82.

Engel, A. K. and Singer, W. (2001). Temporal binding and the neural correlates of sensory awareness. *Trends in Cognitive Sciences*, **5**, 16–25.

Enns, J. T. and Di Lollo, V. (2000). What's new in visual masking? *Trends in Cognitive Sciences*, **4**, 345–52.

Farthing, J. W. (1992). *The Psychology of Consciousness*. Englewood Cliffs, NJ: Prentice-Hall.

Faur, J. (1986). *Golden Doves with Silver Dots: Semiotics and Textuality in Rabbinic Tradition*. Bloomington: Indiana University Press.

Ferrer, J. N. (2000). Transpersonal knowing: a participatory approach to transpersonal phenomena. In: T. Hart, P. L. Nelson and K. Puhakka (eds), *Transpersonal Knowing: Exploring the Horizon of Consciousness*. Albany, NY: State University of New York Press.

Ferrer, J. N. (2002). *Revisioning Transpersonal Theory: A Participatory Vision of Human Spirituality*. Albany, NY: State University of New York Press.

Fishbane, M. (1998). *The Exegetical Imagination: On Jewish Thought and Theology*. Cambridge, MA: Harvard University Press.

Fishbane, M. (2000). The book of Zohar and exegetical spirituality. In: S. T. Katz (ed.), *Mysticism and Sacred Scripture*. Oxford: Oxford University Press.

Flanagan, O. (1995). Consciousness and the natural method. *Neuropsychologia*, **33**, 1103–15.

Fontana, D. (2000). The nature and transformation of consciousness in Eastern and Western psycho-spiritual traditions. In: M. Velmans (ed.), *Investigating Phenomenal Consciousness*. Amsterdam: John Benjamins.

Forman, R. K. C. (1993). Mystical knowledge: knowledge by identity. *Journal of the American Academy of Religion*, **61**, 705–38.

Forman, R. K. C. (ed.) (1990). *The Problem of Pure Consciousness*. Oxford: Oxford University Press.

Forman, R. K. C. (ed.) (1998). *The Innate Capacity: Mysticism, Psychology, and Philosophy.* Oxford: Oxford University Press.

Forte, M., Brown, D. and Dysart, M. (1984–5). Through the looking glass: phenomenological reports of advanced meditators at visual threshold. *Imagination, Cognition and Personality,* 4, 323–38.

Freud, S. (1904/1966). *The Psychopathology of Everyday Life,* trans. A. Tyson. London: Ernst Benn.

Freud, S. (1914/1949). On the history of the psycho-analytic movement. In: E. Jones (ed.), *Sigmund Freud: Collected Papers,* Vol. 1, trans. J. Riviere. London: Hogarth Press.

Freud, S. (1915/1950). The unconscious. In: E. Jones (ed.), *Sigmund Freud: Collected Papers,* Vol. 4, trans. J. Riviere. London: Hogarth Press.

Freud, S. (1915–16/1963). Introductory lectures on psycho-analysis, Parts I and II. In: J. Strachey (ed.), *Standard Edition of the Complete Psychological Works of Sigmund Freud,* Vol. 15. London: Hogarth Press.

Freud, S. (1916–17/1963). Introductory lectures on psycho-analysis, Part II. In: J. Strachey (ed.), *Standard Edition of the Complete Psychological Works of Sigmund Freud,* Vol. 16. London: Hogarth Press.

Freud, S. (1923/1961). The ego and the id. In: J. Strachey (ed.), *Standard Edition of the Complete Psychological Works of Sigmund Freud,* Vol. 19. London: Hogarth Press.

Freud, S. (1930/1961). *Civilization and Its Discontents.* In: J. Strachey (ed.), *Standard Edition of the Complete Psychological Works of Sigmund Freud,* Vol. 21. London: Hogarth Press.

Freud, S. (1933/1964). New introductory lectures in psycho-analysis. In: J. Strachey (ed.), *Standard Edition of the Complete Psychological Works of Sigmund Freud,* Vol. 22. London: Hogarth Press.

Freud, S. (1939/1964). Moses and monotheism: three essays. In: J. Strachey (ed.), *Standard Edition of the Complete Psychological Works of Sigmund Freud,* Vol. 23. London: Hogarth Press.

Freud, S. (1940/1964). An outline of psycho-analysis. In: J. Strachey (ed.), *Standard Edition of the Complete Psychological Works of Sigmund Freud,* Vol. 23. London: Hogarth Press.

Friedman, H. (2002). Transpersonal psychology as a scientific field. *International Journal of Transpersonal Studies,* 21, 175–87.

Gardner, H. (1987). *The Mind's New Science.* New York: Basic Books.

Gay, P. (1988). *Freud: A Life for our Time.* London and Melbourne: J. M. Dent.

Gazzaniga, M. S. (1988). Brain modularity: towards a philosophy of conscious experience. In: A. J. Marcel and E. Bisiach (eds), *Consciousness in Contemporary Science.* Oxford: Clarendon Press.

Gazzaniga, M. S. (1997). Why can't I control my brain? Aspects of conscious experience. In: M. Ito, Y. Miyashita and E. T. Rolls (eds), *Cognition, Computation, and Consciousness.* Oxford: Oxford University Press.

Genesis Rabbah. See *Midrash Rabbah.*

Giller, P. (2001). *Reading the Zohar: The Sacred Text of the Kabbalah.* Oxford: Oxford University Press.

Globus, G. G., Maxwell, G. and Savodnik, I. (1976). *Consciousness and the Brain: A Scientific and Philosophical Inquiry.* New York: Plenum Press.

Glover, J. (1988). *I: The Philosophy and Psychology of Personal Identity.* London: Allen Lane/Penguin Press.

Goertzel, B. (1998). World wide brain: self-organizing internet intelligence as the actualization of the collective unconscious. In: J. Gackenbach (ed.), *Psychology and the Internet.* New York: Academic Press.

Goleman, D. (1991). A western perspective. In: D. Goleman and R. A. F. Thurman (eds), *Mindscience: An East–West Dialogue.* Boston: Wisdom Publications.

Goodwin, B. (1994). *How the Leopard Changed its Spots: The Evolution of Complexity.* London: Weidenfeld & Nicolson.

Goswami, A. (1993). *The Self-Aware Universe: How Consciousness Creates the Material World.* London: Simon & Schuster.

Govinda, A. B. (1975). *The Psychological Attitude of Early Buddhist Philosophy.* Delhi: Nag Publishers.

Gray, C. M., König, P., Engel, A. K. and Singer, W. (1989). Oscillatory responses in rat visual cortex exhibit inter-columnar synchronization which reflects global stimulus properties. *Nature,* 338, 334–7.

Greenwald, A. G. (1992). New look 3: unconscious cognition reclaimed. *American Psychologist,* 47, 766–79.

Gregory, R. L. (1990). *Eye and Brain: the Psychology of Seeing.* 4th edn. London: Weidenfeld and Nicolson.

Griffin, D. R. (2000). *Religion and Scientific Naturalism: Overcoming the Conflicts.* Albany, NY: State University of New York Press.

Groeger, J. A. (1988). Qualitatively different effects of undetected and unidentified auditory primes. *Quarterly Journal of Experimental Psychology,* 40A, 323–9.

Grof, S. (1985). *Beyond the Brain: Birth, Death and Transcendence in Psychotherapy.* Albany, NY: State University of New York Press.

Grossberg, S. (1999). The link between brain learning, attention and consciousness. *Consciousness and Cognition,* 8, 1–44.

Grossenbacher, P. G. and Lovelace, C. T. (2001). Mechanisms of synesthesia: cognitive and physiological constraints. *Trends in Cognitive Science,* 5, 36–41.

Grosso, M. (2001). Psi research and transpersonal psychology: some points of mutual support. In: D. Lorimer (ed.), *Thinking Beyond the Brain: A Wider Science of Consciousness.* Edinburgh: Floris Books.

Guenther, H. V. (No date). *Philosophy and Psychology in the Abhidharma.* Delhi: Motilal Banarsidass.

Hameroff, S. R. (2001). Biological feasibility of quantum approaches to consciousness: the Penrose-Hameroff 'Orch OR' model. In: P. van Loocke (ed.), *The Physical Nature of Consciousness*. Amsterdam: John Benjamins.

Hameroff, S. R. and Penrose, R. (1996). Conscious events as orchestrated space-time selections. *Journal of Consciousness Studies*, 3, 36–53.

Handelman, S. A. (1982). *The Slayers of Moses: The Emergence of Rabbinic Interpretation in Modern Literary Theory*. New York: State University of New York Press.

Hanegraaff, W. J. (1998). *New Age Religion and Western Culture: Esotericism in the Mirror of Secular Thought*. Albany, NY: State University of New York Press.

Haney II, W. S. (1998). Deconstruction and consciousness: the question of unity. *Journal of Consciousness Studies*, 5, 19–33.

Haraldsson, E. (2001). Children and memories of previous lives. In: D. Lorimer (ed.), *Thinking Beyond the Brain: A Wider Science of Consciousness*. Edinburgh: Floris Books.

Hardcastle, V. G. (1995). *Locating Consciousness*. Amsterdam: John Benjamins.

Hardy, A. (1979). *The Spiritual Nature of Man*. Oxford: Clarendon Press.

Harman, G. (1995). Phenomenal fallacies and conflations. *Behavioral and Brain Sciences*, 18, 256–7.

Harman, W. W. (1993). Towards an adequate epistemology for the scientific exploration of consciousness. *Journal of Scientific Exploration*, 7, 133–43.

Harman, W. W. and Clark, J. (eds) (1994). *New Metaphysical Foundations of Modern Science*. Institute of Noetic Sciences.

Harth, E. (1993). *The Creative Loop: How the Brain makes a Mind*. Harmondsworth, UK: Penguin Books.

Harvey, P. (1995). *The Selfless Mind: Personality, Consciousness and Nirvana in Early Buddhism*. Richmond, UK: Curzon.

Hay, D. (1982). *Exploring Inner Space: Scientists and Religious Experience*. Harmondsworth, UK: Penguin Books.

Hayes, L. (1997). Understanding mysticism. *Psychological Record*, 47, 573–96.

Hebb, D. O. (1949). *The Organization of Behavior: A Neuropsychological Theory*. New York: John Wiley & Sons.

Heller, A. (1967/1978). *Renaissance Man*, trans. R. E. Allen. London: Routledge & Kegan Paul.

Helminiak, D. A. (1998). *Religion and the Human Sciences: An Approach via Spirituality*. Albany, NY: State University of New York Press.

Heron, J. (1998). *Sacred Science: Person-Centred Inquiry into the Spiritual and the Subtle*. Ross-on-Wye, UK: PCCS Books.

Hick, J. (1980). Mystical experience as cognition. In: R. Woods (ed.), *Understanding Mysticism*. New York: Image Books.

Hick, J. (2001). *Dialogues in the Philosophy of Religion*. Basingstoke,

UK: Palgrave.

Hilgard, E. R. (1977). *Divided Consciousness: Multiple Controls in Human Thought and Action*. New York: John Wiley & Sons.

Holdrege, B. A. (1996). *Veda and Torah: Transcending the Textuality of Scripture*. Albany, NY: State University of New York Press.

Howe, M. L. and Courage, M. L. (1993). On resolving the enigma of infantile amnesia. *Psychological Bulletin*, **113**, 305–26.

Howe, M. L. and Courage, M. L. (1997). The emergence and early development of autobiographical memory. *Psychological Review*, **104**, 499–523.

Howe, M. L., Courage, M. L. and Peterson, C. (1994). How can I remember when 'I' wasn't there: long-term retention of traumatic experiences and emergence of the cognitive self. *Consciousness and Cognition*, **3**, 327–55.

Hunt, H. T. (1984). A cognitive psychology of mystical and altered-state experience. *Perceptual and Motor Skills*, **58**, 467–513 (Monogr. Suppl. 1-V54).

Hunt, H. T. (1985). Relations between the phenomena of religious mysticism (altered states of consciousness) and the psychology of thought: a cognitive psychology of states of consciousness and the necessity of subjective states for cognitive theory. *Perceptual and Motor Skills*, **61**, 911–61.

Hurwitz, S. (1968). Psychological aspects in early Hasidic literature, trans. H. Nagel. In: J. Hillman (ed.), *Timeless Documents of the Soul*. Evanston: Northwestern University Press.

Idel, M. (1986). Infinities of Torah in Kabbalah. In: G. H. Harman and S. Budick (eds), *Midrash and Literature*. New Haven: Yale University Press.

Idel, M. (1988a). *The Mystical Experience in Abraham Abulafia*, trans. J. Chipman. Albany, NY: State University of New York Press.

Idel, M. (1988b). *Kabbalah: New Perspectives*. New Haven: Yale University Press.

Idel, M. (1988c). *Studies in Ecstatic Kabbalah*. Albany, NY: State University of New York Press.

Idel, M. (1989a). Universalization and integration: two conceptions of mystical union in Jewish mysticism. In: M. Idel and B. McGinn (eds), *Mystical Union and Monotheistic Faith: An Ecumenical Dialogue*. New York: Macmillan.

Idel, M. (1989b). *Language, Torah, and Hermeneutics in Abraham Abulafia*, trans. M. Kallus. Albany, NY: State University of New York Press.

Idel, M. (2002). *Absorbing Perfections: Kabbalah and Interpretation*. New Haven: Yale University Press.

Ito, M., Miyashita, Y. and Rolls, E. T. (eds) (1997). *Cognition, Computation, and Consciousness*. Oxford: Oxford University Press.

Jackson, F. (1982). Epiphenomenal qualia. *Philosophical Quarterly*, **32**, 127–36.

James, W. (1890/1950). *The Principles of Psychology*. 2 vols. New York: Dover.

James, W. (1902/1960). *The Varieties of Religious Experience*. London: Fontana.

James, W. (1909/1977). *A Pluralistic Universe*. Cambridge, MA: Harvard University Press.

Janet, P. (1889). *L'Automatisme Psychologique*. Paris: Alcan.

Jaspers, K. (1923/1963). *General Psychopathology*, trans. J. Hoenig and M. W. Hamilton. Manchester: Manchester University Press.

Jayasuriya, W. F. (1963). *The Psychology and Philosophy of Buddhism*. Colombo: YMBA Press.

Jaynes, J. (1976/1990). *The Origin of Consciousness in the Breakdown of the Bicameral Mind*. Boston: Houghton Mifflin.

Jeffrey, F. (1986). Working in isolation: states that alter consensus. In: B. B. Wolman and M. Ullman (eds), *Handbook of States of Consciousness*. New York: Van Nostrand Reinhold.

Johnson-Laird, P. N. (1983). *Mental Models: Towards a Cognitive Science of Language, Inference and Consciousness*. Cambridge: Cambridge University Press.

Johnson-Laird, P. N. (1988). A computational analysis of consciousness. In: A. J. Marcel and E. Bisiach (eds), *Consciousness in Contemporary Science*. Oxford: Clarendon Press.

Josephson, B. and Rubik, B. (1992). The challenge of consciousness research. *Frontier Perspectives*, **3**, 15–19.

Jung, C. G. (1921/1971). *Psychological Types (Collected Works Vol. 6)*, trans. H. G. Baynes (rev. R. F. C. Hull). London: Routledge & Kegan Paul.

Jung, C. G. (1951/1959). *Aion: Researches into the Phenomenology of the Self (Collected Works Vol. 9ii)*, trans. R. F. C. Hull. London: Routledge & Kegan Paul.

Jung, C. G. (1963/1967). *Memories, Dreams, Reflections*, trans. R. Winston and C. Winston. London: Fontana.

Kant, I. (1781/1968). Trans. N. Kemp Smith as *Immanuel Kant's Critique of Pure Reason*. London: Macmillan.

Kaplan, A. (1990). *Sefer Yetzirah: The Book of Creation*. York Beach, Maine: Samuel Weiser.

Katz, S. T (ed.) (1978a). *Mysticism and Philosophical Analysis*. New York: Oxford University Press.

Katz, S. T (1978b). Language, epistemology, and mysticism. In: S. T. Katz (ed.), *Mysticism and Philosophical Analysis*. New York: Oxford University Press.

Katz, S. T. (ed.) (1992a). *Mysticism and Language*. Oxford: Oxford University Press.

Katz, S. T. (1992b). Mystical speech and mystical meaning. In: S. T. Katz (ed.), *Mysticism and Language*. Oxford: Oxford University Press.

Katz, S. T. (2000). Mysticism and the interpretation of sacred scripture. In: S. T. Katz (ed.), *Mysticism and Sacred Scripture*. Oxford: Oxford University Press.

Kelley, C. F. (1977). *Meister Eckhart on Divine Knowledge*. New Haven and London: Yale University Press.

Kihlstrom, J. F. (1987). The cognitive unconscious. *Science*, **237**, 1445–52.

Kihlstrom, J. F. (1993). The psychological unconscious and the self. In: *Experimental and Theoretical Studies of Consciousness*. Ciba Foundation Symposium no. 174. Chichester, UK: John Wiley & Sons.

Kihlstrom, J. F. (1997). Consciousness and me-ness. In: J. D. Cohen and J. W. Schooler (eds), *Scientific Approaches to Consciousness*. Mahwah, NJ: Lawrence Erlbaum.

Kihlstrom, J. F., Mulvaney, S., Tobias, B. A. and Tobis, I. P. (2000). The emotional unconscious. In: E. Eich, J. F. Kihlstrom, G. H. Bower, J. P. Forgas and P. M. Niedenthal (eds), *Cognition and Emotion*. Oxford: Oxford University Press.

Krippner, S. (1999). The varieties of dissociative experience: a transpersonal, post-modern model. *The International Journal of Transpersonal Studies*, **18**, 81–101.

Krippner, S. (2000). The epistemology and technologies of shamanic states of consciousness. *Journal of Consciousness Studies*, 7, 93–118.

Kunzendorf, R. G. (2000). Individual differences in self-conscious source-monitoring: theoretical, experimental, and clinical considerations. In: R. G. Kunzendorf and B. Wallace (eds), *Individual Differences in Conscious Experience*. Amsterdam: John Benjamins.

Kunzendorf, R. G. and McGlinchey-Berroth, R. (1997–8). The return of 'the subliminal'. *Imagination, Cognition and Personality*, **17**, 31–43.

Lacan, J. (1966/1977). *Écrits: A Selection*, trans. A. Sheridan. London: Tavistock.

Lajoie, D. H. and Shapiro, S. L. (1992). Definitions of transpersonal psychology: the first 23 years. *Journal of Transpersonal Psychology*, **24**, 79–98.

Lambie, J. A. and Marcel, A. J. (2002). Consciousness and the varieties of emotion experience: a theoretical framework. *Psychological Review*, **109**, 219–59.

Lamme, V. A. F. (2001). Blindsight: the role of feedforward and feedback corticocortical connections. *Acta Psychologica*, **107**, 209–28.

Lamme, V. A. F. and Roelfsema, P. R. (2000). The distinct modes of vision offered by feedforward and recurrent processing. *Trends in Neurosciences*, **23**, 571–9.

Lancaster, B. L. (1991). *Mind, Brain and Human Potential: The Quest for an Understanding of Self*. Shaftesbury, Dorset: Element Books.

Lancaster, B. L. (1993a). *The Elements of Judaism*. Shaftesbury, Dorset: Element Books.

Lancaster, B. L. (1993b). Self or no-self? Converging perspectives from neuropsychology and mysticism. *Zygon: Journal of Religion and Science*, **28**, 509–28.

Lancaster, B. L. (1997a). On the stages of perception: towards a synthesis of cognitive neuroscience and the Buddhist Abhidhamma tradition. *Journal of Consciousness Studies*, **4**, 122–42.

Lancaster, B. L. (1997b). The mythology of anatta: bridging the East–West divide. In: J. Pickering (ed.), *The Authority of Experience: Readings on Buddhism and Psychology*. Richmond, Surrey: Curzon Press.

Lancaster, B. L. (1997c). The golem as a transpersonal image: 1. a marker of cultural change. *Transpersonal Psychology Review*, **1** (3), 5–11.

Lancaster, B. L. (1997d). The golem as a transpersonal image: 2. psychological features in the mediaeval golem ritual. *Transpersonal Psychology Review*, **1** (4), 23–30.

Lancaster, B. L. (1999). The multiple brain and the unity of experience. In: J. Rowan and M. Cooper (eds), *The Plural Self: Multiplicity in Everyday Life*. London: Sage.

Lancaster, B. L. (2000a). Book review of Velmans, *Understanding Consciousness*. *Consciousness and Experiential Psychology*, **4**, 17–20.

Lancaster, B. L. (2000b). The psychology of oppositional thinking in rabbinic biblical commentary. *Journal of Semitic Studies*, **S11**, 191–203.

Lancaster, B. L. (2000c). On the relationship between cognitive models and spiritual maps: evidence from Hebrew language mysticism. *Journal of Consciousness Studies*, **7**, 231–250.

Lancaster, B. L. (2001). New lamps for old: psychology and the 13th century flowering of mysticism. *Transpersonal Psychology Review*, **5** (1), 3–14.

Lancaster, B. L. (2002). In defence of the transcendent. *Transpersonal Psychology Review*, **6** (1), 42–51.

Lancaster, B. L. (In press). A Kabbalistic framework for the study of consciousness. In: S. Arzy, M. Fahler and B. Cahana (eds), *Midrash Banefesh: Studies in Jewish Psychology*. Tel-Aviv: Yediot-Aharonot. (Hebrew).

Lao Tzu (1963). *Tao Te Ching*, trans, D. C. Lau. Harmondsworth, UK: Penguin.

Larson, J. G. and Bhattacharya, R. S. (1987). *Samkya: A Dualist Tradition in Indian philosophy*, Encyclopedia of Indian Philosophies, vol. 4. Princeton, NJ: Princeton University Press.

Levine, J. (1983). Materialism and qualia: the explanatory gap. *Pacific Philosophical Review*, **64**, 354–61.

Levine, J. (2001). *Purple Haze: The Puzzle of Consciousness*. Oxford: Oxford University Press.

Leviticus Rabbah. See *Midrash Rabbah*.

Levy-Agresti, J. and Sperry, R. W. (1968). Differential perceptual capacities in major and minor hemispheres. *Proceedings of the National Academy of Sciences USA*, **61**, 1151.

Libet, B. (1994). A testable field theory of mind-brain interaction. *Journal of Consciousness Studies*, **1**, 119–26.

Llinás, R. (1993). Is dyslexia a dyschronia? *Annals of the New York Academy of Sciences*, **682**, 48–56.

Llinás, R. and Ribary, U. (1993). Coherent 40-Hz oscillation characterizes dream state in humans. *Proceedings of the National Academy of Sciences USA*, **90**, 2078–81.

Llinás, R., Ribary, U., Contreras, D. and Pedroarena, C. (1998). The neuronal basis for consciousness. *Philosophical Transactions of the Royal Society of London B*, **353**, 1841–9.

Looren de Jong, H. (2001). Introduction: a Symposium on Explanatory Pluralism. *Theory & Psychology*, **11**, 731–5.

Lorimer, D. (ed.) (2001). *Thinking Beyond the Brain: A Wider Science of Consciousness*. Edinburgh: Floris.

Mangam, B. (1993). Taking phenomenology seriously: the 'fringe' and its implications for cognitive research. *Consciousness and Cognition*, **2**, 89–108.

Marcel, A. J. (1980). Conscious and preconscious recognition of polysemous words: locating the selective effects of prior verbal context. In: R. S. Nickerson (ed.), *Attention and Performance VIII*. Hillsdale, NJ: Lawrence Erlbaum Associates.

Marcel, A. J. (1998). Blindsight and shape perception: deficit of visual consciousness or of visual function? *Brain*, **121**, 1565–88.

Marshall, P. (1992). *The Living Mirror: Images of Reality in Science and Mysticism*. London: Samphire Press.

Matt, D. (1995). Ayin: The concept of nothingness in Jewish mysticism. In: L. Fine (ed.), *Essential Papers on Kabbalah*. NY: New York University Press.

Mavromatis, A. (1987). *Hypnogogia: The Unique State of Consciousness between Wakefulness and Sleep*. London: Routledge & Kegan Paul.

May, R. (1965). Intentionality, the heart of human will. *Journal of Humanistic Psychology*, **5**, 202–9.

McFadden, J. (2002). Synchronous firing and its influence on the brain's electromagnetic field: evidence for an electromagnetic field theory of consciousness. *Journal of Consciousness Studies*, **9**, 23–50.

McGinn, B. (1989). Commentary. In M. Idel and B. McGinn (eds), *Mystical Union and Monotheistic Faith: An Ecumenical Dialogue*. New York: Macmillan.

McGinn, C. (1991). *The Problem of Consciousness: Essays Towards a Resolution*. Oxford: Blackwell.

McGinn, C. (1995). Consciousness and space. *Journal of Consciousness Studies*, 2, 220–30.

MacPhail, E. M. (1998). *The Evolution of Consciousness.* Oxford: Oxford University Press.

Merkur, D. (1989). Unitive experiences and the state of trance. In: M. Idel and B. McGinn (eds), *Mystical Union and Monotheistic Faith: An Ecumenical Dialogue.* New York: Macmillan.

Metzinger, T. (2000). The subjectivity of subjective experience: a representationalist analysis of the first-person perspective. In: T. Metzinger (ed.), *Neural Correlates of Consciousness: Empirical and Conceptual Questions.* Cambridge, MA: MIT Press.

Metzinger, T. (2003). *Being No One: The Self-Model Theory of Subjectivity.* Cambridge, MA: Bradford.

Midrash Rabbah. Vilna edition, first published 1887.

Miller, G. A. (2003). The cognitive revolution: a historical perspective. *Trends in Cognitive Sciences*, 7, 141–4.

Milner, A. D. and Goodale, M. A. (1995). *The Visual Brain in Action.* Oxford: Oxford University Press.

Milner, A. D. and Rugg, M. D. (1992). *The Neuropsychology of Consciousness.* London: Academic Press.

Mindell, A. (2000). *Quantum Mind: The Edge between Physics and Psychology.* Portland, OR: Lao Tse Press.

Minsky, M. (1987). *The Society of Mind.* London: Heinemann.

Morgan, M. J. (1977). *Molyneux's Question. Vision, Touch and the Philosophy of Perception.* Cambridge: Cambridge University Press.

Nagel, T. (1974). What is it like to be a bat? *Philosophical Review*, 83, 435–51.

Narada, M. T. (1956/1975). *A Manual of Abhidhamma.* Kandy, Sri Lanka: Buddhist Publication Society.

Nasr, S. H. (1993). *The Need for a Sacred Science.* Richmond, UK: Curzon Press.

Natsoulas, T. (1995). A rediscovery of Sigmund Freud. *Consciousness and Cognition*, 4, 300–22.

Natsoulas, T. (1999). A commentary system for consciousness? *Journal of Mind and Behavior*, 20, 155–82.

Nelkin, N. (1993). What is consciousness? *Philosophy of Science*, 60, 419–34.

Nelkin, N. (1996). *Consciousness and the Origins of Thought.* Cambridge: Cambridge University Press.

Neumann, E. (1949/1974). *The Origins and History of Consciousness*, trans. R. F. C. Hull. London: Routledge & Kegan Paul.

Newberg, A., d'Aquili, E. and Rause, V. (2001). *Why God Won't Go Away: Brain Science and the Biology of Belief.* New York: Ballantine Books.

Newman, J. and Baars, B. J. (1993). A neural attentional model for access to consciousness: a global workspace perspective. *Concepts in Neuro-science*, **4**, 255–90.

Niebur, E., Hsiao, S. S. and Johnson, K. O. (2002). Synchrony: a neuronal mechanism for attentional selection? *Current Opinion in Neurobiol-ogy*, **12**,190–4.

Nisbett, R. E. and Ross, L. (1980). *Human Inference: Strategies and Short-comings of Social Judgement*. Englewood Cliffs, NJ: Prentice-Hall.

Nissen, M. J., Ross, J. L., Willingham, D. B., MacKenzie, T. B. and Schacter, D. L. (1988). Memory and awareness in a patient with multiple person-ality disorder. *Brain and Cognition*, **8**, 117–34.

Nixon, G. (1999). A 'hermeneutic objection': language and the inner view. *Journal of Consciousness Studies*, **6**, 257–67.

Numbers Rabbah. See *Midrash Rabbah*.

Nunn, J. A., Gregory, L. J., Brammer, M., Williams, S. C. R., Parslow, D. M., Morgan, M. J., Morris, R. G., Bullmore, E. T., Baron-Cohen, S. and Gray, J. A. (2002). Functional magnetic resonance imaging of synaesthesia: activation of V4/V8 by spoken words. *Nature Neuroscience*, **5**, 371–5.

Oatley, K. (1988). On changing one's mind: a possible function of consciousness. In: A. J. Marcel and E. Bisiach (eds), *Consciousness in Contemporary Science*. Oxford: Clarendon Press.

Otto, R. (1917/1923). *The Idea of the Holy: An Inquiry into the Non-Rational Factor in the Idea of the Divine and its Relation to the Ratio-nal*, trans. J. W. Harvey. London: Oxford University Press.

Panhuysen, G. (1998). The relationship between somatic and psychic processes: lessons from Freud's project. In: R. M. Bilder and F. F. LeFever (eds), *Neuroscience of the Mind on the Centennial of Freud's Project for a Scientific Psychology*. New York: New York Academy of Sciences (Annals Vol. 843).

Panksepp, J. (1998). *Affective Neuroscience: The Foundations of Human and Animal Emotions*. Oxford: Oxford University Press.

Parsons, W. B. (1999). *The Enigma of the Oceanic Feeling: Revisioning the Psychoanalytic Theory of Mysticism*. Oxford: Oxford University Press.

Paulesu, E., Harrison, J., Baron-Cohen, S., Watson, J. D. G., Goldstein, L., Heather, J., Frackowiak, R. S. J. and Frith, C. D. (1995). The phys-iology of coloured hearing: a PET activation study of colour-word synaesthesia. *Brain*, **118**, 661–76.

Pearmain, R. (2001). Meditation and the perception of change in long-term meditators: a comparison between meditators and psychothera-pists. Unpublished Ph.D. thesis.

Penrose, R. (1997). *The Large, the Small and the Human Mind*. Cambridge: Cambridge University Press.

Pérez-Remón, J. (1980). *Self and Non-Self in Early Buddhism*. The Hague: Mouton.

Perry, C. and Laurence, J.-R. (1984). Mental processing outside of aware-ness: the contributions of Feud and Janet. In: K. S. Bowers and

D. Meichenbaum (eds), *The Unconscious Reconsidered*. New York: John Wiley & Sons.

Persinger, M. A. (1987). *Neuropsychological Bases of God Beliefs*. New York: Praeger.

Pflueger, L. W. (1998). Discriminating the innate capacity: salvation mysticism of classical Samkya-Yoga. In: R. K. C. Forman (ed.), *The Innate Capacity: Mysticism, Psychology, and Philosophy*. Oxford: Oxford University Press.

Pickering, J. (1999). Consciousness and psychological science. *British Journal of Psychology*, **90**, 611–24.

Pickering, J. and Skinner, M. (eds) (1990). *From Sentience to Symbol: Readings on Consciousness*. London: Harvester Wheatsheaf.

Popper, K. R., Lindahl, B. I. and Århem, P. (1993). A discussion of the mind–brain problem. *Theoretical Medicine*, **14**, 167–80.

Putnam, F. W. (1994). Dissociation and disturbances of self. In: D. Cicchetti and S. L. Toth (eds), *Developmental Psychopathology*, **2**, 251–65.

Radder, H. (2001). Psychology, physicalism and real physics. *Theory and Psychology*, **11**, 773–84.

Radhakrishnan, S. (ed.) (1953). *The Principal Upanishads*. London: George Allen & Unwin.

Rahula, W. (1967). *What the Buddha Taught*. London and Bedford: Gordon Fraser.

Ramachandran, V. S. and Blakeslee, S. (1999). *Phantoms in the Brain: Human Nature and the Architecture of the Mind*. London: Fourth Estate.

Ramachandran, V. S. and Hubbard, E. M. (2001). Synaesthesia: a window into perception, thought and language. *Journal of Consciousness Studies*, **8**, 3–34.

Rao, K. R. (1993). Cultivating consciousness: some conceptual and methodological issues. In: K. R. Rao (ed.), *Cultivating Consciousness: Enhancing Human Potential, Wellness, and Healing*. Westport, CT: Praeger.

Rao, K. R. (2002). Bridging eastern and western perspectives on consciousness. *Journal of Consciousness Studies*, **9**, 63–8.

Revonsuo, A. (1995). Consciousness, dreams, and virtual realities. *Philosophical Psychology*, **8**, 35–58.

Revonsuo, A. (1999). Binding and the phenomenal unity of consciousness. *Consciousness and Cognition*, **8**, 173–85.

Revonsuo, A., Johanson, M., Wedlund, J.-E. and Chaplin, J. (2000). The zombies amongst us: consciousness and automatic behaviour. In: Y. Rossetti and A. Revonsuo (eds), *Beyond Dissociation: Interaction between Dissociated Implicit and Explicit Processing*. Amsterdam: John Benjamins.

Revonsuo, A., Wilenius-Emet, M., Kuusela, J. and Lehto, M. (1997).

The neural generation of a unified illusion in human vision. *NeuroReport*, **8**, 3867–70.

Rhys Davids, C. A. F. (1914). *Buddhist Psychology: An Inquiry into the Analysis and Theory of Mind in Pali Literature*. London: G. Bell.

Ring, K. and Cooper, S. (1999). *Mindsight: Near-Death and Out-of-Body Experiences in the Blind*. Palo Alto: William James Center for Consciousness Studies at the Institute of Transpersonal Psychology.

Rogers, T. B., Kuiper, N. A. and Kirker, W. S. (1977). Self-reference and the encoding of personal information. *Journal of Personality and Social Psychology*, **35**, 677–88.

Rojtman, B. (1998). *Black Fire on White Fire: An Essay on Jewish Hermeneutics, from Midrash to Kabbalah*, trans. S. Rendall. Berkeley: University of California Press.

Rosch, E. (2000). The brain between two paradigms: can biofunctionalism join wisdom intuitions to analytical science? *Journal of Mind and Behavior*, **21**, 189–204.

Rossetti, Y. and Revonsuo, A. (2000). *Beyond Dissociation: Interaction between Dissociated Implicit and Explicit Processing*. Amsterdam: John Benjamins.

Ryle, G. (1949). *The Concept of Mind*. London: Hutchinson.

Sacks, O. (1985). *The Man Who Mistook His Wife for a Hat*. New York: Harper Collins.

Schimmel, A. (1975). *Mystical Dimensions of Islam*. Chapel Hill, NC: University of North Carolina Press.

Schlamm, L. (2001). Ken Wilber's spectrum model: identifying alternative soteriological perspectives. *Religion*, **31**, 19–39.

Scholem, G. G. (1941/1961). *Major Trends in Jewish Mysticism*. New York: Schocken.

Scholem, G. G. (1960/1965). *On the Kabbalah and its Symbolism*, trans. R. Manheim. New York: Schocken.

Scholem, G. G. (1975). *Devarim be-Go*. Tel Aviv: Am Oved. (Hebrew)

Schooler, J. (2002). Re-representing consciousness: dissociations between experience and meta-consciousness. *Trends in Cognitive Sciences*, **6**, 339–44.

Schweizer, P. (1993). Mind/consciousness dualism in Sankhya-Yoga philosophy. *Philosophy and Phenomenological Research*, **53**, 845–59.

Searle, J. R. (1987). Minds and brains without programs. In: C. Blakemore and S. Greenfield (eds), *Mindwaves: Thoughts on Intelligence, Identity and Consciousness*. Oxford: Blackwell.

Searle, J. R. (1992). *The Rediscovery of Mind*. Cambridge, MA: MIT Press.

Searle, J. R. (1997). *The Mystery of Consciousness*. London: Granta Books.

Searle, J. R. (1998). How to study consciousness scientifically. *Philosophical Transactions of the Royal Society of London B*, **353**, 1935–42.

Sefer ha-Bahir. See Kaplan, A. (1979). *The Bahir.* New York: Samuel Weiser.

Sefer Yetsirah. Gruenwald, I. (1971). A preliminary critical edition of *Sefer Yezira. Israel Oriental Studies,* **1**, 132–77 (Hebrew). See also Kaplan (1990).

Sells, M. A. (1994). *Mystical Languages of Unsaying.* Chicago: University of Chicago Press.

Sharf, R. H. (1998). Experience. In: M. C. Taylor (ed.), *Critical Terms for Religious Studies.* Chicago: University of Chicago Press.

Sheldrake, A. R. (1981). *A New Science of Life: The Hypothesis of Formative Causation.* London: Blond & Briggs.

Sheldrake, A. R. (1988). *The Presence of the Past: Morphic Resonance and the Habits of Nature.* London: Collins.

Sherrington, C. S. (1940). *Man on his Nature.* Gifford Lectures, 1937–8. Cambridge: Cambridge University Press.

Shevrin, H. (2000). The experimental investigation of unconscious conflict, unconscious affect, and unconscious signal anxiety. In: M. Velmans (ed.), *Investigating Phenomenal Consciousness: New Methodologies and Maps.* Amsterdam: John Benjamins.

Shokek, S. (2001). *Kabbalah and the Art of Being.* London: Routledge.

Sillito, A. M., Jones, H. E., Gerstein, G. L. and West, D. C. (1994). Feature-linked synchronization of thalamic relay cell firing induced by feedback from the visual cortex. *Nature,* **369**, 479–82.

Singer, W. (1999). Neuronal synchrony: a versatile code for the definition of relations? *Neuron,* **24**, 49–65.

Singer, W. (2000). Phenomenal awareness and consciousness from a neurobiological perspective. In: T. Metzinger (ed.), *Neural Correlates of Consciousness: Empirical and Conceptual Questions.* Cambridge, MA: MIT Press.

Skelton, R. (1995). Is the unconscious structured like a language? *International Forum for Psychoanalysis,* **4**, 168–78.

Skolimowski, H. (1994). *The Participatory Mind: A New Theory of Knowledge and of the Universe.* New York: Penguin Arkana.

Skolimowski, H. (1996). The participatory universe and its new methodology. *Frontier Perspectives,* **5**, 16–23.

Smart, N. (2000). Mysticism and scripture in Theravada Buddhism. In: S. T. Katz (ed.), *Mysticism and Sacred Scripture.* Oxford: Oxford University Press.

Smilek, D., Dixon, M. J., Cudahy, C. and Merikle, P. M. (2001). Synaesthetic photisms influence visual perception. *Journal of Cognitive Neuroscience,* **13**, 930–6.

Smith, H. (1981). Western philosophy as a great religion. In: A. M. Olson and L. S. Rouner (eds), *Transcendence and the Sacred.* Notre Dame, IN: University of Notre Dame Press.

Solms, M. (1997). *The Neuropsychology of Dreams.* Mahwah, NJ: Lawrence Erlbaum Associates.

Solms, M. (2000). A psychoanalytic contribution to contemporary neuroscience. In: M. Velmans (ed.), *Investigating Phenomenal Consciousness: New Methodologies and Maps*. Amsterdam: John Benjamins.

Solms, M. and Turnbull, O. (2002). *The Brain and the Inner World: An Introduction to the Neuroscience of Subjective Experience*. New York: Other Press.

Sperry, R. W. (1969). A modified concept of consciousness. *Psychological Review*, **76**, 532–6.

Sperry, R. W. (1995). The riddle of consciousness and the changing scientific worldview. *Journal of Humanistic Psychology*, **35**, 7–33.

Stace, W. T. (1961). *Mysticism and Philosophy*. London: Macmillan.

Stevenson, I. (1997). *Children Who Remember Previous Lives: A Question of Reincarnation*. Charlottesville: University Press of Virginia.

Stoerig, P. (1997). Phenomenal vision and apperception: evidence from blindsight. *Mind and Language*, **12**, 224–37.

Stoerig, P. and Cowey, A. (1989). Wavelength sensitivity in blindsight. *Nature, London*, **342**, 916–18.

Stoerig, P. and Cowey, A. (1992). Wavelength discrimination in blindsight. *Brain*, **115**, 425–44.

Sullivan, P. R. (1995). Contentless consciousness and information-processing theories of mind. *Philosophy, Psychiatry, Psychology*, **2**, 51–9.

Supèr, H., Spekreijse, H. and Lamme, V. A. F. (2001). Two distinct modes of sensory processing observed in monkey primary visual cortex (V1). *Nature Neuroscience*, **4**, 304–10.

Symons, C. S. and Johnson, B. T. (1997). The self-reference effect in memory: a meta-analysis. *Psychological Bulletin*, **121**, 371–94.

Talmud. *Talmud Bavli*. Standard edition, 18 vols. Vilna: Re'em. 1908.

Tarnas, R. (1991/1996). *The Passion of the Western Mind: Understanding the Ideas that have Shaped our World View*. London: Pimlico.

Tart, C. (1975). *States of Consciousness*. New York: E. P. Dutton.

Tart, C. (2000). Investigating altered states of consciousness on their own terms: state-specific sciences. In: M. Velmans (ed.), *Investigating Phenomenal Consciousness: New Methodologies and Maps*. Amsterdam: John Benjamins.

Taylor, E. (1999a). William James and Sigmund Freud: 'The future of psychology belongs to your work'. *Psychological Science*, **10**, 465–9.

Taylor, E. (1999b). *Shadow Culture: Psychology and Spirituality in America*. Washington: Counterpoint.

Taylor, J. (1999). *The Race for Consciousness*. Cambridge, MA: MIT Press.

Teyler, T. J. and DiScenna, P. (1986). The hippocampal memory indexing theory. *Behavioral Neuroscience*, **100**, 147–54.

Thass-Thienemann, T. (1968). *The Interpretation of Language. Vol 1: Understanding the Symbolic Meaning of Language.* Northvale, NJ: Jason Aronson.

Thatcher, R. W. and John, E. R. (1977). *Functional Neuroscience. Vol. 1: Foundations of Cognitive Processes.* Hillsdale, NJ: Lawrence Erlbaum Associates.

Tin, P. M. (trans.) (1921). *The Expositor (Atthasalini): Buddhaghosa's Commentary on the Dhammasangani The First Book of the Abhidhamma Pitaka,* ed. and rev. Mrs Rhys Davids. London: Pali Text Society.

Tishby, I. (1949/1989). *The Wisdom of the Zohar: An Anthology of Texts.* 3 vols, trans. D. Goldstein. Oxford: Oxford University Press.

Tononi, G. and Edelman, G. M. (1998). Consciousness and complexity. *Science,* **282,** 1846–51.

Trehub, A. (1991). *The Cognitive Brain.* Cambridge, MA: MIT Press.

Turk, D. J., Heatherton, T. F., Kelley, W. M., Funnell, M. G., Gazzaniga, M. S. and Macrae, C. N. (2002). Mike or me? Self-recognition in a split-brain patient. *Nature Neuroscience,* **5,** 841–2.

Underhill, E. (ed.) (1912). *The Cloud of Unknowing.* London: John M. Watkins.

Urbach, E. E. (1969/1979). *The Sages: Their Concepts and Beliefs,* trans. I. Abrahams. Jerusalem: Magnes Press.

Valentine, E. R. (1999). The possibility of a science of experience: an examination of some conceptual problems facing the study of consciousness. *British Journal of Psychology,* **90,** 535–42.

Van der Kolk, B. (1994). The body keeps the score: memory and the evolving psychobiology of post traumatic stress. *Harvard Review of Psychiatry,* **1,** 253–65.

Vanderwolf, C. H. (2000). Are neocortical gamma waves related to consciousness? *Brain Research,* **855,** 217–24.

van Lommel, P. (2002). *The Heart of Death: An interview with Pim van Lommel:* Jill Neimark. http://www.metanexus.net/archives/message_fs.asp?list=views&listtype=Magazine&action=sp_simple_archive_&page=1&ARCHIVEID=5253&searchstring=1/14/2002.

van Lommel, P., van Wees, R., Meyers, V. and Elfferich, I (2001). Near-death experience in survivors of cardiac arrest: a prospective study in the Netherlands. *The Lancet,* **358,** 2039–45.

Varela, F. J. (1996). Neurophenomenology: a methodological remedy to the hard problem. *Journal of Consciousness Studies,* **3,** 330–50.

Varela, F. J. (1999). Present-time consciousness. In: F. J. Varela and J. Shear (eds), *The View from Within: First-Person Approaches to the Study of Consciousness.* Thorverton, UK: Imprint Academic.

Varela, F. J. and Shear, J. (eds) (1999). *The View from Within: First-Person Approaches to the Study of Consciousness.* Thorverton, UK: Imprint Academic.

Varela, F. J., Tompson, E. and Rosch, E. (1991). *The Embodied Mind: Cognitive Science and Human Experience*. Cambridge, MA: MIT Press.

Velmans, M. (1991). Is human information processing conscious? *Behavioral and Brain Sciences*, **14**, 651–69.

Velmans, M. (1999). When perception becomes conscious. *British Journal of Psychology*, **90**, 543–66.

Velmans, M. (2000). *Understanding Consciousness*. London: Routledge.

Vermersch, P. (1999). Introspection as practice. In: F. J. Varela and J. Shear (eds), *The View from Within: First-Person Approaches to the Study of Consciousness*. Thorverton, UK: Imprint Academic.

Vesey, G. N. A. (ed.) (1964). *Body and Mind: Readings in Philosophy*. London: George Allen and Unwin.

von der Malsberg, C. (1997). The coherence definition of consciousness. In: M. Ito, Y. Miyashita and E. T. Rolls (eds), *Cognition, Computation, and Consciousness*. Oxford: Oxford University Press.

Wade, J. (1996). *Changes of Mind: A Holonomic Theory of the Evolution of Consciousness*. Albany, NY: State University of New York Press.

Wallace, B. A. (1999). The Buddhist tradition of Samatha: methods for refining and examining consciousness. In: F. J. Varela and J. Shear (eds), *The View from Within: First-Person Approaches to the Study of Consciousness*. Thorverton, UK: Imprint Academic.

Wallace, B. A. (2000). *The Taboo of Subjectivity: Toward a New Science of Consciousness*. Oxford: Oxford University Press.

Walsh, R. and Vaughan, F. (1993). On transpersonal definitions. *Journal of Transpersonal Psychology*, **25**, 199–207.

Walsh, V. and Cowey, A. (1998). Magnetic stimulation studies of visual cognition. *Trends in Cognitive Sciences*, **2**, 103–110.

Warnock, M. (1987). *Memory*. London: Faber & Faber.

Warren, R. M. (1984). Perceptual restoration of obliterated sounds. *Psychological Bulletin*, **96**, 371–83.

Webb, R. E. and Sells, M. A. (1995). Lacan and Bion: psychoanalysis and the mystical language of 'unsaying'. *Theory and Psychology*, **5**, 195–215.

Weinberger, J. (2000). William James and the unconscious: redressing a century-old misunderstanding. *Psychological Science*, **11**, 439–45.

Weiskrantz, L. (1986). *Blindsight: A Case Study and Implications*. Oxford: Clarendon Press.

Weiskrantz, L. (1992). Introduction: dissociated issues. In: D. A. Milner and M. Rugg (eds), *The Neuropsychology of Consciousness*. London: Academic Press.

Weiskrantz, L. (1997). *Consciousness Lost and Found: A Neuropsychological Exploration*. Oxford: Oxford University Press.

Wertheim, M. (1999). *The Pearly Gates of Cyberspace: A History of Space from Dante to the Internet*. London: Virago Press.

Whyte, L. L. (1962). *The Unconscious Before Freud*. London: Tavistock Publications.

Wiener, P. P. (1951). *Leibniz: Selections*. New York: Charles Scribner's.

Wightman, W. P. D. (1972). *Science in a Renaissance Society*. London: Hutchinson.

Wigner, E. P. (1972). The place of consciousness in modern physics. In: C. Musès and A. M. Young (eds), *Consciousness and Reality: The Human Pivot Point*. New York: Avon.

Wilber, K. (1979). Eye to eye: transpersonal psychology and science. *ReVision*, **2**, 3–25.

Wilber, K. (1996). *A Brief History of Everything*. Dublin: Gill & Macmillan.

Wilber, K. (1997). An integral theory of consciousness. *Journal of Consciousness Studies*, **4**, 71–92.

Wilber, K. (1998/2001). *The Marriage of Sense and Soul: Integrating Science and Religion*. Dublin: Gateway.

Wilber, K. (1999). *Integral Psychology (Collected Works, vol. 4)*. Boston and London: Shambhala.

Wilber, K. (2000a). *A Theory of Everything: An Integral Vision for Business, Politics, Science, and Spirituality*. Boston, MA: Shambhala.

Wilber, K. (2000b). Waves, streams, states and self: further considerations for an integral theory of consciousness. *Journal of Consciousness Studies*, **7**, 145–76.

Wilhelm, R. (trans.) (1962). *The Secret of the Golden Flower: A Chinese Book of Life*. London: Routledge & Kegan Paul.

Wolfson, E. R. (1994). *Through a Speculum that Shines: Vision and Imagination in Medieval Jewish Mysticism*. Princeton NJ: Princeton University Press.

Woody, J. M. and Phillips, J. (1995). Freud's 'project for a scientific psychology' after 100 years: the unconscious mind in the era of cognitive neuroscience. *Philosophy, Psychiatry, Psychology*, **2**, 123–34.

Wright, P. (1998). Gender issues in Ken Wilber's transpersonal theory. In: D. Rothberg and S. Kelly (eds), *Ken Wilber in Dialogue: Conversations with Leading Transpersonal Thinkers*. Wheaton, Ill: Quest.

Yadin, A. (2003). The hammer on the rock: polysemy and the school of Rabbi Ishmael. *Jewish Studies Quarterly*, **10**, 1–17.

Yates, F. A. (1964). *Giordano Bruno and the Hermetic Tradition*. London: Routledge & Kegan Paul.

Yerushalmi, Y. H. (1991). *Freud's Moses: Judaism Terminable and Interminable*. New Haven and London: Yale University Press.

Zajonc, A. (1993). *Catching the Light: The Entwined History of Light and Mind*. New York: Bantam Press.

Zeki, S. (2003). The disunity of consciousness. *Trends in Cognitive Sciences*, **7**, 214–18.

Zeki, S. and Bartels, A. (1999). Toward a theory of visual consciousness. *Consciousness and Cognition*, 8, 225–59.

Zimmer, H. (1960). On the significance of the Indian tantric yoga. In: J. Campbell (ed.), *Papers from the Eranos Yearbook: Eranos 4. Spiritual Disciplines*. Princeton, NJ: Princeton University Press.

Zohar. (1978). Ed. R. Margoliot. 6th edn. 3 vols. Jerusalem: Mosad ha-Rav Kook.

Zohar Hadash. (1978). Ed. R. Margoliot. 2nd edn. Jerusalem: Mosad ha-Rav Kook.

Author index

Subject index

accessibility, 208–9, 221, 223, 261–2, 277
Active Intellect, 24, 26, 87, 242, 249, 253, 258, 267–8, 269, 276, 306 n6
adaptive resonance theory, 132–3, 136
All-Self, 71–2, 129, 172–3, 298 n14
archetypes, 25, 26, 44–5, 52, 228, 271–2, 277
associative thinking, 108–9, 221–2, 233–4, 241, 244
see also memory and associations; multiplicity of meaning; 'wheel of associations'
astrophysics, 63
attachment to God, 172
attention, 66, 83–4, 125, 140, 152

blindsight, 151, 187–92, 198, 200–1, 295 n2
brain function, 46–7, 67, 96, 103, 114, 120, 123–41, 145–7, 148, 150, 152–6, 160, 185–6, 199–200, 204, 224–5, 262, 264, 283 n5
in dreaming, 224–5
quantum theory and, 34, 116–22
reflective of higher realms, 13–15, 144–7
see also neural correlate of consciousness; neurophysiology;

re-entrant processing
Buddhism, 12, 16–19, 48, 71, 77, 79, 81, 83–6, 104–7, 111, 112, 125, 164, 246, 256, 280 n9, 287 n2, 293 n7, 295 n3, 297 n8
Abhidhamma, 17–18, 104–13, 170–5, 244, 251, 264, 271, 291 n13, 291 n14, 299 n15
Zen, 170
see also no-self

Christianity, 47, 52, 216, 217–18, 219, 275, 282 n3, 305 n15
Christian mysticism, 102, 230, 236–8, 256
cognitive neuropsychology, 114, 148–92
cognitive psychology, cognitive approach, 8, 11, 25, 66, 148–92, 194–7, 204–5, 221, 244, 251, 264, 277, 295 n1
see also cognitive neuropsychology; representation
commentary system, 190–1
conscious access hypothesis, 151–63
see also consciousness, access; global workspace theory
consciousness
access, 68–73, 106,

170, 198, 220, 222, 264, 297 n7
in animals, 170, 285 n8, 308 n11
and belief, 41, 60–5, 82, 162, 262, 278, 296 n5, 301 n3
as biological only, 4, 56
causation and explanation of, 21–35, 39, 115, 261–2
and coherence, 129, 137
and computation, 41, 56, 285 n8, 296 n5, 301 n2
cosmic, 129
defined, 65–73, 98, 100, 144, 261
dimensions of, 195, 198–202, 205–9, 220, 261–2, 277
see also accessibility; intentionality 1; intentionality 2; phenomenality
as divine, 3
field theory of, 34, 121
fringe, 9, 301 n4
hard problem of, 51, 63, 72–3, 92, 160
'higher', 7, 79
informational, 68–9
integrative theory of, 10, 34–5, 37–8, 51, 57–60, 73, 107, 113, 261, 276–8
light as metaphor for, 67, 92, 284 n7
and meaning, 197, 297 n7
microconsciousness, 17

337

Printed in Poland
by Amazon Fulfillment
Poland Sp. z o.o., Wrocław